D1526687

Jesuit on the Roof of the World

Jesuit on the Roof of the World

Ippolito Desideri's Mission to Eighteenth-Century Tibet

TRENT POMPLUN

OXFORD
UNIVERSITY PRESS
2010

OXFORD
UNIVERSITY PRESS

Oxford University Press, Inc., publishes works that further
Oxford University's objective of excellence
in research, scholarship, and education.

Oxford   New York
Auckland   Cape Town   Dar es Salaam   Hong Kong   Karachi
Kuala Lumpur   Madrid   Melbourne   Mexico City   Nairobi
New Delhi   Shanghai   Taipei   Toronto

With offices in
Argentina   Austria   Brazil   Chile   Czech Republic   France   Greece
Guatemala   Hungary   Italy   Japan   Poland   Portugal   Singapore
South Korea   Switzerland   Thailand   Turkey   Ukraine   Vietnam

Published by Oxford University Press, Inc.
198 Madison Avenue, New York, NY 10016

www.oup.com

Library of Congress Cataloging-in-Publication Data
Pomplun, Trent.
Jesuit on the roof of the world : Ippolito Desideri's mission to eighteenth-century
Tibet / Trent Pomplun.
p.   cm.
Includes bibliographical references (p.   ) and index.
ISBN 978-0-19-537786-6
1. Desideri, Ippolito, 1684–1733.   2. Missionaries—Tibet—Biography.
3. Missionaries—Italy—Biography.   4. Missions—Tibet.
5. Jesuits—Italy—Biography.
6. Tibet—Church history.   I. Title.
BV3427.D38P66 2010   266'.2090—dc22   [B]   2009009570

For my father, Gordon H. Pomplun, who first inspired my love of learning

Contents

Preface

What follows is a study on the Western fascination with Tibet, which aims to complement the work of other scholars in Tibetan Studies with an account of the life and times of Ippolito Desideri, the man often thought to be the first practitioner of our art. My principal concern is to offer a thick description of Desideri's intellectual world, especially as it concerns his membership in the Society of Jesus, the Roman Catholic apostolic order more commonly known as the Jesuits. Although I will follow the missionary's journey across Tibet—his story is too good not to tell—this study will concern itself primarily with the peculiar European ideas and emotions that accompanied him on his travels. If, to borrow a phrase from Peter Brown, my study allows readers to experience a bit of the "disturbing strangeness" of the chief ideas that preoccupied Ippolito Desideri, I will have achieved my purpose in writing it.

The difficulties of interdisciplinary writing are balanced by attendant pleasures, not least of which is the shared company of scholars from two quite different fields of study. My dual existence, as both a scholar of Tibetan Studies and a historian of the early Society of Jesus, has thus allowed me to live Ippolito Desideri's encounter with Tibetans in miniature. It has also caused me to accumulate scholarly debt in two fields, so the thanks and acknowledgments that I owe my teachers, colleagues, and friends far exceed my abilities to express them all. Several people played important roles in the genesis of this project, and I would like to single them out for special thanks. First, I must thank

Anne Klein of Rice University for introducing me to all things Tibetan and nurturing my love of Tibetan religion and philosophy. I must also thank my good friend Bryan Cuevas, who first insisted—against my repeated protestations—that I undertake this study of Ippolito Desideri. I had no intention of doing so, and his encouragement has shaped my academic life considerably. I will always be grateful for the opportunity to work privately with Jeffrey Hopkins, who patiently translated sections of the *Chos lugs kyi snying po* with me. I must also thank Richard Sherburne and Thomas Reddy, both priests of the Society of Jesus, for kindly providing me with mounds of Desideriana at important points in my research, Father Sherburne from his own personal microfilm copies and Father Reddy from the massive treasury of the Archivum Romanum Societatis Iesu, of which he served as chief archivist. Finally, I must thank Michael Sweet, Leonard Zwilling, and Enzo Gualtiero Bargiacchi, whose new research on Desideri—and generous conversations—have done much to change the way I think about Ippolito Desideri. Although all of the translations of Desideri's writing that follow are my own, I have checked them against Michael Sweet's translation of Desideri's *Notizie istoriche*, which he kindly shared with me as I finished this project. Rather than cite Michael's work in every footnote on the *Notizie istoriche*, I would like to acknowledge here the pervasive influence of his work upon my own. A number of people also read drafts of this manuscript, and I would like to single them out for thanks as well: Gene Rogers, who read the version that I submitted as a dissertation at the University of Virginia; Michael Sweet, who kindly took time away from his own translation to offer *più di commenti*, and Matthew Kapstein and Bryan Cuevas, who both served as readers for Oxford University Press and later waived their anonymity. Bryan's orthographical rigor greatly improved my manuscript. I owe a great deal to Matthew, too, whose offhand comment about Mary Carruthers's work led me to rewrite significant portions of my first and final chapters.

Several institutions have also assisted its publication. The American Philosophical Society provided me with a Franklin Research Grant for a crucial summer of writing. The Center for the Humanities at Loyola College in Maryland provided me a junior faculty sabbatical for one semester of research and writing, and its Office of Grant Services provided two summer research grants. I am forever indebted to libraries galore. Special thanks to Nawang Thokmey and the staff at the University of Virginia, Peggy Feild at Loyola University Maryland, Heidi Herr at Special Collections in the Eisenhower Library at Johns Hopkins University, Leon Hooper at the Woodstock Theological Center Library, John Buchtel and Ted Jackson of Special Collections at Georgetown University, Patrice Kane at Fordham University, Jennifer Lowe at the Pius XII Memorial Library of Saint Louis University, Susan Meinhoff at the Library of Congress, Edite Bandos and Cristina Santos at the Santa Casa Misericordia in Lisbon, Cornelius Lochschmidt at the Bayerische Staatsbibliothek in Munich, and finally J. F. X. Pratt and the kind staff at the Archivum Romanum Societatis Iesu. I must also acknowledge Father Francis Tiso and the University of Hawai'i Press for allowing me to use portions of an article that I first published as "Divine Grace and the Play of Opposites," in *Buddhist-Christian Studies* 26 (2006), pp. 159–72, as well as portions of another article, "The Holy Trinity in Ippolito Desideri's *Chos lugs kyi snying po*," *Buddhist-Christian Studies* 29 (2009), pp. 95–97, 115–27. I am grateful to Bryan Cuevas, Kurtis Schaeffer, and E. J. Brill for allowing me to use parts of "Ippolito Desideri, S.J. on Padmasabhava's Prophecies and the Persecution of the Rnying ma 1717–1720," which first appeared in Bryan Cuevas and Kurtis Schaeffer, eds., *Tibetan Society and Religion: The Seventeenth and Eighteenth Centuries* (Leiden: E. J. Brill, 2006), pp. 33–45. Tsering Wangyal Shawa of Princeton University made the maps for this book, and I thank him for his patience and skill. Thanks, too, to Cynthia Read and the staff at Oxford University Press for seeing this book through to publication.

I owe special thanks to the family of friends and scholars at the University of Virginia who first guided this study, especially to David Germano, Bill Magee, Karen Lang, Paul Groner, Erik Midelfort, Carlos Eire, John and Alison Milbank, Augustine Thompson, and Robert Wilken. I must also thank the chorus of Tibetologists who kindly assisted me along the way, especially Janet Gyatso, Ronald Davidson, José Cabezon, Dan Martin, Gray Tuttle, Elaine Robson, and Simon Wickham-Smith. The Jesuits played their part, and so my thanks go to Charles Borges, Jim Connor, Joseph Rossi, John Conley, and Dominic Maruca. Thanks, too, to my especially patient friends, Brian Sholl, John Betz, Grant Kaplan, David Hart, Joseph Harder, Beth McManus, Greg Hite, Martin Kavka, Bill Gorvine, Frances Garrett, Travis McCauley, Rebby Sharp, David Newman, David Kalil, Scott Boltwood, Paul Hackett, Derek Maher, Jon Malesic, Paul Long, Colin Campbell, Aaron Stutts, Paul Zachary Yeager, James Harrington, Donovan Thomas, Kate and Paul Daniels, Rainey Knudson, Susan Miller, Fritz Bauerschmidt, Stephen Fowl, Bill Donovan, Michael and Seemee McShane, Heather Lyons and Zak Fusciello, Erin Goss, Caitlin Lynch-Huggins, Nate Bowditch, and Eden Unger (Julius, Lyric, Cyrus, and Olive, too).

Finally, I must thank my family: my father, my mother, Amy, Tara, Michael, Lauren, Luke, Emily, and Katie.

Technical Notes on Translation and Transliteration

I will render Tibetan terms that occur in the body of this text following the simplified phonetic transliteration scheme developed by David Germano and Nicolas Tournadre for the Tibetan and Himalayan Digital Library (THDL). For specialists, I will also render Tibetan terms in the orthographic transliteration system developed by Turrell Wylie in his article "A Standard System of Tibetan Transcription," *Harvard Journal of Asiatic Studies* 22 (1959), pp. 261–67. When quoting passages from Desideri's Italian writings that contain transliterations of Tibetan terms, I will use the THDL phonetic transliteration rather than Desideri's own. Transliterations of Chinese are in Pinyin rather than Wade-Giles, and transliterations of Mongolian follow the example of Christopher P. Atwood in his *Encyclopedia of Mongolia and the Mongol Empire* (New York: Facts on File, 2004). The names of cities, regions, and such are given their modern forms: *Beijing* rather than *Peking*, *Kolkata* rather than *Calcutta*, *Chandannagar* rather than *Chandernagore*, etc. I have not standardized the orthography of the various Latin texts I quote. For quotations from the Bible, I have usually followed the Vulgate, since Ippolito Desideri would have done the same. I often translate the Latin passages myself to emphasize certain features. All translations are my own unless otherwise noted.

Chronology

Jesuit on the Roof of the World

Introduction: Snow and Mirrors

His whole figure was so utterly unlike anything of this world that
those who never saw a Jesuit took him for one, and others believed
him some high priest of the Jews.

—Alexander Pope, *Scriblerus*

When I attended the University of Virginia, a strange tale circulated
among the graduate students in Tibetan Studies. The fourteenth
Dalai Lama once visited the university and came upon the statue of
Thomas Jefferson that stands in front of the Rotunda. His Holiness
stopped, gazed upon the statue, and asked, "Who is this man?"
Someone explained, with pious embarrassment, that Thomas
Jefferson was one of the founding fathers of the United States of
America, the author of the Declaration of Independence, and the
man responsible for the mental and physical architecture of the
university. The Dalai Lama listened carefully, considered the statue
at length, and solemnly announced that he had been
Thomas Jefferson in his past life.

   Such a startling revelation needs little explanation for the spiritual
elites familiar with Tibetan Buddhism. After all, Tenzin Gyatso, the
spiritual leader of Tibet and recipient of the Nobel Peace Prize, is also
an emanation of the omniscient bodhisattva Avalokiteśvara. In an
earlier incarnation, perhaps eons ago, he had foreseen the Chinese
invasion of Tibet that would bring him to the United States. Armed
with this foreknowledge, he chose to incarnate in the line of living

bodhisattvas that would come to be known as the Dalai Lamas of Tibet. Having the power to exist in several bodies simultaneously—one of his many divine prerogatives—the omniscient bodhisattva Avalokiteśvara also chose to exist as the seventh Dalai Lama's near contemporary Thomas Jefferson. On his visit to the University of Virginia, the fourteenth Dalai Lama intimated that the United States of America was first conceived in the mind of an omniscient bodhisattva to serve as a haven for Tibetan refugees in the latter half of the twentieth century. Thomas Jefferson, himself an emanation of the divine bodhisattva, thus turned his own omniscient gaze upon the events of the twentieth century and saw that he needed an institute of higher learning to prepare the citizens of the United States for their future acceptance of Buddhism. He needed sympathetic professors and graduate students—so the tale goes—to translate the holy scriptures of Buddhism from Tibetan into English, thereby preserving Buddhist religion and culture in the United States much as the translators of yore had preserved the heritage of lost Pali and Sanskrit texts, unmolested for centuries, on the Tibetan plateau.

The fourteenth Dalai Lama is a consummate missionary. He grants interviews, makes television appearances, endorses products, and writes a seemingly endless stream of books. He also gives public teachings about philosophy and initiates masses into the secret rites of Tibetan Buddhism. In all these things, the Dalai Lama faces the problems of any large-scale missionary endeavor. He must schedule itineraries, secure travel accommodations, manage his bank accounts, and generate a steady flow of cash. He must also express Tibetan truths in other languages, translate Buddhist concepts into Western ones, and accommodate Buddhism to various foreign cultures, accepting some things, rejecting others, and hiding anything that might shock potential donors. What is more important, he must judge how to do so in the most effective manner. He must ask himself, for example, whether the people of other cultures are capable of understanding Buddhist teachings and, if they are, under what conditions. All missionaries face these problems; one need only turn on the television to see how the Dalai Lama has begun to solve them.

What one does not see on television is the highly refined scholastic worldview that serves as the foundation of the Dalai Lama's mission. When Tenzin Gyatso hinted that he was Thomas Jefferson in his past life, he spoke to a select group of professors and graduate students who shared his uniquely Tibetan worldview. He did not tell this tale in public. Why should he? Few Americans would consider accepting a religion whose teachings involve the simultaneous existence of two men who are both emanations of a single omniscient spiritual being—especially when one of these men was Thomas Jefferson. Some might find the contamination of politics by religion—especially such an exotic one as

Tibetan Buddhism—downright frightening. Nothing in the Dalai Lama's story, however, would ring strange in Tibetan ears, least of all the use of reincarnation as a political stratagem. Since the fifteenth century, many of Tibet's most powerful political figures are discovered as children who are thought to be reincarnations of previous leaders, and the Dalai Lama is but one among many such incarnations. Tibetan educational institutions train monks from the earliest age to master the complex metaphysical system that provides warrant for this belief, and the Dalai Lama himself is a product of these institutions. Were someone to think reincarnation primitive or mythological, Tibetans would expect him to master their own extensive philosophical literature. Then—and only then—could one dispute the possibility that Kelzang Gyatso, the seventh Dalai Lama, was not also Thomas Jefferson, the third president of the United States of America.

Ippolito Desideri and the Myth of Tibet

The first Westerner to attempt such an internal critique of Tibetan Buddhist metaphysics was the Jesuit missionary Ippolito Desideri, who lived in Tibetan-speaking regions from 1715 to 1721. During his stay, the Jesuit missionary witnessed several events of particular interest for the history of modern Tibet: the Zünghar invasion, the persecution of the Nyingma, and the establishment of the Manchu protectorate. He composed philosophical and theological treatises in Tibetan, including a middling-sized catechism and an immense refutation of reincarnation.[1] Four different accounts of his journey, written in Italian, lay unfinished when he died in 1733.[2] Tibetologists have long considered these writings, which are quite rich in geographic and ethnographic detail, among the first works of modern Tibetan Studies. They remain an important source for historians of early modern Tibet and are quite colorful besides. They are also a natural place to begin consideration of the Western fascination with Tibet, not least because Tibetanists often have seen themselves—or their enemies—reflected in them. As a result, Ippolito Desideri has undergone a series of remarkable transformations in the academic literature: he has been a spy, an explorer, a historian, a proponent of interreligious dialogue, and, finally, a cipher for our own anxious fantasies about the land of snows.

Like one of Padmasaṃbhava's treasures concealed for future generations, the bulk of Desideri's writings was unknown until the late nineteenth century. Discovered among the papers of the Pistoian gentleman Filippo Rossi Cassi-goli in 1875, the first manuscript of Desideri's account suffered a painful parturition and was only published by Carlo Puini in fragments beginning at the end of the century, to mixed acclaim.[3] Although Clements Robert Markham took an interest in the manuscript, other British scholars ignored its publication or made scanty and furtive reference to it, even though Puini's publications made a significant contribution to the Tibetan studies then being published by Schlagintweit, Rockhill, Waddell, and Wegener.[4] Sandberg, Landon, and Holdich openly criticized Desideri, claiming that his journey to Tibet was part of a nefarious Jesuit plot to discredit the Capuchins—a fine charge indeed from apologists for the Younghusband expedition.[5] Neither Ryder nor Rawling, captains of the Younghusband expedition themselves, make any mention of the Jesuit missionary.[6] David Macdonald seemed largely unaware of Desideri's writings.[7] Sir Charles Bell gave Desideri a cursory, if belated, glance in *The Religion of Tibet*, more than thirty years after the missionary's writings were first published.[8]

Jesuit scholars saw Desideri in a different light. Henri Hosten and Cornelius Wessels, attracted by the citation of Puini's publications in Carlos Sommervogel's *Bibliothèque de la Compagnie de Jésus*, uncovered more Desideriana in the Society's archives.[9] Following the directives of the twenty-fourth general congregation of the Society of Jesus in 1892, both Hosten and Wessels treated the missionary primarily as a source for the institutional history of the Society of Jesus.[10] Like Puini, they believed the Jesuit's importance lay in his contributions to the history of geography and what we might now call ethnography, an interpretation that mirrors the concerns of the next generation of non-Jesuit scholars who read Desideri's manuscripts. Sven Hedin judged Desideri "one of the greatest explorers ever to set foot in Tibet."[11] Filippo de Filippi, who partially translated Desideri's account into English, felt that it had "a scientific value of the first importance."[12] Giuseppe Tucci, arguably the greatest Tibetanist of the twentieth century, said simply, "Tibetan Studies was born with Desideri."[13] Although Tucci never wrote more than small notes on Desideri, usually in surveys of Italian exploration, we owe most of our general images of the Jesuit missionary to his imagination. It is from Tucci that we came to see the Jesuit's encounter with the monks of Sera as an encounter between "Buddhist dogmatics and St. Thomas Aquinas."[14] It is also from him that many Tibetanists came to see Desideri in noble, even heroic, terms as a sympathetic interpreter of Tibetan religion who possessed profundity, clarity, and a certain largesse.[15] Robert Fazy believed him to be "humble."[16] Luciano Petech, who completed the critical edition of Desideri's Italian writings, echoed Tucci's judgment that the Jesuit missionary was "the first Tibetologist in history" but also expanded the catalogue of his virtues to include "spiritual maturity" and "apostolic zeal."[17] The author of the classic work on Tibetan politics of the eighteenth and nineteenth centuries, Petech also saw Desideri as an important historical source for Tibetan politics.[18]

Despite Tucci's tantalizing association of Desideri and St. Thomas Aquinas, few scholars of his generation really explored the theological aspects of Desideri's writings. Given the general political profile of neo-Thomism before the 1960s, it would have been hard for his readers to imagine a Thomist possessed of such *larghezza*. After the Second Vatican Council, however, Roman Catholic Tibetologists, such as Richard Sherburne, S.J., Giuseppe Toscano, S.X., and Robert Goss, promoted Tucci's characterization anew, but specifically as a precursor of the interreligious dialogue championed at the council.[19] Pedro Arrupe, the minister general who guided the Society of Jesus in the wake of the Second Vatican Council, even wrote the preface for the second volume of Giuseppe Toscano's *Opere Tibetane di Ippolito Desideri, S.J.*[20] To be sure, a missionary and a theologian committed to interreligious dialogue face similar challenges: each must search for the shared assumptions that make dialogue possible while recognizing and respecting the very real differences between the two religions in the interreligious encounter. Consequently, those scholars who saw Desideri as a precursor to modern interreligious dialogue generally explored his metaphysical arguments against specific Buddhist teachings such as emptiness (*stong pa nyid*) and were concerned to demonstrate links between older Jesuit missiological practices and contemporary interreligious dialogue.[21]

The Jesuit missionary has enjoyed a bit of a renaissance lately. Among the most controversial works in the last decade of Tibetan Studies have been those about the Western fascination with Tibet and, by extension, with the history of Tibetan Studies as an academic field. Not surprisingly, such works have sparked interest in the earliest Western writers on Tibetan religion and culture, Ippolito Desideri especially.[22] These studies, propelled along the path broken by Donald Lopez, treat the posthumous founder of Tibetan Studies as one of the first perpetuators of the "myth of Tibet." "Tibet and Tibetan Buddhism," Lopez says, "have long been objects of Western fantasy. Since the earliest encounters of Venetian travelers and Catholic missionaries with Tibetan monks at the Mongol court, tales of the mysteries of their mountain homeland and the magic of their strange—yet strangely familiar—religion have had a peculiar hold on the Western imagination."[23] Lopez discovers at the root of Western fantasies of Tibet a mirrorlike "play of opposites" between "the pristine and the polluted, the authentic and the derivative, the holy and the demonic, the good and the bad."[24] In Lopez's telling, Ippolito Desideri becomes the sum and surrogate of our own anxieties, a cipher, or a mirror in which we might see our own fantasies reflected. The missionary's entry into the Tibeto-Mongol court in Lhasa is one among "several emblematic moments in which foreigners positioned themselves before Tibetan lamas, sometimes standing, sometimes sitting, moments to which the present-day scholar of Tibetan Buddhism is inevitably heir."[25] The missionary cannot but be victim and proponent of a violence that represents his Tibetan interlocutors in terms that foreshadow the modern Orientalist, who looks upon the past with nostalgia and his present interlocutors with contempt. The missionary directs an urgent, suspicious gaze at his native Tibetan informants while he casts a blind eye toward Tibet itself. Roman Catholic missionaries play a starring role in this genealogy, and Lopez depicts them as prisoners to the play of opposites par excellence. This should not take away from the lasting value of Lopez's work; indeed, it should serve as its confirmation. One cannot deny the missionary zeal coursing through Desideri's writings, nor the urgency born of it. But neither can one deny that Lopez is caught in some strange—yet strangely familiar—fantasies about Roman Catholics.

Ippolito Desideri and the Myth of the Jesuit

The suspicion with which Lopez views Desideri—and the suspicion with which the apologists for the Younghusband expedition viewed him—hints at another myth of fine standing. Straw men in much European and American literature, both Catholic and anti-Catholic, members of the Society of Jesus have enjoyed a long run as hoarders, fanatics, meddlers, and murderers.[26] Blamed for the Gunpowder plot, the Franco-Prussian war, and the Dreyfus affair—and these are only the highlights of a very distinguished curriculum vitae—blindly obedient Jesuits, their strict military organization disguised by secrecy and subterfuge, swept over the European imagination like overeducated Tartars. There has hardly been a corpus so literary in its vitriol as that directed against the Society of Jesus. John Donne contributed genuinely anti-Jesuit classics with *Ignatius, His Conclave* and *Pseudo-Martyr,* John Oldham his own *Satyrs upon the Jesuits,* and Phineas Fletcher *The Locusts, or Apollyonists.* Other works, such as *St. Ignatius' Ghost,* a tract from 1700, were less poetic but equally hateful:

> Had I been there when Charles had changed his state
> I'd decked the House of Death with bloody scenes
> As strangling ravish'd maids not in their teens;
> So great had been my spleen I should deflower
> Virgins which lifeless lay besmirched with gore;

Laughed at young infants springing from their womb
To meet their mothers in a flaming tomb
Vomited flame upon the reeking stage
Without respect to greatness, sex or age.

There was more than a little doggerel, too. Sample titles include *Pyrotechnica Loyolana: Ignatian Fire-Works, or the Fiery Jesuit's Temper and Behavior* (which blamed the Jesuits for the great fire of London in 1666); *The Wanton Jesuit, or Innocence Seduced; The Jesuits Character, or, a Description of the Wonderfull Birth, Wicked Life, and Wretched Death of a Jesuite; Authentic Memoirs of the Exquisitely Villainous Jesuit, Father Richard Walpole*; and (my personal favorite) *Trust a Papist and Trust the Devil.*[27] Such works were not unique to England; on the Continent, Zaharowski's *Monita secreta* and Etienne Pasquier's *Le catéchisme des jésuites* provided the foundations upon which the great *philosophes* built their anti-Jesuit diatribes.[28] By the mid-nineteenth century, the popular image of the Jesuit reached its apogee: a man—sometimes even a woman—given to stalking subterranean passages and appearing through secret doors, the Jesuit of the French imagination possessed such a rare strain of diabolical magnetism that he might topple the nation as easily as he might bed a pious but unsuspecting maid.[29] Eugène Sue's *Juif errant* put the final touches on this phantasmagoric portrait; in the annals of literature, his work stands alongside its American cousin, *The Tales of Maria Monk*, as one of the most outrageous anti-Catholic works ever written. Jesuits in the United States inevitably would be accused of having assassinated William Henry Harrison, Zachary Taylor, James A. Garfield, William McKinley, and Abraham Lincoln.

The Jesuit myth entered the academy in a mitigated but clearly discernible form during the *Kulturkampf* in late nineteenth-century Germany.[30] Academic historians, often Lutheran, identified the Jesuits with the Council of Trent and the so-called Counter-Reformation, and the history of early modern Europe has labored under a double yoke since.[31] On one hand, it has opposed Ignatius of Loyola to the modern world of Protestantism, as a militant demagogue bent on dragging a newly liberated Europe back into the Dark Ages. Although he did much to clarify the terms of the debate, even Hubert Jedin, much like Leopold von Ranke before him, singled out the Council, the papacy, and the Society of Jesus as the primary players of what he termed the "Tridentine Era," and he described the Council of Trent as a "defense" against Protestantism rather than as the culmination of several trends within Catholicism itself.[32] As a result, the Jesuits were identified with the Council even though the first attempt to convoke a general council was in 1537, three years before Pope Paul III ratified the Society of Jesus. On the other hand, much early scholarship on the Jesuits labored under the excesses of periodization. The Society of Jesus was often identified solely with the baroque, even though the artistic style did not appear for more than a half century after the order itself. This facile identification served much the same ideological purpose as the identification of the Society of Jesus with the Counter-Reformation: it allowed scholars the liberty of contrasting the arts and literature of Counter-Reformation Catholicism with the allegedly more individualistic and secular Renaissance.[33]

Recent research on the Society of Jesus has attempted to dismantle the identification of the Society of Jesus and the Counter-Reformation. In John O'Malley's fine formulation, many historians now ask not "How was the Society of Jesus an agent of the Counter-Reformation?" but rather "What were Jesuits like?"[34] In attempting thick descriptions of Jesuit thought and culture, new works have shifted their focus away from the history of the Church conceived as an institution comprising the papacy, episcopacy, synods, and inquisitions to include popular religion, ritual studies, and microhistories of forgotten events, individuals, or movements. This shift allows scholars to conceive Jesuits less as ecclesiastical agents than as practitioners and promoters of wider currents of spirituality, literature, and the arts. In this regard, the global efforts of the early Society of Jesus have garnered a great deal of attention from contemporary historians, particularly in the multicultural perspective implied in the missions in Asia and the Americas, perspectives that largely have been ignored in the historiography of the Catholic Reformation.[35] In short, the methods used to study the Society of Jesus are expanding in much the same direction as those used to study Tibetan religion and culture—from the history of ideas to social history, cultural anthropology, art history, and the history of science and technology.[36]

Still, members of the Society of Jesus often seem a bit too "modern" in the most recent works on Jesuit history, and most such works seem to protest too much against hagiography. In some respects this canard is true—the new Jesuit historiography is far from the spirit of old standbys such as George Dunne's *Generation of Giants*—but several important studies eschewed hagiographical narratives long ago. John Witek, for example, outlined all manner of Jesuit machinations, both Portuguese and French, in his work on Jean-François Foucquet, and one certainly does not come away from reading his work with any sense that the Jesuit figurist was a saint. Nor did Jonathan Spence piously omit mention of Matteo Ricci's flaws or the dementia that overtook him as he died.[37] In fact, much of the new Jesuit historiography seems beholden to clichés from the thirty-second General Congregation of the Society of Jesus, held in 1975, even when it is written by non-Jesuits. It protests the old hagiography of the heroic soldier for Christ even as it subtly—or not so subtly—promotes a new hagiography of the progressive, humanistic, business-savvy Jesuit. It would have us believe that the Jesuits placed no stock in Rome or that they had little interest in the scholastic heritage of the Middle Ages.[38] It distances the Society from its militaristic metaphors and promotes the multicultural "cooperation" of the missions. Such interpretations ironically labor under the same periodization that beset those that identified the Society with the Council of Trent or baroque art, but with the terms reversed. Their new humanistic Jesuit seems as eager to escape his scholastic confines as a young Martin Luther, and the new Jesuit's Renaissance seems more like Burkhardt's than Ignatius's own.

Such protests against hagiography risk an academic overcorrection, in which the genuine theological concerns of seventeenth- and eighteenth-century Jesuits, missionaries or otherwise, are ignored in favor of other topics more suited to twenty-first-century tastes. Interestingly enough, the hagiography that scholars such as John W. O'Malley, Gauvin Bailey, and Liam Brockey rightly deplore— whether from the 1920s or from the 1960s—avoids discussing the theological issues inherent in the missionary enterprise as studiously as they themselves do.[39] Except for a few isolated references to the Jesuit promotion of free will— which is denuded of its theological trappings and seen as a harbinger of modernity—the speculative theology of the Jesuits is still terra incognita in the twenty-first century.[40] In this respect, the academic literature of the 1950s and the 1960s did not break with tradition but continued the general practice of Jesuit historiography that followed the directives of the twenty-fourth General Congregation of 1892. To be sure, it ignored many of the topics that the new Jesuit historiography treats so wonderfully, but not because the older historiography was aggressively theological; rather, just like the new Jesuit historiography, it consistently took its cues from secular academic trends.

The scholarly work on Ippolito Desideri is a case in point. One may assume that British apologists reared on Donne would sniff mightily at a Jesuit's religious sensibilities, but both Henri Hosten and Cornelius Wessels emphasized the geographical and ethnographical aspects of Desideri's writings at the expense of other topics. Filippo Filippi's 1937 translation of Desideri's *Notizie* omitted its overtly theological sections altogether. Apart from Giuseppe Tucci's (unsubstantiated) evocation of Desideri's Thomism, writings of the 1940s and 1950s treated Desideri as a historian or explorer. Scholars acknowledged the religious aspects of Desideri's writing only after the Jesuits' thirty-second General Congregation, in 1975, which promoted inculturation and interreligious dialogue, along with lay collaboration and social justice, among its directives. But here, too, the religious themes addressed by these scholars reflect their own twentieth-century concerns more than Desideri's own. Indeed, the pictures of Desideri found in Tibetan Studies and those of twentieth-century Jesuit historiography are curious mirror images. In both,

Ippolito Desideri is the heroic explorer of the early twentieth century and the tolerant multiculturalist of the 1960s, but rarely is he a man of his times, theological warts and all.

Outline of the Present Work

I hope to present a somewhat more balanced view in the work that follows. I will treat Desideri as an explorer, a historian, and a theologian—I will even consider whether he was a spy—but I will also treat him for what he was: a missionary of the Society of Jesus in the early eighteenth century. In doing so, I hope to introduce readers to the elemental constituents of Desideri's world in six chapters, which I have arranged chronologically to allow readers to see how his feelings about Tibet changed, deepened, or remained static. I will begin with Desideri as a novice in Rome, and accompany him on his maritime adventures to Goa; we will march across the great western deserts of Tibet, into the court of Lhazang Khan, and on to the debate courtyards of Ramoché and Sera monasteries; we will listen to his account of the Zünghar invasion of 1717, the persecution of the Nyingma, and the beginnings of the Manchu Protectorate; and we will follow him back through India and Europe as he battles his Capuchin rivals for control of the Tibetan mission. As we retrace Desideri's steps, we will have occasion to ask the very questions that he himself asked about Tibetans, their religion, and their culture: Had Christianity been introduced into Tibet at some earlier time? Did Tibetans worship the Holy Trinity? Did they enjoy the invisible graces of God in their daily lives and, if so, under what circumstances? Desideri's answers to these questions will take us into the far reaches of seventeenth-century debates about the genealogies of nations, the varieties of divine grace, and the problem of the salvation of non-Christians. They will also give us occasion to assess his contributions to Tibetan Studies.

My account begins in 1715 as Ippolito Desideri and his traveling companion Manoel Freyre make their way across the great deserts of western Tibet in the company of a mixed Mongol-Tibetan caravan. As we follow Desideri and Freyre on their journey, we will read the accounts of their exploration in light of the Jesuits' own understanding of mission. I will thus introduce readers to Ignatius Loyola, the Jesuits, and their religious institutions in the first chapter. In light of the work already done by scholars such as Mary Carruthers and Jonathan Spence, I will devote special attention to the Jesuits' own emphasis on images and image production in iconography, in literature, and in meditation. This account of *phantasia* and *phantasmata* in the Society of Jesus is essential for understanding Desideri's central preoccupations, but it is also meant to provide the historical context necessary to understand Desideri's own fantasies about Tibet and Tibetans. I hope it will contribute to the work of other historians on Jesuit self-understanding in the time from the foundation of the Society in 1540 to its suppression in 1773.

Desideri sails for India in the second chapter, and we will follow the missionary as he arrives in Goa, meets Manoel Freyre, ascends into Ladakh, and enters Lhasa. In this chapter, I will concern myself primarily with Desideri's epistolary efforts. We will see that the Jesuit's rather exuberant letters follow the themes of the *Spiritual Exercises* quite readily, and a closer analysis of them will give us occasion to peer into the spirituality of the missions. We will see how Europeans viewed Tibet before Desideri and Freyre embarked on their mission and discuss some of the salient myths about the land of snows already in circulation. The two Jesuits, then, will cross Tibet accompanied not only by other missionaries but also by a small cabal of humanist cartographers. While in Ladakh, the two Jesuits will also argue about whether to continue to Lhasa, an episode that will illuminate some of the political mysteries of Desideri's career that I will take up in the fifth chapter.

My third chapter begins with Desideri in the court of Lhazang Khan. In this chapter, we will tackle the problem of the resemblances between Roman Catholicism and Tibetan Buddhism as Desideri himself understood it. Several important seventeenth-century theological debates about the possibility of salvation among non-Christians will require our attention here, and this chapter will touch upon early modern theories of idolatry, discussions of the survival of primitive revelation in traditional societies, and Jesuit accounts of grace and free will. If, in my reading of Desideri, the barren plains of Tibet become overgrown with the thickets of Jesuit scholasticism, it is only because I believe that the speculations of Francisco Suárez, Gabriel Vásquez, and Luis de Molina help us understand Desideri better. In re-creating some of their questions, I hope to show that their speculations come alive when returned to their original soil. If one has the patience to work through the technical language, one can discern in the Jesuits' philosophical and theological speculations an intellectual program for Christian living among strangers. We will see that Desideri did indeed anticipate certain aspects of the Second Vatican Council; at the same time, we will see that he is hardly the model of modern pluralism.

Desideri flees the capital to escape the Zünghar invasion of 1717 in the fourth chapter, which will largely be taken up by Desideri's narrative of the carnage that followed. Through his eyes, we shall see that the wars that lacerated Tibet in the early eighteenth century were not fought between discrete national groups of Tibetans, Mongols, and Chinese. While most scholars are content to separate these groups racially and explain the conflicts accordingly, Desideri's account quite clearly demonstrates that the conflicts were largely the result of competition among factions of the Geluk monastic order. These factions—from central, southern, and far-eastern Tibet, respectively—not only opened their nation to Manchu control but largely decimated Tibet's oldest monastic order, the Nyingma, in the process. Desideri's account has the added virtue of being confirmed by the Tibetan accounts, especially those that were written by Nyingma or Tsangpa Geluk who were sympathetic to their persecuted friends. In this chapter I will outline the dominant ideological and political myths of seventeenth- and early eighteenth-century Tibet, especially those involving the Dalai Lamas, and address the missionary's understanding of the uniquely Tibetan understanding of reincarnation. This approach allows me to synthesize much of the new research being done in Tibetan Studies today, as well as introduce the reader to many of the ideas that the young Jesuit would later present to his European readers. The violent political struggles of seventeenth- and eighteenth-century Tibet also allow us to discern the political motives behind Desideri's writing, which I will outline in the fifth chapter and which will set the stage for an assessment of his capacities as a historian. As we shall see, the young missionary had every reason to avoid the excesses of Jesuit accommodation, not merely to win his legal battle with the Capuchin friars but also to avoid choosing sides in the battles that followed upon his arrival in the land of snows.

The fifth chapter follows Desideri back to India after church authorities have informed him that he must cede the Tibetan mission to the Capuchins. Since scholars of Desideri have often seen him as a practitioner of the Jesuit missiological method of "accommodation" or "inculturation" promoted by the Jesuits Matteo Ricci and Roberto de Nobili, my account will dwell on the politics underlying the Chinese and Malabar Rites controversies. If we follow the various trails that branch from the battle between Desideri and the Capuchins, we will be led into the underbelly of these controversies, the cloak-and-dagger world of Jesuit espionage, and all manner of early modern bureaucratic machinations. Desideri's role in these controversies will give us reason to question several of the virtues that scholars have attributed to the Jesuit missionary. After a close analysis of what sources we have, I cannot but think that some of these trails lead to shadowed corners in our portrait of Desideri that cannot be illuminated by the sources now available to us. In any event, what historical realities we can discern will turn out to be a tad murkier than the luminous chiaroscuro that Tibetologists favor for their portraits of Desideri and his rivals.

My account ends in Rome as Desideri prepares the account of his journey for publication. In this final chapter, I assess Desideri's manuscripts in light of similar literature written by Jesuits in the seventeenth and early eighteenth centuries. I hope to show that the missionary's descriptions of Tibetans, their religion, and their culture rest firmly in the literary trends and intellectual assumptions of the time, especially Tartar romances and the baroque vogue for all things Egyptian. I will argue that Desideri manipulated these literary tropes to paint a sharp contrast between the natural virtues of Tibetans and the diabolical sins of the sixth Dalai Lama, a contrast that he intended to further his own argument for rights to the Tibetan mission. Despite the minor quibbles registered above, this final chapter will also serve as a vindication of Donald Lopez's work on Western fantasies about Tibet, for in Desideri's literary presentations of Lhazang Khan, the sixth Dalai Lama, and Padmasaṃbhava, we will see that the Jesuit missionary did indeed view the Tibetans through a glass darkly—very, very darkly—and that he did so with an uncommon spiritual urgency. Whether the Jesuit missionary remains a cipher for our own anxieties or dreams will be left to the reader's judgment.

Each of my six chapters stands alone as an independent investigation of one aspect of the missionary's thought, and each chapter has an independent thesis about how to better understand his place in the history of Tibetan Studies. My first two chapters advance upon the terrain already covered by Cornelius Wessels and Henri Hosten. In them, I hope to suggest something of the depth of Desideri's spiritual vocation, especially in light of the *Spiritual Exercises*, which formed his views of Tibet—a context that is strangely lacking in the writings of these two great Jesuit historians. My third and fourth chapters, which take up Desideri's encounter with Tibetan religion, address Giuseppe Tucci and Luciano Petech's portraits of the missionary. In the third, I hope to give a fuller sense of Desideri's dependence on theological reasoning than a mere evocation of Thomism allows. In the fourth, I hope to show the ways that religious concerns, both Desideri's own and those of the Nyingma order, influenced the way the missionary interpreted the historical events in which he found himself. I outline Desideri's political and social context in my last two chapters. The fifth chapter aims to correct the common misunderstanding of Desideri as a progressive proponent of accommodation, while the sixth chapter returns, if only obliquely, to our own preoccupations with the alleged fantasies of Europeans about Tibetans. I will touch on various economic, political, and social factors that influenced Desideri's conceptions of Tibet, but the predominant strain in my work is the rather old-fashioned history of ideas. If the Jesuit entertained fantasies about Tibet or encouraged certain myths when he wrote the account of his journey—I believe he did both—we need to understand how those fantasies were part of the larger intellectual context of early modern Catholicism. In this respect, my work is intended as much for historians of the Society of Jesus as for scholars of Tibetan Studies.

A few scholarly caveats: I will make use of the full spectrum of Desideri's writings to tell his story, although I will favor the Italian texts generally, since I am concerned most with how Desideri viewed Tibetans and how he presented their culture to his European readers. I hope this approach will be of interest to both scholars of Tibetan Studies and historians of the Society of Jesus. I will reserve a fuller discussion of Desideri's Tibetan writings for a future study. I do not intend to enter into controversies about periodization. The terms "Middle Ages," "Renaissance," "Reformation," and "baroque" have borne too much weight in the last century of European historiography. When I characterize Ippolito Desideri as a "late baroque" figure, I take it for granted that much of what was of intellectual interest during the Middle Ages and the Renaissance can be found—sometimes changed, sometimes not—during his day. I will use these terms loosely to refer to well-recognized trends in the intellectual history of Europe, and no more.

Certain difficulties attend the writing of a work intended for more than one scholarly audience. Scholars of Tibetan religion and culture will note that I review events with which they are long familiar, but may find my citations of primary sources in Western languages excessive or off-putting. To some extent this is unavoidable. My goal in doing so is to demonstrate, in the most obvious manner, the challenges of taking the measure of a man whose times differed so markedly from our own. Historians of early modern Europe must likewise endure the shock of Tibetan language and history after reviewing familiar material about the Society of Jesus. If they balk at the frequent citation of Tibetan sources, or marvel at the religious and cosmological views expressed therein, I ask only that they imagine the shock of encountering such ideas in the early eighteenth century, alone, on the roof of the world.

As regards pace, I should warn the reader that this book is rather brisk. Ippolito Desideri ascends the Tibetan plateau and is whisked back to Europe in the space of two chapters. My work cannot pretend to be a comprehensive study of the missionary. Such a study would include a detailed reconstruction of his ecclesiastical relations in both Europe and Asia. While we know Desideri's itinerary with some certainty—there are still some fascinating lacunae—until an ambitious scholar spends a healthy spell in several archives, especially the various archives of the Portuguese Assistancy, many of the missionary's social, personal, and political ties will elude us. A truly comprehensive study of Ippolito Desideri would also include an exploration of his philosophical and theological writings in Tibetan, especially his magnum opus on reincarnation. Although I will introduce readers to these writings, I will do so only within the larger context of the Jesuit's battle with the Capuchins for the rights to the Tibetan mission. A thorough index of these works and their citations, carefully compared to the primary sources that Desideri may have read, would allow scholars to interpret some of the Jesuit missionary's rather puzzling statements about Madhyamaka, especially if scholars located these primary sources in the catalogues of the monasteries Desideri visited. Such work would need to be supplemented by a rigorous study of scholastic and humanistic theology in the West. This, too, is well beyond the scope of this present study.

My aims are more modest. I hope in what follows to give the reader some sense of just how complex the feelings of one man might be for the men and women of another culture. In doing so, I also hope to introduce scholars of Tibetan Studies to the world of its first son, a world every bit as strange as the one he encountered on the roof of the world—or announced by the fourteenth Dalai Lama on his own missionary journey to the University of Virginia.

I

Jesuit *Phantasia*

The first point is to see with the eyes of the imagination.
　　　　　　　　　—St. Ignatius Loyola, *Spiritual Exercises*

On November 22, 1715, the Jesuit Manoel Freyre lost his way in a snowstorm in western Tibet. Freyre and his traveling companion, a young Tuscan Jesuit named Ippolito Desideri, were riding with a large caravan of Mongols and Tibetans from Trashigang to Lhasa when Freyre stopped to rest his mount. The caravan had almost reached its campsite, so the Jesuit did not worry himself too much when he discovered a thick stream of blood flowing from his horse's nostrils. He ordered all but one of his servants to continue without him into the snowy night, abandoning him to the elements like a solid-state Jonah. The Jesuit's sluggish horse resumed its tired march but slowed under Freyre's spurring and eventually collapsed in the snow. Stranded at night in western Tibet, the Jesuit might as well have been howling for help on the face of the moon.[1] Assuming that Freyre had dropped from the third rank of the caravan to the fourth, Desideri pitched their tent while he waited for his fellow missionary to appear. Years later, when he wrote his account of their hazardous trek across Tibet, Desideri recalled that Freyre was nowhere to be seen when the fourth rank arrived with the trailing servants and pack animals. A search party mobilized in the "blink of an eye" and found Freyre and his servant a few hours later, half frozen and buried in the snow. The Jesuit had escaped death by snuggling against the warm body of his dying horse.[2]

I often imagine Manoel Freyre as he slowly disappears under the western Tibetan snows. Why would a Jesuit missionary—or anyone, for that matter— brave such a fate? It seems frivolous to attribute such behavior to something so whimsical as fantasy. But in its broadest sense this is true. A host of men from the Society of Jesus exposed themselves to the dangers of the overseas missions during the sixteenth and seventeenth centuries. Nor did they do so passively; they actively sought, even fantasized about, the missions and the martyrdom they promised. This collective fantasy, traces of which can be seen in the fourteen thousand letters in the Roman Archives of the Society of Jesus requesting assignment to the missions, was born in the earliest history of the Society.[3] Fueled by the *Spiritual Exercises* of St. Ignatius and encouraged by the splendors of Jesuit art and architecture, young members of the Society of Jesus dreamt of traveling to the most distant lands and realizing the Society's deepest ideals in doing so.[4] The Jesuits promoted such images by cultivating their novices' *phantasia*, and a great deal of the resulting *phantasmata*, both inner and outer, depicted the overseas missions. Ippolito Desideri imbibed these images as part of his formation as a Jesuit, and they significantly affected the way he conceived Tibet and its people. These curious Jesuit *phantasmata* accompanied the Jesuit missionary to Tibet, and—as we shall see—they loyally followed him all the way back to Rome.

The Society of Jesus and the Missions

Ippolito Desideri was born at approximately 7:00 p.m. on December 20, 1684, at what is now 6 Via Pietro Bozzi, in Pistoia, Italy.[5] He was the fourth child of the doctor Iacobo Desideri and Maria Maddalena Cappellini, who gave their son the name of Maria Maddalena's father, Ippolito, as well as the names Gaspar, Romulus, and Thomas, the last after the apostle believed to have been sent by Christ to India, whose vigil was celebrated in the liturgical calendar of the Tridentine Church on the night Desideri was born. We know precious little more about Desideri's early life. The Desideri family had lived originally in Gora, a small town about two miles northwest of Pistoia, where they had made a comfortable living as millers. By the time Ippolito was born, they had earned patrician status as Pistoian citizens and moved within the city walls. His older siblings, Francesco, Anna Maria, and Giuseppe, were born yearly starting in 1681, and his mother died when she was twenty-eight years old, on April 15, 1687, after giving birth to her fifth child, Giovan Battista, the previous year. His father was remarried to Costanza Dragoni of Prato, and all of the children entered the religious life except Giuseppe, who pursued a degree in medicine at the University of Pisa like his father. Ippolito received the sacrament of confirmation from Bishop Leone Strozza in the town cathedral on May 12, 1693, and enrolled in the minor seminary at the Jesuit college at Pistoia.[6] In 1700 Ippolito, a young man of sixteen, traveled to Rome in the company of the college's rector, Giovanni Battista Nembrini, S.J. He arrived smartly attired, and entered the Jesuits' novitiate church, Sant'Andrea al Quirinale, to begin the period of discernment that preceded formal entry into the Society.[7]

It was a tempting prospect. If we trace the power of the Society of Jesus as an arc that ends with its suppression in 1773, Desideri was about to enter an institution that had just passed its topmost point. From 1680 to 1710, the Jesuits grew from about seventeen thousand men to just under twenty thousand.[8] When Desideri entered the Society, it was 160 years old. Its founder, Ignatius Loyola, and its greatest missionary, Francis Xavier, had been canonized. Its members had the ear of kings and queens, and its great power drew charges of calumny from Catholics and Protestants alike. The Society was perhaps best known for its missions, and indeed, such missions were essential for the Jesuits' own self-understanding. The first written statement of the Society's intentions, the *Formula Instituti*, says,

> Whoever desires to serve as a soldier of God beneath the banner of the Cross in our society, which we desire to be designated by the name Jesus, and to serve the Lord alone and his Vicar on earth, should after a solemn vow of perpetual chastity keep what follows in mind. He is a member of a Society founded chiefly for this purpose: to strive especially for the progress of souls in Christian life and doctrine and the propagation of the faith.[9]

This text was the centerpiece of Pope Paul III's bull *Regimini militantis ecclesiae* of September 27, 1540, which recognized the Society of Jesus as a legitimate apostolic order, and it appeared again in a second bull, the *Exposcit debitum* of Pope Julius III, on July 21, 1550. In addition to the well-known military nomenclature and the explanation of the Society's name, these documents share the expressed goal of success in the missions.[10] Although the word *mission* is now common, it was almost a distinctly Jesuit word in the heady days of the early Society, referring not merely to evangelization overseas but to any task to which a Jesuit might be sent, under obedience, by a superior, the father general, or even the pope himself.[11] It summarized the itinerant style of ministry that the earliest Jesuits imagined for themselves, a vision that received its final confirmation in the Jesuit Constitutions: "Our vocation is to travel through the world and to live in any part of it whatsoever where there is hope of a greater service of God and the good of souls."[12]

The source of this evangelical wanderlust was Iñigo de Oñaz y Loyola, the founder of the Society of Jesus.[13] Unlike the typical saint of the Middle Ages, Iñigo did not play at holiness, nor did he have any intention of entering or founding a religious order. Rather, he entertained himself with tales of knights, dragons, and damsels in distress from popular Spanish romances such as *Amadís de Gaula*, which besotted the young man much as they did Cervantes's Don Quixote.[14] As a young gallant, Iñigo had the pleasure of acting out these fantasies, engaging in various military exercises, jousting, hunting, and making pleasant conversation with ladies of the court. Iñigo Loyola even had the opportunity to put his fantasies to the test: refusing retreat at the Battle of Pamplona on May 20, 1521, he took a cannon shot to the right leg as he resisted the soldiers who poured through the breached wall. The victorious French were kind enough to set Iñigo's shattered leg and eventually carried him back to his ancestral castle. Despite the best efforts of surgeons at Loyola, his leg was badly deformed. Still desiring to return to polite society, but distressed that his deformity would forever prevent him from cutting an elegant figure, the vain young man insisted upon undergoing a gruesome operation in which his leg was deliberately broken again and the spurs that resulted from the previous operation shaved away.

During the protracted convalescence that followed, Iñigo requested some romances to read, but the only volumes available were Ludolph of Saxony's *Life of Christ* and the *Flos sanctorum*, a Spanish-language edition of Jacobus de Voragine's compilation of hagiographies. Ludolph's *Life of Christ* contains an embryonic theology of both the missions and the imaginative meditations that would later characterize the Society of Jesus:

> At the end of the twenty-nine years during which the Lord Jesus had spent his life in hiddenness and sorrow, Jesus said to His Mother: It is now time for me to go, reveal, and glorify My Father, and to show myself to the world from which I have until now been hidden and effect the salvation of souls for which My Father sent me into the world. And so the Lord of the world departed barefoot on such a long journey, solitary and alone. Look upon Him lovingly and devoutly. Share in His sufferings with your heart's deepest affections.[15]

Iñigo was particularly sensitive to imaginative impressions, and he was deeply moved by Christ's mission and suffering. He was also impressed by the saints, such as Dominic and Francis of Assisi, who imitated Christ and conformed themselves to Him in ascetic annihilation and compassionate service to the poor. Looking upon Christ lovingly and devoutly in his convalescence, Iñigo came to think of himself as a knight of an altogether different sort and resolved to imitate the great saints in the service of Christ their King. In March 1522, ten months after the cannonball shattered his leg, Iñigo set off on a series of itinerant adventures that took him to Montserrat, Manresa, Venice, and eventually Jerusalem. Rebuffed at the Holy City, he returned to Europe and at the wizened age of thirty-three engaged in a Latin grammar class for children. Embarking on an unlikely career in theology, Iñigo studied at the University of Alcalá, the chief institution of the reforms began by Cardinal Cisneros, and eventually at the University of Paris, where he met the six other men who would form the core of the Society of Jesus. On the Feast of the Assumption 1534, these seven men pronounced vows of poverty, obedience, and chastity in front of a consecrated host and set off to evangelize Muslims in the Holy Land.

Ignatius—Iñigo first used the name in 1537—would not realize his dreams of evangelizing the Holy Land. He and his companions went to Rome instead and pledged themselves to the service of Pope Paul III, who soon approved them as an apostolic order. Christened the Society of Jesus, Ignatius's band joined the explosion of new religious orders during the Catholic Reformation. The Theatines, who soon enjoyed almost unrivaled power in Rome, were founded in 1524. The Capuchins followed in 1525 as a reform movement within the Observant Franciscans. Smaller orders and congregations such as the Barnabites, Somaschi, and Lazarites (among men) and the Angelics, Ursulines, and Visitandines (among women) also date from the reforms of the sixteenth century. Like many of these newer orders, the Society of Jesus emphasized active, apostolic ministries. The Piarists and Ursulines advocated education and social work; the Theatines, Barnabites, Oratorians of St. Philip Neri, and Oblates of St. Charles Borromeo preached the need for missions and the reform of the clergy; and all of the new orders taught a mystical abandonment to God in service to the poor. The Society of Jesus combined this apostolic zeal with pedagogical reform so potently that its schools soon speckled the globe.

Much of this success, at least in the eyes of the early modern Jesuits, could be attributed to the special graces received by St. Francis Xavier. As the Jesuit superior of the East Indies, Xavier spent ten years traveling in India, Indonesia, and Japan. Teaching catechism and baptizing thousands, the saint became the model for the Jesuit overseas much as Ignatius became the model for the Jesuit at home. Xavier's letters from Asia inspired young Jesuits from the first printing of two letters from Goa in 1545 to the near-complete collection of Tursellinus in 1596.[16] By Desideri's day, the Jesuits had championed their missions in a full century's worth of ideologically motivated histories, such as Pietro Maffei's *Historiarum Indicarum libri XVI* and Luis de Guzmán's *Historia de las misiones*.[17] Biographies and panegyrics of Jesuit saints also went through several editions, as did Jesuit martyrologies such as Philippe

Alegambe's *Mortes illustres* and Jean Nadasi's *Heroes et victimae caritatis*. Everywhere these works identified the spiritual successes of the Society with its temporal ones, as though the overseas missions were but the necessary historical manifestation of the inner emotion of the enraptured Jesuit. When Ippolito came to decide whether he wished to join the Society, it could boast of hundreds of colleges in Europe and extensive missions in Canada, Maryland, Florida, California, Mexico, Brazil, Argentina, Peru, Paraguay, Bolivia, Chile, India, China, and Japan. Members of the Society who braved all to span the world, especially in dangerous and exotic locales, imitated the apostolic zeal of Ignatius and Francis Xavier in a way that the Society's various professors, paper shufflers, and functionaries could not. No fewer than four thousand Jesuits volunteered when Nicolas Trigault, a veteran of the Chinese missions, appealed for recruits on a return mission to Europe from 1613 to 1622.[18] A glance at the Indipetae, the collection of letters requesting assignment to the overseas missions, reveals that many of the brightest lights in the Society, including several of those whom we will meet later in these pages, such as Athanasius Kircher, the last great Jesuit polymath, and Francisco Suárez, the frail, absentminded prince of Jesuit scholasticism, petitioned for the privilege of martyrdom in the Indies. The various fathers general of the Society of Jesus usually informed their petitioners that they would find their "Indies" in Europe and their martyrdom in more ordinary tasks such as teaching.[19] Jesuits who were chosen for the overseas missions could imitate Christ in ways that not even Ignatius himself imagined.

A Would-be Missionary's Spiritual Exercises

Ippolito entered the novitiate on May 9, 1700, after the minimum number of days required for the initial probation. As part of the novitiate, he would have risen early, made a brief visit to the chapel, meditated on a pious subject chosen the previous night, and assisted at the Mass held before breakfast. He would have read devotional works such as *The Imitation of Christ* by Thomas à Kempis and the *Vitae patrum*, a collection of the lives of early martyrs and confessors. As part of his nightly routine for the next ten years, Desideri would have listened as a Jesuit brother read after dinner in the Jesuit houses.[20] Letters from missionaries were commonly chosen for these nightly readings; in them, the deeds of the ancient martyrs were enacted anew to the astonishment of the novices and to the continued admiration of older Jesuits. Xavier led a gruesome procession of slain Jesuit missionaries marching straight into Desideri's day, such as Isaac Jogues and Jean de Brébeuf in Quebec, or Juan Bautista Maciado and Sebastian Vieira in Japan.[21] Such tales could not have made very appetizing after-dinner entertainment: Jogues had a few fingers chewed off by Mohawks, only to be tomahawked to death later. Vieira was suspended upside down in a pit filled with filth and excrement, small slits being made in his scalp to allow a trickle of blood just large enough to prevent him from lapsing into unconsciousness. After enduring this torment for three days, Vieira was taken down and burned alive. Leonardo Cinnami, who founded the Jesuit mission to Mysuru in 1648, offered a succinct summation of this spirituality when he wrote to his brothers in Europe: "The bravest and most generous among the soldiers of Christ will seek the place of greatest danger."[22]

Desideri's day's work would have included a conference led by the novice master—in this case, Giovanni Battista Conti—on some topic of Jesuit life and some form of manual labor.[23] Young novices were also subjected to tests that would allow their superiors to assess the strength of their vocation. It is not unlikely that Ippolito taught catechism in a village church, tended the dying in a hospital, or undertook a pilgrimage or small mission without money. We might presume that he excelled in whatever task was given him, for such tasks allowed Jesuit superiors to determine whether the novices were ingenious enough to succeed as missionaries overseas. Ippolito also would have made a thirty-day retreat based on the *Spiritual Exercises* of St. Ignatius during his two-year novitiate.[24] A collection of prayers, meditations, and directives that was compiled by St. Ignatius during his mortifications at Manresa and later codified, the *Spiritual Exercises* formed the backbone of Jesuit spirituality and culture.[25] All Jesuits would have made a pair of thirty-day retreats and yearly eight-day retreats based on the *Exercises* as part of their formation. Its methods for prayer and the examination of conscience would have been part of daily and, in especially diligent Jesuits, hourly life.[26] Such meditations taught young Jesuits such as Ippolito Desideri to do all things with the crucified Christ present before their every thought, word, and action—a contemplative presence that extended and prolonged the real presence of Christ in the Eucharistic celebrations in which the young Jesuits participated—but the *Exercises* also taught young Jesuits to make themselves present for Christ, to answer His call with the selfsame answer of the ancient patriarchs and prophets, the "here I am" of Abraham on Mount Moriah and Isaiah before the fiery seraphim. Such apostolic availability required a fearless abandonment to God's providence and a decisive choice to take upon oneself the greatest share in the sufferings of Christ. Such were the fantasies of a young Jesuit at the turn of the eighteenth century.

The thirty-day retreat that Ippolito underwent as part of his novitiate consisted of four "weeks" of meditation—the designation derives from the common practice of dividing the four sections of the exercises over a month, although the length of each "week" varied according to the needs of the retreatants—with each week devoted to specific supernatural realities. Each week looked to the next, and each individual exercise orchestrated the rising tide of spiritual exhilaration in a tight routine of prayers and guided meditations that would recapitulate in the willing novices St. Ignatius's own conversion from a worldly dilettante to a soldier battling foes on planes of existence not normally visible to the human eye. The novices did not read the *Spiritual Exercises* themselves; rather, the Jesuit who directed the novices through the various meditations used the text, along with supplementary material such as the *Directorium in Exercitia*, as a guide for his own preaching in order to leave the novices free to experience its spiritual realities more fully. In all likelihood Ippolito made the exercises with the other novices during a retreat in darkened quarters that the Society set aside for such purposes, while listening as their director guided their meditations. During their retreat, Ippolito and the other novices observed strict silence except for conversations with their spiritual director and the spoken formulae necessary for participation in the sacraments of penance and the Eucharist. They made five daily meditations, each of which lasted about an hour, with the first at midnight, the second at daybreak, the third before the morning celebration of Mass, the fourth during the early evening hours, and the fifth just before supper. As part of this regimen, the novices made daily examinations of conscience after the noon and evening meals in a deliberate effort to root out personal sins and shortcomings, and they met daily with their spiritual director to discuss their progress. Night fell with a final examination of conscience and a brief consideration of the midnight meditation. Since a fifteen-minute reflection followed each of the five meditations, what little free time the novices had would have been given to acts of reflection and penance. Although Ignatius himself curtailed severe penances later in his career, the novices were probably made aware of the heroic achievements of earlier Jesuits. Pierre Favre, when he first made the exercises under St. Ignatius's direction, fasted for several days, meditated in the snow, and slept, scantily clad, on a pile of wood. Francis Xavier, in addition to his own fasting, bound his body and legs tightly with cords, and made his meditations in this sorry state.[27] We have no idea what acts of penance might have attracted Ippolito himself, although his director would have suggested the typical mortifications of the early modern period, such as wearing a hair shirt, wrapping his body in chains, or scourging himself lightly. Following the principle of moderation suggested by St. Ignatius himself, the novices' spiritual director would have admonished them to take care that they felt the pains caused by such austerities "only in their flesh, and not in their bones."[28]

Such penances were but a small part of the *Exercises*, whose programmatic goal was to assist the novices in their task of "conquering" themselves, of ridding their souls of any disturbing or distracting desires, and of seeking and finding God's own providential guidance in their lives. The method for doing so is outlined in its famous *Principio y Fundamento*:

> Man is created to praise, reverence, and serve God our Lord, and save his soul thereby. All things on the face of the earth are created for man to help him fulfill the end for which he is created. Man is thus to use these things to the extent that they might help him attain this end. Similarly, he must rid himself of them insofar as they prevent him from attaining it. Therefore we must make ourselves indifferent to all created things, insofar as it is left to the choice of our free will and is not forbidden. For our part, we should act accordingly, preferring not health more than sickness, riches more than poverty, honor more than dishonor, a long life more than a short one, and so in all things we should desire and choose only those things that will best help us attain the end for which we were created.[29]

To initiate the process by which the novices would learn to rid themselves of unruly desires and discern the will of God in their lives, their spiritual director would have instructed them to stop a few paces short of the place in which they made their meditations, raise their minds to God, and place themselves in His presence. Following his director, Ippolito would then begin with a preparatory prayer, petitioning God for the grace that all of his intentions, actions, and works might be wholly devoted to God's praise and service. He would then visualize the "place" of his meditation, whether it be visible or invisible. Having set the stage for their first meditation with this *compositio loci*, the director would bid the novices to ask God to fire their hearts with feelings appropriate for the subject matter of their meditation, in this case, for "shame and confusion" at their own sins. The first point of the meditation proper was the sin of the angels, to which Ippolito would have applied the three powers of his soul— memory, intellect, and will—recollecting every detail of their refusal to serve God, considering each detail repeatedly, and rousing his affections, so that he might be "more ashamed and confounded" when he compared the angels' single sin with his own. The novices' first meditation progressed to a consideration of the single sin of Adam and Eve, which brought about the fall of mankind and required such lengthy and rigorous penance, and finally to the single sin of any person, who might well have been justly consigned to hell despite an otherwise exemplary life. As this first meditation neared its end, Desideri's director would have exhorted the novices with a final colloquy:

Imagine Christ our Lord before you, hanging on the cross. Speak with Him of how, being the Creator, He became man, and how, possessing eternal life, He submitted to this death for our sins. Then consider your life and ask yourself, "What have I done for Christ? What am I now doing for Christ? What ought I to do for Christ?"[30]

This highly charged meditation was just the first of a week's worth of meditations on sin and hell, but its dynamic was typical of the subsequent meditations, which added to the overall effect like a brimstone fugue, not unlike one of the sermons of Jonathan Edwards. For his second meditation, Ippolito would have called to mind his past dalliances, year by year, imagining in lurid detail the sins he had committed at home, at the minor seminary in Pistoia, and even since arriving in Rome. His director would ask him to imagine his relationships and weigh the malice of each sin he had committed against his parents, siblings, friends, and teachers. Ippolito Desideri would measure himself and his sins against the entire cosmos, seeking to make himself smaller and smaller, a mere "sore and abscess" that did nothing but infect the once-pure world. In fear and trembling, he would pace out the very dimensions of God's immeasurable Being. All this prepared Ippolito for the famous *exclamatio admirativa* of the first week, the "cry of admiration," in which the young Jesuit, staggering under the weight of a lifetime of sins, contemplated all creatures, from the tiniest grain of sand to the highest angel, against the backdrop of the incomprehensibility of sin, suffering, and death. Ippolito would see with the eyes of his imagination all creation split asunder at its most elemental level. On one side, he would consider the sun, moon, and stars, the plants and animals, as they took their stand under Christ with the saints and angels. On the other side was Ippolito Desideri, his head bowed under the raised swords of the avenging angels and his soul suspended bodily over the "new hell" that would have opened under him had it not been for the sustaining force of God's love, which stayed the angels' hands and mysteriously turned judgment into mercy.[31]

Lest the novices lose their fervor, the remaining exercises of the first week deepened the sense of contrition and the desire to amend one's life through a series of repetitions and reviews that culminated in a meditation on the "length, breadth, and depth" of hell, in which the novices applied each of their physical senses to the meditation in turn, imagining the sights, sounds, smells, tastes, and tactile sensations of hell in the most excruciating detail. This type of meditation, which is often mistakenly seen to be unique to the Society of Jesus, is called an "application of the senses" (*applicatio sensuum*).[32] Asking

God for a "deep awareness" of the pains suffered by the damned, Desideri would have been instructed

> with the gaze of the imagination, to see the immense fires, and the souls, as it were, in bodies of fire; to hear the wailing, the screaming, the cries and blasphemies against Christ our Lord and all His saints; to smell the smoke, the brimstone, the stench and rottenness; to taste bitter things, tears, sadness, and the sting of conscience; with the sense of touch, to feel the flames that envelop and burn souls.[33]

The depth of remorse brought on during the first week of the exercises led naturally to a consideration of one's choice of a path of life in the second. Ippolito's director would have asked the novices to imagine Christ's personal call to them through a series of meditations, from Christ's personal existence as the Divine Word before His incarnation through His triumphal entry into Jerusalem on the Sunday before His crucifixion. These meditations treated the novices to a dramatic enactment of salvation history in which they themselves were asked to assume prominent, even heroic, roles. Two of them, the call of the king and the meditation on the two standards, are particularly important for understanding the great desire that young novices had for the overseas missions. The meditation on the call of the king stood outside the cycle of individual exercises during the second week; in a sense, it was its principle and the foundation. Ippolito Desideri would have made this meditation twice daily, once immediately upon rising in the morning and again about an hour before supper. In it, he would envision a king deserving of every respect and honor, who addressed him directly:

> It is my will to conquer all infidel lands. Whoever wishes to come with me must be content to eat as I eat, drink as I drink, and dress as I dress. He must be willing to work with me by day and watch with me by night. He will then share the spoils of victory inasmuch as he has toiled with me.[34]

Asked to consider what response a faithful subject would give to such a virtuous king, Desideri would imagine the shame of refusing such an honorable ruler. The Jesuits would then repeat the meditation, placing the divine king before their mind's eye. Christ now addressed all mankind, including the young Jesuit himself:

> It is My will to conquer the whole world and all of my enemies, and thereby enter into the glory of My Father. Whoever wishes to come

28   JESUIT ON THE ROOF OF THE WORLD

with Me must toil with Me, so that following Me in suffering, he may follow Me in glory.[35]

Desideri would then consider that those who wished to show the greatest affection for Christ, and those who wished to distinguish themselves in His service, would offer themselves entirely for the work, gladly following Him in whatever suffering was necessary to accomplish His task. Feeling himself chosen for great things, and called by God to accomplish them, he would consider what sort of answer a young Jesuit should give.

With this foundation, Desideri contemplated the Incarnation for the first meditation of the second week. He would see in his imagination "the great extent and space of the world, where so many people and nations dwell."[36] With spiritual ears, Desideri would hear blasphemies whispered and roared; with a spiritual sense of smell, he would detect the stench of obscene rites. With spiritual sight, he would see people descending into hell. But imagining the feelings of God Himself as He witnessed this pageantry of destruction, Desideri also would have been encouraged by his director to feel compassion for this great loss of souls in the same way that he had felt the immense burden of his own sins. And just as Ippolito had experienced God's mercy "with mounting feeling" in the first week of exercises, so now he would be deeply touched by God's own desire to save all men and women from sin, suffering, and death. He would see Christ, His mother, and the saints in his imagination; listen to what they were saying and doing to effect God's will; smell and taste the fragrance and sweetness of God's infinite compassion; and devoutly embrace or kiss the places in which Christ enacted the salvation of the world in order to gather more spiritual fruit from his meditations.

On the fourth day of the second week, Desideri and the other novices would have made the meditation on the two standards. If the meditation on the call of the king showed the novices what was expected of the soldier of God, the meditation on the two standards showed them their enemy: "Imagine how the evil leader of all the enemy forces seats himself in the center of the vast plain of Babylon, on a great throne of fire and smoke—a horrible and terrible sight to behold."[37] The novices would see the Devil haranguing and scattering his troops, "some to one city, some to another, throughout the whole world, missing no province, no place, no state of life, nor indeed any single person."[38] The spiritual director would ask the novices to consider the Devil's armaments, dwelling on the riches of the world, its empty honors, and the fateful pride that arose when they lured one away from God. To these temptations, the director contrasted Christ, meek but beautiful, choosing men from every age and nation to teach his doctrines, charging His soldiers sweetly to help all men and women, and arming them with the failsafe weapons of spiritual warfare. A novice might even glimpse the demonic Goliath intended for him by the Devil himself.

For the meditations of the third week, the novices would have prepared for the rigors of the newfound discipleship by marching in their imaginations on an extended Good Friday procession, following Christ step by step during His passion to His death on the Cross, making stops in Gethsemane, the houses of Annas, Caiaphas, and Pontius Pilate, Golgotha, and the sepulcher in which Christ was buried. These meditations tempered their previous excitement to a mute, smoldering passion, preparing the would-be missionary to accept the harshest toil and to cast aside his life for the Gospel. John Helyar's notes on the *Spiritual Exercises*, which some believe to be Ignatius's own words, express this passion bluntly: "Christ, the supreme captain, promises no outward joys, nor even anything agreeable, but only what is rough, hard, and bitter. He promises constant war."[39] Ippolito and the other novices would pray accordingly for tears and deep suffering in imitation of Christ, to be, in Ignatius's words, "heart-broken with Christ heartbroken" (*dolor con Christo doloroso*).[40] A young man brought low by penance might then experience a magnificent conversion like the one brought about during Ignatius's own convalescence, rising from his bed as a soldier in God's army.

One can imagine the emotional release when, after three weeks of silence and darkness accompanied by fasting and other acts of mortification, the novice director threw open the windows for the fourth and final week of meditations. As light flooded the room, Desideri and the other novices would be encouraged to feel the apostles' joy as the resurrected Christ sought them and commissioned them to go into the world and baptize people in the name of the Holy Trinity. These exercises brought the novices to the resurrected Christ as he appeared to each of His disciples in turn, communicating to the novices the victory that they themselves might win over death, were they but passionate enough to follow Christ like Ignatius and his original companions. Praying for this spiritual power, Ippolito Desideri would end this meditation, most likely made in the fall or winter of 1700, begging the Virgin Mary to intercede for him to her divine Son, that the young Tuscan might be found worthy to serve under the banner of Christ.

Meditation and Mnemonics

It would be difficult to overestimate the effect that the *Exercises* had on young novices such as Desideri. Dull as they seem when simply read, put into practice the *Exercises* offered a powerful means to inculcate the virtues necessary to be a good Jesuit and—if a young man was particularly talented—a missionary and martyr of the Society.[41] Their efficacy required exceptionally vivid *phantasia* and *imaginatio*, the faculties, according to early modern scholastic philosophers, that enabled the soul to produce and process images.[42] Before every meditation of the *Exercises*, Desideri would have made a *compositio loci*, in which he visualized the place where the events upon which he was about to meditate took place, even down to the smallest detail.[43] If the meditation was on Christ's birth, for example, Desideri might have imagined the width of the road from Nazareth to Bethlehem or the size of the cave in which Christ was born. In the event that the subject of meditation was itself invisible, such as in the meditation on sin that he made in his first week, Desideri would have imagined a corresponding figure or symbol. St. Ignatius, for example, recommended imagining oneself as imprisoned in a valley of tears surrounded by brute, threatening beasts. Desideri also would have fired his imagination with the meditative technique called *applicatio sensuum* to create especially vivid and affecting mental images. In this respect, spiritual directors encouraged their charges to "color" their images with deeply emotional associations in order to instill the "feeling" and "savoring" of spiritual realities (*el sentir y gustar de las cosas internamente*).[44] Of course, a Jesuit of the early eighteenth century did not think himself to be merely imagining such realities any more than a Tibetan monk who similarly engages his own *phantasia* or *imaginatio*. Concessions to the imagination were necessary only because the supernatural realities depicted in such meditations defied human comprehension.

The techniques of the *compositio loci* and *applicatio sensuum* situate Ignatius's *Spiritual Exercises* in the traditions of therapeutic philosophy that date back to the Stoics and ancient Church fathers.[45] Such philosophical traditions were mnemonic; they assumed that the pursuit of wisdom required the philosopher to keep important matters—particularly his own death and a rule for living accordingly—before his eyes through the disciplined exercise of memory (*mneme*) and meditation (*melete*).[46] In Christian antiquity, the unifying form of these spiritual exercises was the "memory of God" (*mneme theou*), an all-encompassing spiritual practice that included exercises of self-mortification (*ascesis*) and moral education (*paideia*).[47] As a mnemonic practice, Christian meditation was also indebted to ancient rhetoric, especially the rhetoric of Cicero, which listed memory, along with invention, arrangement, style, and delivery, as one of the five canons of rhetoric. The first of these canons, *inventio*, is particularly important in this regard: a monk meditating in his cell developed his *memoria* not in order to regurgitate information as a student might on an examination for a class that interested him little, but rather as would an orator or musician who needed to improvise upon a theme to move his listeners. Building upon the advice to place memory images in architectural settings, medieval Christian authors even developed mnemonic techniques in which the meditator built mental "superstructures" (*superaedificationes*) on two- or three-dimensional architectural plans. In this way, the monk laid a path for his memory just as an architect used his lines (*linea*) to measure the iconic proportions (*rationes*) of a building. After the meditator raised such structures in his mind, he then traced a "way" among them, with various stages or steps being strongly marked by affection and emotion.

Unlike the monks of late antiquity or the friars of the Middle Ages, the Jesuits had a large reserve of printed images to assist them in their meditations, as well as several fully fledged theories about their use in meditation.[48] Drawing upon the Renaissance fascination with emblems, members of the Society of Jesus typically used combinations of mottos, images, and longer texts for their meditations, even in the Asian missions, where they prepared illustrations of Christ's life, depictions of heaven and hell, and maps imbued with apologetic and polemical purpose.[49] Emblems allowed the Jesuit to familiarize himself with the topic of meditation before going to sleep and recall it during his formal meditation in the morning. More important, they allowed spiritual directors and preachers to anchor their sermons with a single scriptural text, which could be repeated for dramatic effect, and also to embellish them with vivid images freely adapted to the needs of their listeners. A spiritual director who wished to preach on Christ's descent to hell while he was leading his young charges through the *Spiritual Exercises* might have turned for inspiration to a common Jesuit emblem book such as Jerónimo Nadal's *Adnotationes et meditationes in Evangelia* (or, as it is known in some editions, *Evangelicae historiae imagines*).[50] Figure 1.1 shows each of the main aspects of ancient mnemonic practice set out in visual form: the topic of the meditation, Christ's descent to hell, is announced at the top of the page, and three scriptural passages are provided for the body of the meditation, in this case the ninth chapter of Zechariah, the twenty-fourth chapter of Ecclesiasticus (or Sirach), and the fourth chapter of St. Paul's Epistle to the Ephesians. An image is provided to assist the *compositio loci*, and each point for meditation is labeled in the picture and listed below the image.

A Jesuit who wished to preach or meditate on this image had considerable freedom in applying it according to his own needs. He might, for example, choose any one of the scriptural passages, a section from one or more of them, or a different passage altogether. He might use an entire chapter or select a single verse. Indeed, the three passages cited show us something of Nadal's own choices in this regard; he does not select the two passages that have

QVÆ GESSIT CHRISTVS DESCENDENS AD INFEROS.
131
Zach. ix. Eccle. xxiiij. ad Ephes. iiij.
ciiij

A. Christi anima nulla mora interposita, venit in Limbum Patrum.
B. Omnium sanctorum Patrum animæ, animam IESV supplices venerantur.
C. Anima latronis, paulo post mortui, portatur ab Angelis ad Limbum.

D. In Limbo infantû nulla pars huius lætitiæ.
E. E Purgatorio multæ animæ liberantur, quod significant radij lucis inde ad limbum Patrum prodeuntes.
F. In inferno inferiori Lucifer cum suis, ipsoque Iuda grauáter fremit.

FIGURE 1.1. Christ's Descent to Hell from Jerónimo Nadal, *Adnotationes et meditationes in Evangelia* (Antwerp: Martinus, Nutius, 1595). Courtesy of Special Collections, Pius XII Memorial Library, St. Louis University.

garnered the most attention from twentieth-century commentators on Christ's descent to hell, namely, the mention of Christ's preaching to the "spirits in prison" (1 Pet 3:18–20) and the proclamation of the gospel to the dead (1 Pet 4:6), although a Jesuit very well could have constructed a sermon around them using the same *compositio loci* and closely following the points identified by Nadal. A preacher who chose to follow Nadal's suggestions, however, likely would have highlighted two verses from the ninth chapter of Zechariah, which is a prophetic oracle delivered against Israel's enemies. Speaking of Tyre, Zechariah's oracle says,

> Behold, the Lord will possess her,
> And hurl her wealth into the sea,
> And she shall be devoured by fire. (Zech 9:4)

A preacher of the early modern period—a Christian preacher in any case—likely would have turned to the following verse after elaborating upon the first oracle:

> The Lord God shall be seen over them,
> And His arrows shall go forth as lightning:
> And the Lord God will sound the trumpet,
> And march forth in the whirlwinds of the South. (Zech 9:14)

Nadal's image alludes to this last verse with its depiction of the cloud of angelic ministers who accompany Christ to the underworld, since Christian exegetes and iconographers usually associated the whirlwinds that accompany God's actions, most famously in the theophany in Job, with angelic spirits. Nadal's image also clues us in to why he chose the twenty-fourth chapter of Sirach to illustrate Christ's descent to hell. Christian theologians, especially Franciscans and Jesuits, generally interpreted this praise of Wisdom as an allusion to the Incarnate Word, who "came forth from the mouth of the Most High" (Sir 24:5). Here, Wisdom covers the earth "as a cloud" (Sir 24:6), a text that is mirrored in the *compositio loci*, which shows the broad expanse of the earth and its nether regions. The cloud, which echoes God's primordial watering of the earth in Genesis, also dovetails with the imagery of Zechariah:

> I dwelt in the highest places,
> And my throne was in a pillar of cloud
> I alone have compassed the circuit of heaven
> And have penetrated the depths of the abyss,
> And walked upon the waves of the sea. (Sir 24:7–8)

This text from Sirach alludes to the text Nadal has chosen from St. Paul:

> Grace was given to each of us according to the measure of Christ's gift.
> Therefore it is said, "When he ascended on High He led a host of
> captives, and he gave gifts to men." In saying, "He ascended," what
> does it mean but that he had also descended into the lower parts of the
> earth? He who descended is He who also ascended far above all the
> heavens, that he might fill all things. (Eph 4:7–10)

A preacher could embellish each or any of these passages with the points
depicted in the image; he could consider the Holy Soul of Christ [A], the
souls of the holy fathers who venerated His Holy Name before the Incarnation
[B], the soul of the good thief who gained his salvation on the cross and was
promised the wine of paradise [C], the souls of infants in limbo [D], the souls
liberated from purgatory [E], and finally, Lucifer himself seated amidst the
blazes of the lowest hell [F]. A skilled preacher, sensing fatigue on the part of
the Jesuits making their retreat, might even exhort them to greater diligence in
their mnemonics by returning to the text of Sirach:

> Come over to me, all ye who desire me,
> And be filled with my fruits.
> For my spirit is sweet above honey,
> And my inheritance above honey and the honeycomb.
> The memory of me is unto everlasting generations. (Sir 24:26–28)

Events narrated in Scripture often required rather elaborate emblems, like
those found in Nadal's *Evangelicae historiae imagines*, to help the Jesuit remember everything that he might consider during his sermon or meditation.
Compositions of invisible realities, such as we see in figure 1.2, depiction of
the seven deadly sins from a late seventeenth-century edition of the *Spiritual
Exercises*, are often simpler. In this case, a young Jesuit would need to remember the various classifications of sin to make his frequent examinations of
conscience and to ensure that he made a good confession when he participated
in the sacrament of penance. And so this image is a textbook example of the
injunction commonly found in mnemonic manuals to compose uncluttered
backgrounds against which to place discrete, easily recalled images. For the
compositio loci, a Jesuit would be asked to imagine the bottomless pit (*puteus
abyssi*), mentioned at the opening verse of the ninth chapter of the Apocalypse
(Rev 9:1), followed by a sinner pierced by seven swords, and over whose head
hangs the sword of justice (*gladius ultionis*). The text of the meditation is "In a
moment they descend to hell" (Job 21:13). Here, too, there is a tight correlation
between the image and the text: a skilled Latinist certainly would have noted
that the *in puncto* of the passage from Job derives etymologically from *pungere*,

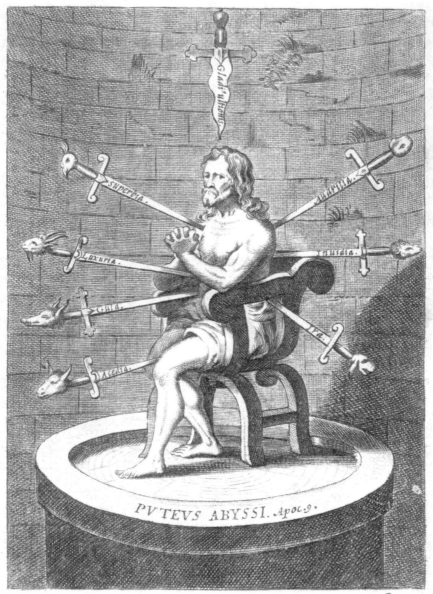

In pũĉto ad inferna defcēdunt. Iob 21.

FIGURE 1.2. Mnemonic image for the seven deadly sins, from *Esercitii spirituali di S. Ignatio* (Rome: Nella Stamperia del Varese, 1673). Courtesy of Special Collections, Pius XII Memorial Library, St. Louis University.

which means "to stab." The seven deadly sins are imagined accordingly as seven swords. While each of the swords is labeled, note that the hilt of each also mnemonically depicts an animal often associated with the sin in question: pride (*superbia*) is shown as a rooster, lust (*luxuria*) as a goat, gluttony (*gula*) as a pig, sloth (*acedia*) as a stubborn mule, and so forth. Figure 1.3, an image of the four sins that cry out for divine justice from Jan David's popular emblem book *Veridicus Christianus*, shows the same mnemonic injunction carried out with maximum efficiency. The four sins—which a Jesuit would have known to be oppression of the poor, defrauding a laborer of his wages, willful murder, and sodomy—are arranged as four putti who hover in the sky over a barren, deserted landscape. Each issues an identical cry for vengeance (*vindica*), which rises to God as the heavens open and the divine Father moves to respond.

Hardly any discussion of the second imaginative technique, the *applicatio sensuum*, can avoid mentioning James Joyce's *A Portrait of the Artist as a Young Man*, where Father Arnall develops his sermon on hell in Clontarf Chapel over several hair-raising pages. In our case, Joyce's oft-quoted meditation on the fires of hell allows me to end my digression on Jesuit mnemonics and return to Desideri's own spirituality:

> Our earthly fire again, no matter how fierce or widespread it may be, is always of a limited extent: but the lake of fire in hell is boundless, shoreless, and bottomless. It is on record that the devil himself, when asked the question by a certain soldier, was obliged to confess that if a whole mountain were thrown into the burning ocean of hell it would be burned up in an instant like a piece of wax. And this terrible fire will not afflict the bodies of the damned only from without but each lost soul will be a hell unto itself, the boundless fire raging in its very vitals. O, how terrible is the lot of those wretched beings! The blood seethes and boils in the veins, the brains are boiling in the skull, the heart and breast glowing and bursting, the bowels a redhot mass of burning pulp, the tender eyes flaming like molten balls.[51]

Although the final touch—"tender eyes flaming like molten balls"—is Joyce's own, it is now well established that the great Irish modernist borrowed Father Arnall's sermon from another Jesuit from Pistoia, Giovanni Pietro Pinamonti.[52] Such a sermon would have been standard fare in northern Italy during the late seventeenth and early eighteenth centuries, especially in the rural missions. Pinamonti's master and traveling companion Paulo Segneri preached similar sermons, barefoot, to as many as twenty thousand people at a time.[53] Antonio Baldinucci, another Florentine Jesuit sometimes associated

FIGURE 1.3. Mnemonic image for the four sins that cry out for divine justice, from Jan David, *Veridicus Christianus* (Antwerp: Ex Officina Plantiniana, apud Ioannem Moretum, 1601). Courtesy of Special Collections, The Sheridan Libraries, The John Hopkins University.

with Segneri and Pinamonti, began his own hellfire sermons with a robust self-scourging and closed his missions with bonfires in which weapons, playing cards, and dice surrendered by his audiences were burned in the town square.[54] Desideri himself mentions the work Joyce used as the model for Father Arnall's sermon, Pinamonti's *L'inferno aperto*, which imaginatively "opens" hell to its readers with a spine-tingling meditation for each day of the week.[55] On Sunday, the reader could consider his imprisonment in hell, its darkness, and its stench; on Monday, he could consider the fire, its quality, quantity, and intensity; on Tuesday, he could consider his hideous companions in eternity; on Wednesday, the pain that accompanies the loss of divine favor; and so on for the remainder of the week.[56] Figure 1.4 shows two of the images

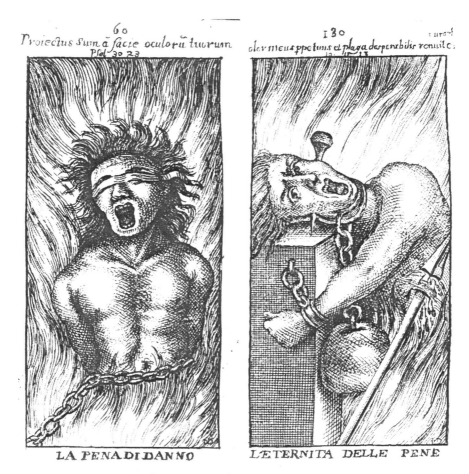

FIGURE 1.4. Two images for meditation from Giovanni Pinamonti, *L'Inferno aperto* (Milan, 1693). Courtesy of the Bayerische Staatsbibliothek, Munich.

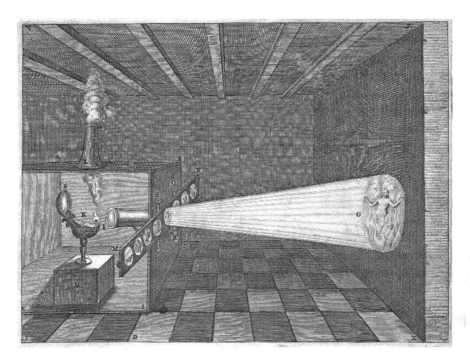

FIGURE 1.5. Kircher's "Magic Lantern" from Johannes Stephanus Kestlerus, *Physiologia Kircheriana experimentalis* (Amsterdam: Ex Officina Janssonio Waesbergiana, 1680). Courtesy of Special Collections, The Sheridan Libraries, The John Hopkins University.

that accompanied Pinamonti's meditations in some editions of his work, and it is in this context that Desideri mentions his fellow Pistoian Jesuit.[57]

In Desideri's day, Jesuits apparently used the latest technology to produce even more vivid images of the sort that frightened young Stephen Dedalus. If one looks closely at the image projected on the wall by Athanasius Kircher's magic lantern, as we see in figure 1.5, one can see that it closely resembles those found in Pinamonti's text. I suppose Kircher, who was known for his love of practical jokes, chose this image to get a chuckle from fellow Jesuits, but we cannot discount the possibility that a few spiritual directors might have frightened their charges with Father Kircher's gadget.

Outer *Phantasia*: Jesuit Iconography and the Missions

Desideri pronounced his vows of poverty, obedience, and chastity on April 28, 1702, and entered the prestigious Collegio Romano, near the Jesuits' Church of Sant'Ignazio. He completed his course of studies in philosophy over the next four years and taught the Greek and Latin classics in the Jesuit colleges in Orvieto and Arezzo from 1706 to 1710 and later at the Collegio Romano itself. In autumn 1710 he began his theological studies and began supervising younger students in logic. On August 14, 1712, he petitioned the Jesuit father general, Michelangelo Tamburini, for permission to become a missionary to the Indies. Knowing that the father general would read his petition on the following day, Ippolito took care to point out that the Feast of the Blessed Virgin Mary's Assumption into heaven was also the same day that Francis Xavier had landed at Kagoshima and initiated the fabled Jesuit mission to Japan.[58] Showing himself keenly aware of the Society's history, the young Jesuit noted that it had been exactly one hundred years since Christianity had been forbidden in Japan.[59] Declaring himself a "worthless sinner" (*indegno peccatore*), but also pointing out that Christ Himself called not the just but rather sinners, the young Jesuit begged the general to grant him the "most-longed-for power" (*facoltà sospiratissima*) and send him to the Indies.

Lacking any earlier testimony, we cannot know when Desideri first heard the call to the missions. His later account says simply that the Jesuit had felt a strong inner impulse to become a missionary to the Indies for "a number of years" (*per lo spazio di varij anni*).[60] He may have dreamt of such a life from an early age, or it may have been among the resolutions that he would have made as a normal part of his practice of the *Exercises* during his novitiate. At any rate, his desires came to a head when Ippolito made a pilgrimage to the Holy House of Loreto and practiced the *Spiritual Exercises* there in late September 1711. Whenever he may have first resolved to enter the missions, he could have found no better confirmation than the vaulted ceiling of Sant'Ignazio. The young Jesuit would have gazed up at Andrea Pozzo's recently completed tour de force, *The Allegory of the Universal Mission of the Jesuits*, a small section of which is reproduced in figure 1.6.[61] The Jesuit painter, taking as his theme the missionary spirit of the Society of Jesus, depicted God the Father sending forth a blazing ray of light upon Christ, who communicated His fire to Ignatius Loyola upon a vast illusionistic fresco that made it seem that the church had no ceiling at all. The illustrious founder, refracting Christ's light as a prism, then sends four beams that enlighten Europe, Asia, Africa, and the Americas. The words of Christ that surround the fresco and announce its theme are from the Gospel of Luke: "I came to cast fire upon the earth, and would that it were already kindled" (Lk 12:49).[62]

The imaginary cities of the novices' *Spiritual Exercises* could hardly have compared to the fantastic qualities of Rome itself. In the hundred years before Desideri was born, the eternal city underwent an urban renewal that involved the construction of plazas and palaces, the completion of St. Peter's Basilica,

FIGURE 1.6. Asia with Saints Ignatius Loyola and Francis Xavier from Andrea Pozzo's *Allegory of the Universal Mission of the Society of Jesus*, Chiesa di Sant'Ignazio, Rome. Scala/Art Resource, NY.

and the erection of several Egyptian obelisks as symbols of the Church's triumph over paganism.[63] Although one loses sight of the early Society when one identifies it with the baroque, the Society that Desideri entered largely set the standard by which baroque extravagance is measured. Two of its churches in Rome, Sant'Ignazio and the Gesù, are undisputed masterpieces of baroque architecture, and the Jesuits regularly patronized artists such as Gianlorenzo Bernini and Peter-Paul Rubens. Bernini, the quintessential baroque artist, was a close friend of the Jesuit general Giovanni Paulo Oliva and regularly made the exercises under his direction.[64] In addition to designing the surreal, undulating *baldacchino* in St. Peter's, Bernini finished the chapel for the Jesuit novitiate, Sant'Andrea al Quirinale, just thirty years before Desideri journeyed to Rome.[65] The programmatic iconography of these Jesuit churches bolstered the meditations of the *Spiritual Exercises* with such vehemence that many scholars have not hesitated to label Jesuit art propaganda, even if the multileveled irony of this designation seems lost on some of them.[66] The *Spiritual Exercises* found its greatest reinforcement in the iconographical program of the Gesù itself.[67] But this is no less true of smaller chapels such as Bernini's Sant'Andrea al Quirinale, which boasted several vivid scenes of martyrdom for Desideri to contemplate.[68] One would be seriously mistaken if one imagined that the artistic and architectural extravagance typical of these baroque masterpieces mitigated the stark emotional impact of the *Exercises*. The golden oval of Sant'Andrea al Quirinale stood above its own life-sized depiction of the crucifixion of St. Andrew as Christ's resurrection stood above His Cross, and the exaltation of the fourth week of the *Exercises* raised the young novices from the austere passions of the third. The gravity-defying domes and impossible skies of Jesuit architecture evoked, with precise deliberation, the interior extravagance of generous abandon.

One cycle of paintings is particularly important in this regard, if only because we can be reasonably sure that Desideri laid eyes upon it before departing for India. In the sacristy of São Roque, the main Jesuit church in Lisbon, Desideri would have seen André Reinoso's twenty paintings depicting the life of St. Francis Xavier.[69] The events of Xavier's life depicted in the sacristy of São Roque curiously anticipate Desideri's own adventures. The first painting depicts Xavier receiving the apostolic blessing of Pope Paul III, and subsequent images show Xavier bravely enduring the dangerous overseas passage, preaching the Gospel to exotically dressed locals, celebrating Mass, battling demons, and confounding Buddhist monks in the Yamaguchi court. A frank exoticism suffuses these scenes. Reinoso shows evident delight in portraying the bold patterns on the Indian spectators' clothing, their brightly dyed turbans, and the shaved heads of the Japanese monks. The cycle culminates with Reinoso's melancholy composition of Xavier's death off the coast of China (figure 1.7). The saint's eyes roll back just slightly, showing that the heavenly scene of Christ and the Virgin upon which he gazes is situated not in the physical space depicted in the painting but in the interior space of his own ecstasy. Xavier's mouth opens just enough to utter a final prayer as his shipmates leave without him.

The dominant theme of this painting, which Desideri could have contemplated as he waited for his own ship in Lisbon, is abandonment. On the

FIGURE 1.7. André Reinoso, *Death of St. Francis Xavier*, c. 1619. Oil on canvas, 34.6 x 61.4 inches. Church of São Roque, Lisbon. Courtesy of Júlio Marques, SCML/Museu de São Roque.

material level, the saint is left to die alone on the shore of the South China Sea, but on the spiritual level, Xavier resigns himself to divine providence. Not many Jesuits were chosen to follow in the footsteps of St. Francis Xavier. Ippolito Desideri was one of the few, lucky Jesuits who were given the opportunity to live this fantasy to the fullest.

2

From Rome to Lhasa

Are they servants of Christ? I am a better one—I speak as a
madman—with far greater labors, far more imprisonments, with
countless beatings, and often near death. Five times I have received
the forty lashes less one. Three times I have been beaten with rods;
once I was stoned. Three times I have been shipwrecked; a night and a
day I have been adrift at sea; on frequent journeys, in danger from
rivers, danger from robbers, danger from my own people, danger
from gentiles, danger in the city, danger in the wilderness, danger at
sea, danger from false brethren; in toil and hardship, through many a
sleepless night, in hunger and thirst, often without food, in cold and
exposure.

—2 Corinthians 11:23–27

Ippolito Desideri received permission to become a missionary to the
Indies on August 15, 1712. A month later, the young Jesuit kissed
the feet of Pope Clement XI, received the apostolic benediction, and, at
the age of twenty-seven years and nine months, embarked from
Rome. We do not know whether Desideri himself knew anything of
Tibet before he embarked on his journey, nor do we know whether he
intended to open the Tibetan mission.[1] Sent into the far country like
Abram, he left for a land that appeared only sporadically on maps,
when it appeared at all. Herodotus had said little about the regions
north of India, except to report a curious tale about gold-digging ants.[2]
Alexander the Great left no descriptions of lands north of the Hindu

Kush, nor did Strabo or Ptolemy. Cosmas Indicopleustes—a writer known by Desideri—mentions the region only as a source of yak tails and musk.[3] To a young Jesuit with humanistic leanings, steeped in the travel literature of the day, a land beyond India unknown to the historians of the ancient world must have seemed terribly exotic. But missionaries' letters also show us how such fantasies stretched or snapped when Jesuits faced the unpleasant realities of the evangelical life in such faraway lands. Missionaries who had dreamt of escaping bureaucracy at home often found themselves embroiled in its machinations overseas, thwarted by incompetent superiors, crippled by rivalries, or simply overburdened by the responsibilities of leading fledgling Christian communities. Ippolito Desideri is no exception in this regard. As heroic as his adventures often sound, the Jesuit was saddled with several rather mundane problems during his journey. Trials were commonplace enough: a missionary aiming to be a true servant of Christ was judged successful if he withstood them and humbly submitted to the grace of God. In this respect, Tibet was a blank screen upon which the would-be missionary projected the larger fantasies of the *Spiritual Exercises*, but it was also a field of spiritual battle upon which the missionary could prove himself an ideal missionary and martyr of the Society of Jesus.

Rumors of Cathay

Medieval writers fared little better than their ancient ancestors when they attempted to describe Tibet.[4] The twelfth-century Jewish traveler Benjamin of Tudela mentioned the land of snows but was satisfied to repeat the ancient claim that it was a prime source of musk.[5] Arabic writers largely echoed Benjamin.[6] Iohannes de Plano Carpini, a Franciscan friar dispatched by Pope Innocent IV as an envoy to Chinggis Khan in 1245, provided some of the first reports of Central Asia to medieval Europe and is probably the source of the medieval association of cannibalism with Tibet. Carpini also seems to have been the first Western writer to use a cognate of the word *Tibet*, at least in the forms *Burithabet*, *Buritabet*, and *Burithobec*.[7] Another Franciscan, Guillelmus of Rubruc, traveled in Central Asia during the middle of the thirteenth century. While he used the forms *Tebet* or *Tebec*, Guillelmus offered little more than the interesting anecdote that the Tangut, a tribe that lived north of Tibet near the western border of China, made goblets of their parents' skulls to call to mind the inevitability of death.[8] Guillelmus was also the first to report on the famous prayer *oṃ maṇi padme hūṃ*, although he did not link the prayer to Tibet itself.[9] Another friar, Odoricus de Portu Naonis, added details about the mastiffs of the land he calls *Tibor, Tibon*, or *Tibot* and its funerary customs.[10] An anonymous Spanish Franciscan of the mid-fourteenth century used the form *Trimic*.[11] Marco Polo was scarcely more detailed.[12] Maps based upon these accounts, as well as those of John Mandeville and John of Montecorvino, were confused about Tibet's location; sometimes they placed it on the far coast of East Asia, near the newly discovered California.[13] Depending on their sources, the maps of the sixteenth and seventeenth centuries calculated the location of Tibet with varying degrees of success as well.[14] Curiously enough, as cartographers assimilated new information from Portuguese sailors and Jesuit missionaries, Tibet disappeared from these maps. In their efforts to adhere to greater scientific standards, mapmakers erased regions that seemed mythical or needlessly obscure. Like depictions of the Garden of Eden or the kingdom of Prester John, Tibet receded from the world of empirical realities and entered the rarefied world of the imagination.

Except for the very recent entry of Capuchins into Tibet—an entry of which Desideri may have been unaware until embarking on his own journey—the land of snows was known only to a small coterie of humanist cartographers and missionaries in the early eighteenth century. At this point in European history, it would be a bit of an exaggeration to speak of a particular "fantasy" of Tibet. While the Jesuits showed some interest in the regions between the Mughal and Manchu empires, there is little to suggest that the land of snows excited the fantasies of Europeans in the way that China did at this time, or India did later. The Jesuits did have considerable hearsay of the land of snows, even before António Andrade's account was published in 1626. Matteo Ricci himself called for an exploration of those lands once known by the medieval Franciscans in a letter from Nanjing on October 12, 1596.[15] Jesuit missionaries in the Mughal Empire, including Antonio Monserrate, Rodolfo Acquaviva, and Jerónimo Xavier, also knew of Tibet in the late sixteenth century.[16] Acquaviva spoke of the land of Bottan, beyond the Himalayas, as early as 1582.[17] In a justly famous passage of the *Mongolicae legationis commentarius* from 1591, Monserrate wrote of vestiges of Christianity to be found in the deep recesses of the Himalayas, where priests in linen garments read from the Holy Scriptures and distributed consecrated wine and bread from golden vessels, although he did not believe them to be the Bothi or Bothentes, who were "governed by magicians."[18] Xavier wrote in two letters from 1598 about rumors of a considerable Christian population in Marco Polo's Cathay.[19] After consulting Ortelius's *Theatrum orbis terrarum*, Xavier sent his companion Bento de Góis from Lahore through Peshawar, Kabul, Yarkand, Khotan, Turfan, and eventually to Suzhou (now Jiuquan), near Dunhuang. Although de Góis only skirted the borders of Tibet, he did solve the vexing problem of whether the

Cathay of the medieval travelers was in fact China. This discovery nearly went unheeded, for de Góis died under mysterious circumstances, most likely the victim of poisoning in Suzhou. The weary Jesuit held on just long enough to meet the lay brother sent by Matteo Ricci to intercept him; the brother saved a few pages of de Góis's diary from the fire.[20]

Excited by Monserrate's mention of Christians living in the Himalayas, António Andrade entered western Tibet in 1624.[21] Andrade discovered no Christians, but he felt that the territory was ripe for evangelization. After returning to Agra for more missionaries, the Portuguese Jesuit made a second journey from Agra through Delhi to Tsaparang with two other Jesuits, Gonzales de Souza and Manoel Marques, and established the first Christian mission to Tibet on August 28, 1625. Joined by João de Oliveira, Alano dos Anjos, and Francis Godinho (and later by António Pereira and António da Fonseca), Andrade gave relatively detailed accounts of Tibetan religion and culture, noting, for example, the differences among Tibetan religious orders and the ubiquitous mantra oṃ maṇi padme hūṃ.[22] He also thought that Tibetan religion bore traces of the mysteries of Christianity. In Andrade's telling, the Holy Trinity, the Incarnation, the Mother of God, the angels, and the sacraments all had correlates in Tibetan religion.[23] Tibetans, too, were a good-natured and pious people.[24] In one of the more sympathetic missionary accounts of non-Christian iconography, Andrade points out that the wrathful depictions of Buddhist deities are but their outer forms, which they display to frighten demons.[25] In all likelihood, the Jesuits believed the Tibetans to have once been Christian. Godinho fairly gushes, "It is impossible to say how much they cherish the Cross, and this is the best proof of their ancient religion."[26]

The Jesuit mission in Tsaparang was not without its problems; both Marques and Godinho returned to Agra owing to the difficulties of living in such a brisk climate. Still, Andrade learned of the central Tibetan regions of Ü and Tsang—which he called the kingdom of Ütsang—from traders and promoted it as a new mission field to his superiors in Goa. Andrade and Pereira returned to Goa in 1630, and Andrade soon sent two more missionaries, Domenico Capece and Francesco Morando, to Tsaparang in the company of Pereira. Yet another Jesuit, Francisco de Azevedo, arrived in Tsaparang on August 25, 1631, only to discover that the king of Leh in the nearby region of Ladakh had since overthrown the king at Tsaparang, his armies sacking the church and enslaving many of the four hundred Christians in the process. Two of the fathers were taken as captives to Leh, the capital of Ladakh, but released after a short imprisonment. Azevedo, now with de Oliveira, made the journey to Leh and petitioned the king to allow the missionaries to continue their work in Rudok. Satisfied to have gotten the mission back on its feet, Azevedo and

Oliveira returned to Agra on January 3, 1632.[27] Andrade, being relieved of his duties as superior in Goa in 1634, resolved to return to the Tibetan mission himself but apparently was poisoned on March 19, 1634. One disaster followed another in the Tsaparang mission after Andrade's death. Owing to the famine plaguing the Mughal Empire, only one of the six missionaries who accompanied Nuño Coresma to Tsaparang in 1635 arrived safely. Shortly thereafter, Coresma and Marques were banished from the country. By December 11, 1635, they were back in Agra. Undaunted, the Jesuits marshaled another mission to Tsaparang, but dos Anjos died in Srinagar before reaching Tsaparang. Against the suggestions of both Coresma and the provincial Alvaro Tavares, the Jesuit general, Muzio Vitelleschi, asked that a fresh expedition be mounted, but both Stanislaus Malpichi and Marques were captured trying to enter Tibet in 1640.

Jesuits had also entered Tibet from Bengal. In 1625, Andrade had suggested that the Society attempt to penetrate Ütsang from its station in Chandannagar, just north of Kolkata on the Hugli River, and the Jesuits wasted no time in making an attempt. On July 10, 1626, Estavão Cacella wrote from Chandannagar that he had recently arrived at the Jesuit station and hoped to continue his journey northward. Cacella also seems to have harbored hopes of secret Christians living in the mountains. Like Monserrate, his statements were more cautious than they would first appear. The Jesuit merely reported that the people of Cathay "behaved like Christians."[28] In February 1627, Cacella and his companion João Cabral entered Bhutan, where they were promptly imprisoned and robbed. Cacella's *relatio* of their travels even gives a detailed account of the first king of Bhutan, Ngawang Namgyel, the Drukpa Kagyü monk who had fled from Tibet to Bhutan in 1616 after a dispute about his claim to be the reincarnation of the great Drukpa scholar Pema Karpo.[29] Cacella and Cabral made enquiries about the surrounding regions while in the court, and were inspired to learn of a place called Shambala in addition to Tibet, Tartary, and China.[30] Cacella also described Tsaparang, Zhikatsé, Gyantsé, and Lhasa, effectively connecting the dots between Andrade's mission and his own. In December 1627, Cacella obtained supplies from a lama who was sympathetic to Ngawang Namgyel's rival from Ütsang, Karma Tenkyong Wangpo, and, with no small amount of resistance from Ngawang Namgyel, obtained permission to depart for Zhikatsé that month.[31] Owing to difficulties on the road, Cabral joined his Jesuit confrere in Zhikatsé on January 20, 1628. Karma Tenkyong Wangpo received the missionaries with great liberality, but two Bhutanese lamas soon stirred up trouble against the missionaries. Cabral, who had gathered enough information about entering Tibet from Bengal, left after a few days, thereby becoming the first Westerner to visit Nepal. Cacella himself returned to Patna in the summer of 1629. His second journey to Zhikatsé, in the company of Manuel Diaz, ended with the death of both men. Cabral returned to Ütsang in 1631, where he wrote to Azevedo in Tsaparang about the deaths of Diaz and Cacella. After Azevedo relayed the news to the provincial Gaspar Fernandes, Cabral was recalled to Chandannagar in 1632, effectively ending the mission to Ütsang just before the fifth Dalai Lama engulfed it in war.

Azevedo retired, his arms permanently deformed by repeated falls during his journeys in the mountains, but the Society of Jesus did not abandon hope after the dismal failure of the Tsaparang mission. In the *Litterae annuae* of 1643, one of Cacella's friends, Simon de Figueiredo, wrote to Europe recalling the efforts of his Jesuit brothers:

> Lack of men and money has forced us to give up the mission, but we cannot leave the land to itself. Great sacrifices have been made, Brother Bento de Góis has died in discovering it; Fathers Cacella and Diaz have passed away. Let us not be less generous. The people are worth our effort; they are really good; and the state of things is better there than in Japan or Ethiopia. Let those who ask be sent to these countries. Do not forget the poor Tibetans! *Ite angeli veloces, ite ad gentem expectantem!*[32]

By this point the Jesuits clearly believed themselves to be the sole proprietors of the Tibetan mission. Figure 2.1, from the first edition of Athanasius Kircher's *Ars magna lucis et umbrae*, shows the various assistancies, provinces, and missions of the Society of Jesus growing as a tree from the saint; if one looks at the detail of this image in figure 2.2, one can see that the Jesuits still felt that "Tebeth" was a mission of the Society in 1646. Looking at this stylized representation of the Jesuits' worldwide expansion, one can see why Kircher remarked, "The sun never sets on the actions of the Society of Jesus."[33]

The next two Jesuits to enter Tibet, Johannes Grueber and Albert D'Orville, were not missionaries. The first modern Europeans to come to Lhasa, the two men stayed for just under two months en route from Beijing to India. Grueber and D'Orville were to have a far-reaching influence on European conceptions of Tibet, an influence quite disproportionate to the time they had spent in the country and the scanty knowledge they conveyed.[34] It appears that their entire reason for entering China was to attempt an overland return that might supplant the dangerous sea voyage to Asia. Neither man stayed long at Beijing; after receiving the necessary technical training at the Imperial Observatory, D'Orville joined Grueber in a trek that took them from Beijing to Kökenuur and south across the great eastern deserts of Tibet, arriving in Lhasa on October 8, 1661.[35] Grueber's sketches of his travels, which found

FIGURE 2.1. Jesuit Missions from Athanasius Kircher, *Ars Magna lucis et umbrae* (Rome: Sumptibus Hermanni Scheus, 1646). Courtesy of Special Collections, Fordham University Library.

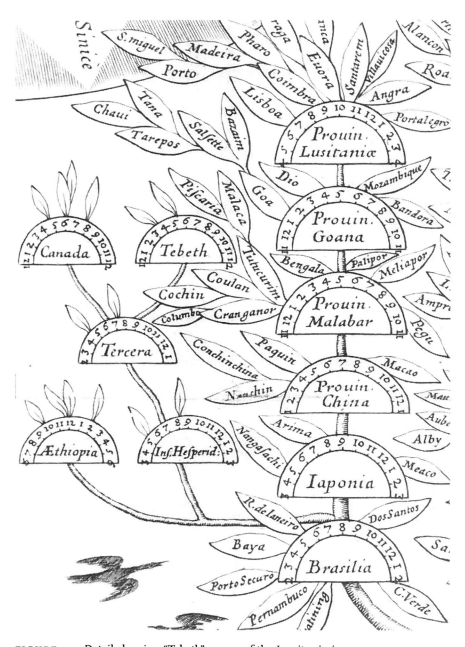

FIGURE 2.2. Detail showing "Tebeth" as one of the Jesuit missions.

their way after some unfortunate alterations into Kircher's *China illustrata*, served as the primary pictures of the Dalai Lama and the Potala until the first photographs of Lhasa and its environs were published in the twentieth century.[36] Figure 2.3 shows Grueber's somewhat fanciful depiction of the Potala—several commentators have noted that the wheeled cart in the foreground is an anachronism—which was still under construction when the two Jesuits passed through Lhasa. The Dalai Lama and his supplicants are shown, again in an imaginary setting, in figure 2.4. Grueber and D'Orville added to the already confused European knowledge of the mantra *oṃ maṇi padme hūṃ* and also offered accounts of the prayer wheel and certain scatological practices that would scandalize European readers for years to come. After quitting Lhasa toward the end of November, they traveled through Zhikatsé, Dingri, Nyalam, Kathmandu, and along to Agra via Patna and Varanasi, a route very similar to the one Desideri himself took when he left Lhasa in 1721. Arriving in Agra in the second half of March 1662, D'Orville took to his bed and expired on Holy Saturday, April 8, 1662. Grueber continued overland with another Jesuit, Henry Roth, and set foot in Rome on February 20, 1664. A true peripatetic, Grueber had hardly arrived in Rome when he set off for China again, although

FIGURE 2.3. The Potala, from Athanasius Kircher, *China illustrata* (Amsterdam: Joannem Janssonium à Waesberge & Elizeum Weyerstraet, 1667). Courtesy of Special Collections, Georgetown University Library.

for reasons unknown he remained in the Austrian Province of the Society of Jesus, carrying on an epistolary war with Kircher about mistaken details in the *China illustrata* until his death in 1680.

It was not until the eighteenth century, with the appointment of Miguel de Amaral as the visitor to the Goa Province, that the Jesuits decided to reopen the Tibetan mission in earnest.[37] In fact, the Jesuits made several attempts to open the Tibetan mission in the years immediately preceding Desideri's arrival in India. Amaral dispatched Manoel Monteiro to find the most suitable route to Tibet in 1704, although Monteiro died in 1707, having gathered no additional information about some difficult roads from Armenian merchants in Agra.[38] In the same year, two Jesuits from the Goa Province, João Carvalho and Peter Gill, petitioned the Jesuit general, Michelangelo Tamburini, to be sent to the Tibetan mission. Shortly thereafter, the provincial, Manoel Sarayva, wrote Tamburini to inform him that he had appointed Carvalho and Peter de Torres to open the Tibetan mission at Amaral's insistence, but the two missionaries had to be sent to Mysuru instead. On July 6, 1709, Tamburini wrote again to recommend the opening of the Tibetan mission. In the meantime, Saraya commissioned two more missionaries stationed at Agra, Giuseppe Martinetti

FIGURE 2.4. The Dalai Lama, from Athanasius Kircher, *China illustrata* (Amsterdam: Joannem Janssonium à Waesberge & Elizeum Weyerstraet, 1667). Courtesy of Special Collections, Georgetown University Library.

and Francis Koch, to prepare for the new undertaking. We know nothing of Koch, but Martinetti abandoned the mission amid unnamed "disgrace and calamities" and wrote Tamburini begging to return to Europe just as Desideri was completing his studies.[39] Wessels, true to the spirit of the Society, says of Martinetti, "Evidently, this man was not the stuff of which missionaries are made."[40] This rather partisan judgment—true as it might be when measured against the supernatural goals of the Society of Jesus—obscures the very real fact that the missions were often understaffed, and complaints often surfaced about the unwillingness of the professed Jesuits to undertake them or about the ignorance of the unprofessed Jesuits who were sent on them.[41] Neither of these flaws could be attributed to Desideri, who was still an unprofessed Jesuit, but he, too, would have his own problems with the Society's administration in India.

Ippolito Desideri in India

On September 27, 1712, Desideri embarked from Rome—a date, he would later remind his readers, that was exactly one year after he had departed for the Holy House of Loreto to consider his calling to the Indies. The would-be missionary was almost detained by Cosimo III, the grand duke of Tuscany, who relented when he learned of the seriousness of Desideri's resolve, and allowed the missionary to continue on his journey after giving Desideri some spiritual advice. From Florence Desideri traveled to his hometown and on to Livorno, where he boarded a ship traveling up the coast to Genoa. On November 23, Desideri left Genoa aboard *La Madonna delle Vigne*, a ship commanded by Giovanni Lorenzo Viviani, where he was given the opportunity to practice his submission to the divine will. The storms were violent enough that Viviani asked Desideri and the other Jesuits to gather on the deck and perform an exorcism against the demons that caused the storm. After exorcising the waves, Desideri broke off a small piece of an Agnus Dei, a small wax medallion bearing an image of the Lamb of God that was consecrated for just such purposes, and one of the other priests tossed it into the sea. As soon as the holy crumb hit the waters, the sea grew calm and the winds became favorable, a fitting display of divine power on the vigil of St. Francis Xavier. Even so, storms beset them again, and a Turkish ship shadowed them for several days along the Barbary Coast. While all on aboard remained alert in the face of the threat, the attack never materialized, and *La Madonna delle Vigne* arrived safely in Portugal in the middle of March.

Desideri sailed from Lisbon on April 8, 1713. The voyage from Lisbon to Goa, the primary Portuguese port on the western coast of India, required a half year at sea.[42] In addition to the grinding monotony of sea travel, passengers squeezed into claustrophobia-inducing quarters, ate putrid comestibles, and did their best to avoid puddles of vomit.[43] Desideri's ship almost sank as it passed Pernambuco and the Bay of All Saints, and it drifted for eight days in the intense heat around Madagascar. Regaining its sails, the missionaries' ship safely entered the channel and landed on Mozambique on July 25, 1713. The island boasted a large fortress equipped with a cannon, a church, and—much to Ippolito Desideri's delight—an abundance of medicinal herbs. In Mozambique, the ship picked up shipments of gold, silver, ivory, black amber, and several slaves who were to be sold in Goa. Of the slaves, Desideri wrote that a silver coin and a taper were given for the baptism of each, even though the slaves lacked catechetical instruction and the languages necessary to understand it. In a note of fellow feeling, the Jesuit missionary lamented such "traffic in the life and liberty of men."[44]

Desideri's account is filled with the typical tidbits of Jesuit seafaring. In order to satisfy the curiosity of those who believed that people died crossing the equator unless they were "copiously bled," he noted that although the seafarer encountered several days of great heat when crossing the line from the north, one did not need to resort to bloodletting to deal with the resulting insomnia or languor. For those who worried about food and water, the Jesuit advised that water from Mauritius kept reasonably well over a long journey, while water from Martinique quickly filled with worms and had to be exposed to sunlight and filtered through linen to become potable.[45] The Jesuits held public catechism several times during the week, preached on feast days, and taught the sailors and soldiers lessons from the life of the Blessed Virgin Mary every Saturday. They recited the Rosary at night, heard confessions, and celebrated the Eucharist on deck. Not surprisingly, the Jesuits were often called upon to mediate in arguments that broke out over card games and "other sinful things." Unlike other Jesuit accounts, Desideri's also lingered on some of the less trying features of sea travel, such as the festivities that occurred when ships crossed the equator. The young Jesuit does not tell us what roles he and his companions, being priests, played in these nautical rituals, nor does he mention whether the priests were exempt from the tariffs playfully imposed on those who had not previously crossed the line, but his enthusiasm suggests that they turned a blind eye to the hazing that was common on the occasion.[46]

Desideri arrived in Goa, the "Rome of the Orient," on September 20, 1713. The provincial and his fellow Jesuits greeted them at the doors of the Church of the College of Saint Paul and led the newly arrived missionaries inside to kiss the relics of the Holy Cross and of the local saints while the assembly sang psalms of thanksgiving.[47] Of the ten priests who arrived at Goa, eight from Europe and two who were picked up in Mozambique, two died, some were in extremis, and all but Desideri and Ildebrando Grassi fell gravely ill during their voyage at sea.[48] After a brief tour of various churches and the site of Rodolfo Acquaviva's martyrdom on the island of Salcette, Desideri returned to Goa, where he passed the necessary examination and pronounced his solemn vows on October 28. Thus beginning his tertianship, the Jesuit made another twelve-day retreat with the *Spiritual Exercises*.[49] On November 12, Desideri wrote to Michelangelo Tamburini, the Jesuit general, informing him that the provincial in Goa, António de Azevedo, had "destined" him to the new Tibetan mission.[50] Echoing the second week of the *Spiritual Exercises*, Desideri wrote:

> Our Father, God calls me to Tibet. If I do not go there, it will certainly not be on my account. If at the Judgment, God should ask me, "Why did you not go?" how would I answer him? Might I say I had no authority to do so, since men prevented me? That, then, would be my fault, since I did not procure such authority.[51]

In a more conspiratorial tone, the young Jesuit also complained about

> other impediments, which the experience of what happened at other times to other missionaries teaches me to be the most bothersome and thus the most to be feared, and thus, too, the most to be guarded against, and the wills of Ours, which bind the runner, and clip the flyer's wings and, in a word, oppose as with a drawn sword, the wishes of Your Paternity's zeal, and thus the manifest intentions of God.[52]

We do not know exactly what Desideri feared from his fellow Jesuits, to which he refers with the famous moniker "Ours," nor do we know with any certainty why he felt them to be opposed to the wishes of the general. Desideri hints that he and Tamburini shared some intimate understanding that he should not commit to writing. Whatever that may have been, Desideri's letter requests "absolute, total, and independent" permission to leave for Tibet.

Desideri soon discovered a letter in the Society's archives that the general had written to Manoel Sarayva on July 6, 1709, expressing his desire to reopen the Jesuit mission to Tibet. Desideri wrote the general again on the fifteenth. After repeating the information in his last letter—a hedge against the poor postal practices of the early eighteenth century—Desideri mentioned the letter he had discovered and quoted the general's words: "And let no difficulties frighten us, *nam causa Dei est*. Ah, our father, I cannot express what courage, what vigor, these beautiful words give: 'It is God's cause!'"[53] Barely able to contain his excitement, Desideri requested from the general a patent, or letter of approval, that would explicitly order him to open the Tibetan mission.[54] In this letter, too, Desideri added the somewhat ominous note that the unnamed obstacles of which he had previously written "detained missionaries in the past and will do so in the future."[55]

For reasons as yet unknown, Desideri left Goa without the patent on November 16, 1713. He traveled through Daman with Melchior dos Reys before arriving at Surat on January 4, 1714. Owing to disturbances caused by internecine strife among the Mughals in nearby Ahmadabad, Desideri stayed for three months at the Capuchin hospice in Surat, where he met the Jesuit visitor of the Agra mission, José da Silva. We do not know much about the atmosphere at the Capuchin hospice, but it must have been somewhat tense, as the two religious orders had just recently engaged in an acrimonious dispute about which order could rightfully evangelize the city.[56] In any case, Desideri must have revealed his ambitions to the Jesuit visitor at Surat, since this same letter to Tamburini remarked that the visitor did not wish Desideri to go to such distant places alone.[57]

A third letter that Desideri addressed from Surat—but which, oddly, is dated December 30—continued the epistolary war with his unnamed opponents. "To this point, I have spoken in the common cause of this province and the Company," Desideri wrote. "Let me now add something in my own cause."[58] Again he requested a patent placing him under the general's sole supervision. This letter also hinted at some manner of direct interference, whether imagined or not: "Both in Goa and in the rest of the province, I have experienced much that is contrary to my wishes, and I know so many others who were sent but later detained, so that, to speak directly, I am greatly afraid that I will receive a solemn order to stop at Agra."[59] Desideri did not say why a delay in his journey would prove so disastrous, except to imply that it would endanger the salvation of Tibetans. To pique the general's curiosity, Desideri mentioned that a substantial sum had already been given for the cause of the Tibetan mission. He even dangled before the general some tantalizing but inconclusive information on the various routes to Tibet before continuing his plea for a patent. Here, at least, Desideri named the "impediments caused by Ours," including contrary orders and instructions that the missionary "might receive from these local superiors and provincials."[60]

Desideri decided that the Society was "under grave obligation to reopen the mission by any means possible." Quoting from Tamburini's 1709 letter to Amaral, Desideri exclaimed, "*Ecce ego, mitte me.* I am ready to go without subsidy, without *viaticum*, without anything, my faith in the divine assistance being enough for me, since I hold, engraved in my heart, the words of Your Paternity, written to the Superiors of this province, ordering them to open new missions and to consider with greater earnestness, *de reditu ad Thibetum.*"[61] The quotation of the general's own words in Latin reveals no small amount of

Desideri's own seriousness. The phrase *ecce ego, mitte me* ("here I am, send me"), a quotation from the commissioning of the prophet Isaiah (Is 6:1–8), only reinforces it. By early 1714, "returning to Tibet" had become an idée fixe for the young Jesuit.

Desideri left Surat in late March 1714 with José da Silva and Melchior dos Reys, who was to take over as rector of the Jesuit college at Agra.[62] Desideri was separated from the other Jesuits when the caravan divided along the imperial caravan route of Rajasthan, accosted by officials who thought he was hiding some vast wealth, and briefly imprisoned—a common enough peril for missionaries. After a city official in Jaipur intervened on his behalf, Desideri was released and, traveling alone, arrived at Delhi on May 11.[63] In Delhi, Desideri witnessed the magnificent court of the Mughal Empire and a thriving Christian community led by Dona Giuliana Diaz da Costa, the "foundation and ornament of our Holy Faith in the Empire."[64]Although Desideri later discounted the tale that Dona Giuliana had effected the emperor Bahadur Shah's deathbed conversion, the missionary admitted that the emperor held some tenets of the Catholic faith. He had, for example, a lively faith in the efficacy of consecrated palms, a sentiment born in his heart after Dona Giuliana miraculously quenched a raging fire by casting one in its midst. In Delhi Desideri found another Jesuit shepherding a flock of about three hundred Christians. Manoel Freyre welcomed Desideri with "great courtesy and love."[65] As the letter continues, it becomes clear that Desideri hoped for more than simple hospitality from Freyre. "You should know, that having obtained permission in Goa to attempt to open a new mission to Tibet, I was destined, but alone, without any companion, on a very arduous enterprise, to places so remote from our own fathers and from any other Christian."[66] Desideri's somewhat melodramatic tone notwithstanding, he had in fact asked the provincial at Goa for a companion when he was first commissioned to the Tibetan mission. The provincial acquiesced but ordered the missionary to stay in India and wait for the arrival from Goa of another Jesuit, who probably would not be available for at least a year—a decision that must have tormented the restless Jesuit. Ippolito Desideri took Freyre's offer to accompany him to Tibet as "a gift from the compassionate hand of God."

Freyre, having lived his entire adult life in India, appeared to be an ideal companion. Born at Ancião, Portugal, in 1679, Freyre had entered the Society of Jesus in Goa and was a veteran of the mission at Agra.[67] One minor technicality stood in the way of a speedy departure: Freyre, being in charge of three hundred souls, could not abandon them for his newfound companion's Tibetan adventure. Nor would it be easy to find a replacement during the monsoon, which was fast upon them. Not to be diverted, Desideri hurried to

Agra, a seven-day journey, where he found two priests, probably the new rector, Melchior dos Reys, and the old, Manoel Durão, who was returning to Goa to find some rest. With apparently providential concision, Durão agreed to take charge of the Christians at Delhi, and the matter was settled. On August 15, 1714, Desideri received a patent allowing him to go to Tibet from José da Silva, who had recently traveled to Delhi for the feast of the Assumption of the Virgin. Although it would have been normal for the visitor to issue a patent in the general's stead, Desideri does not mention whether it granted him the independence he desired. Two days later, Desideri received a letter from Manoel Freyre informing him that he was now ready to embark on their journey. He, too, presumably received permission from da Silva as the visitor passed through Delhi.[68] Freyre, the older of the two Jesuits by five years, was deemed Desideri's superior.[69]

The monsoon prevented the two Jesuits' immediate departure. With time to spare, Desideri wrote to a dear friend in Rome, his fellow Jesuit Volomnius Piccolomini, on August 21, 1714. This single letter is so suffused with the rhetoric of Jesuit spirituality that it is difficult to imagine that Desideri did not intend it to be chosen for a devotional reading after dinner at the Jesuit house in Rome. Written on the eve before his departure, Desideri's letter to Piccolomini shows the fullest extent of the fantasies that he entertained about Tibet. After detailing the adventures that brought him from the Capuchin hospice in Surat to his present detainment in Delhi, the Jesuit wrote of the difficulties of learning the languages of India, noting that even the "small sacrifice of such labor" became sweet when he fixed his eyes upon Christ and the possibility that Tibetans might be redeemed by His Blood, "the two condiments that render easy all that is difficult, and make sweet all that is bitter."[70] Warming to his theme, the Jesuit offered his old friend a meditation that reads, for all intents and purposes, like a variation on the instructions for making decisions in the second week of the *Spiritual Exercises*:

> The pain is sharper when I see before my eyes the steady ruin of
> precious souls, and so many and such great offenses committed
> against the Infinite Goodness, when I see I cannot take a single step to
> prevent such lamentable confusion. This is like being tortured on a
> rack, strong ropes drawing the body in one direction, while ropes
> simultaneously draw the body with equal violence in the opposite
> direction, the two totally opposed strains causing a cruel torment, just
> as I feel in my own heart. It pleases His Divine Majesty to lead my
> whole heart away *in vinculis caritatis* and with sweet, amorous
> violence, to where there is great loss of souls, and where His most

friendly goodness is more outraged. At the same time, my feet are bound with the tightest fetters and I am carried elsewhere, while I can do nothing but send, alone and unaccompanied, the powers of my soul, where the body cannot follow. But soon enough they return, disconsolate like dogs that beg the huntsman to pierce with his weapons the prey for which they have so longed but which they themselves cannot seize.[71]

Being led to Tibet bound "in chains of love," Desideri recounted an imaginary itinerary in which he "sent forth the powers of his soul" to the wonders that awaited him, recalling the places he would go, calculating the distances he would travel, and arousing his affections for the tasks that lay before him.

Let the Devil, let hell, do all that they might. Let them mount all their force in opposition; it does not frighten me, for I know whom I believe. I know that it is God's cause, and I know that I am steeped in sins and ingratitude for the divine mercies, yet with the Lord's help the intention is right; and so I cannot for a moment doubt that God will always be with me.[72]

One might expect Desideri's letter to end on this crescendo; instead it ascends higher and higher peaks of fervor. After resolving to die in the midst of his labor, Desideri abased himself with a recollection of his many sins, asking that holier Jesuits offer Masses for the success of his mission; he "brought before his eyes" the worst of iniquities committed by infidels; he saw "the poor blind people in all Tibet" locked in the "sweetest wounds of Jesus"; and finally, "imitating the example of the most glorious apostle to the Indies, St. Francis Xavier," he resolved to offer all of his prayers to the divine Majesty, that the missionary might make God known and loved by all. After riding on the wings of his fancy for so long, Desideri abruptly returned to the more prosaic details of his journey for Piccolomini and established his friend as the official procurator for the Tibetan mission in his province. With a long list of their mutual friends, Desideri brought his letter to a close:

Goodbye, my dearest Father Piccolomini. I salute you with all my affection and I beg you to pray for me continually.... May the Lord in His mercy deign to fill Your Reverence with His holy love, with a grand and constant fervor in His holy service, and in zeal for the salvation of souls, and with every consolation, so that we receive the grace of meeting again in His Holy Paradise. Farewell! Farewell! Farewell![73]

Desideri's heroic tone soars, if on somewhat artificial wings, several measures above Freyre's comparatively earthy and indulgent account of their
travels. It is not always so; sometimes the Tuscan can be very matter-of-fact,
and this stylistic duality is found in all of his Italian writings. When he
consciously—self-consciously—opens his heart for the edification of his brethren, his style takes flight. Consider the following passage:

> *Ecce ego, mitte me.* Even if I must walk through the flames, even if
> I must pass through the whole of hell, in order to succeed in
> imparting the knowledge of God and the holy Catholic faith to those
> poor people of Tibet, through the flames I shall walk, and through the
> whole of hell I shall pass, confident in my God, so that the Company
> may not remain the least bit burdened, to exalt the glory of God and to
> procure the eternal salvation of those souls.[74]

Such pathos might seem excessive to modern sensibilities. An exuberant style
was not at all uncommon for Jesuits of his day—their rhetoric depended on
highly emotional appeals to the tangible world of Christ that formed the basis
of the *Spiritual Exercises*—but the letters Desideri wrote as he approached Tibet
display an emotional pleonasm that is excessive even by early eighteenth-
century standards. Still, Ignatius instructed Jesuits to write letters in this very
fashion.[75] Jesuits who intended to edify and inspire readers and listeners, he
maintained, should narrate events of apostolic significance—sermons
preached, confessions heard, spiritual exercises made, good works performed
on behalf of others—but then write from an "abundance of heart," expressing
graces, consolations, trials, and tribulations, especially as they related to the
Jesuits' service in the Society, without being overly concerned with style.
Ignatius also instructed missionaries to "amplify" their letters by including
words of exhortation for Jesuits back home, and Juan Polanco urged his
brothers to color their letters after the manner of the Jesuit *compositio loci*
and *applicatio sensuum*.[76] Even Desideri's repeated quotation *ecce ego, mitte me*
("here I am, send me") contains a theology of mission in miniature. While the
original meaning of this text (Is 6:1–8) concerns the commissioning of the
prophet Isaiah in 742 BCE as Assyria annexed the Northern Kingdom during
the Syro-Ephramite War, the prophet's vision of the heavenly throne and the
six-winged angels that attend it, his fiery purgation, and his solitary commission to preach to obstinate and uncaring people were themes that missionaries
readily assimilated.[77]

Desideri's next letter to Tamburini, written as he passed through Delhi
again on the way to Lahore, returned to more mundane affairs. He thanked
José da Silva, who had secured for Desideri sufficient money from Dona

Giuliana.[78] Desirous of a speedy departure, the young missionary also asked the general to grant a rescript if the superiors in Goa requested that Freyre make the profession of his final vows. One gathers from Desideri's request that Freyre had not completed his tertianship, the twelve-month course of study that lay between ordination and the profession of final vows—although one suspects that he was ordained if he shepherded a Christian community of three hundred at Delhi.[79] Both the patent granting Desideri independence and the rescript permitting Freyre to delay the profession of his final vows would free both Jesuits for the mission Desideri so desired. The patent being granted by the visitor, neither Jesuit felt a need to wait for further instructions. On September 23, 1714, they set off for Lahore, where they arrived on October 9. From Lahore, the two Jesuits crossed the Indus River and stood at the foothills of the vast Himalayan range.

Climbing the *Dorsum Orbis*

From Lahore, the two Jesuits ascended the road to Srinagar in Kashmir, whose mountains Desideri compared to "staircases piled one atop another." "The highest point," he later wrote, "which is called Pir Panjal after the name of a daimon much revered by these people ... is very high and steep, being covered for several months of the year with deep snow, while a perpetual layer of ice, with the duration and hardness of marble, fills its deepest valleys."[80] The Jesuits also forded streams of ice-cold water—"nay, molten snow"—between Lahore and Srinagar that weakened the Jesuit such that he later suffered an attack of dysentery "with loss of blood."[81] After a brief respite around Christmas 1714, Desideri fell ill again in February, evoking concerns from Freyre that he would not survive the winter. Despite the hardships brought on by the cold, Desideri found the mountains in Srinagar pleasant on account of their great variety of trees and foliage, and dutifully noted the abundance of fruit ("grapes, pears, apples, walnuts, peaches, apricots, plums, cherries, almonds, pistachios, quinces, and similar fruits") and flowers ("roses, tulips, anemones, narcissi, hyacinths, and the like"). He also delighted in the city itself. Beautiful lakes and ponds, upon which one could sail "with much amusement," surrounded its splendid buildings and well-laid streets, which its inhabitants judged a true paradise. If his own enthusiasm is any indication, the young Jesuit felt much the same, although he would not entertain the Kashmiris' suggestion that King Solomon himself had founded the city, a belief that Desideri declared "superstitious" and "absolutely imaginary" (*superstizioso e assolutamente favoloso*).[82]

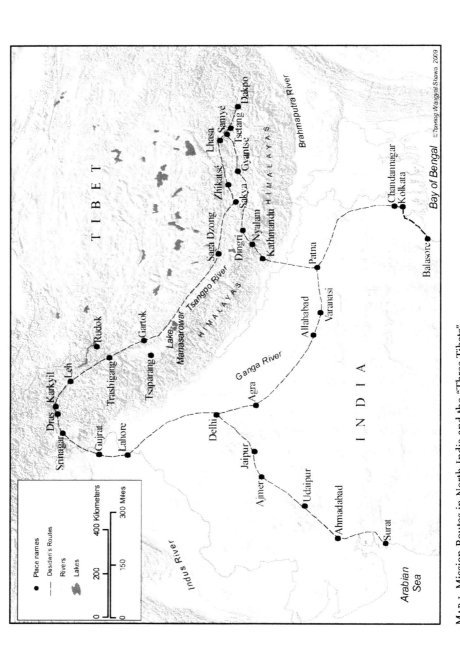

MAP 1. Mission Routes in North India and the "Three Tibets"

The snow began to melt in the middle of May 1715, and the two Jesuits left Kashmir on the seventeenth. The trees and flowers that delighted Desideri soon gave way to more rugged terrain. On May 29, 1715, the travelers found themselves at the foot of a "formidable" mountain, the Zoji. "From the base of this mountain," the missionary wrote, "it is nine months' journey to China, during which the earth's fertility and pleasantness quite cease, and one meets naught but desolation and the barren horror of the Caucasus Mountains, which are called by geographers the *dorsum orbis*."[83] Of all their trials, none terrified Desideri like the mountains. The paths upon which the missionaries traveled were so narrow that they walked single file, in constant fear of falling. Crossing the gorges was similarly perilous. With every step, the ramshackle bridges swayed to and fro, and the rush of the water below dazzled the missionaries and made them dizzy. Sometimes they did not even have the comfort of bridges but only a few unstable planks or ropes plaited with small green willow branches.[84] Faced with such primitive means, the missionaries often had to remove their footwear to get a better hold. "Trust me," Desideri later wrote, "I still shudder at the slightest thought of those frightful passages!"[85] The playful festivities of crossing the equator must have seemed very far away indeed.

Forty days' travel separated Srinagar and Leh, the capital of Ladakh, and Desideri faced even greater trials during this journey.[86] In late June or early July, he was afflicted with snow blindness and had to be led around by a fellow traveler, his eyes bandaged with a cloth blackened with charcoal from their cooking fires. This small indignity seems to have injured Desideri's pride, for he often wandered off without his guide. On one occasion, he stumbled off to investigate a large elephant-shaped rock, and had barely gone twenty paces when a huge block of ice crashed from the mountain onto the very spot where he had been. Freyre could hardly comprehend their porters' own remedies for snow blindness: "Our porters then put down their loads and washed their feet and foreheads in the river, hoping to stop the fluid that flowed from their eyes, but we, not being accustomed to the cold, only sprinkled our faces with water."[87] The party passed its nights without shelter until finally arriving in Leh on June 26. In Desideri's account, the Ladakhis received him and Freyre with great hospitality. Desideri judged the Ladakhis virtuous and well disposed to receive the Christian faith, two qualities that would later come to occupy his more advanced conceptions of Tibetan religion and culture. After this rudimentary encounter, Desideri wrote Tamburini with his first descriptions of Tibetan religion and culture. Tibetans, he claimed, were "gentiles," neither Jews, Muslims, nor Christians, although they were not as superstitious as gentiles were in other parts of India—this is almost certainly a reference to the rejection of the ritual ablutions and dietary restrictions he would have witnessed among Hindus.[88]

Freyre was less interested in the finer points of Tibetan religion. Exhausted from their travels, the Jesuit started to ask whether there was another road back to the Mughal Empire.[89] In the meantime, they had several interviews with Nyima Namgyel, the petty king of the region, and the regional governor. Each meeting was increasingly hospitable: a first involved copious amounts of tea and butter, and a second treated the Jesuits to a feast of roast kid. With each interview, Desideri's desire to stay in Ladakh grew. During his second interview, he asked for permission to stay and preach. Freyre, on the other hand, wishing to escape the "filthy and famished" region, desired only a passport that would allow him to continue to warmer regions, and consequently demanded conditions for staying that the Ladakhis could not meet—although Desideri took care not to name them. The conflict of the two Jesuits' interests came to a head during a later interview, in which Desideri claimed the regional governor expressed a "great desire" that the Jesuits should learn his language, so that they might converse more easily about religious topics, an opportunity that Desideri wished to seize. Freyre was none too pleased by this turn of events and, according to Desideri, "made much difficulty."[90] If we are to believe Desideri's account, the Ladakhis caught wind of Freyre's displeasure and changed the subject.

In the meantime, Freyre learned that there was a "third Tibet" that was a four-month journey from Ladakh. This third Tibet was the Tibet that the Capuchins had visited and, more important, was closer to the Mughal Empire, thus providing the speediest route by which Freyre could escape his hardships. Desideri found himself in distress (*io mi trovai in angustie*) after Freyre's suggestion that they journey to this third Tibet, but the younger Jesuit held his tongue and—somewhat grudgingly—acknowledged that Freyre was his superior. Still, the younger Jesuit bristled as he acquiesced: "I wished to lie as still as a stone and die a thousand times, but *melior est obedientia quam victimae.*"[91] Although "obedience is better than sacrifices," Desideri still wrote Tamburini to complain about the man that he had testily demanded earlier. The younger Jesuit protested, quite against the tone of his earlier letters, of the evident dangers and financial impossibility of a mission to this third Tibet. His letter made "strong arguments" for remaining in the second Tibet, whose people were already "well disposed" to his evangelical overtures. Desideri particularly feared that Capuchins might still reside in the third Tibet, a presence that Freyre mysteriously seemed to welcome.[92] Desideri's doubt was strong enough that he wrote Tamburini about it. Apparently, Freyre had little use for such scruples. The older Jesuit let it be known that he would discuss the issue no further, and if Desideri wished to stay, he would have to explain his actions to their superiors. Facing the alternatives, Desideri followed Freyre, but he also made sure to let Tamburini know that he was not particularly happy about it.[93]

Freyre and Desideri left Leh on August 17, 1715. After wandering for days through the mountains, their caravan entered the northern plains that stretch between Ladakh and Tibet. Struck by its eerie, stagnant pools and sulfurous springs, the Jesuit warned of the "dead, putrid water" (*acque morte e putride*) and the "noxious air" (*aria infetta*) that inflamed the lips and gums and occasionally killed a pack animal.[94] To reduce the swelling, Desideri's guides chewed medicinal herbs and mixed them with the barley flour that they fed their horses. On September 7, they arrived at Trashigang, where they sought a guide to take them across the great western deserts to Lhasa, the capital of the third Tibet. Soon they learned about a remarkable woman whom Freyre called Casal.[95] The widow of a recently deceased district governor, Casal commanded a strong body of Tibetan and Mongol troops that defended the Trashigang fortress from bandits. Lhazang Khan, the Khoshud Mongol chieftain who ostensibly ruled central Tibet, had recently summoned the widow to Lhasa, but she did not intend to leave anytime soon. Desideri and Freyre camped on the plain in the meantime. Freyre's account of their travels is especially rich for this period of their journey and quite attentive to a few details left out by Desideri. When relating how icicles froze into Desideri's beard, Freyre cannot help exclaiming, "What a sight!" (*admirabile spectaculum*). He also includes several less-than-heroic episodes. On the next to last day of September, it snowed so hard that the two Jesuits' tent collapsed. Desideri, "fearing that the Last Day had come," rushed out of the tent, forgetting his walking stick in the process, and fled to the mess tent in confusion.[96] For his own part, Desideri summed up their experiences with glum romanticism: "The ground was our bedding, the sky was our roof, and snow rained upon us."[97]

The widow obtained an astrologically favorable day to depart and instructed the Jesuits to bring yaks and several horses, many of which would not survive the journey. Satisfied with this advice, the two Jesuits joined her retinue, which left for Lhasa on October 9, 1715, and passed Mount Kailash exactly a month later. The two missionaries traveled in the third rank of the widow's caravan, sandwiched between the ministers and military officers in the second rank and the pack animals and foot travelers in the fourth. They rarely deviated from routine: at daybreak, they struck their tent, saddled their horses, drank a bowl of buttered tea, and rode until sunset. When they found a suitable campsite, they pitched their tent and searched for dung to make fires.

The two Jesuits said matins and lauds for the following day while their servants prepared dinner. They watered and fed their horses, then retired to bed. Frostbite sorely afflicted the travelers, who were forced to wear lice-ridden coats, and they constantly picked at vermin. Freyre, who had spent the whole of his adult life in India's warmer weather, cursed the wind, thereby inviting the sympathies of the widow, who occasionally brought the two Jesuits into her tent and shared tea with them. "The night," Desideri later wrote, "was more a cessation of fatigue than a real repose."[98] On November 22, 1715, Manoel Freyre had his near-fatal encounter in the snow. Back in camp, the thawed missionary was fed and given another horse, and the two Jesuits continued undaunted.

> Amid these trials and torments, sensibly comforted by the loving kindness and paternal assistance of God, by whose singular love we had undertaken all of these things, we yielded to everything in good spirits. With a cheerful and healthy disposition and constant heartfelt contentment, with serene conversations between ourselves and with others, we passed through this desert free of alacrity, as though we had gone on a voyage for our amusement and recreation.[99]

Desideri and Freyre arrived in Lhasa on March 18, 1716. Having seen her charges arrive safely, the widow quit the world for a convent in Zhikatsé. In recounting her many kindnesses years later, Desideri was moved to write one of his most poignant passages.

> If only I had been fluent in the language while I traveled with her, I might have won her over to the Holy Faith, to which she was most inclined, as I had so intensely desired. I pray most insistently that God may enlighten her now and lead her to eternal salvation.[100]

Lhasa

In the half century before Desideri's arrival, Lhasa had been transformed from a small town known primarily for the Jokhang temple to the capital of the new Tibetan government under the fifth Dalai Lama. Adorned with the recently built Potala palace, the capital quickly became the wellspring of the greatest cultural and artistic flourishing in Tibetan history, replete with fresco cycles, refined poetry, and increased patronage of classical scholarship. Lhasa also became a thriving trade center, and among its narrow alleys, Ippolito Desideri would have jostled with merchants who had arrived in caravans from India,

Mongolia, Ladakh, China, and Russia; encountered other travelers making their pilgrimages as part of the cult of Avalokiteśvara promoted by the Dalai Lama; or chanced upon a troupe of actors and dancers, or an itinerant Tibetan preacher not too unlike himself.[101] On April 16, Freyre placed Desideri in charge of the Tibetan mission and resumed his journey southward to Nepal and India, in search of the warmth and heavier air of lower altitudes. "I remained alone for a while," Desideri later wrote, "the only missionary, indeed the only European, in the vast stretch of the three Tibets."[102]

A customs official soon accosted Desideri, but the irritation would prove fortuitous. On his way to a meeting with the officials, the Jesuit missionary chanced to pass under a balcony where a minister attended Lhazang Khan, the Mongol chieftain who had exercised a shaky rule over Tibet since 1705. The Khoshud Mongol inquired about the strangely dressed European. As luck would have it, the minister happened to know something of Desideri and informed the chieftain of the missionary's troubles with the customs house.[103] Lhazang Khan summoned the Jesuit to appear before him, and Desideri visited the palace on April 28. Arriving at the khan's quarters, the Jesuit found the minister who had recommended him to the khan. The minister, whom the missionary called Targum Trashi, heard that he was outside, came out, and invited Desideri to his own private apartments, where he gave the Jesuit many "cordial assurances of their enduring friendship."[104] Desideri assured his readers that these offers were not obsequious, and claimed that from that day, the minister showed so many proofs of true friendship that all were astonished to see such familiarity between two men of different races.[105] The minister playfully rebuked him for not having presented himself to Lhazang Khan and offered to present Desideri to the khan in a private audience, but Desideri cannily refused, hoping to incite the khan's curiosity, and protested that had no gift suitable for such nobility. The missionary's excuse was ignored, and a meeting was secured. The Jesuit then slipped down to the market and bought some suitable presents. To these small gifts, he added a few choice items of his own, including two pots of balsam and two bezoar stones.

On May 1, Desideri returned to the palace. In the antechamber, he found "more than a hundred people of consequence" awaiting the khan. An official took down his name as court attendants admitted guests two by two and accepted their presents on behalf of the khan. The missionary was soon brought into the khan's presence along with a highly esteemed lama. The lama's gift was "considerable" and Desideri's "insignificant," but Lhazang Khan ordered that the lama's gift be laid aside at the entryway and Desideri's gift brought before the throne, an action that Desideri did not fail to note "is considered an exceptional mark of favor in the court."[106] The khan, Desideri told his readers, was "cheerful," "affable," and "of a generous disposition, too."[107] The Khoshud chieftain asked the missionary to be seated next to his throne and peppered him with questions for two hours. Seeing his chance, the missionary expressed his desire to preach the Gospel in Tibet. Much to his surprise, Lhazang Khan granted Desideri's wish with great enthusiasm and—if we are to believe Desideri's account—no small amount of paternal sentimentality. He even relaxed the normal restrictions placed upon foreigners in Lhasa and permitted the missionary to buy a house.[108] When Desideri left the audience, people crowded around him with congratulations. Many visited his apartments and sent encouraging notes. "Having been granted God's graces for the happy commencement and success of my mission," he would later write,

> I applied myself with an incredible ardor, with the whole of my strength, to the exercise of my work and a study of the language especially. From that time until the final day I spent in the kingdom, I worked toward my goal and continued in this fashion for almost six years, studying from the early morning until my nightly repast, sustained throughout the day—except on solemn feasts or extraordinary occasions—on a most useful and nourishing beverage called *cha*.[109]

The Jesuit soon had another opportunity to impress himself upon the khan, who—along with his minister—was suffering recurrent effects from a poison administered to him and his minister during an attempt on their lives more than ten years earlier. Desideri sent them a highly valued vase of medicine with his best wishes and instructions for the proper dosage. The medicine, the Jesuit panacea *teriaca*, had its desired effect: Lhazang Khan and his minister slept soundly and felt strong when they awakened.[110] The Khoshud ruler, duly impressed—or influenced—by the opiatic qualities of Desideri's drug, showed him even greater affection and consideration. Desideri was later summoned to the palace to speak with Döndrup Tsering, the "generalissimo" of the Tibetan armies at Lhasa.[111] The general asked Desideri where he was from, who he was, and why he had come to Tibet. The young Tuscan answered him with gusto, announcing that he had "come from a far distant land, separated from Tibet not only by stretches of land but also by immense stretches of ocean, from the West to the far East, from Europe to Tibet." He identified himself as a Christian, priest, and lama bound to rescue those in error and guide them to Christianity, which was the "only true and lawful path, apart from which there was no way to reach heaven and eternal salvation."[112] Asked how long he intended to stay, the missionary answered that he intended to stay until his death, a response that caused some commotion among those present. In another evocation of the *Spiritual Exercises*, the missionary answered, "I sought none of their honor, none of their grandeur, none of their riches, and in sum no temporal or personal advantage whatsoever, but only the glory of God and their eternal salvation."[113]

Lhazang Khan was later informed of this conversation and—again according to Desideri's reckoning—pledged that should he be convinced by a mature discussion and examination of the missionary's religion, he and his subjects would convert to Christianity. Lhazang Khan was not a Christian king—not yet, in any case—but Desideri's heart must have leapt at the thought.

3

Tibetan Religion in Theological Perspective

All the gods of the gentiles are demons.

—Psalm 95:5 LXX

Three Capuchin fathers arrived in Lhasa on October 1, 1716. Despite the rivalry between the two religious orders, Desideri went to greet the Capuchins on their arrival. After introducing himself to Domenico da Fano, the Capuchin prefect of the mission, and the other two Capuchin fathers, Francesco Orazio della Penna and Giovanni Francesco da Fossombrone, Desideri conducted the friars to his apartment and showed them what little hospitality his situation allowed. They celebrated the feast of St. Francis of Assisi together on the fourth, and the Capuchins soon arranged to rent the apartments next to Desideri's own. A letter from Desideri to Tamburini tells us that the men lived together "with exemplary uniformity in all things and with mutual and fraternal charity."[1] This fraternal charity did not prevent the Capuchin fathers from pointing out that the Congregation for the Propagation of the Faith, the bureaucratic office in Rome that coordinated the overseas missions, had appointed the Tibetan mission to their order in 1703. Desideri had little desire to relinquish the hardwon fruits of his journey, and the question was referred to Rome for settlement. Having "satisfied the dictates of hospitality," Desideri took up the composition of his first refutation of Tibetan religion.

Desideri finished his small work toward the end of December, added a dedication to Lhazang Khan, and had the entire work nicely copied. He then sent a message to the Khoshud chieftain telling him that he would like to present his gift. The khan responded that he preferred to receive the gift in a solemn public audience, and that he would leave the choice of the day to the missionary. After celebrating Mass and praying for success, Desideri was received by the khan on January 6, 1717, the Feast of the Epiphany. When Desideri presented his gift, which was wrapped in silk brocade, the khan took it into his own hands and untied its wrapping. Lhazang directed the missionary to sit next to his throne as he read the book's dedication and first few pages himself. He then handed Desideri's gift to an "influential" monk, who continued reading where the khan left off. Two things perplexed the chieftain: Christians' belief in a single supreme being and their denial of reincarnation. A hearty debate followed and continued to midday. After considering Desideri's arguments, Lhazang Khan decided the moment was inopportune to make a decision about the future religion of Tibet; rather, he suggested that the Tibetan monks and the Jesuit missionary hold a public disputation, but only after Desideri had thoroughly studied Buddhist dialectics. He also decreed that the Jesuit should attend the disputations held in the universities and choose a monastery at which to study, where all the necessary books would be made available and all the proper tutors engaged. To this end, the khan adjourned the audience so that the Jesuit could begin preparing the defense of his strange doctrines. The missionary lost no time obeying the khan's commands, which "agreed so perfectly" with his own.

Apes, Idols, and the Holy Trinity

Desideri was a quick study. When he had first arrived in Lhasa, he wrote a long letter to another Jesuit missionary, Ildebrando Grassi, who was stationed in Mysuru. Desideri recounted his adventures since the two men had last been together, three and a half years earlier at the Jesuit residence in Goa. Desideri told Grassi of his travels to Surat, Delhi, Lahore, Leh, and Lhasa, and recalled his first impressions of Tibetan religion and culture. Tibetans, he said, were gentle and docile, but coarse and uncultivated. They had neither arts nor sciences, and they had no contact with other nations, but they did reject the doctrine of transmigration and appeared to have some knowledge of the Christian faith.[2] "Here is what I learned about the Tibetans' religion," he wrote.

> They call God könchok [dkon mchog], and they appear to have some notion of the adorable Trinity, for at times they call Him könchok chik [dkon mchog gcig], that is, the One God, and at other times they call

Him *könchok sum* [*dkon mchog gsum*], that is, the Triune God. They also use a kind of chaplet, over which they repeat the words *oṃ āh hūṃ*, and they say that the word *oṃ* signifies knowledge or an arm, that is, power; *āh* is the word, and *huṃ* is the heart, or love, and that these three words mean God. They also worship a being named Padmasaṃbhava, who was born some seven hundred years ago. When asked if he was God or man, some people replied that he was both God and man, having neither father nor mother, but having been born from a flower. Even so, they have statues representing a woman with a flower in her hand, whom they call Padmasaṃbhava's mother, and they venerate several others whom they treat as saints. In their churches, one finds an altar covered with cloth and ornaments, and a sort of tabernacle sits in the middle of the altar, where they say Padmasaṃbhava dwells, though they also assert that he is in heaven.[3]

This letter, which survives only in a French translation, is noteworthy, if only because Ippolito Desideri would later repudiate almost everything he affirmed in it. In a matter of months, the Jesuit would change his mind about Tibetans' capacities for art, science, and culture. He would also change his mind considerably about their religion. As we shall see, the missionary's change of heart was not simply a matter of the accumulation of knowledge or an increased sensitivity to Tibetans and their culture; it was part of a larger missionary strategy that depended in turn on several complex theological doctrines about the possibility of salvation for non-Christians.

The Jesuit missionary did come to appreciate Tibetan religion more deeply during his stay in the land of snows. His later account praised Tibetans' ability to memorize long prayers, their attentiveness to sermons, their repeated fasts, and their devotion to daily rituals. Tibetan religion, in the Jesuit's estimation, had all the trappings of an authentic faith, including contemplation, penitence, and spiritual direction.[4] The only virtue lacking in Tibetan religion, he noted, was humility.[5] Two divine figures dominated his conception of Tibetan religion: Padmasaṃbhava, the semimythical exorcist who won Tibet over to Buddhism, and Avalokiteśvara, the bodhisattva whom Tibetans had increasingly associated with their nation beginning in the eleventh century.[6] Tibetans associated both figures with the old Tibetan empire, linking Padmasaṃbhava to the reign of Trisong Detsen and Avalokiteśvara to the reign of Songtsen Gampo, but both myths so thoroughly defined Tibetan religion by the early eighteenth century that we cannot draw firm conclusions about Desideri's earliest tutors in Tibetan religion and culture, the facts of which would become quite a point of contention between him and the Franciscans.

On his own admission, Desideri seems to have studied a series of texts associated with Padmasaṃbhava:

> Among the many ancient books that are in general circulation in Tibet, two especially talk of Padmasaṃbhava. The first is entitled *lungten* [*lung bstan*], or the prophecies of Padmasaṃbhava—this was the first book that was translated to me word by word after I arrived in Lhasa and began to study the books of this people. The other book, which I also studied word by word, tells of the life of Padmasaṃbhava, his arrival in Tibet, and his stay there. In the first book and some of the chapters of the second, there is an extensive series of prophecies in the form of a dialogue between the king of Tibet and Padmasaṃbhava, in which the latter predicts those things that shall happen in the kingdom after many centuries have passed.[7]

I will discuss the important of the prophecies associated with Padmasaṃbhava and their influence on Desideri in the next chapter; at present, it is sufficient to note that the second book to which Desideri refers is most likely *The Testimonial Record of Padmasaṃbhava* (*Padma bka' thang*), which served as the stylistic model for the book that Desideri presented to Lhazang Khan on Epiphany.[8] Nor did the Jesuit missionary hesitate to draw upon Padmasaṃbhava myth to promote himself and his message. In his first work, the *Allegory of the Dawn That Dispels Darkness* (*Tho rangs mun sel nyi ma shar ba'i brda*), the Jesuit missionary presented himself as a "treasure revealer" (*gter ston*), like Padmasaṃbhava, and the Gospel as a "treasure" (*gter ma*), drawn not from the earth but from heaven itself.[9] As he read *The Testimonial Record of Padmasaṃbhava*, Desideri was puzzled that many of the events in the life of the Tibetan saint bore an uncanny resemblance to events in Christ's own life or to stories from his own Holy Scriptures. Padmasaṃbhava had been born from a lotus blossom; he remained in a fiery blaze without being burned; he stopped the natural course of the sun; he ascended into heaven. Faced with such parallels to the miraculous birth of Christ, the story of Shadrach, Meshach, and Abednego praising God in the fiery furnace, Joshua's miracle outside the walls of Jericho, and Christ's own ascension, the missionary was forced to confront several rather tricky theological questions. Did Tibetans preserve a remnant of the primitive revelation made to Adam and Eve or one of the ancient patriarchs? Were such tales the historical remnants of a once-existing Christian church, possibly from the early ministry of the apostle Thomas or later Nestorian groups that had migrated to China?[10]

For a Christian theologian of Desideri's day, the very salvation of Tibetans was at stake in these questions. Theologians had long puzzled about the fate of those who, through no fault of their own, had never heard the Gospel. Their Holy Scriptures apparently admitted no compromise in this matter; without faith, it was impossible to please God (Heb 11:6), and faith came only from hearing the word of God (Rm 10:17). Even Christ had said, "He who believes and is baptized will be saved; but he who does not believe will be condemned" (Mk 16:16). Although theologians of the Dominican and Franciscan orders sometimes accused Jesuits of avoiding mention of hell in their missions, Desideri did not. He notes with approval that the Jesuit missionary Jerónimo Xavier clearly laid out the reasons why "such a large part of humanity" is damned, and he continued to teach the same thing in his last Tibetan work, *The Essence of Christian Doctrine (Ke ri se ste aṇ kyi chos lugs kyi snying po)*.[11] But Christian theologians also held the admittedly more comforting doctrine that God sincerely "desired all men to be saved and to come to the knowledge of the truth" (1 Tim 2:1–4) and that Christ would draw all men to himself (Jn 12:32).[12] Since it was impossible to please God without faith, and yet God desired the salvation of all men and women, Roman Catholic theologians concluded that God necessarily gave all men and women grace sufficient to make an act of saving faith. Not all theologians agreed on exactly how such saving faith was possible. Theologians of the Middle Ages required those who lived after Christ to confess the mysteries of Christian faith such as the Holy Trinity and the Incarnation explicitly.[13] But, following Augustine, they assumed that, except for a small group of "exceedingly depraved people," the whole of humankind believed in God's existence and providence.[14] A medieval theologian such as Thomas Aquinas could safely assume that the number of honest unbelievers who had not heard of the Gospel was exceedingly small. The exceptional person, Aquinas reasoned, might receive a revelation of the truths necessary for her salvation from an angel.[15] The Jesuit Francisco Suárez even went so far as to deny that such angelic revelations were miraculous, and saw them as a normal part of God's providence.[16]

Upon the discovery of vast numbers of people in Asia and the Americas who had not had an opportunity to hear the Gospel, Roman Catholic theologians became less satisfied with recourse to private revelations. While admitting the truth of such revelations in limited circumstances—they had scriptural warrant, after all—theologians felt that newer theories better explained the possible salvation of non-Christians. Generally, they relaxed the necessary conditions for faith among newly discovered people, allowing them the possibility of an implicit faith in the Trinity and the Incarnation, while upholding the necessity of an explicit faith in God and His providence—the same requirements that Thomas Aquinas allowed for those who lived before the Incarnation. Theologians of the sixteenth and seventeenth centuries soon applied a great thicket of scholastic distinctions to determine the necessary and sufficient conditions for these two requirements—belief in God's existence and belief in His providence—that might help the missionary discern the implicit faith of those who did not outwardly accept the Gospel. The Jesuits were particularly ingenious at formulating such theories, and the apostolic impulse went hand in hand with them.[17] If they easily imagined the possibility that others might be damned, it was because they considered the possibility of their own damnation so fervently in the meditations of their own *Spiritual Exercises*; similarly, experiencing the surge of emotion that came with the experience of God's infinite compassion, they naturally sought to discern its presence in the lives of others.

Desideri puzzled over *The Testimonial Record of Padmasaṃbhava* because discerning whether the Tibetans possessed implicit faith depended on the resemblance their religion bore to Christianity. If Desideri first thought that Tibetans had been Christian once, he soon had doubts:

> One might well doubt whether Christianity was founded in these
> regions or whether some apostle came here long ago. Such suspicion
> may be reasonably grounded by a great many things in the Tibetan
> sect and religion that bear a great resemblance to the mysteries of our
> holy faith, to our ceremonies, institutions, ecclesiastical hierarchy, to
> the maxims and moral principles of our holy law, and to the rules and
> teachings of Christian perfection.[18]

We do not know if Desideri had answered this question to his satisfaction when he presented his first book to Lhazang Khan. Even if he had then thought that Tibetans had once been Christian, he still would have felt it necessary to correct their apostasy from the apostolic doctrine to which they had once adhered. At some point, however, he decided against it. "I have found no credible indication," he later wrote, "that Tibetans once had a notion of Christianity and our holy faith, but rather find it much more likely that the religion and false beliefs of Tibet can be found among the ancient Indian nations."[19] Although Desideri knew that Tibetans looked to India as their spiritual fatherland, the missionary says that they abolished much that was unintelligible in the tenets and retained only "what appeared to be true and good."[20] After commenting on what he considers the Indian proclivity to adore promiscuous and vengeful gods, Desideri compares Tibetan deities to forgeries that are so clever that only a refined eye can detect the fraud.[21]

Desideri's denial of historical contacts between Christianity and Tibetan Buddhism did not rule out other sources for the resemblances he detected in the two religions. Barring the distant influence of the Apostle Thomas, four theological possibilities remained. The resemblances could be the result of God's direct inspiration of ancient Tibetan authors; they could be the remnant of the primitive religion revealed to Adam and Eve and passed through virtuous pagans such as Seth, Noah, Enoch, and Job; they could be unconscious expressions of the natural desire that all men and women had for Christian revelation; or they could come from demons intent upon ruining souls with idolatrous parodies of the true faith. All of these theories received quite a good deal of attention in sixteenth- and seventeenth-century theology, although scholars seem exercised exclusively by the notion of "demonic plagiarism," since it allegedly demonstrates a natural "Western" proclivity for racism, colonialism, intolerance, and such sins.[22] In an oft-quoted passage, the seventeenth-century Jesuit polymath Athanasius Kircher described Tibetans' veneration of the Dalai Lama in these words:

> Strangers at their approach fall prostrate with their heads to the ground, and kiss him with incredible Veneration, which is no other than that which is performed upon the Pope of Rome; so that hence the fraud and deceit of the Devil may easily and plainly appear, who by his innate malignity and hatred, in way of abuse hath transferred, as he hath done all the other Mysteries of the Christian Religion, the Veneration which is due unto the Pope of Rome, the only Vicar of Christ on Earth, unto the superstitious Worship of barbarous people.
>
> Whence as the Christians call the Roman High-Priest Father of Fathers, so these Barbarians term their false Deity the Great Lama, that is, the Great High-Priest, the Lama of Lamas, that is, the High-Priest of High-Priests, because that from him, as from a certain Fountain, floweth the whole form and mode of their religion, or rather mad and brain-sick idolatry, whence also they call him the Eternal Father.[23]

It is important that we not make too much of such language. It cannot be denied, of course, and we will see some of Desideri's own statements to this effect presently. Still, none of the theories that accounted for resemblances between Christianity and other religions necessarily excluded the others, nor can they be reduced to an artificial dialectic or "play of opposites." Missionaries' feelings for the cultures they evangelized were personal and often contradictory. Heirs to a Renaissance culture that valorized the gods and goddesses of the ancient world, the men most likely to condemn the "mad and brain-sick idolatry" of other cultures were also those with the keenest appreciation of them and—it must be said—the deepest desire to learn from them.[24] Some pagan authors—Aristotle comes to mind among the scholastics, Plato among the humanists—possessed an authority in Christian theology surpassed only by Scripture and the Church fathers. Much of the educational reforms of the early modern period were built upon a foundation of pagan classics, and the ancient gods were duly celebrated in academic and literary culture.[25]

Nowhere is this domestication of the gods more apparent than in the learned fascination with vestiges of the Holy Trinity. Renaissance philosophers delighted in the triads of ancient religions and even believed that they promised the cognoscenti a deeper understanding of the Christian mysteries.[26] Even so, the voyages of discovery and the Protestant Reformation stood between the easygoing attitudes of Renaissance humanists and Desideri's encounter with Padmasaṃbhava, and missionaries often had mixed feeling about the Trinitarian vestiges they discovered. While missionaries had been educated in a culture that revered pagan antiquities, the ancient gods of Greece and Rome were no longer rivals. Missionaries in Asia and America confronted living gods and goddesses. José de Acosta reacted quite harshly to the three sun gods that he discovered in Cuzco, and Matteo Ricci attributed false trinities in China to the Devil's handiwork.[27] Quoting the testimony of Spanish missionaries who saw a "three-headed male idol" in Beijing, Athanasius Kircher felt that isolated vestiges of the Christian faith existed in Asia, although he did not share Ricci and Trigault's enthusiasm for ancient Chinese monotheism.[28] Figures 3.1 and 3.2

XVII. Idolum *Manipe* in urbe *Barantola* Regni *Lassa.*   XXI. Aliud Idolum *Manipe.*

FIGURE 3.1. A "monstrous" divinity from Athanasius Kircher, *China illustrata* (Amsterdam: Joannem Janssonium à Waesberge & Elizeum Weyerstraet, 1667). Courtesy of Special Collections, Georgetown University Library.

show two examples of Kircher's renderings of multi-limbed Asian deities that excited such speculations. Jesuit figurists such as Joachim Bouvet, Jean-François Foucquet, and Joseph Henri-Marie Prémare went so far as to claim that the ancient Chinese classics revealed supernatural mysteries of the faith such as the Holy Trinity and the Incarnation.[29] Las Casas thought that the Christian Trinity was known in much of the Yucatán and the Americas, although he believed that various rites of weather magic were evidence of pacts made with demons.[30]

Trinitarian vestiges in Indian religions exerted a continuous fascination on Jesuit missionaries.[31] Both António de Andrade and Francisco Godinho, like Desideri early in his own estimation of the Ladakhis' religion, believed that Tibetans worshiped the Holy Trinity. Godinho is most explicit:

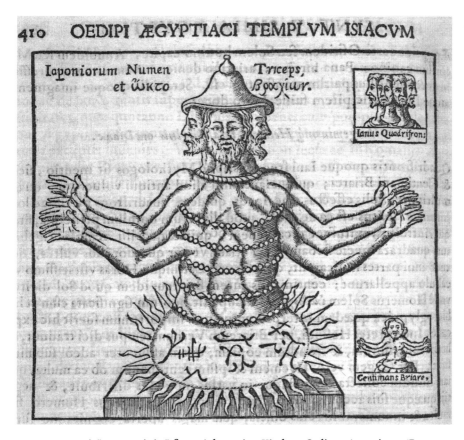

FIGURE 3.2. A "pagan trinity" from Athanasius Kircher, *Oedipus Aegyptiacus* (Rome, Vitalis Mascardi, 1652). Courtesy of Special Collections, The Sheridan Libraries, The John Hopkins University.

> The peoples of this great Tibet are not idolaters, since we have found
> that they acknowledge the adorable Unity and Trinity of the true God;
> they know that there are three hierarchies of angelic spirits, which are
> divided into nine choirs according to their different excellencies and
> dignities; that there is a hell which awaits the wicked and a paradise to
> reward the good. But these truths have become mixed up with so
> many clouds of error, which, through their nearness to pagans, have
> spread like a plague.[32]

As this passage indicates, the discovery of vestiges or resemblances of Christianity did not guarantee that missionaries would tolerate the religious practices they discovered; in fact, such discoveries were almost always accompanied by a severe condemnation of contemporary Asian religious expressions, even when missionaries celebrated the ancient Asian classics. In such cases, missionaries faulted Asians or Americans not for having fallen away from Christianity but for having fallen away from the religious truths expressed, albeit symbolically or allegorically, in their own most ancient religious texts.

This genealogical analysis was de rigueur for missionaries during the seventeenth century. The Jesuit Roberto de Nobili claimed that the Sanskrit term *brahman* was not the proper name of an idol but a general name for God even as he identified himself as a "guru of the lost law" who preached a "lost Veda" to the Indians.[33] Protestant missionaries did much the same. The Dutch Calvinist Abraham Roger thought that Hindus had once possessed a pristine knowledge of the "invisible things of God" but judged that the depravity he witnessed had led to its decay.[34] Bartholomaeus Ziegenbalg and Thomas Burnet advanced similar arguments.[35] Far from dismissing other religious traditions, such genealogical analysis presupposed the religious authority of their ancient texts. It did not assume that a given religion was demonic, but rather held that demons had obscured its true nature. Ricci, for example, believed that the ancient Chinese rightly worshiped God but rejected Song neo-Confucianism as a distortion of the most ancient Chinese texts. Jean Bouchet, who later would be Desideri's superior in Puducherry, believed that Hindus retained a confused notion of the "adorable Trinity which was formerly preach'd to them," a clear indication that he felt that the various sacred triads he encountered were historical remnants of the Gospel proclaimed by the Apostle Thomas in India. In a letter to Pierre-Daniel Huet, he explains further.

> A few Years ago, a *Brachman* thus expounded his notion of the
> fabulous Trinity of the Pagans: We are to represent to ourselves, said
> he, God and his three several names [Brahma, Vishnu, and Rudra],
> which answer to his three principal attributes, much in the Nature of

those Triangular Pyramids we see rais'd before the Gates of some
Temples.

   You are sensible, my Lord, that I do not pretend to tell you this
Imagination of the Indians answers exactly to the Truth which
Christians profess; but, however, it makes us sensible that they once had
a clearer Light, and that they are grown darker, by Reason of the
Difficulty which occurs in a Mystery so far above Man's weak Reason.[36]

Catholic theologians, especially after Thomas Aquinas, generally felt that
all religious experiences, with the possible exception of the very highest states
of rapture such as experienced by Moses and St. Paul, were accompanied by
acts of imagination. While the mystery of the Holy Trinity surpassed the weak
reason of men and women, it still offered itself to imaginative depictions. Jesuit
authors loved artfully concealed depictions of the Trinity and commonly chose
them for emblems. As a result, Europe was awash in triple-faced suns, Janus
figures, and staring triangles.[37] Images of the Holy Trinity as a Janus-Christ
with three mystically conjoined faces were especially common in Hermetic
circles, even after Antoninus of Florence and Pope Urban VIII denounced
them in 1628. Although some art historians have expressed their inability to
understand this condemnation, its theological reason seems evident enough.
It was unfitting to represent that which transcends human nature with a
"monstrous" image, that is, a representation of the perversion of human
nature.[38] We see much the same reasoning at work in missionaries' responses
to the multi-limbed "trinities" of the Hindu and Buddhist pantheons, such as
the image of Guhyasamāja depicted in figure 3.3. As we saw above, European
humanists generally compared such representations to those of Janus, which
allowed them to treat all religions as part of the history of the world outlined in
the Bible. But such pagan images were themselves often thought to be imaginative anticipations of Christian mysteries, and educated men and women in
early modern Europe commonly decorated their books with such emblems.
Figure 3.4 shows that Jeremias Drexel, one of the most renowned authors of
Jesuit emblem books, depicted Hermes Trismegistus, the mythical pagan
magician who was thought by many to have been blessed with prophetic
foreknowledge of the Holy Trinity, in just this fashion. For all intents and
purposes, it would have been difficult for missionaries not to draw formal
comparisons between the multiheaded deities of the Tantric pantheons and
such emblematic depictions of the Holy Trinity. To make matters even more
confusing, European authors such as Athanasius Kircher adjusted certain
iconographic features of Buddhism—for example, the lotus—to fit the iconographical conventions of Roman Catholicism. Compare figure 3.5, Kircher's

rather fantastic rendering of the Amida Buddha, to figure 3.6, two examples of Marian iconography from the emblem books of the Jesuit Maximilianus Sandaeus.[39] That Christian depictions of demons often took Trinitarian form, as in figure 3.7, from a contemporary life of St. Ignatius Loyola, only compounded their difficulties.

FIGURE 3.3. Guhyasamāja, Central Tibet, seventeenth century. Ground Mineral Pigment, Fine Gold Line on Cotton, 29.75 x 22.75 in. Collection of Rubin Museum of Art (HA 487).

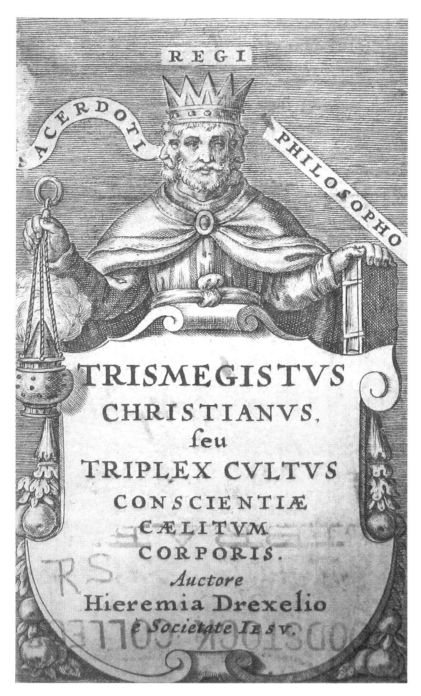

FIGURE 3.4. An allegorical depiction of Hermes Trismegistus, from Jeremias Drexel, *Trismegistus Christianus* (Cologne: Apud Cornel. ab Edmond, 1631). Courtesy of the Woodstock Theological Library, Georgetown University.

FIGURE 3.5. The Amida Buddha from Athanasius Kircher, *Oedipus Aegyptiacus* (Rome, Vitalis Mascardi, 1652). Courtesy of Special Collections, The Sheridan Libraries, The John Hopkins University.

86

Ut florem in partes cirat Sol pravius omne
A Iesu-trahitur, virgo parensq, suo.

Hanc Violam lege Virgo puer, lege virgo puella.
Non venit calathis pulchrior ulla tuis.

FIGURE 3.6. Two devotional images from Maximilianus Sandaeus: (1) *Maria flos mysticus* (Moguntia: s. n., 1639);(2) *Maria gemma mystica* (Moguntia: s.n., 1631). Courtesy of the Bayerische Staatsbibliothek, Munich.

Desideri, having rejected apostolic influence on Tibetan religion, took a different approach, although we can see how firmly he stands within this general theological tradition. When he composed his first account of the Trinity in the final months of 1716, the missionary did not attempt to explain the Trinity, nor did he offer any analogies that might assist Lhazang Khan and his court. He simply asserted that God is one and that God is three (*de yang gcig pu de yang nyid 'dug*). In fact, the Tuscan Jesuit would wait until his very last Tibetan work, written more than four years later, to offer a more detailed explanation of this fundamental Christian mystery. When writing later for his European audience, Desideri addressed the hermeneutic difficulty directly, trying in all likelihood to correct any misunderstanding caused by his previous letter to Ildebrando Grassi:

> The three complex objects of adoration, namely, their primary and supreme saints, the books or laws they have given to the world, and the most faithful and perfect observers of those laws, I declare are

Sæpe noctu inter orandum, aut qui=
escendum à Dæmonibus verberatur.

67

FIGURE 3.7. A demonic "trinity" from *Vita beati P. Ignatii Loiolae, Societatis Iesu fundatoris* (Rome, 1622). Courtesy of Special Collections, Georgetown University Library.

totally separate from and opposed to the three persons of the Holy
Trinity, Father, Son, and Holy Spirit, but if one considers the principle
attributes of the Most Holy Trinity on the one hand with the quality of
these three complex objects of adoration on the other, one might
wonder whether this complex trinity may be an obscure symbol or
blind fable of the true and most august divine Trinity.[40]

In this passage, the Jesuit missionary is outlining possible theological interpretations of the Three Jewels of Buddhism—the Buddha, the dharma, and the
sangha. The phrases "obscure symbol" and "blind fable"—like the frequently
employed terms "idolatry" and "superstition"—bear technical meanings in
Christian theology, and it is doubtful that Desideri would have used such
highly charged words without knowing their theological significance. Were
the Three Jewels an "obscure symbol," they would be a remnant of the
primitive revelation made to Adam and Eve that implicitly (or "obscurely")
pointed to the Trinity—this is a positive valuation, recognizing not only some
truth but even the possibility of salvation for Tibetans, if not in Tibetan religion
itself. Were the Three Jewels a "blind fable," Tibetan religion would be what
Christian scholastics and humanists called a type of "Greek" idolatry—as
opposed to "Egyptian" or "Chaldean" types—in which a nation mistakenly
deified its long-dead heroes.[41] Ironically, this well-known classification of
idolatry, which Desideri would have found summarized in the work of Thomas
Aquinas or that of Jesuit missionaries such as José de Acosta, is taken from a
pagan author, Diodorus Siculus. Although the identification of Tibetan Buddhism as a type of "Greek" idolatry is a negative valuation, it is in fact quite
mild, since Catholic humanists idealized ancient Greco-Roman culture. For
our purposes, we need only note that Desideri outlines two possible theological
interpretations of the Three Jewels, one positive and one less so, but neither
necessitates the recourse to demonic plagiarism.

Desideri's later rendering of the "curious" tale of the bodhisattva Avalokiteśvara alludes to the same typology of myth:

A woman lost her way in these mountains and could not find the road.
After much affliction and inconsolable grief, deploring her
misfortune, she noticed a large monkey, which in Portuguese is called
monos, who with many demonstrations of joy and good cheer, brought
wild fruit to sustain her, and finally became intimate with her, such
that she bore him several sons. Then, wandering to a ledge, she came
to a small stone mountain, which was later called Potala, very close to
the place where the city of Lhasa would later be founded. There she
discovered a certain Avalokiteśvara—an imaginary idol!—who told her

that he was custodian of the place and guardian of the land. He gave
her some grains of wheat, rice, and barley along with various
vegetables and then commanded her and her sons to sow the earth
with grain, thus multiplying them, which would serve them as
sustenance year by year in future harvests. . . . This opinion is found in
several Tibetan books and the same authors call Tibetans
"descendents of the monkey."[42]

Here, too, when Desideri refers to Avalokiteśvara as an "imaginary idol" (un
idolo favoloso) his terminology suggests that he identified Tibetan religion as a
form of "Greek" or "mythical" theology, that is, the idolatrous worship of long-
dead heroes as gods. His reference to Tibetans as "descendents of the monkey,"
however, allows him to combine his typology with a strong account of demonic
plagiarism. The monkey, a symbol of the ars simiae naturae during the Renaissance, more often connoted the figura diaboli during the baroque age. Athanasius Kircher, in a picture excellently explained by David Mungello in another
context, used this trope in his China illustrata. Figure 3.8 shows a Chinese man
writing with a monkey prominently displayed in the foreground. It is no
accident that Kircher, who had been so critical of Chinese "hieroglyphs,"
would depict a monkey aping the Chinese sage while he wrote, for in doing
so the monkey shows the pagan nature of Chinese culture.

Desideri, who was familiar with Kircher's work, used the metaphor to
explain the similarity of some episodes in the Jataka tales to Christian spirituality, and so described the Buddha's election of his mother as "another copy,
made by that infernal ape, of what our ascetics and contemplatives say about
the Divine Word's election of the Most Holy Virgin."[43] In this regard, the
presence of a monkey in the Tibetan origin myth is a historical irony of no
small importance, since it allowed Desideri to fit the Tibetan story of Avalokiteśvara seamlessly into his own theology.

The Paradox of Buddhist Atheism

From March 25 until the end of July 1717, Desideri walked every day to the
Ramoché monastery, where he "read, nay, devoured" Buddhist texts.[44] Desideri
quickly found the library at Ramoché inadequate, and moved in August 1717 to
the great university attached to Sera monastery, where he was given a good
house and permission to construct a chapel. Desideri compared the monastery
to a large town, duly noting its walls, streets, squares, and temples, as well as its
priests, masters, doctors, and several thousand monks. The lively intellectual

FIGURE 3.8. Chinese "hieroglyphs" and the aping of nature, from Athanasius Kircher, *China illustrata* (Amsterdam: Joannem Janssonium à Waesberge & Elizeum Weyerstraet, 1667). Courtesy of Special Collections, Georgetown University Library.

culture at Sera impressed the missionary, especially its public disputations, and he took pains to describe their choreography, their role in the community, and the methods of argumentation used in such disputations.[45]

> Tibetans have their own dialectics, interpretations of terms, definitions, divisions, and arguments, all in the form of simple enthymemes; a way of starting arguments, of convincing by implication, of denying and conceding points, of denying the supposition, of distorting an argument, and so forth.[46]

The great sport with which Tibetans enjoyed such disputations also attracted the Jesuit.[47] Desideri was no stranger to disputations himself; in addition to a curriculum including theology, philosophy, classics, and the sciences, young Jesuits engaged in rigorous yet stylized debates not unlike those found in the monastic courtyards of Tibet.

The Tibetan writings that immediately followed Desideri's period of study at Sera, such as *The Origin of Sentient Beings and Other Phenomena (Sems can*

dang chos la sogs pa rnams kyi 'byung khungs), show that Desideri was familiar
with about forty different works, including Nāgārjuna's *Refutation of Objections*
(*Vigrahavyāvartanīkārikā*), *Sixty Stanzas of Reasoning* (*Yuktiṣaṣṭikākārikā*), *The
Precious Garland* (*Ratnāvalī*), and *Treatise on the Middle Way* (*Madhyamakakārikā*). Not surprisingly, the *Madhyamakakārikā* is the most frequently cited
work, and Desideri expounds Nāgārjuna's thought most often through Candrakīrti's commentaries, including the *Clear Words* (*Prasannapadā*), his introduction to the *Madhyamakakārikā* (*Madhyamakāvatāra*), and his commentary on the *Sixty Stanzas* (*Yuktiṣaṣṭikāvṛtti*). Desideri was also familiar with
Bhāvaviveka's commentaries, including both the *Prajñāpradīpa* and the
Madhyamakahṛdayakārikā. Āryadeva's *Four Hundred Stanzas* (*Catuḥśatakaś
āstrakārikā*) is another a favorite source, which the missionary cites almost as
frequently as he cites the *Madhyamakakārikā*.[48] He was also familiar with
works by Asaṅga, Aśvaghoṣa, Buddhapālita, Śāntideva, and Atiśa.[49] Desideri
treats these texts as forming a single unified tradition, not unlike the Greek and
Latin classics of his own education, and he appeals to them with a certain
delicate humanist reverence. He does not merely attempt to refute Madhyamaka positions by demonstrating their logical flaws, but rather appeals to
various passages in the canonical texts to support his own position, as if an
esoteric meaning that he alone understood lay hidden deep within the ancient
Indian texts. He would later treat the Buddhist teaching on selflessness similarly, as a cipher for the meditative virtues associated with asceticism.

The missionary's account of these studies is often quoted:

Occasionally I attended their public disputations, and above all I
applied myself to study and really attempt to understand those most
abstruse, subtle, and intricate treatises they call *tongpanyi*, or vacuum,
which are not to be taken in a material or philosophic sense, but in a
mystical and intellectual one; their real aim being to exclude and
absolutely deny the existence of any uncreated and independent Being
and thus effectively do away with any conception of God. When I
began to study these treatises, the doctor who had been appointed my
master protested that he could neither understand nor explain them.
I judged this merely a pretext to impede my knowledge of the subject,
so I begged and implored him repeatedly to teach me what I wanted.
Seeing that I was not convinced that he was as incapable as he
claimed, he appealed to some of the most notable lamas to satisfy my
wishes, and offered to bring other doctors, declaring that he would be
well pleased if I found any one who could throw light on these
intricate and abstruse questions. In fact we both applied to several of

the most esteemed masters and doctors and all gave me the same
answer, but they all confessed together, as my previous teacher had,
that their treatises were too recondite and complex to explain. I
resolved to penetrate the real meaning contained in these treatises,
and seeing that no one could help me, I warmly recommended myself
to God, the father of light, for whose glory alone I had undertaken this
work, and applied myself with all intention and composure to reading
the books' headings, but always without results, for they were most
obscure. But I did not lose my spirit, and again I read most attentively,
but with the same result. Persuaded, however, that *labor improbus
omnia vincit*, I began with renewed courage, and returned to all most
carefully, reading from the top to the bottom, but to no avail. Little by
little, I pressed on with the task that had been given me, until a faint
ray of light pierced the darkness. This incited in my heart a living hope
of seeing, and finally the sun emerged into a fine, morning
brightness. Not a point was lost, but with a new and ever-growing
vigor, I read and reread, scrutinized and searched, until, thanks be to
God, I not only understood, but held most carefully, and—all glory
being to God—masterfully comprehended all the subtle,
sophisticated, and abstruse subjects that were so necessary and
important for me to know.[50]

Desideri undertook his study of Madhyamaka with some relish; presumably
the missionary hoped that the proper use of natural reason might combat the
errors that had crept into Tibetan religion. But Desideri's study of the chief
philosophical system of the Tibetan monasteries soon alerted him to a trou-
bling fact: Tibetans did not admit God's existence or His providence. Lhazang
Khan's doubt about Christians' belief in a supreme being and their denial of
reincarnation was not an isolated instance or individual aberration: it was the
religious law of the land of snows. Desideri is absolutely clear on both points:

The primary error of the Tibetans' sect, and the wellspring of all the
false dogmas they believe, is to deny positively, directly, and expressly
the existence of a being in itself, uncreated and independent, and the
first and universal cause of all things. It was the infernal enemy's
malice that created such a shrewd and subtle artifice that hides the
extreme monstrosity and irrationality contained in this error with a
pretty covering of tinsel. . . . It is almost as if the Devil has hidden
behind a skillfully embroidered curtain of gold, whose beauty and
luster had bedazzled his spectators, and thereby blinded their minds
with an artificial and beggarly light.[51]

Tibetans acknowledge no supreme judge who distributes rewards to the good and punishments to the wicked. Instead, they claim that the good receive a reward in proportion to their virtue, by the power of their merit alone, and that the wicked receive a just punishment in proportion to their vice in a like manner, without the judgment of any judge or the decrees of any supreme regulator of the world.[52]

The paradox of Tibetan atheism, as seen by Catholic theologians such as Desideri, stemmed from the common scholastic assumption that salvation, whether of Christians or non-Christians, required certainties of reason in addition to certainties of faith.[53] Christian scholastics did not think that such knowledge required explicit philosophical foundations, and although such certainties did not admit of probability or imprudent doubt, scholastics admitted degrees of certainty.[54] Even so, post-Tridentine theologians thought that the intellect's assent to the virtual proposition "God exists" might very well remain obscure, but it could never be present if the proposition itself was denied. There was always an element of actual sin involved in every profession of atheism, and its sinfulness extended even to acts that, consciously or unconsciously, prepared a man for its open avowal. Even a belief in the existence of God held for invalid reasons implied a mistaken idea about the divinity.[55] Buddhists, too, presented a further problem, for they seemed to deny the existence of God for what they thought were entirely valid motives. The Tibetan philosophers that the missionary encountered at Ramoché or Sera did not deny the existence of God furtively; they denied Him fully convinced of their need to do so. Still, the Jesuit had learned in his own philosophical training that one could never attain rational certitude about a false proposition. Absolute certainty of an evident falsehood was a chimera. The Buddhist denial of God did not—and could not—rest on such firm footing as the Tibetans thought. The philosophical reasoning that Buddhists felt separated them from Christianity was precisely that aspect in which Desideri saw the greatest connection between his own religion and that of his interlocutors. This is why Desideri attacked Madhyamaka philosophy: by denying the two minimum requirements necessary for faith, the monks of Sera stripped the symbols of Tibetan worship of their very capacity to lead Tibetans to salvation.

Later, Desideri himself would evoke the Augustinian doctrine of the scarcity of true atheism. Through an imaginary interlocutor, Desideri wonders whether any nation on earth could be so "uncultured and barbarous" as not to recognize some deity, even if it is imaginary and monstrous.[56] His imaginary interlocutor protests calling Tibetans atheists: "Will you say then that the Tibetans are atheists? This is a rather capricious claim, for there are no people on earth who wholly and explicitly profess atheism, and it would patently contradict the information you have already provided about their religion."[57] Desideri offers three responses to this objection. He first notes that Tibetans cannot be considered atheists if by that term one intends the "blind Epicureanism of *edamus et bibamus cras enim moriemur et post mortem nulla voluptas*" (let us eat and drink, for tomorrow we may die and there is no pleasure after death). Such nihilists accept neither reward for virtue nor punishment for vice, nor do they recognize any deity whatsoever, and so one would commit a grave injustice against Tibetans if one were to call them atheists in this sense. If one means, however, merely that Tibetans deny the existence of God with their words and believe themselves to be atheists, Desideri thinks the appellation fitting enough. But he continues,

> If by atheist you mean a person or people who neither signally or reflexively (to follow the manner of speaking in the schools) nor implicitly and confusedly, indeed neither theoretically nor practically, recognize any true or false deity in any way, I say that Tibetans, in my judgment, do not merit the hateful title of atheists.[58]

Desideri appealed here to well-known scholastic distinction: a practical atheist lives as though God does not exist—this is what he had already rejected as an Epicurean atheism—even if he intellectually concedes that God exists. A theoretical atheist, on the other hand, denies that God exists intellectually, even though he or she may very well lead a morally exemplary life. In scholastic discussions of atheism, this hypothetical atheist has never seriously considered the problem of God's existence. The ambiguity of such theoretical atheism, once admitted, leads to a number of possible solutions to the problem of the salvation of non-Christians, and here we see Desideri struggling mightily to leave all of his theological options open. Of course, Tibetan philosophers would have heartily rejected the implication that they had not seriously considered the existence of God, but Desideri is willing to entertain the possibility, if only to hold on to the hope that Tibetans might, in the deepest recesses of their hearts, still search for the God Who remained unknown to them. Although he strictly separated the true Trinity from the false trinity found in the Three Jewels of Buddhism, Desideri still noted that Tibetans confessed an object of refuge and prayer that possesses most of God's attributes: goodness, peace, omniscience, omnipotence, and infinite compassion. He also noted that Tibetans recognize that no one is really able to do good or avoid evil without the assistance of this very object of refuge. Despite the missionary's frequent recourse to the doctrine of demonic plagiarism, we see here a view considerably more progressive than that found in other theologians of his day. By recognizing that Tibetans might have an implicit faith in God's existence and providence—even as they explicitly denied both—Desideri granted Tibetans the possibility of a grace that many previous theologians would have denied.

Epiphany in the Court of Lhazang Khan

The Christian doctrine of grace in general—and the Jesuit doctrine of grace particularly—allows us a final glimpse into the complexity of Desideri's views of Tibetan religion and culture. Desideri explicitly mentioned grace "animating and inciting" Lhazang Khan and his court as the missionary was composing his first refutation of Tibetan religion:

> Already touched and penetrated by the power of divine grace—far more than by what I myself said—their ears sought God's voice in their own hearts, and they asked me continually whether there was any great difference between our holy law and their sect. In response, I explained to them many times that one discovers two things in any law: first, some principles, maxims, or dogmas to be believed and, secondly, precepts and directions about what to do or not to do. With regard to the first, our laws were totally opposed, and a total change in their beliefs was absolutely necessary. With regard to the second, our laws largely agreed on teaching what to do, and we could not find much difference. This explanation gave them much consolation and encouragement, and they outwardly displayed the impulse and operation of divine grace that secretly animated and incited them.[59]

Desideri's words to Lhazang Khan contain a Jesuit theology of grace *in nuce*. Ippolito Desideri had every reason to encourage the khan and his court in their practice of virtue; preserving and respecting the natural integrity of those evangelized allowed the missionary to assist them to predispose themselves negatively for the reception of grace—insofar as it was possible—or cooperate with prevenient grace should God grant it.[60] The peculiar understanding of the relationship of virtue and grace, or nature and supernature, marks Desideri's theology as Molinist or, more properly, as a species of Molinism called congruism, which is usually associated with the Jesuit theologians Francisco Suárez and Robert Bellarmine. Congruism placed a special premium on the role of the missionary in evangelization, and so highlighted the importance of discernment in the practical application of the various theologies of the salvation of non-Christians during Desideri's day. In this respect, congruism was the perfect theological expression of the mnemonic world of the *Spiritual Exercises*.

It treated the entire world as an oracular composition, a never-ending book of emblems to be interpreted by the Christian who wandered across its pages. Congruism cast God as the supreme rhetorician, with the missionary as both mouthpiece and listener, in a supreme drama of salvation history. Just as with the technical vocabulary of idolatry and superstition associated with these theologies, Desideri's *Notizie istoriche* is peppered with references to the language of grace and the discernment that attended its application in the missions. The missionary judged Casal, the woman who led his caravan from Ngari to Lhasa, to be "most inclined" (*inclinatissima*) to accept the true faith and Lhazang Khan to have formed an "almost certain conviction" (*quasi ferma persuasione*) that the Gospel was true.[61]

The distinctive Jesuit contributions to the theology of grace are found in the *Concordia liberi arbitrii cum gratiae donis* of Luis de Molina and the various works that followed in its wake.[62] In keeping with the Thomistic tradition loosely shared by Dominicans and Jesuits, Molina taught that God drew men and women to Himself through prevenient graces that elevated the will beyond its own capacities and endowed it with the faith that all Christians believed was necessary for salvation. Molina also taught that this salutary act happened only when the man or woman animated or excited by such graces freely cooperated with them. Also in keeping with the wide Thomist tradition, Molina felt that the person who freely cooperated with God in no way added to the power of grace when he or she consented, since it was God's grace that prepared, aided, and elevated the will in making the act of faith. In contrast to Dominican interpretations of Thomas Aquinas, however, Molina argued that the sufficient grace that God gives to all men and women is made efficacious by the free consent of the will, sufficient grace thus remaining inefficacious or merely sufficient if the man or woman does not freely consent to God's salvation. As a result, Molina felt that one and the same grace might be efficacious in one case and inefficacious in another—theoretically speaking.[63] His teaching led to one of the most hotly contested doctrinal debates in an age known for its controversies. Molina's opponents objected to his emphasis on the free consent of the believer because it appeared to compromise the infallibility of God's grace. It seemed, in other words, to make salvation dependent upon the believer's own merits rather than upon the gratuitous gift of God.

Molina's response to this objection was one of the cleverer bits of theologizing in the early modern period, if not necessarily the most intellectually satisfying. He affirmed that God's grace was both efficacious and infallible not because God had predetermined how men and women would respond in His grace but because He knew how they would respond from all eternity through a *scientia media*, a "middle knowledge" that was neither His own knowledge of

His eternal decrees nor a direct knowledge of the believer's free response, but rather an omniscient knowledge of how a free man or woman will respond when placed in the specific contingent situations He decreed. God, knowing both hypothetically free acts and absolutely free acts, infallibly and eternally knows how every man, every woman, and every child might respond in every possible situation. As a result, He creates the world in order to secure, as it were, the free response of each man, woman, or child He wishes to save. God's grace then proves efficacious according to His foreknowledge of how the person might possibly respond rather than how he or she actually responds. In other words, efficacious grace is infallible because God creates, conserves, and providentially governs the entirety of human history, and those who freely respond to His call are chosen and predestined because the scope of God's *scientia media* embraces all possible worlds. Men and women who then re-spond—or fail to respond—truly exercise their free will, insofar as God has not physically predetermined their responses. From the point of human reason, God makes us an offer that we can in fact refuse. Seen *sub specie aeternitatis*, God makes us an offer that we can refuse only if He so permits.

This highly controversial account of the relationship of grace and free will was championed and clarified by another Jesuit theologian, Robert Bellarmine, and it is largely through his influence that the general Jesuit position on grace and free will was disseminated.[64] Grace, Bellarmine argued, included both the state of affairs providentially ordered by God as well as the interior excitation and movement of the will. If the same grace was hypothetically offered to two men, and one accepted it while the other rejected it—while one believed and was moved to love God and one was not—this was not because the man who believed did so without grace, but because he received the impulse of grace in the manner, place, and time that God saw to be congruous with his own intent to save humanity.[65] Bellarmine thus widened the concept of grace to include the whole of God's providence, and it is here that we can see its importance for the missions. Opponents of congruism objected that God did not adapt himself slavishly to situations in order to enact His eternal decrees. Grace worked in men and women, they claimed, with little or no regard to the congruity of the states in which men and women found themselves. Its Jesuit defenders retorted that such congruity, which was truly known by God alone, would remain hidden for those without eyes to see. Mysteries such as the Incarnation and Crucifixion could hardly be thought fitting without the illuminating grace of faith. Indeed, the mystery of God's providence, the Jesuits argued, was made manifest precisely when apparently weaker impulses of grace were conferred in favorable circumstances. Likewise, apparently stronger impulses might very well be thwarted by unfavorable affairs. *Deo volente,* a single stone might accomplish more than legions—or faith might move mountains.

Jesuit theologians gave this insight its greatest possible extension. In the world they envisioned, the smallest acts—such as choosing to unwrap a gift with one's own hands—might very well be the state of affairs that God deemed congruous for the salvation of a soul, even the soul of Lhazang Khan. Such an act might be the first of many prevenient graces that led, under the proper circumstances, to the very act of faith that saved a Khoshud chieftain. Timing is of the essence here, for both the missionary and the people he evangelized, for he had to seize the remotest possibility of faith and nurture it if God's hidden graces were to become manifest in the lives of Tibetans. The missionary was required not only to discern the best methods for guiding a soul to salvation through God's grace but also to discern and root out any obstacle that his own sins might place in God's way. He was required to wage spiritual warfare not merely against the demons that deceived Tibetans but against the demons that manufactured idols within his own heart. The Jesuit who believed that God had providentially ordered history in order to secure the free response of men and women could thus see himself as part of a grand drama. Since the free response of an unbeliever could happen at any time, even one that appeared incongruous, the missionary had to attune himself to the grace that made him an actor in this cosmic drama. He must, in other words, commit himself to the practice of Christian love, cooperating with God's grace in the discernment not only of the spiritual state of his charges but also of the graces he would need for the drama's successful completion. If God lovingly created the world to over-come any possible refusal—as congruism implies—then the Jesuit who failed to become a perfect instrument of God's grace would be responsible for any soul lost on account of his failure, and so find himself not at Christ's right hand but at His left. Christ was speaking to him not from the works he carried from Europe but through those very people he evangelized: "Depart from me, ye cursed, into the eternal fire prepared for the Devil and his angels; for I was hungry and you gave me no food, I was thirsty and you gave me no drink, I was a stranger and you did not welcome me, naked and you did not clothe me, sick and in prison and you did not visit me" (Mt 25:41–43). Far from ensuring the missionary a privileged pole in the play of opposites—a presump-tion that would be the very definition of mad and brain-sick idolatry—the theology of the Society of Jesus cast him in the role of slave to the people he evangelized. "One who saves a sinner from the error of his ways," after all, "saves his own soul from death" (James 5:20). According to the theology of his order, Ippolito Desideri would work out his own salvation on the roof of the world.

Such theological notions naturally led Desideri to emphasize the importance of Tibetans' own natural virtues, a position that was similarly controversial in Desideri's day. Shortly after he had left for India, Pope Clement XI condemned Pasquier Quesnel's assertion "All natural knowledge of God, even that found in pagan philosophers, can come from nowhere but God, and without grace produces nothing but presumption, vanity, and opposition to God Himself, instead of adoration, gratitude, and charity."[66] Asserting that no one could perform morally good actions except in a state of perfect infused charity, theologians such as Quesnel accepted the consequence that all acts of non-Christians were in fact sins. In this, he was but one of a line of early modern theologians, usually labeled Jansenists, who expressed great skepticism about the natural powers of non-Christians. Another, Michel Baius, had taught, "All of unbelievers' actions are sins and all of philosophers' virtues are vices," a position that also had been condemned as unorthodox.[67] Cornelius Jansen, the figurehead of the later Augustinian movement, supported these arguments with a bewildering number of quotations from Augustine himself. Among his favorite quotations was "If the way of truth is hidden, free will avails for nothing except sin."[68] Jansen even claimed St. Paul among his supporters: "Whatever does not proceed from faith is sin" (Rm 14:23).[69] The bishop of Ypres interpreted these words to mean that whatever a man does in a state of mortal sin—such as Tibetans would inevitably find themselves in without faith—was sinful on account of his not being in a state of grace. His followers asserted that God is the cause of all good but denied that any good could be found in non-Christian cultures. The later Jansenist Antoine Arnauld even claimed that "pagans, Jews, heretics, and others of the same kind receive no influx from Christ at all, and it is rightly inferred that in them there is but a naked and helpless will, without any sufficient grace."[70] As a result, he also argued that unbelievers necessarily sin in all of their actions, a position likewise condemned by Pope Alexander VIII.[71] This denial of pagan virtue followed from a distinctive teaching on the relationship of grace and free will. Essentially, Jansen taught that the will of fallen men and women is overcome by grace in the exact manner in which it is overpowered by concupiscence in the absence of grace.[72] While Adam and Eve enjoyed freedom of the will in paradise, they lost that freedom entirely when they sinned, and so become subject to a twofold delectation—the *delectatio coelestis victrix* and the *delectatio terrena sive carnalis*. When the *delectatio coelestis* is stronger than the *delectatio terrena*, grace efficaciously overcomes the will. When the *delectatio coelestis* is weaker, earthly delights overcome the will—and the person sins of necessity. As a result, Jansen effectively denied the doctrine of sufficient grace and evacuated the sphere of natural virtue altogether.[73]

Jesuit theologians resisted these conclusions with evident ferocity. They argued that virtue must be defined to include those acts that order one to participation in God's life; that virtue includes acts that are neither supernatural nor salutary; that the natural virtues might yet be elevated by supernatural grace; and that God gives non-Christians sufficient grace to make salutary acts whether they choose to do so or not. To support their arguments, they also produced quite a few statements from Augustine that countered Jansen's interpretation and provided support for their own doctrines of sufficient grace and the freedom of the will.[74] Following the lead of Thomas Aquinas, they argued that some actions of unbelievers are in fact good, as the story of Cornelius in the tenth chapter of the Acts of the Apostles indicates, because human nature retains its integrity after the Fall.[75] Indeed, it was the common teaching of Roman Catholic theologians that God did not deny grace to men or women who did what they could to follow the natural law.[76] Jesuit theologians stressed this point to such a degree that some, such as Juan Martínez Ripalda and Gabriel Vásquez, argued that prevenient grace always accompanied natural virtues in the present economy of salvation.[77] Here, too, Desideri's vocabulary suggests a deeper consideration of these issues. By distinguishing between prevenient graces (*gratia preveniens sive operans*) and subsequent graces (*gratia subsequents sive cooperans*), Desideri carefully avoided granting salvation to Lhazang Khan—such a grace not being his to give—since only cooperating grace is salutary, strictly speaking.[78] At the same time, the missionary recognized the possibility of the khan's natural virtue and, if he followed the general theological trends of the Society, almost certainly would have felt that prevenient grace oriented such natural virtues to the performance of those that are supernatural and salutary. While the missionary would have had no way of knowing whether Lhazang Khan had received such grace—the effects of grace, like karma, are very hidden—the theology of his order would have given him reason to hope. In the Jesuit's heart, the Feast of the Epiphany in 1717 might have been the day when Lhazang Khan had been baptized with the implicit faith of desire.

The twin acknowledgments that grace animated and incited Tibetans and that their natural virtues were ordered to a supernatural fulfillment in no way lessened the missionary's need to refute Buddhist doctrines; if anything, it heightened it. If Tibetans had faith in the Buddhas' merits, if they hoped for their assistance or loved them for their perfections, the missionary had still to uncover the truth hidden at the heart of their actions and to demonstrate to his interlocutors that these very actions spoke of an infinite, providential God, all while using their own methods of argumentation. On November 28, 1717, Desideri began writing a treatise entitled *The Origin of Sentient Beings and Other*

Phenomena, the first of a series of works of increasing length in which he would attempt to demonstrate the existence of God to the Tibetans who denied Him, and show them the rewards of believing in His providence. Unfortunately, Ippolito Desideri would not have time to convince the monks of Sera of their philosophical errors, for he would soon be forced to hide in the monastery as Lhazang Khan lost the country he had conquered twelve years earlier. When he recounted these events years later, the missionary ruefully remarked that, whatever virtues Lhazang Khan may have had, he would have been better served by "that other quality, quite necessary for rulers, of suspicion, the lack of which cost him his kingdom, his family, and his very life."[79]

4

The Zünghar Invasion

Sometimes one monastery will wage war against another, and
sometimes these ecclesiastical swash-bucklers will pour into towns
and seize and hack to pieces some unpopular governor.
                              —William McGovern, *To Lhasa in Disguise*

The tangled affairs of early eighteenth-century Tibetan politics are impossible to describe in a single chapter. The Geluk monastic order that
dominated the central government was divided into several competing
factions, each with complex and ever-shifting alliances with various
Tibetan aristocrats, Manchu nobles, and Mongol chieftains. Between the
regent Sangyé Gyatso and the secular "king" Lhazang Khan in central
Tibet—and the Manchu Empire and Zünghbe its borders—
these factions bound Tibet to its increasingly unstable neighbors as they
battled for control within the Lhasa government. Even as Desideri stood
in Lhazang's court on the feast of Epiphany, several Tibetans were
engineering the khan's downfall. When the Zünghars, a group of Oirat
Mongol tribes from the northwest, invaded central Tibet in 1717, the
tension between these factions broke into open conflict, and Tibet was
plunged into war. Desideri left a flawed but fascinating account of the
carnage, which he described with an apt mythopoetic comparison:

> Tibetans compare the shape of Tibet to a prone person with his
> torso chained, in the position in which poets describe the fabled
> Prometheus on the horrid peaks of the Caucasus, which are

precisely this long, unending stretch of Tibetan mountains. When the poets speak of Prometheus, condemned to have his torso and entrails torn and torn again by the gluttonous and insatiable bird, he is shown bound in chains, prone, and helpless. This is certainly what one reads in Martial's epigram that begins *Qualis Caucasea religatus rupe Prometheus adsiduam nimio pectore pascit avem.*"[1]

Desideri's account of the Zünghar invasion allows us to put one of the most prominent fantasies of Tibet to the test, namely, that it was a land untouched by violence or religious persecution. On this score, Ippolito Desideri is a refreshing exception; he fantasized no more about Tibetans than did most modern historians and, indeed, quite a bit less than many.[2] He rightly understood that there were differences between the Tibetan monastic orders and that a great deal of the religious persecution that he witnessed was politically motivated. He did not record every historical detail accurately, nor did his attention to such mundane affairs prevent him from giving them a supernatural interpretation, but the sympathy the missionary showed for those who suffered the most during these persecutions is noteworthy. Desideri's relationship to adherents of the Nyingma order, or the "Ancient Ones," not only explains his description of the Zünghar invasion but also gives us a vantage point from which to view the evolution of his Tibetan works and the rather surprising ways he manipulated Tibetan religious claims for his own apologetic purposes. In fact, the Nyingma men and women who resisted Taktsepa and the Zünghar government after the invasion came to play an important role in Desideri's own understanding of Tibetan religion.

Tibet Under the Dalai Lamas

The seeds of Lhazang Khan's demise were sown in 1682, when the fifth Dalai Lama, Ngawang Gyatso, died in the Potala. Knowing the political tensions that surrounded the selection of a new Dalai Lama, the regent, Sangyé Gyatso, concealed the Dalai Lama's death as he groomed a candidate for the vacated throne. The regent had every reason to protect his share of Ngawang Gyatso's legacy. With the Dalai Lama hidden safely away, the regent now sat alone atop the pyramid of the new Tibetan tax structure, the final fruit of long years of political maneuvering. This complex state of affairs depended on the peculiar Tibetan interpretation of the doctrine of reincarnation (*yang srid*). Before the late fourteenth century, monastic titles and estates were usually passed from uncle to nephew, with neither needing to break his vow of celibacy. Estate disputes among the Kagyü order led to a novel interpretation of the doctrine of reincarnation in the late fourteenth or early fifteenth century.[3] According to this interpretation, one could discover among the living the reincarnation of a recently deceased titleholder by interpreting various omens and carefully testing several children. This ingenious interpretation, which quickly became prominent among most of the monastic orders in Tibet, had a powerful effect on Tibetan politics. It allowed religious orders to thwart the claims of heirs traditionally considered, but it also enabled them to seek successors among powerful aristocratic families who had been allied with other religious orders. In other words, it allowed celibate monks to "marry" into families who owned extensive estates but who patronized other orders. For a strictly celibate and relatively young monastic order such as the Geluk, the discovery of child reincarnations allowed them to compensate for their lack of aristocratic patronage and displace—or claim—the biological succession by which various Tibetan clans controlled the monasteries. The third Dalai Lama, Sönam Gyatso, for example, came from a distinguished family with ties to the older Sakya order and other powerful families such as the Pakmodrü. The second Panchen Lama came from a prominent Bönpo family. Unlike other orders, the Geluk combined this doctrine with real military firepower, often recognizing the reincarnations of prestigious lamas among Mongol warlords: the fourth Dalai Lama was the great-grandson of Altan Khan, the powerful chief of the Tümed Mongols. Whether one thinks the coincidence to be divine mandate or political expediency, the third Dalai Lama had met Altan Khan ten years before his reincarnation was discovered, and both the Dalai Lama and the Mongol khan believed themselves to be recapitulating the priest-patron (*mchod yon*) relationship between the Pakpa Lama and Qubilai Khan in the thirteenth century.[4]

The fifth Dalai Lama was himself a fruit of such doctrines. Born at Chongyé, the burial place of the old Tibetan kings, Ngawang Gyatso was from a Nyingma family with ties to Samyé monastery and the powerful Pakmodrü family. Upon meeting the Khoshud chieftain Güüshi Khan in 1638, Ngawang Gyatso gained military might enough to extend the political unity forged by the third Dalai Lama and Altan Khan over the central Tibetan regions of Ü and Tsang. After emerging victorious over his rivals in 1642, the Dalai Lama united central Tibet and initiated epochal reforms in Tibetan literature, medicine, government, and land polity.[5] He also rewrote Tibetan history with himself, as the reincarnation of Avalokiteśvara, at its center.[6] This wholesale construction of a central Tibetan myth included the visionary "discovery" of ancient texts called "treasures" (*gter ma*), the promotion of new liturgies and oracles, and the patronage of arts that supported the Dalai Lama's political agenda.[7] The Dalai Lama crowned his own apotheosis by building the Potala palace upon the sacred mountain Marpori (*dmar po ri*). With the ostensible reason of "purifying" the battlefield sins of Güüshi Khan, the Dalai Lama even brought to Lhasa the very image of Avalokiteśvara, the bodhisattva of compassion, that his armies had carried from battleground to battleground.[8] After ascending the throne, he visited monasteries across Tibet with the Khoshud army, taking a census of the monks and making a complete survey of monastic estates, sometimes forcibly converting monasteries of other orders, particularly the Jonang order, into Geluk institutions, and often replacing local government officials with his own supporters. Perhaps what is more important, the new government reformed and centralized the system of taxation and tax officials and redirected several streams of tribute.[9] The fifth Dalai Lama also endowed several Nyingma monasteries, most notably Mindröling and Dorjé Drak (*rdo rje brag*), two institutions that would play important roles in the events that Desideri witnessed, allowing the Nyingma to enjoy a cultural resurgence under his patronage. Terdak Lingpa and Lochen Dharmaśri at Mindröling unified several scattered lineages under the liturgical reforms centered on the Sutra Empowerment (*mdo dbang*) tradition, while Pema Trinlé at Dorjé Drak encouraged the Northern Treasure school (*byang gter*), whose proponents Desideri would chance to meet.[10]

The regent's methods of concealing the death of the fifth Dalai Lama were as complex as his motives; he staged audiences for Tibetan aristocrats and Mongol emissaries in which a monk disguised as the dead Dalai Lama celebrated mock rituals. Terdak Lingpa, the Nyingma priest who was privy to the regent's secret, routinely faked initiations and ordinations in which the pseudo–Dalai Lama participated. As abbots and aristocrats inquired about the Dalai Lama's increasing secrecy, Sangyé Gyatso signed a pact with the Zünghars, a prominent tribe among the western Mongols.[11] While the relations between the Zünghars and their Khoshud brethren in Tibet were ambiguous at best, the Zünghars were openly hostile to the Qing Empire.[12] The borders of China expanded considerably during Qing rule, covering the Gobi Desert and Manchuria to the north as far as Nerchinsk and Irkutsk and stretching to the west over the Altai Mountains to Lake Balkash and the Karakorum Mountains.[13] This expansion brought them into the areas around the Atlai Mountains controlled by the Zünghars, namely, Tianshan and the Tarim Basin.[14]

The regent's pact with the Zünghars did not rest well with other Geluk authorities. Many, particularly noblemen from Tsang with favorable ties to the Nyingma order, objected to the regent's alliance because it threatened their own relations with the Khoshud Mongols and the Qing Empire. Other Geluk leaders, especially clergy from powerful monasteries in Ü who resented the Nyingma influence on Ngawang Gyatso, sought to cast off the Khoshud and

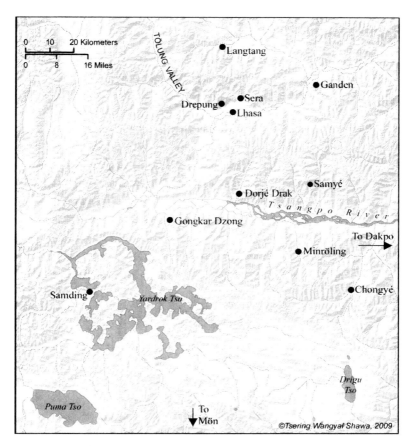

MAP 2. Central Tibet and Its Monasteries

Manchu yoke altogether. Powerful Geluk leaders from Amdo, the far-eastern Tibetan province that borders Mongolia and China, enjoyed stronger ties to the various Mongol tribes than any of the other Tibetan factions and were increasingly pro-Qing. If the regent hoped that an alliance with the Zünghars would weaken the influence of the Manchu and Khoshud in central Tibetan affairs, he tragically underestimated both the Manchu emperor Kangxi and the Amdo Geluk who supported him. Worse still, he underestimated the resentment many central Tibetan Geluk held for the Nyingma.

Sangyé Gyatso had already secretly chosen the child who was to become the sixth Dalai Lama.[15] The child's mother was from an old Nyingma family, the Berkhar, whose ancestors had received special revelations from Padmasaṃbhava and had endowed many ancient Nyingma temples. He was also from Mön, a region quite rich in resources that could not be obtained on the

Tibetan plateau and that provided the only direct trade corridor to the Indian subcontinent. The child seemed ideal in every way: if he could be easily controlled, the regent could then continue the fifth Dalai Lama's program of political and economic expansion southward while retaining the aristocratic connections to the old Tibetan Empire, an important ingredient in the central Tibetan myth he had helped to create. The regent's machinations continued unhindered until 1694, when Zünghar prisoners of war informed Kangxi that the regent had been concealing the death of the fifth Dalai Lama. His ruse discovered, Sangyé Gyatso delayed as long as he could and then placed Tsangyang Gyatso, a boy who was already thirteen years old, on the throne of the Dalai Lama. Kangxi was not pleased that the regent had chosen the sixth Dalai Lama without his consent, nor was he happy that the regent had secretly supported the Zünghars, apparently with the assistance of the second Panchen Lama. The emperor neither questioned the regent's choice nor objected to the Panchen's infidelity. He quietly selected Changkya Ngawang Lozang Chöden to represent him as proxy at the enthronement ceremony and silently awaited his report.

To all outward appearances, Sangyé Gyatso had maintained Ngawang Gyatso's own political alliances. The enthronement ceremony of the sixth Dalai Lama was a portrait of Tibetan politics in miniature. The Panchen Lama represented Geluk from Tsang with strong diplomatic ties to the Nyingma, the Khoshud, and the Manchu—ties that did not escape Desideri's notice. The Changkya Qutuqtu represented Tibetan and Mongolian Geluk interests from Amdo. Two powerful Nyingma hierarchs, Terdak Lingpa and the Dorjé Drak abbot Pema Trinlé, were also present. These two Nyingma masters initiated the young Dalai Lama into the mysteries of their own order; the Tibetan aristocracy maintained its influence in Geluk affairs, and the Khoshud chieftain Tenzin Wangyel succeeded his father, Dalai Khan, as the military protector of Tibet. The regent flooded Lhasa with the late seventeenth-century equivalent of political pins and bumper stickers, including clay molds of the fifth Dalai Lama's ritual dagger and small portraits of the sixth, whom they feted with great pomp in the capital. As the Panchen Lama prepared the young man for the tonsure, Tsangyang Gyatso wept. Much to the chagrin of the monks, it quickly became apparent that the boy had little interest in his office, and scandal soon enveloped the young incarnate lama. He refused to take his final vows and was often seen in the streets of Lhasa in situations that did not befit the divine ruler of the Tibetan government. Sangyé Gyatso, disturbed by the Dalai Lama's exploits, even arranged to have the source of the troubles, a friend named Targyené, eliminated. The regent's thugs, fooled because the Dalai Lama and his friends often wore each other's clothes during their nighttime revels, botched their assassination attempt and killed the wrong man.[16]

Desideri's Patron Lhazang Khan

Lhazang Khan entered this world with some rather unsavory machinations of his own: desiring to assume the role of Tibet's military protector, traditionally afforded to the Khoshud chieftain, he poisoned his brother Wangyel in 1703. Fearing the change in the Khoshud ranks, Sangyé Gyatso in turn poisoned the Khoshud chieftain, who survived the attempt on his life when given an antidote by the Amdo Geluk Jamyang Zhepa, the head of Gomang College at Drepung monastery.[17] Not to be outdone, Sangyé Gyatso incited the monks at Sera monastery to riot against the khan during the New Year's festivities in 1705. Proposing that the monks seize and slay the Khoshud chief, the regent was again opposed by Jamyang Zhepa. In an attempt to cool the quickly escalating tensions, the Lhamo oracle of the Panchen Lama, the powerful Geluk reincarnate who controlled the Tashilhunpo monastery in Zhikatsé, issued a double prophecy that Sangyé Gyatso would retire to an estate far removed from the political stage and that Lhazang Khan would join his Khoshud brethren in Kökenuur, in far northeastern Tibet.[18] The Mongol chieftain pretended to acquiesce, stocked a caravan, and set off. The caravan halted north of Lhasa, Lhazang Khan distributed arms to his tribesmen, and his forces turned to Lhasa. The Panchen Lama intervened in the hopes of preventing an altercation and offered to mediate the dispute between the regent and the khan.[19] Both men rejected the Panchen's offer. The regent massed troops from Ü, Tsang, and Ngari; Lhazang Khan, for his part, marched to Langtang, crossed the mountains north of Lhasa, and advanced his army toward the capital in three columns. Leading the right column of Lhazang Khan's army through the Tölung Valley was none other than his wife, Tsering Trashi. In the fighting that followed, the khan routed the regent's armies. As a result, Sangyé Gyatso relinquished his powers and was banished to the Gonkar fortress. On September 6, 1705, Tsering Trashi had Sangyé Gyatso brought to the Tölung Valley. The monks of Drepung must have sensed her ill intentions, since Jamyang Zhepa was soon en route to intercede on behalf of the regent. He arrived, tragically, just after Tsering Trashi had Sangyé Gyatso beheaded.[20]

After assuming his full powers as the sole ruler of Tibet, Lhazang Khan sought the help of Kangxi. The Manchu emperor knew that the regent's death did little to dampen central Tibetan support for the Zünghars. If anything, it and the Dalai Lama's waywardness created a void that the Zünghars could fill more easily. The emperor had little time to lose, especially if the Khalkha or

Khoshud in Kökenuur formed an alliance with Züngharia to oust their Mongol brethren in central Tibet. To avoid such a conspiracy, the emperor needed the support of the Khoshud in Ü and Tsang. Kangxi gave the khan an imperial title and feigned sympathy for his moral qualms about Tsangyang Gyatso. He even agreed to investigate the authenticity of the incarnation. Even if he thought Tsangyang Gyatso an imposter, Kangxi knew well enough that the Kökenuur Mongols greatly revered the Dalai Lama.[21] With well-calculated diplomacy, the emperor asked that the Dalai Lama be sent to Beijing to be evaluated personally. Lhazang Khan was trapped, needing the emperor's support but fearing that the newly conciliated monasteries would protest the Dalai Lama's removal, and so he stalled. Kangxi ignored the delay and sent an envoy to escort the Dalai Lama to the capital. Lhazang Khan, confident that he had enough support among the central Tibetan Geluk, attempted to settle the matter himself by coercing a party of leading Geluk to declare Tsangyang Gyatso an imposter. He successfully secured the aid of the Lhamo oracle—who effectively served as the voice of the Panchen Lama—in his plan, but failed to garner any other supporters. The plan came to naught when the noble Taktsepa convinced powerful Geluk hierarchs to declare the ordination valid. Not one to be deterred by such supercilious diplomacy, Lhazang Khan marshaled his troops and kidnapped the Dalai Lama. When the khan's party passed near Drepung, its monks stoned the party and rescued the Dalai Lama. The khan retaliated by raining artillery on Ganden, the monastery of the Tri Rinpoché, and the Dalai Lama surrendered to prevent the monastery's destruction. Although Desideri and the Capuchins were later to spread the rumor that Lhazang Khan murdered Tsangyang Gyatso after his surrender, both Tibetan and Chinese accounts maintain that he died of small-pox on the way to Beijing on November 14, 1706.

After the death of the sixth Dalai Lama, Lhazang Khan attempted to pass off one Ngawang Yeshé Gyatso as the "authentic" sixth Dalai Lama. The monk from the Chakpori medical college in Lhasa was rumored to be Lhazang Khan's natural son, and although the Panchen Lama ritually consecrated him as the new Dalai Lama, he was never really accepted by many Tibetans.[22] Lhazang Khan's rash attempt to place a puppet Dalai Lama on the throne also angered the Mongol tribes in Kökenuur, who felt spurned when he did not consult them about his selection. In the meantime, a group of Geluk discovered the sixth Dalai Lama's "true" reincarnation near Tupchen Jamling, a monastery that had been founded by the third Dalai Lama, in Kham near the border of Amdo.[23] The new Dalai Lama's father, Sönam Dargyé, was from Chongyé, the birthplace of the fifth Dalai Lama, and had minor political connections at Drepung.[24] Hearing that another Dalai Lama had been discovered closer to home, Kangxi prudently decided to withhold his support for Lhazang Khan's puppet. He issued an edict demanding

Tibetan fealty to the khan and the Dalai Lama, while cleverly leaving the latter unnamed. As support for the child spread to central Tibet, Lhazang tried unsuccessfully to declare the child a fake. The Kökenuur chieftains appealed to the Manchu emperor to recognize their candidate.

Kangxi well understood the importance that the Mongols attached to the office of the Dalai Lama. Beginning with the relationship of the third Dalai Lama, Sönam Gyatso, and the Altan Khan of the Tümed Mongols, the desire of various Mongol chieftains to unite their brethren under a single khanate was inexorably linked to the religious concerns of the Geluk order. As a result, both the Manchus and the Zünghars understood the necessity of controlling the Dalai Lama, since their competition to win the various groups of eastern Mongols to their side depended on securing the young incarnate. Kangxi ordered that the child be brought to Beijing. In the meantime, he sent an envoy to the Panchen Lama to question him about the child. As the Kökenuur chieftains stalled, word arrived that the Panchen Lama disavowed the new incarnation, and the tension between the Geluk parties in Tsang and Amdo grew accordingly. Kangxi asked the Kökenuur chieftains to remove the child and his father to another, more heavily armed monastery at Kumbum, near Xining. The emperor's demand excited the chieftains considerably. Although Lhazang Khan still enjoyed the emperor's favor, many Kökenuur Mongols desired to put an end to the Khoshud hegemony in central Tibetan politics. Others, despite their dislike of the khan, felt it wiser to submit to the emperor for the time being. After a spirited debate, the Kökenuur chieftains told the emperor that the young Dalai Lama could not travel, since he had not yet had smallpox. As Kangxi and the Kökenuur chieftains settled on a compromise—the young child would be held at the Kumbum monastery—Züngharia and Manchu China went to war.

Lhazang Khan, "by nature kind and unsuspicious," in Desideri's estimation, seems not to have anticipated the conflict. His placement of Ngawang Yeshé Gyatso on the Dalai Lama's throne so enraged some of the Geluk in Ü that they appealed to the Zünghars for assistance. Sensing an opportunity, the Zünghar ruler Tsewang Rapten proposed a marriage between his daughter and Lhazang Khan's eldest son, a proposal that was met with some suspicion until the khan's son threatened suicide—an act that suggests Ganden Tsering himself had more than a little to gain by the death of his father. When Lhazang Khan acquiesced, the Zünghar ruler demanded a sizable sum to pay for the wedding ceremonies, a sum he then used to supply two large armies, the first of which marched to Kumbum to capture the "true" Dalai Lama. The second army, under the pretense of avenging the death of Sangyé Gyatso, marched through northwestern Tibet hoping to surprise Lhazang Khan in his summer camp. Lhazang's generals discovered the plot as he prepared for the wedding, and they retreated to Lhasa to fortify its walls. Kangchené Sönam Gyelpo, the man whom Lhazang had appointed as district governor of Ngari after the husband of the woman who escorted Desideri and Freyre across Ngari died, also got word of Zünghar troops moving through western Tibet, although they evaded his forces and continued their march toward Lhasa. Polhané, another supporter of Lhazang Khan who would play a great role in Tibetan politics, also gathered armies to defend Lhasa against the impending siege. The Manchus meanwhile repulsed the Zünghar army in Kökenuur and maintained their grasp on the young Dalai Lama.

In Desideri's judgment, the Zünghars were forced to choose between attacking a well-fortified city with only six thousand men or retreating into the on-slaught of the "justly irritated" Manchu army. Truth be told, Lhasa was not particularly well fortified. Seeing no practical way to accomplish their mission in eastern Tibet, the Zünghars spread the rumor that they had defeated the Manchus at Kumbum and marched upon Lhasa. "No sooner did the squadron appear," Desideri remarked, "than with shouts of joy, acclamation, and inexplicable happiness," the monks of Drepung, Sera, and Ganden ran to cheer the Zünghars and bring them "provisions, arms, and ammunition."[25]

> After midnight on November 30, 1717, the walls of Lhasa were attacked on all sides, and in accordance with a premeditated conspiracy, ladders were let down that enabled the enemies to scale the walls of the city in various places while the northern and eastern gates were opened. The Zünghars entered that unhappy city, a bloody fight began, and by daybreak they were masters of the city.[26]

Desideri spared no deprecations in describing the atrocities of the Geluk monks who participated in the sack of Lhasa, which lasted for two days and spread into the nearby regions. With their Zünghar allies, the monks stormed private residences, robbed monasteries, and looted temples. Desideri also claimed that the monks tortured people indiscriminately in order to force confessions about the location of hidden wealth:

> The monks who had joined the soldiers in a spirit of solidarity rushed into the houses with a sordid greed, drawn weapons in their hands, and robbed their brethren in accordance with their secret plan. Not content to satisfy their lust, they returned to the houses and sought those things that had been conserved and hidden in the monasteries. With an insatiable and inexplicable greed, they returned again and again to the houses, sparing neither the elderly nor women nor any sort of person whatsoever, stabbing some with the points of their swords, wounding others over the whole of their bodies with cruel

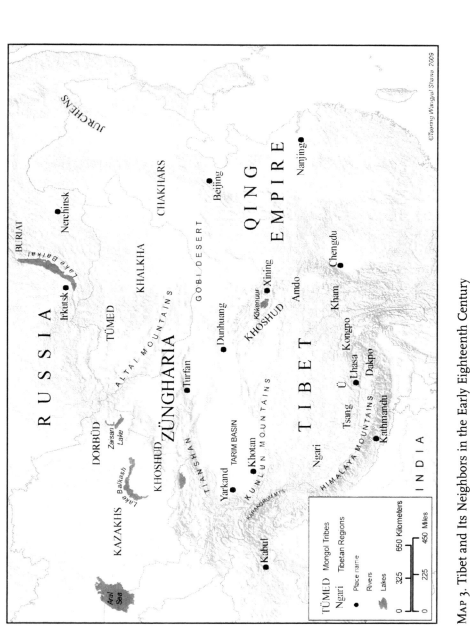

MAP 3. Tibet and Its Neighbors in the Early Eighteenth Century

FIGURE 4.1. A Tartar siege from Martino Martini's *Regni Sinensis a Tartaris devastati enarratio* (Amsterdam: Aegidius Janssonius, 1661). Courtesy of Special Collections, The Sheridan Libraries, The John Hopkins University.

> saber blows, tying others by their hands, suspending them from the beams of the ceiling, and whipping them repeatedly, and in other barbarous ways inhumanely torturing all with unspeakable abuse to make them reveal the whereabouts of their riches. The monks carried on in this way for two days and two nights until everything that could be unearthed, gathered up, and stolen, indeed everything precious and valuable, had been taken from Lhasa and the surrounding regions.[27]

Desideri's tone is highly romantic, and one can presume that he wished to take advantage of the European taste for Manchu military exploits—figures 4.1 and 4.2 are prime examples of such literature—but the atrocities he reported were very real. One of the Capuchin fathers was stripped naked and whipped so severely that his wounds took several months to heal. The other Capuchins were robbed of 500 scudi, an amount that constituted almost their entire means of support. In the midst of the chaos, Lhazang Khan retreated into the Potala. The Zünghars scaled its southern walls but could not enter the

FIGURE 4.2. The horrors of war, from Martino Martini's *Regni Sinensis a Tartaris devastati enarratio* (Amsterdam: Aegidius Janssonius, 1661). Courtesy of Special Collections, The Sheridan Libraries, The John Hopkins University.

palace in which the khan hid. The attackers "called fire to their aid" to drive the khan from his hiding place, but he escaped through a secret passage on its northern side. The nobleman Taktsepa offered the khan and his family refuge but quickly betrayed him to the Zünghars. Lhazang's flight was soon discovered, and a chase ensued. The khan's horse, spooked by a ditch, stumbled and went down, and the Zünghars fell upon the khan, who, in Desideri's telling, "fought gloriously and memorably until the last moment of his life."[28]

Prophecies in Dakpo

New Year's 1718 did not bode well for the Zünghars. They controlled Lhasa but had no Dalai Lama. Wasting no time, the conquerors deposed Lhazang Khan's puppet Dalai Lama—thereby denying his consecration at the hands of the Panchen Lama—and left the government in the hands of Taktsepa. As the Panchen Lama and other Tsangpa Geluk retired to the south, Taktsepa and the Zünghar government began a systematic persecution of Nyingma and Kagyü monks under the direction of Lozang Püntsok, a Zünghar lama at Gomang.[29] Beginning in December 1717, the Zünghars and their allies from Drepung, Sera, and Ganden sacked and pillaged monasteries along the Tsangpo River, reaching as far east as Daklha Gampo. Although we have yet to untangle the complex reasons for these persecutions—I believe they are best understood in terms of land polity and family conflicts—one thing is clear: the monasteries sacked were predominantly Nyingma and Kagyü institutions in Ü, Tsang, and Dakpo, and the most notable among these were the Nyingma monasteries—Samding, Mindröling, and Dorjé Drak—that had intimate ties to the fifth Dalai Lama.[30] While some scholars see this persecution in racial terms—as a policy imposed upon Tibetans by the Zünghars—Desideri believed it to result from internal Tibetan conflicts. Luciano Petech also seems at pains to assert that the Tibetans had little to do with the persecution and implies that the Geluk merely allowed the pillaging of Nyingma monasteries as they waited for the rightful Dalai Lama to appear. The Jesuit is a more severe critic and—at least in this regard—a more interesting historical source. He observed, for example, that the Geluk differed in their opinions about the Nyingma, some being content to edit or suppress works about Padmasaṃbhava, and others engaging in gratuitous iconoclasm:

> The enraged persecutors confiscated the whole of their riches, seized their estates, sacked their palaces, and destroyed a great part of their monasteries and temples, demolishing some, using others as stables, and stripping others bare. They smashed statues and sniffed out images and books of Padmasaṃbhava, which they then burned, and forbade Tibetans under the penalty of death from keeping or preserving any of these things, from reciting prayers to him, invoking him in any way, or merely pronouncing his name.[31]

As a result, many of the most esteemed Nyingma lamas were deposed, banished, or murdered. Many, Desideri related, "fled like vagrants, stripped of everything, and sought refuge in hidden caverns."[32]

Fearing that his friendship with Lhazang Khan would cost him his life, Ippolito Desideri fled to Dakpo and took up residence in the Capuchin hospice there. He traveled widely in eastern Tibet over the next three years, visiting the Daklha Gampo monastery and the holy mountain Tsari. The missionary's evident relief was reflected in his exuberant descriptions of the countryside, which he painted in sharp contrast to the sterility of the western deserts. He took care to note its abundance of fruit, clover, juniper, and rich butter. He recounted his discovery of how to make wine from Tibetan grapes with some degree of self-satisfaction, as though he were passing down a recipe for future missionaries.[33] In Dakpo the missionary also befriended a "rosy and rotund" man he called the "Lungar Lama." "We enjoyed a great friendship and close familiarity," Desideri wrote, "and he often invited me to pass two or three days in his company, being very generous, offering me presents time and time again, especially great quantities of gold."[34] Sadly, the joint Tibetan-Zünghar government expanded its pillaging into Dakpo. Awakened one night by shouts outside his door, the Lungar Lama snatched his son and hurried through a secret passage, disappearing under cover of the night. They descended a steep path down to the river and made a daring escape by boat. It chanced that, in their flight, the Lungar Lama and his son passed the Jesuit's house and borrowed some money. "Not without compassion and tears," Desideri told his readers, "I assisted the flight of the Lungar Lama, who was miserably destitute and in great pain, that he might escape the hands of his barbaric persecutors."[35]

Such escapes were all too common during the Zünghar persecution. Mingyur Peldrönma, the daughter of the Mindröling abbot Terdak Lingpa, fled the Zünghars and found refuge in the hidden valley Dremo Jong in present-day Sikkim.[36] When faced with such trials, Nyingma such as Mingyur Peldrönma and the Lungar Lama turned for solace to the very prophecies that Desideri read in the court of Lhazang Khan. Although scholars in recent years have doubted the veracity of such "treasure texts" (*gter ma*), they provided the ideological framework of much of Tibetan politics during the seventeenth and eighteenth centuries, especially in times of political crisis.[37] While the biographies of Padmasambhava were well known by all the participants in this drama, special mention should also be made of the mystical cartographies of hidden sanctuaries that are often associated with the teachings of the Northern Treasure school, which flourished at Dorjé Drak under Pema Trinlé, one of the Nyingma lamas singled out by the Zünghars for extreme persecution.[38] Although such *beyül* (*sbas yul*) texts differ in specific details, as a whole they describe a period of stable Mongol rule, after which invaders conquered Tibet and social and spiritual disintegration ensued. They also reveal hidden sanctuaries on the southern slopes of the Himalayas where devotees could preserve royal lineages and ancient teachings during apocalyptic times. Such sites were, like *terma* (*gter ma*), concealed by Padmasambhava, only to be discovered by later visionaries. Nestled within deities' bodies according to mystical cartographies, such sanctuaries were unassailable on account of their divinity and made ideal fortresses from which Tibetans could practice their war magic, especially the "sorcery of protection, expulsion, and suppression" (*bsrung bzlog mnan pa'i las sbyor*). Nor should this come as any surprise: Tibetans were greatly feared for their arsenal of harmful magic (*drag las*) and took great pride in it.[39] The Nyingma were particularly feared for their prowess in battlefield sorcery, especially the adepts of the Northern Treasure traditions. Mingyur Peldrönma is a case in point.[40] In fact, no Tibetan school was without its practitioners. The pious Geluk apologist Tuken credited the Manchu victory over Bönpo insurgents during the Gold Stream Expedition of 1772 to the weapon *tormas* (*gtor zor*) of a later incarnation of the Changkya Qutuktu.[41] With the help of his allies among the Northern Treasure traditions, especially Rindzin Ngagi Wangpo and Zur Chöying Rangdröl, no less a figure than the fifth Dalai Lama engaged in its practice against the Choktu allies of the Karmapa in his struggle for control of Tibet in 1637–42.[42] In his visions Ngawang Gyatso also received teachings about black magic performed with ritual daggers, and these rituals would eventually be performed publicly, under state sponsorship, by the monks of Namgyel monastery.[43] Of course, the most famous practitioner of war magic and supernatural border patrol was none other than Padmasaṃbhava himself.[44]

Desideri, working within this general framework, saw the rise in Mongol influence, the Zünghar invasion, and the establishment of the Manchu protectorate foretold in the prophecies. While I cannot yet say exactly which of the treasure texts the Jesuit father may have studied—beyond the dialogues in the *Testimonial Record of Padmasaṃbhava*—it is sufficient for our purposes that he perused them, since little ingenuity is needed to read the events of the seventeenth and early eighteenth century into them.[45] All of those who suffered saw themselves in the texts. Those in Tsang and Dakpo who had supported Lhazang Khan could thus see in his death the end of stable Mongol rule that the texts prophesied. The Zünghar conquest, the spoliation of Tibet, and the religious persecutions followed with equal necessity. Unfortunately, similar religious persecutions continued with enough consistency during the first half of the eighteenth century to align with the prophetic vagaries and ensure the survival of the genre. The Nyingma polymath Katok Tsewang Norbu, writing in the aftermath of a fresh wave of persecutions in 1726, could see in the fifth Dalai Lama's alliance with the Khoshud but one sign of the times that culminated in the persecution of his own order.[46]

Although it is difficult to say what the Jesuit thought of such *terma*, there is little reason to think that they would have offended his religious sensibilities. Similar phenomena were by no means scarce in Christianity. Augustine, in an episode in his *Confessions* that surely would have been known by Desideri, tells how Ambrose of Milan miraculously discovered the relics of the

saints Gervasius and Protasius. Giovanni Nanni of Viterbo, the secretary of
Pope Alexander VI, "discovered" twelve ancient texts that proved his rather
ingenious theories about the Egyptian origins of the Italian people and bestowed a heroic genealogy upon his papal patron by showing how the Borgia
family descended from Hercules.[47] In any case, Ippolito Desideri did not doubt
the prophecies' veracity. When he first arrived in Tibet, he thought them
ridiculous and "fit for a few good laughs." Later, when he saw monasteries in
Dakpo decimated by the Zünghars and their allies, Desideri felt compelled "to
prostrate myself upon the earth and adore the supreme, most just, most holy,
and inscrutable Providence of God, and repeat the words of the Holy Prophet
David time and time again: *Justus es, Domine, et rectum iudicium tuum.*"[48] If
God was just and His judgments right, the Jesuit missionary still did not
believe that Padmasaṃbhava was privy to any special graces. The Jesuit missionary, like his fellow Tuscan Dante Alighieri, knew that demons could predict
the future, and this was precisely how he explained Padmasaṃbhava's uncanny prophetic accuracy. Tibetan religion—and his own—remained thoroughly
preternatural.

Desideri's belief that demonic voices guided Padmasaṃbhava's prophecies
seems not to have affected his friendships in the least. He may very well have
been convinced of their truth by a friendly and garrulous treasure revealer such
as the Lungar Lama, especially if Desideri's unnamed friend is none other than
Chöjé Lingpa, the *tertön* from Lumkar (*klu mkhar*) in Dakpo.[49] Initiated into
both Nyingma and Kagyü lineages, Chöjé Lingpa opened hidden sanctuaries
in Kongpo in order to escape the Zünghars[50] and had ties to Lhazang Khan.[51]
He fits the age and, apart from details about his girth and complexion,
the description of Desideri's Lungar Lama. If Desideri knew the *tertön*
from Lumkar, we can reasonably place him within the ambit of some of
the most fascinating political characters of his time, most notably Mingyur
Peldrönma,[52] her Geluk ally Lelung Zhepé Dorjé,[53] and Polhané himself.[54] If
Chöjé Lingpa was Desideri's Lungar Lama, he would also be the most obvious
source for Desideri's continued fascination with the prophecies of Padmasaṃbhava as well as his sympathies for those who suffered so at the hands of
the Zünghars. He might even be the source of other prophecies the Jesuit
missionary may have read.[55]

The "Sad Error of Metempsychosis"

Desideri completed *The Origin of Sentient Beings and Other Phenomena* in
Dakpo on June 21, 1718, and promptly began his magnum opus, the *Questions*

Concerning Reincarnation and the View of Emptiness Offered to the Scholars of Tibet by the Christian Lama Ippolito (Mgo skar bla ma i po li do shes bya ba yis phul ba'i bod kyi mkhas pa rnams la skye ba snga ma dang stong pa nyid kyi lta ba'i sgo nes zhu ba), on June 24, 1718.[56] Irenic in tone—Desideri opens with a poem praising the great scholars of Tibet—the *Questions on Reincarnation and Emptiness* is a wholesale scholastic assault on the doctrine of reincarnation. Its title page can be seen in figure 4.3. He would not write his refutation of emptiness until the beginning of *The Essence of Christian Doctrine*, abandoning the *Questions* half completed after 464 folios. Desideri's *Notizie istoriche* also displays an uncommon fascination with the topic, and quite a good bit of knowledge about its political ramifications. The Jesuit was familiar with the tests by which Tibetans chose young incarnates and had a fairly solid grasp of Tibetan beliefs about the Dalai Lama and his importance for Tibetan politics, knowing that the bodhisattva cultivated Tibet especially, that the Dalai Lama was Avalokiteśvara incarnate, and that he reincarnated "always as the Grand Lama of Tibet."[57] His account even included ethnographic details about how the doctrine influenced mortuary and hunting customs.[58] The "sad error of metempsychosis" (*il pessimo errore della metempsicosi*), to which the Dalai Lama owed his civil status, most perturbed the Jesuit missionary, who called it a "most intricate and inescapable labyrinth" (*un intricatissimo e inestricabile laberinto*) and "an unlimited chaos and vast fathomless sea" (*un chaos illimato e un immenso mare senza fondo*).[59]

In all likelihood, the Jesuit missionary chose to attack emptiness and reincarnation because he thought that these two doctrines stood in the way of the two minimum requirements for implicit faith, namely, belief in God and belief in His providence, and so hoped the *Questions*, like the other manuscripts he wrote at Dakpo, would serve as metaphysical prolegomena to the Christian mysteries. The scope of Desideri's *Questions* allows us to glimpse the magnitude of his feelings about reincarnation, but its writing may have served a practical purpose as well: in such a charged political atmosphere, the *Questions* allowed Desideri the luxury of not having to choose sides in any of the controversies that surrounded the person or office of the Dalai Lama—a luxury made all the more important by the recent loss of his patron. Refusing to countenance the religious underpinning of the political controversies he witnessed, the Jesuit could bemoan the exploits of the sixth Dalai Lama while distancing himself from Lhazang Khan's puppet; he could rejoice at the destruction of the Padmasaṃbhava cult as he lamented the persecution of Nyingma and Kagyü Buddhists by the Tibetan-Zünghar government; he could finally feign indifference in the midst of his fiercest religious polemics.

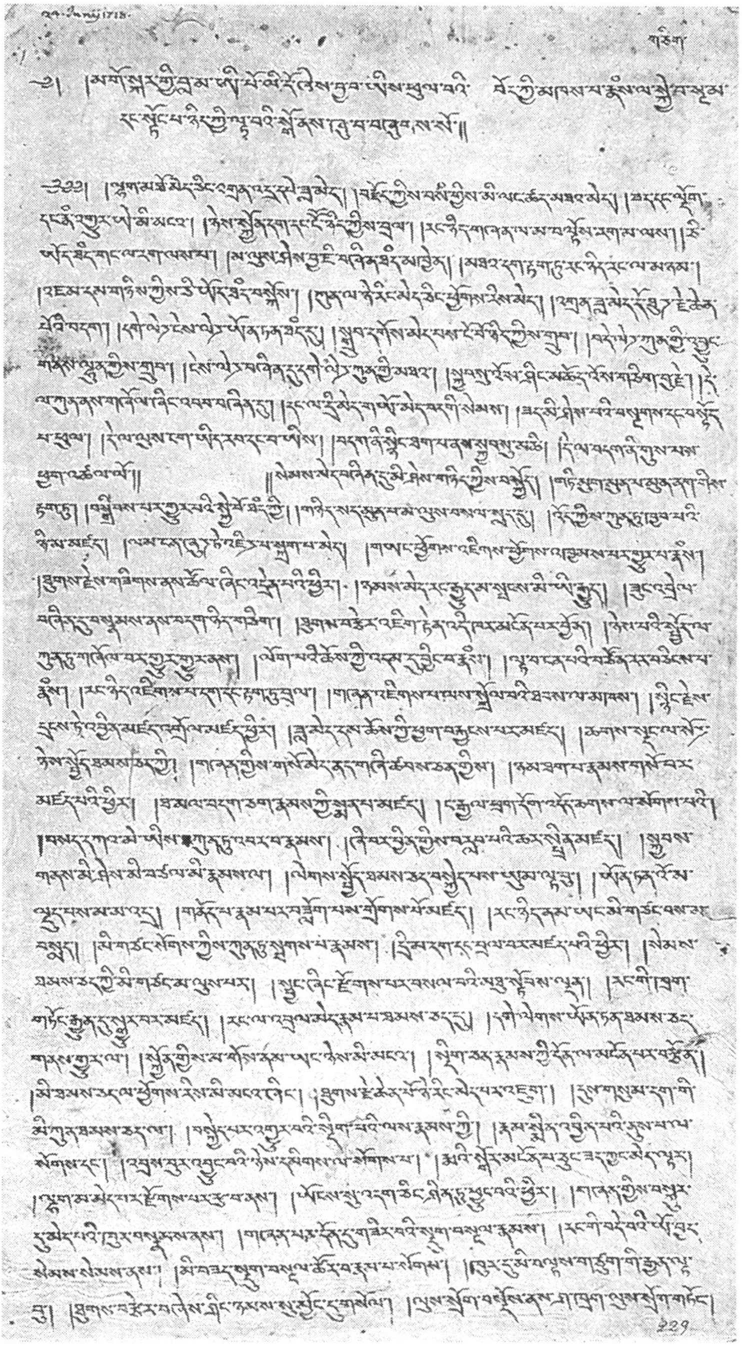

229

FIGURE 4.3. Title page of Ippolito Desideri's *Questions on Reincarnation and Emptiness* (ARSI Goa 75). Courtesy of the Archivum Romanum Societatis Iesu.

In this respect, no one is so roundly criticized in Ippolito Desideri's *Notizie istoriche* as the sixth Dalai Lama. While the missionary praised the moral and intellectual virtues of ordinary Tibetans, he much of the gossip about the shenanigans of the sixth Dalai Lama that circulated in the khan's court and the streets of Lhasa when the missionary lived there. He noted, for example, that the name of the Dalai Lama's palace reflected his love of the ladies and that Lhasa's yellow houses marked his numerous sexual conquests.[60] For the Jesuit, Tsangyang Gyatso was "a most dissolute youth" (*un giovane molto dissoluto*), "of an excessive lust and detestable liberty" (*d'una troppo sfrenata libidine e di una detestibile libertà*), and—if such slurs were not enough—"utterly irremediable" (*più irremediabile*). In Desideri's account, the sixth Dalai Lama, against the inviolable monastic customs of Tibet, fussed over his hair, drank, and gambled to such an extent that "neither wives nor maidens nor a pretty person of either sex could escape his unbridled licentiousness."[61] If such charges did not convey his insidiousness strongly enough, the missionary repeated the scandalous charge we have already seen in Athanasius Kircher: "These blind, deluded people actually beg for the excrement of the Grand Lama, which is made into small pills, sought as relics, devoutly conserved in reliquaries, and swallowed as a powerful remedy against malady and misfortune of every sort."[62]

If the tone of Desideri's *Questions* is irenic, his account of the political uses of reincarnation that he wrote for his European audience can only be called extreme. Lest there be any mistake, the Jesuit missionary highlighted the demonic importance of the Dalai Lama in his later account of Tibetan religion. It begins, "To give an account of this most particular religious sect, or rather, this mixture of most strange dogmas that are but a monstrous parody of religion, unlike any other in the world that I know, it is fitting to begin with its head, the Grand Lama, who is this people's Pope."[63] It is telling that Desideri wrote so passionately about a man he had never met. In the *Notizie istoriche*, he expended no small amount of energy attempting to demonstrate that the office of the Dalai Lama was directly engineered by satanic powers. He wrote two chapters refuting a hypothetical opponent who objects that the apparently miraculous deeds of the child Dalai Lama were simply fables or the result of human trickery, and the second of these is, like his magnum opus on the same topic, unfinished.[64] It was not, Desideri argued, "incredible and laughable"—as he himself had once thought Padmasambhava's own prophecies—but probable and well founded that the "direct author of this lie" was the Devil, who prompted the young child and spoke for him when he was put to the test. Otherwise, Desideri reasoned, it is impossible that so many learned and wise men, from among so many different nations, would be outwitted by a small child, even if he were taught by the most devious collection of men. These were no country bumpkins, but skilled and feared governors, vigilant judges, a sovereign king, and a huge number of scholars who were "wholly alert in their observations" and "very shrewd in opposing the claims and arguments of others." Nor, Desideri insisted, could such a fraught process come off so peaceably without violent disagreements and civil wars.[65]

A mere child who displayed such utter equanimity, even when scolded, threatened, or tortured, must be possessed by a diabolical spirit:

> There is a firm reason to believe that the Devil is the motor and immediate agent of this deceit, because he very well understands men, including the temperament, constitution, and physiology of each one, and can thus purposely nurture and deliberately choose such-and-such a boy to be the agent of his deceit rather than some other boy, since he could foresee that the one boy would in all likelihood live longer by virtue of his superior character and physiological organization. The Devil can guard the boy against dangers, protect him against falls, cure him of maladies, and concur in conserving his life in a thousand different ways, deliberately scheming in such a way to make more credible the error that this boy is the dead lama brought back to life.[66]

The magnitude of the Devil's involvement in Tibetan politics went well beyond his tampering with the "melancholic humors" of the children selected to be the Dalai Lamas; it produced such a "many-wheeled machine" of lies and subterfuge that an entire nation of civilized and sharp-witted people was fooled into believing these "baseless illusions and nonsense." Responding to an interlocutor who objects that such widespread demonic tyranny would detract from the glory of Christ's victory over evil, Desideri says,

> To the contrary, the majesty of that divine victory is made that much greater by the affirmation that there are even today peoples dominated by infernal tyranny and mysteriously submerged in unheard superstitions as a punishment for their sins, for these people await an evangelical ministry that will unfurl Christ's banner against the malign enemy, put him to flight, and continue in the farthest regions the triumph of Christ over the demons, which began centuries ago in Europe and has been so happily carried to the rest of the world.[67]

It would be little exaggeration to say that the Jesuit missionary largely blamed the sixth Dalai Lama for the death of his patron and the carnage that followed the Zünghar invasion of 1717. In the Jesuit's telling, an "inexplicable, universal grief" overtook the land of snows with the death of the sixth Dalai Lama, and all classes of people, the ecclesiastical dignitaries and monks especially, felt an "extremely bitter hatred" toward Lhazang Khan. These were the "first sparks," Desideri noted, "which, after years of prolonged and covert plots, ignited the blaze that claimed the king's life and kingdom."[68] When a young child spoke on the Chinese border near Xining and announced that he was the Great Lama who had been murdered by Lhazang Khan, now reborn just as he had promised before his death, the "spirit of revolt" caught fire in Tibet. The Zünghar invasion, according to Ippolito Desideri, was caused by an act of demonic ventriloquism. Such, for a missionary of the early eighteenth century, was the power of the enemy.

The Missionary as Historian

Desideri's distrust of the doctrine of reincarnation led him to misinterpret more mundane political affairs. He implied, for example, that Lhazang Khan disapproved of reincarnation as much as he disapproved of the Dalai Lama's ribaldry when he remarked that the Khoshud chieftain, at wit's end, took violent measures to "stamp out the evil that was contaminating the country."[69] While Lhazang Khan may have lost a little sleep over the Dalai Lama's exploits, we find no hint that the Khoshud chieftain ever considered abandoning the doctrine of reincarnation. He was well aware of the political uses of reincarnation and immediately set to work rebuilding his allegiances through the ritual empowerments that governed them, swiftly convincing—or coercing—the Panchen Lama to consecrate the puppet Dalai Lama he had placed on the throne after the sixth Dalai Lama's death and setting in motion the institutional machinery that would thwart other claimants. If anything, the khan's rule crumbled not because he believed in reincarnation but because he too hastily manipulated the political world it supported. Desideri also saw cooperation between the emperor and the khan when there was none: he claimed, for example, that they arranged for the seventh Dalai Lama to be placed under armed protection. This claim was simply false, unless Lhazang Khan installed his own puppet lama only as a decoy until the emperor could produce a candidate. Tibetan sources also fail to confirm Desideri's claim that Lhazang Khan imposed a death sentence on the sixth Dalai Lama, much less that he was actually executed. While factions opposed to the Khoshud khan might very well have circulated such a rumor, it seems odd that one of his most ardent supporters would repeat it. I suspect that the missionary exaggerated the conflict between Lhazang Khan and Tsangyang Gyatso not so much out of loyalty to his own patron—although that too may be true enough—but to present Tibet as a still fertile mission.

Desideri's rendering of the events that led to the regent's death is worth noting, too. Desideri claims that enemies of the regent forged a letter from the sixth Dalai Lama by sneaking into the drunken Dalai Lama's chambers and stealing the seal from around his neck, and that they then used the forged letter to trick the regent into surrendering to the khan.[70] This admittedly odd detail has puzzled scholars. The Panchen Lama, whose family would later suffer greatly at the hands of the Zünghars, certainly had favorable relations with Lhazang Khan, but the historical sources disagree about the nature of his mediation between the regent and the khan. Petech mentions that the Panchen's party had hardly left the monastery when the final battle between the regent and the khan broke out.[71] Shakabpa, however, notes that the Panchen Lama, on his way to mediate the dispute personally, received a letter from the sixth Dalai Lama informing him that a cease-fire was in effect and that mediation was no longer necessary. Petech thinks that this is the forged letter to which Desideri refers, but he also notes that the Panchen Lama received gifts from Tsering Trashi after the affair.[72] Jamyang Zhepa's role in these events is similarly ambiguous. The regent Sangyé Gyatso had asked the Gomang abbot to refute the teachings of Panchen Sönam Drakpa in order to remove them from the curriculum of Loseling College at Drepung, a ploy to bolster the regent's influence over the monasteries—two goals that Jamyang Zhepa did not support.[73] In light of these tensions, one might legitimately wonder whether the great abbot lingered on his way to the regent's execution site. There is ample evidence of tensions among the Geluk during the New Year's riot. Perhaps the Lhamo oracle ordered rather than advised Lhazang Khan to retreat—as Petech suggests.[74] If a central Tibetan faction bribed the oracle in order to avoid an armed clash with Lhazang Khan, it could only be at the expense of the Tsangpa, whose ties to the Manchu emperor and the Kökenuur Mongols would weaken without Khoshud allies. It seems just as likely that a bribe—if indeed there was one—came from forces in Amdo. Nor can foul play from within Sera itself be ruled out. While the monks of Sera suffered greatly at the hands of Lhazang Khan after the New Year's riot—Lhazang Khan executed the head of Sera Mé College on his way to do battle with the regent and would have razed the monastery had not Jamyang Zhepa restrained him— the monastery also received endowments from the khan after his rise to power, including the regent's own estate at Drongmé.[75]

The sixth Dalai Lama sat at the center of these affairs. After the regent attempted to assassinate his friend Targyené, the Dalai Lama went to the Lhamo oracle, who gave him an arrow decorated with five-color tassels. Michael Aris rightly notes that this was an obvious pointer to the "arrow captain" Gachakpa.[76] I suspect that the Dalai Lama saw more in the oracle's clues than Aris did. The regent, after all, had an abiding interest in archery. In describing the remarkable series of events that led to the regent's death, Luciano Petech was content to remark that Tsering Trashi "seemed to harbour a personal hatred against the fallen regent."[77] Petech's delicate understatement echoes one of his sources, Sumpa Khenpo, who remarks that Lhazang Khan's wife was "a nasty person."[78] Hugh Richardson tells another, juicier story: according to oral tradition (*ngag rgyun*), the regent had once enjoyed a dalliance with Tsering Trashi, who became Lhazang's wife only after the regent lost her in a game of chess. Lhazang Khan won the match and the lady, who, deeply offended by the regent's insensitivities, waited patiently until she could exact her final revenge.[79] The tale admittedly has little basis in fact. Most likely, Tsering Trashi simply possessed the hard-nosed qualities that Desideri found lacking in her husband—qualities that were fast becoming necessary for surviving central Tibetan politics. Still, if Desideri's tale of the forged letter is true, it raises the sad possibility that the sixth Dalai Lama's drunkenness was exaggerated in the oral tradition in order to absolve him from the rather obvious motives he had for conspiring with Lhazang Khan to destroy the regent. These two tales from the oral tradition—the chess match between the regent and the khan and the forged letter from the sixth Dalai Lama—might have offered the popular Tibetan imagination a way to shift the blame for the swift dissolution of Tibetan autonomy away from Tsangyang Gyatso and onto an easier target. In this case, Tsering Trashi had the misfortune of being a woman in bed with the enemy, a collaborator for whom few would feel much sympathy, especially in an increasingly apocalyptic landscape.

Desideri imagined this apocalypse primarily in terms of "red hats" and "yellow hats," a blunt but not incorrect way of interpreting the historical realities of early eighteenth-century Tibet. The missionary repeatedly condemned the cruelty of the central Tibetan Geluk for their complicity in the Zünghar invasion, and he consistently expressed his admiration for the piety and virtue of the Nyingma who remained steadfast during the persecutions.[80] He even suggested that the Geluk persecuted the Nyingma because ordinary Tibetans found them more inclined to virtue.[81] While the division of Tibetan orders into red hats and yellow hats is a common model of indigenous history, at least when we view it in terms of the fifth Dalai Lama's *Song of the Queen of Spring* (*Spyid kyi rgyal mo'i glu dbyangs*), it often obscures the fruitful tension between royalty, patronage, and political power.[82] Many families had ties to various sectarian traditions (*chos lugs*); more important, several families within the same tradition, such as the Geluk, had rather significant political differences among themselves.[83] Such tensions were arguably at their greatest between the great central Tibetan monasteries and the Dalai Lama's government, the Ganden Podrang.[84] The three great Geluk monasteries in central Tibet, Sera, Ganden, and Drepung, often criticized the government when they felt that it had slighted the interests of their order.[85] While scholars often explain this tension as one between the rigorist religious concerns of the Geluk and the more syncretic concerns of the "secular" government, it should be pointed out that the tensions were also the result of family relations and regionalist sympathies.[86] Also, while it is tempting to see the three seats as narrowly rigorist and somehow representative of "Tibetan" culture as a whole, the religious authority of the Geluk monasteries united a great diversity of regional and ethnic interests, including Khoshud, Khalkha, and Zünghar, spanning the Zünghar khanate to the sea of Manchuria, against the comparatively provincial interests of noble families and older religious orders in Ü, Tsang, and Dakpo.[87]

I am inclined to think that the real fault line among the Geluk lay in the differences between the rigorists themselves, especially insofar as they supported Zünghar or Qing interests. In retrospect, it appears strange that Jamyang Zhepa counted among his disciples both Dokgewa, the heretical Nyingma sympathizer, and Lozang Püntsok, the Zünghar lama at Gomang responsible for much of the bloodshed during the religious persecutions, but in the rough-and-tumble world of Tibetan politics, such odd bedfellows were necessary for survival.[88] Desideri, though, had only a rudimentary understanding of these relationships. He seems to have attributed the unification of Ü and Tsang, for example, not to the fifth Dalai Lama and Güüshi Khan but to his own patron, Lhazang Khan. But Desideri well understood the ambiguous relations between the Tibetan aristocracy, the monasteries, and the various regional and ethnic interests in the conflicts he witnessed. He was immune to the strangest of the Western myths about Tibet—that it was a land untouched by religious violence. He is also one of the only Western sources who noted the possibility of a real Khoshud-Zünghar alliance, even as he cast the Zünghars as the villains in his rather romantically told story.[89] On this one point especially, the missionary displays a particular historiographical subtlety. Living as he did in the midst of these events, Desideri could not judge the Ganden Podrang's support of Galdan and the Zünghar khanate in the light of hindsight. He naturally avoided the temptation to which many later accounts, both Asian and European, succumbed, and so avoided their mistakes. The Manchus were untested rulers when the Ganden Podrang government began courting the Zünghar khanate.[90] As the fifth Dalai Lama neared death, Kangxi was still rooting out the last of the Ming loyalists in south China. He even accepted, with no small amount of grudging caution, Galdan's own announcement of the title bestowed upon him by the Ganden Podrang. When Sangyé Gyatso chose to support Galdan and the Zünghar khanate, he had no idea that the Qing would expand so quickly and so successfully. Like Kangxi, he did not realize that Galdan would be so volatile. Had Galdan been more successful in his campaigns against the Qing, or had he been a tad less unpredictable, the tensions between Khoshud and Zünghar might never have devolved into the chaos that engulfed Tibet in the early eighteenth century.[91]

The Establishment of the Manchu Protectorate

Kangxi, planning his final stratagem, dispatched the Manchu general Erentei with seven thousand men, most of them Chinese and Muslims, along the northern route to Lhasa from Xining. He also sent the general Namujar with ten thousand Tangut troops along the southern route from Chengdu in Sichuan. Erentei's force was destroyed in September 1718, prompting Kangxi to assemble three hundred thousand troops in Xining. Kangxi supplied the Manchu army with a great amount of silver ingots, provisions that would eventually disrupt the Tibetan economy. Thus replenished, Yanxin, one of the emperor's nephews, and Galbi marched this massive army toward Lhasa in February 1720.[92] Kangxi's fourteenth son, Yinti, followed Galbi's force with a rear guard in May, with the blessed presence of the child Dalai Lama. Desideri narrowly escaped being conscripted into Galbi's army as it marched to Lhasa in September. The missionary was visiting the "governor's palace" when two armed men arrived and ordered that all men age twelve or over were to be enrolled, armed, and employed in the service of the emperor. According to the missionary's account, the men gave him arms, assigned him a horse and pack animals, and began to escort him to their encampment "under penalty of death." His status as a Christian "lama" was of no avail, since the Manchu forces had forcibly conscripted Tibetan priests into the army. The "vice governor," whom Desideri noted to be a "distant relation" of the Manchu general, interceded on Desideri's behalf, and the missionary's short stint in the army ended on his way to the encampment.

Kangxi recognized the "true" incarnation of the Dalai Lama only as the child led the Manchu armies toward Lhasa. His official statement was no mean feat of diplomacy: the emperor failed to mention either Tsangyang Gyatso or Ngawang Yeshé Gyatso, both of whom he had implicitly recognized. The emperor placed in the service of the Dalai Lama a powerful Amdo Geluk named Tuken Qutuqtu Ngawang Chökyi Gyatso, who met with emissaries of the Panchen Lama and other powerful central Tibetan Geluk monasteries. The tide of central Tibetan support now shifted decisively to the Manchu emperor rather than the Zünghars. Both Polhané and Kangchené gathered armies for a revolt, the latter capturing the Gartok pass, which led back to Zünghuria, with a tricky ambush recounted by Desideri in a highly romantic strain. Indeed, this is one of the few times in his narrative in which the personalities of his friend Targum Trashi and Kangchené coincide. The southern front of the Manchu army suffered two stinging defeats in the meantime, but the Zünghars were so severely depleted that they retreated from Lhasa without incident, not in fear of the poorly organized Tibetan-Manchu alliance marching from the south, but of the northern front of the Manchu army, which was stiffened by significant numbers of Kökenuur Khoshud. "After almost twenty years of tumult and catastrophe," Desideri narrates, "this third and principal Tibet passed in October 1720 from the Tartars to the Chinese emperor, with whom the present government and great power resides."[93] As a result, abbots of the great Geluk monasteries relieved Zünghar lamas of their duties and turned them over to the Manchu troops. In order to prevent future troubles, the emperor established a council to handle intra-Tibetan affairs and a military government in Lhasa to ensure its success. The traitor Taktsepa was discovered and executed, along with several of his co-conspirators.[94] Five of the lamas appointed by Tsering Döndrup were decapitated—a relatively civil form of Tibetan capital punishment. Taktsepa and his followers suffered a more common fate: they were tied to gallows and shot with arrows until dead. The new government also removed Ngawang Yeshé Gyatso, Lhazang Khan's puppet Dalai Lama, to Beijing as a precautionary measure.[95] In December, the Panchen Lama and the Tri Rinpoché consecrated the young Kumbum incarnation as the seventh Dalai Lama and bestowed upon him the name Lozang Kelzang Gyatso.

With peace restored—albeit briefly—the Jesuit interrupted work on his magnum opus and returned to Lhasa. When he arrived, the Capuchin fathers showed him the legal decision from Rome granting them exclusive rights to the mission and orders from Tamburini commanding him to leave. With ample time before the spring thaw, Ippolito Desideri paid Chöjé Lingpa one last visit. Recounting their reunion years later, the loquacious Jesuit found himself at a loss for words:

I cannot describe the tears and expressions of friendship with which the good lama described his disgrace and deprivation, our old friendship not having suffering in the slightest, but being made stronger and more robust. He wished not only to return the money he had borrowed but also to give me copious presents, but I refused to take either, which cut him to the quick with the loss that comes with the departure of a most sincere friend.[96]

5

The Fight with the Friars

Hagiography is out.

—John W. O'Malley, S.J.

Ippolito Desideri left Tibet on April 28, 1721, with Giuseppe Felice Morro da Jesi, one of the Capuchin fathers with whom he had lived in Dakpo. They traveled on horseback over the Tung pass and through Dingri, the small town that is still used today as a base from which to approach Mt. Everest. On May 13, they arrived at the Nyalam fortress, near the border of Nepal. Desideri wisely determined to stay until December to allow an easier transition between climates; Father Felice Morro went on without him and perished in an influenza epidemic raging in Kathmandu. Safe in Nyalam, Desideri wrote a long appeal to the pope protesting the decision of the Congregation for the Propagation of the Faith. In the meantime, the Capuchin Felice da Montecchio arrived from Lhasa, and the two men departed together for Kathmandu on December 14. Desideri pointedly remarked that he enjoyed the Capuchin's "spirited conversation" but was pained to see him obliged, at sixty years of age, to face such difficult roads.[1] They rested for a time at the Capuchin hospice in Patna, where Desideri received a letter from Tamburini ordering him to report to a Jesuit house in Delhi or one of the other main cities under the jurisdiction of the Goa Province of the Society. Just before he left the Capuchin hospice, the Jesuit mailed a formal citation that summoned Felice da Montecchio and Domenico da Fano to appear before the Sacred

Congregation for the Propagation of the Faith to argue their case for the mission to Tibet. Sufficiently restored—and with a newfound sense of purpose—Desideri continued alone to Varanasi and finally arrived at the Jesuit community in Agra on April 20, 1722, seven years and seven months since he had been there last. Finally among brethren, the Jesuit made his solemn profession of the fourth vow but took ill and was forced to move again, this time to Delhi.

Desideri lived in Delhi for the next three years, having learned Hindustani and Persian well enough to preach fluently. He planted a garden adjoining the church, with shade trees and the "most popular" flowers to attract visitors, leaving his door open until nightfall, welcoming all who dropped by, listening to complaints, and appeasing quarrels among the townspeople. The Jesuit's routine was interrupted again by an order to return to Goa. As political strife overtook the Mughal Empire, the Jesuit decided to avoid riots along the usual southern road to Goa and to trace his way back to Patna on November 21, 1725—most likely a convenient excuse to avoid further involvement with his superiors in Goa.[2] Desideri then embarked from Balasore for Puducherry, the French colony in south India, where he arrived on January 11, 1726. He found the Jesuits there "very austere," abstaining from savory foods and intoxicants and living on meager amounts of milk, fruit, herbs, and rice. In Puducherry, Desideri met a Jesuit of similar taste and temperament, Jean Bouchet, who seems to have made a great impression on the newly arrived missionary.[3] The French colony, having been funded by Louis XIV and granted independence from the Portuguese mission in Madurai, sheltered Desideri from the authorities, and Bouchet used his power as head of the Puducherry mission to prevent Desideri from returning to Goa. Later that year, Joseph Pinheiro, the bishop of Mailapur, summoned Desideri to his diocese and ordered him to carry documents for the canonization of João de Brito, a Jesuit martyr of the missions, to Rome. Having successfully skirted the authorities at Goa, Desideri now had the opportunity to return to Rome, where he could vindicate himself and the Society of Jesus against his Capuchin rivals.

On the Virtues of Missionaries

Desideri arrived in Rome on January 23, 1728, and was soon followed by Felice da Montecchio. Their legal battle, which occupied the whole year, involved a complicated call and response in which Desideri published three *difese* against the arguments of da Montecchio.[4] Their dispute was not the first between a Jesuit and a Franciscan: it was but one of many that stretched back to the very beginnings of the Catholic missions in Asia and the New World.[5]

François-Marie de Tours, the prefect of the first Capuchin mission to Tibet, was known to the Jesuits long before Desideri arrived in Goa. An old mission hand, de Tours lived in Surat in the 1690s, where he succeeded in ousting the Jesuits from the mission; in Puducherry at the turn of the century, where he initiated a formal investigation against Jesuit missionary methods; and then in Rome, where he published a treatise indicting Jean Bouchet and the Jesuits in Malabar for violating the previous papal censure of Jesuit methods. In fact, Franciscans had coveted the Tibetan mission for quite some time. Bonaventura Ibañez mentioned it as early as 1668.[6] A letter from Agostino a S. Paschali mentions Tibet again in 1680.[7] Like the Jesuits, the Franciscans were interested in an overland route to China by way of Surat and Agra, and their missionaries in China remained in contact with their brethren in the first Tibetan mission.[8] Both François-Marie de Tours and Domenico da Fano held long-standing grudges against the Jesuits before they entered the Tibetan mission; for all practical purposes, they were the public face of Capuchin opposition to the missionary methods of the Society of Jesus. Much later, although admittedly for their own political reasons, the English apologists for the Younghusband expedition accused the Jesuits of meddling in the Capuchins' affairs. Sandberg, who described Desideri as "an agent of the Society," suspected him of actively working to discredit the Capuchins.[9] Sir Thomas Holdich believed the Jesuits to have been sent, presumably by Tamburini himself, "to inquire into the workings of the Capuchin missions and to discredit them as far as possible."[10] Landon distilled his colleagues' fear to a purer draught: Desideri and Freyre were no more than "Jesuit spies."[11] Desideri's role in this is still unclear, but one thing is certain: the loss of the Tibetan mission would humiliate the Jesuits and force them to acknowledge their Franciscan rivals.

Despite the suspicions of the British apologists, Tibetologists generally celebrate the Jesuit's many virtues, in contrast to the imagined faults of the friars. A typical portrait can be found in Snellgrove and Richardson's *A Cultural History of Tibet*. "Christian religious authorities," the authors write, "in ignorance of the nature of Tibetan civilization, sent missionaries who with one notable exception, the great Jesuit Father Ippolito Desideri, were incapable of understanding the depths of Tibetan feelings and convictions."[12] In contrast to the man who "studied and taught and recorded Tibetan life and religion as no foreigner has done before and since," Snellgrove and Richardson present the Capuchins as tentative journeymen who led a furtive existence in Tibet until inspired by the example of Desideri. "This," they assure the reader, is "surely evidence" of Desideri's "transparent piety, sincerity, and strength of character." Snellgrove and Richardson continue:

Desideri was an educated man of penetrating intellectual powers, able within a short space of time to master sufficient Tibetan to write an account of the essentials of Christianity, and a little later to master the content and meaning of Tibetan Buddhism, as expounded to him by *dGe-lugs-pa* teachers, and to write in Tibetan his refutation of their doctrines. In his *Account of Tibet*, although he necessarily condemns those doctrines of Buddhism which conflict with his faith and philosophical conceptions, he never indulges in abuse, and although he criticizes what he sees as the weak points of Tibetan character, he is full of praise for the greater good which he sees in it.

The Capuchins, on the other hand, happened to be men of far less education, trained rather for the emphatic preaching of slogans than for the intellectual discussion and analysis of their own and other people's religious beliefs. All but one of them, Orazio della Penna, who lived for twenty years in Tibet, found it impossible to learn Tibetan sufficiently well to discuss religious matters. Their proselytizing efforts consisted in the translation of a few simple catechisms containing for the most part moral views and injunctions with which Tibetans would in any case be in complete agreement. Ignorant of Tibetan religion, they regarded the acceptance of these points as signs that the faith of the Tibetans, even of the Dalai Lama himself who expressed kind agreement, was wavering and that a mass conversion of Tibet was imminent. They even wrote with satisfaction how they had proved to several reincarnating lamas that such a kind of rebirth was impossible, and that the lamas expressed "great interest." Meanwhile they did not trouble to understand the theory and practice of Tibetan religion, but simply condemned it with extravagant abuse. Serious tension was bound to develop between such simple but pretentious men and the truly religious intellectual Desideri, with the result that they did not hold back from the most un-Christian accusations against him in their letters to superiors.[13]

On the whole, Snellgrove and Richardson's account is not false, but neither is it entirely trustworthy. It rests upon judgments that these eminent Tibetologists have made about the respective virtues of the men in question. Desideri is educated, while the Capuchins are uneducated. The Jesuit displays mastery, but the Capuchins show their ignorance. The Jesuit is full of praise for what he finds good in Tibetans, while the Capuchins can only heap extravagant abuse upon their religion. The cool tones of Desideri's intellectual analysis contrast with the heated nature the Capuchins display in their emphatic preaching of slogans. In sum, Desideri is a truly religious intellectual beset by a veritable horde of simple but pretentious Franciscans.

Snellgrove and Richardson can be forgiven this somewhat simplistic portrait. Although it is somewhat ironic that heirs to the Younghusband expedition would adopt such a sympathetic view of a Jesuit, the contrast between the progressive views of missionaries from the Society of Jesus and the hidebound medieval world of the mendicant orders is a commonplace, especially among energetic Jesuit historians, who often present friars as robed conquistadors who had neither sympathy nor respect for the intellectual achievements of cultures other than their own.[14] The degree to which Snellgrove and Richardson distort the historical record depends upon what sort of men we imagine the missionaries to have been. If the historian grants that the Jesuit Desideri possessed transparent piety, sincerity, and strength of character, then the ire of his Capuchin rivals might serve as sure evidence of their deeper jealousy and spite. But if the historian does not grant that Desideri was so saintly—if he adopts a more skeptical view—the battle between the Jesuits and Capuchins for the Tibetan mission might well be taken as sure evidence that the Tuscan missionary was vain, manipulative, or deceitful. On such a reading, Ippolito Desideri might very well have been everything that other orders feared in the Society of Jesus.

Il Modo Soave

Desideri is sometimes presented as a proponent of Jesuit "accommodation," "inculturation," or "adaptation," all terms meant to identify the commendable process by which a missionary—usually a sensitive, enlightened Jesuit—accommodates certain aspects of indigenous culture to Christian worship. This notion allows historians to distinguish Desideri from his Capuchin rivals, but it also allows them to number him among the greatest Jesuit missionaries in Asia, such as Roberto de Nobili in India, Matteo Ricci in China, and Alessandro Valignano in Japan.[15] For all intents and purposes, Desideri did likewise; when we read of him adorning his garden with flowers and teaching little children in Delhi, it is difficult to imagine that he was not a practitioner of il modo soave, the "gentle manner" for which Italian Jesuit missionaries were famous.[16] But determining the extent to which Desideri practiced or defended the accommodative practices associated with his order is no easy task, especially when we investigate the controversies more carefully. This difficulty is compounded when we attempt to untangle the sad history of conflicts between Jesuits and Franciscans that led to Desideri's expulsion from Tibet and his eventual legal battle with Felice da Montecchio.

Jesuit accommodation is most commonly associated with Matteo Ricci. Faced with the complex literary and political culture of the Ming Dynasty, Ricci recommended that Christianity adapt itself to the existing culture in order to further the Jesuits' evangelical efforts.[17] Such adaptation consisted of learning the appropriate languages, studying literature, and adopting the rituals and etiquette necessary for success among the nobility and literati. Ricci succeeded dramatically in his endeavor, and his vast learning culminated in a history-making directive that permitted certain Chinese civic rituals, such as the veneration of Confucius and ancestors, to exist alongside Christian worship. Ricci based his accommodative practices on a larger genealogical criticism of Chinese culture that we saw in the third chapter, and he assumed that the rites by which the Chinese venerated Confucius and their ancestors could be separated from the surrounding religious practices that Christianity was meant to supplant. Not surprisingly, this principle proved difficult to apply consistently. In 1615, Nicolas Trigault secured permission from Pope Paul V for the Chinese to participate in their ancestral rites and for the Mass to be celebrated in literary Chinese.[18] But unlike Ricci, who famously found the rites "certainly not idolatrous, and perhaps not even superstitious," friars such as the Franciscan Antonio Caballero de Santa María and the Dominicans Juan Bautista Morales and Domingo Navarette judged them to be superstitious and most likely idolatrous, on account of the altar, red wax candles, incense tapers, joss sticks, food and flower offerings, and ritual prostrations that accompanied them. Friars also objected to the Jesuits' silk robes and elevated sedans as unbefitting Christians committed to serving the poor.

Ricci's methods arguably had their most dramatic effect in the south Indian missions. In the sixteenth century, south Indian neophytes were ex-pected to behave, dress, drink, and eat as a well-bred Portuguese might. Such demands disgusted south Indians because they violated several of their laws of ritual purity. In order to address these difficulties, Roberto de Nobili accommodated certain Hindu ablutions, vestments, and initiations to Christianity in the Madurai mission.[19] He dressed in ochre robes, marked his forehead with sandalwood paste, and accustomed himself to the high wooden sandals favored by Hindu ascetics. He restricted his diet to rice, fruit, and herbs and lived very modestly in a single small hut—the very austerities later mentioned by Desideri when he visited Puducherry. He justi-fied the caste system and its ritual prohibitions, somewhat too enthusiastically perhaps, as a reflection of the social hierarchies of contemporary Rome. Nobili also pioneered the reflection on the "civil" sphere as distinct from the "religious," and defended Brahmanical customs as social practices rather than superstition.[20] Nobili even designated a special class of Jesuits to evangelize the lowest castes. João de Brito, the martyr whose canonization papers Desideri would take to Rome, was one of these "pandaraswamis." If St. Paul could become "all things to all men, that he might save some" (1 Cor 10:22), it only made sense that the Jesuits should become Brahmins to the Brahmins and outcastes for the outcastes.

Nobili's Portuguese colleagues were less than thrilled by this turn of events. Gonçalo Fernandes denounced Nobili in 1618, and a lengthy investigation ensued. The archbishop, Cristóvão de Sá, was flabbergasted: "A Father of the Society of Jesus has gone over to paganism, and he asks me to connive in his apostasy."[21] Nobili defended himself well with Scripture and Aquinas, but Pope Paul V required him to appear before the Inquisition at Goa, where the Jesuits voted in his favor but the Dominicans, Franciscans, and secular clergy voted against the new methods. The case was referred to Rome, prompting Nobili to write one of the classic texts of Jesuit missionary methodology, the *Answer to the Objections Raised Against the Method Employed in the New Madurai Mission.* Nobili eventually emerged victorious with a papal approval of Jesuit *accommodatio* in the apostolic constitution *Romanae sedis* of Pope Gregory XV in 1623. As a result, the number of converts in Madurai, Mysuru, and Tiruchirapalli increased dramatically.

In 1645, the Holy See condemned the Chinese rites as superstitious. In 1656, however, Pope Alexander VII endorsed the Jesuit method, and the floodgates of controversy were opened.[22] In 1673, Pope Clement X forbade the publication of any writing on the missions without a patent granted by the Sacred Congregation for the Propagation of the Faith, an injunction that went unheeded, even though it threatened violators with excommunication.[23] Kangxi seemingly had settled these debates before Desideri arrived in Asia, having issued an edict proclaiming that the Confucian rites were civil ceremonies with no religious importance. Just when it appeared that the Jesuits had emerged victorious, however, Charles Maigrot, the vicar apostolic of Fujian, launched an indictment of the Jesuits' missionary methods in 1693.[24] A member of the Société des Missions étrangères, a largely Jansenist-run competitor of the Jesuits, Maigrot judged the endorsement of Pope Alexander VII to be inapplicable to the present situation in China, largely because he believed that Martino Martini, the Jesuit missionary and procurator who had argued on behalf of the Jesuit methods in the 1650s, did not provide an accurate description of the rites for Roman authorities.[25] Maigrot also prohibited the use of the Chinese words *Tian* and *Shangdi* to refer to God. This already precarious situation was worsened by the visit of the papal legate, Charles de Tournon. The legate found great hostility to the Jesuits among the Société des Missions étrangères, who insisted that de Tournon recall the Jesuits from China.[26] Against the suggestions of the Bavarian Jesuit Kilian Stumpf, de Tournon ignored Chinese interpretations of the issues at hand, and his visit was a disaster for all concerned. Kangxi forcefully rebuked the papal legate in his second audience, and dispatched two Jesuits, António de Barros and Antoine de Beauvollier, to Rome for the ensuing legal battle.[27]

For the next decade, Popes Innocent XII and Clement XI sponsored repeated commissions to resolve the debate. Several witnesses and polemical briefs were brought before the Congregation for the Propagation of the Faith. The pope's decree of November 20, 1704, criticized the Jesuits' choice of words to translate Christian concepts and, while allowing simple commemorative tablets for ancestors, prohibited all other Confucian rituals for the dead. Clement XI supported the Jesuit line of reasoning but denied that it applied to the rites in question. While condemning the practices within the context of Confucianism, the decree left untouched the most pressing concern of all—whether such rites might be accommodated to Christian worship. To the Jesuits, the pope's decree implied that practices that were neither idolatrous nor superstitious could be accommodated to Christianity. It almost need not be said that this finely nuanced solution satisfied no one. Even the Jesuits agreed that Confucian rites should be condemned inasmuch as they were religious. They appealed the decision, maintaining that if the decree agreed with their missiology in principle, then it must apply to the rites in question. Had not Kangxi himself deemed the rites to be civil ceremonies?[28]

De Barros and Beauvollier, traveling in separate ships as a precautionary measure, were drowned in shipwrecks off the Portuguese coast on January 20, 1708.[29] As Desideri neared the end of his studies in Rome during the spring of 1709, Pope Clement XI prohibited the Chinese rites, confirmed de Tournon's judgments on September 25, 1710, and rejected any further appeals from China, thereby reducing the missionaries to a state of shock. Tamburini was informed on October 11, and the general pledged the obedience of his subjects. The following year, on November 20, 1711, the pope received Tamburini and the procurators of the Jesuit missions for a papal audience in which the general promised that the Society "reprobates and repudiates" any Jesuit daring to disobey the pope's orders, "and that such a one deserves punishment, and is not to be acknowledged a genuine son of the Society. The Society will hold him, as she has ever held and now holds such persons, for degenerate and no child of hers; and will ever restrain, repress, and crush him to the extent of her power."[30] Clement's aggressive rebuke of Tamburini fueled tensions with the French and Portuguese monarchies, since both had heavily invested in the Jesuit missions.[31] The king of Portugal prohibited Miguel de Amaral, the visitor at Goa who dispatched Manoel Monteiro to find a route to Tibet in 1704, from publishing the pope's confirmation of Tournon's decree within the confines of the Padroado when he was provincial of Japan.[32]

Clement responded by reaffirming the previous decree in his apostolic letter *Ex illa die* on March 19, 1715, which included a mandatory oath of obedience for anyone entering the mission fields. For the most part, the Jesuits simply could not believe that the Holy See would endanger the mission in such a way if it knew the necessary facts. Further appeals were rejected when *Ex illa die* arrived in Canton aboard English ships in 1716.[33] By commanding the priests to administer the sacraments to Chinese Christians only in cases where there was a danger of death, Clement forced the missionaries to risk offending Kangxi. The decree placed missionaries in such a delicate situation that friars and Jesuits registered their doubts about its promulgation. The Augustinian missionary Alvaro de Benavente, himself a vicar apostolic of Jiangxi, submitted a juridical appeal to de Tournon's decree.[34] Kilian Stumpf wrote a spirited defense of the Jesuit position in 1717, entitled *Informatio pro veritate*, and the Jesuits in China were again investigated in 1719 by another papal legate, Carlo Mezzabarba.[35] While the legate apparently assured the Jesuits there that he found nothing wrong with their methods, he rebuked them sharply upon returning to Rome.[36] On September 13, 1723, Tamburini was given three years to answer the charge that the Society had been negligent in the service of prompt obedience to the Holy See. Until he did so, a three-year ban was placed on sending novices to the Far East.[37]

Several of the men involved in the controversy over the Chinese rites were directly involved in the last phase of the Malabar Rites controversy, so it comes as no surprise that it had a similar denouement. In 1703, shortly before embarking on the first Capuchin mission to Tibet, François-Marie de Tours submitted a criticism of the Puducherry Jesuits to the Congregation for the Propagation of the Faith. Pope Clement XI appointed the same man, Charles de Tournon, to investigate de Tours's claims, and the pope's decision was again to prove disastrous. Tournon, who knew neither Tamil nor Portuguese, stayed at Puducherry for six months. Being sick for most of his stay, he never really had the opportunity to investigate the mission firsthand. Satisfied by interviews with Jean Bouchet and Charles Bertoldi, Tournon delivered sixteen censured propositions concerning Jesuit missiology to the pope on June 23, 1704, and the Holy Office confirmed Tournon's censure on January 7, 1706. Bouchet and another Jesuit, Francisco Laínez, journeyed to Rome to battle the decision. At first, it seemed that the tides would shift in the Society's favor. Laínez published his *Defensio indicarum missionum madurensis* and was appointed as bishop of Mailapur, but he was again opposed by Capuchin polemicists. The pope, much as he had done in the Chinese Rites controversy, offered a compromise. By an *oraculum vivae vocis* granted to the procurator of the Madurai mission, the pope confirmed Tournon's censure on September 25, 1710, and obliged the missionaries to observe the decree "insofar as the divine glory and the salvation of souls would permit." Not surprisingly, this solution satisfied no one. The Jesuits, appealing to this notorious clause in the oraculum, continued to tolerate the very practices that Tournon outlawed. The Capuchins, for their part, continued to pressure the pope, who on September 17, 1712, renewed the decree of the Holy Office and reprimanded Laínez for willfully disobeying it. On July 24, 1715, this brief was sent to the Jesuits in Pondicherry, who again sent two missionaries, Pierre Martin and Broglia Brandolini, to protest the decision in Rome. In the meantime, the new pope, Innocent XIII, appointed a special congregation to investigate the issue, with Prospero Lambertini, later Pope Benedict XIV, as secretary. Lambertini's investigation of the Malabar Rites continued for the duration of Desideri's stay in Asia and eventually involved the men who had sheltered Desideri from the Portuguese authorities at Goa. It is impossible to imagine that Desideri did not hear the latest about the controversies from these disgruntled Jesuits.

Initial Qualms

With one notable exception, there was little outward hostility between Desideri and the Capuchins. A letter that Desideri wrote to Tamburini on February 15, 1717, even tells the general that the Capuchins "surpass me not only in courtesy but in an abundance of courtesy" and requests that the general ask the procurator of the missions at the Congregation for the Propagation of the Faith to send some thanks to them.[38] Desideri could not have been entirely unaware of the political battle that lay ahead, and he expressed his desire to enlighten the Congregation for the Propagation of the Faith about the conflict—and arm the Society—by enclosing a letter to the pope. (Never one to miss a diplomatic opportunity, Desideri apologized in advance for the poor quality of paper on which his letter to the pope was written.) There seem to have been some unspoken tensions, however. Desideri's letter to Tamburini insinuated that the Capuchins were tentative, even sheepish, about their mission. He claimed that the Capuchins did not have the courage to show him the decree of the Congregation for the Propagation of the Faith that awarded them the mission "some sixty years ago," and reported that Domenico da Fano had considered turning back when he heard—probably from Freyre as he returned to the Mughal Empire—that the Jesuit was in Tibet. Desideri added, almost as an afterthought, that the friars were at least good enough to show him their patents "with much humility," and he even remarked—with an air of indifference—that the Capuchin prefect intended to turn away with his companions if Desideri expressed even the slightest claim of priority.

Desideri's letter to Tamburini implied, perhaps disingenuously, that he was ready in principle to grant the force of the decree, but his own strategy was to bypass the Sacred Congregation altogether and appeal to the authority of Pope Clement XI, an undertaking that apparently depended on the familiarity—probably imagined—between the pontiff and the missionary. Desideri supported this rash strategy, which he would follow to its bitter end, with only the flimsiest of arguments. In this initial stage of their conflict, Desideri simply felt that the Capuchins had forfeited their rights to the mission because Domenico da Fano had abandoned it earlier. Apparently Desideri had forgotten, or was never aware, that da Fano had been in Rome before the Sacred Congregation serving as both the prefect and procurator of the Tibetan mission.[39] Desideri staked his claim to the mission on the mere fact that he had cultivated it for one year and twenty-four days before the friars arrived. He did not at this point appeal to the presence of any previous Jesuits, even Andrade. Discerning that he was well endowed for the mission "by a special favor from God," the Jesuit decided that he could in no way abandon it. He had progressed so well in his Tibetan writings that to do so would be a most grave violation of conscience.

Desideri wrote directly to the pope that February. While Desideri did not fill this letter with the rhetorical flourishes of his letter to Tamburini, he gamely requested that the pope allow the Capuchins to stay in Tibet. "Where my weakness fails," Desideri implored the pontiff, "the talent, the fervor, and the zeal of such worthy and select apostolic missionaries will supply strength."[40] The Jesuit noted, apparently without irony, how he himself had served the helpless Capuchins by teaching them Tibetan and by arranging, "at their request," a catechism, a grammar, and a dictionary. Desideri let his desires fly ahead of his actual accomplishments here; in the letter to Tamburini that he wrote two days later, Desideri says merely that he hoped to write the catechism, grammar, and dictionary.[41] In both cases, he deliberately omitted the fact that the Capuchins had already written a catechism and had begun compiling the dictionary on their own.

Had it ended there, Desideri's letter to Tamburini would have been innocuous enough. Although his rendering of events slights the Capuchins, he presents their view fairly and expresses his own doubts openly. But Desideri's letters often betray a peculiar analytical quality, especially as he resolves a doubt or reaches a conclusion. This process is so transparent in some of Desideri's letters that it is almost as if the Jesuit discovers a divine confirmation for his decisions in the very act of writing the letter. After resolving to stay in Tibet,

Desideri tells Tamburini, "I do not speak for my own sake, for I am *aes sonans et cimbalum tinniens*," but God, who is *"mirabilis in consiliis suis,* chooses the weak ones of the world in order to make the infinite power of his divine majesty shine all the more."[42] If God is "wonderful in his counsels," and chooses the weak ones of the world, one might wonder why God could not work his wonderful counsels through the very Capuchins that Desideri had just accused of timidity. Desideri's transition from abstracted self-abasement to strategic questioning of the friars' lack of courage is seamless. Although the Jesuit protested that he in no way meant to cast a slur on the zeal of the Capuchin fathers, he leads the reader to conclude that their own weakness would give way to God's power, acting, of course, through the Jesuit himself.

Tensions surfaced in an exchange of letters between Desideri and Felice da Montecchio in early 1718. The point of contention between the Capuchin prefect at Patna and the Jesuit in Tibet was the Manchu envoy who had arrived in Lhasa the previous May as part of the joint Jesuit-Manchu cartography expedition.[43] Dignitaries of the Manchu court, being accompanied by a lawyer, apparently attempted to transfer the missionaries to Beijing against their will, rousing the Capuchins' suspicions that Desideri had engineered the plot to remove them from Tibet. Such schemes were not unknown. Jesuits had taken rather comical measures to keep the Franciscans out of China, and it is unimaginable that these charades did not burn brightly in the collective memory of the Franciscan missionaries.[44] Felice da Montecchio wrote to Desideri on December 23, 1717, evoking a sharp retort from the Jesuit on August 4, 1718.[45] We know from Desideri's letter that the Capuchin asked the Jesuit to write letters of recommendation to the Jesuits in Beijing on behalf of the Capuchin fathers who had been forcibly removed to the Manchu capital. Piqued by the Capuchin's thinly veiled sarcasm, Desideri wrote that however much he wished "with all his heart" to comply with the prefect's requests, he "rejoiced exceedingly that he had not the slightest chance of doing so," for neither Orazio della Penna nor Domenico da Fano was to be conducted to Beijing against his will. Still, the Jesuit missionary could not help protesting:

> With ardent humility and all possible urgency I beg Your Very
> Reverend Paternity kindly to write some correspondent of your own in
> Beijing and recommend my own self to him, since the Chinese
> pressed me much more fiercely than they pressed the Very Reverend
> Capuchin Fathers and attempted to conduct me to that metropolis
> against my will.[46]

Desideri then told da Montecchio, with feigned sincerity, "That I might more surely obtain the favor of such a recommendation, Your Very Reverend

Paternity will pardon me if, in all truthfulness, without changing even the smallest thing and without the least admixture of passion, I subjoin here a most faithful account of what happened."[47] Desideri was surely offended by da Montecchio's request, and we can presume the offense was intended. Cooler heads might have prevailed in other circumstances. If we accept Desideri's account, it appears that the misunderstanding about the Manchu envoy provoked suspicions that simply could not be remedied. Nor does it appear that Desideri or da Montecchio sought to alleviate them. Desideri could not resist pouring salt on the wound:

> I now beg Your Very Reverend Paternity to excuse me if, in all candor, I
> confidentially reveal my own suspicion to you. On reading Your Very
> Reverend Paternity's aforementioned commands, I suspect that, not
> from any ill intent, no, but because you had not received enough
> information about my position, you wished under otherwise
> courteous expressions to give me the unmerited mortification of
> pricking me politely and covertly rather than honoring me with your
> most welcome and revered orders.[48]

Such bluntness was common enough in the polemical literature of Desideri's day but rather uncommon in the perfumed correspondence of the early modern period. The Jesuit missionary continued, "Such a suspicion is not without foundation, because each of the members of your mission has too warmly and too openly admitted it, except for the Superior." If the Capuchins suspected that Desideri would sow dissension among their ranks, we can only imagine da Montecchio's feelings when the Jesuit implied that he himself was on closer terms with the other Capuchin fathers than the procurator himself. Note, too, that Desideri's letter suggests that four of the Capuchin fathers, Orazio della Penna, Giovanni Francesco da Fossombrone, Angelico da Brescia, and Buonaventura da Pedona, were more honest with him than Domenico da Fano was. The implication is that the Jesuit was chummy enough with these four Capuchins that they would willingly reveal what their superior would not.

On December 21, 1719, Desideri wrote Tamburini to inform him that he felt "seriously obliged" to appeal to both the Sacred Congregation and the pope himself.[49] Expressing his desire to return to Rome to defend the Society, Desideri claimed that he alone possessed the evidence necessary to refute the unjust charges leveled against the Society. It was Desideri's turn to be infuriated when the decree from the Congregation finally arrived. The decree enjoined Tamburini to give up any mission in the three kingdoms of Tibet, which had been assigned "long before" to the Capuchins, and "without any tergiversation or delay" recall and remove any Jesuit who "without consulting the Sacred Congregation, nay even against its decrees, went to cultivate those missions."[50] The words, "nay, even against its decrees," wounded Desideri, and he wrote a long, passionate letter to the general again asking to come to Rome to defend the honor of the Society. Tamburini, for his part, proclaimed his innocence, protesting that he did not know that the Capuchin fathers had been assigned to the Tibetan mission when he permitted Desideri to cultivate it.

Desideri was hard-pressed to believe that Tamburini had not known about the Capuchins.[51] Adopting much the same tone with Tamburini that he previously used with da Montecchio, Desideri scolded Tamburini for not writing more than one letter, forestalling any postal excuse by noting that he had received letters from several other Jesuits in Rome, and darkly hinted that the Society might not always enjoy his ardor: "Humanly speaking," Desideri continued, "this is the very thing that discourages missionaries, and which might make them grow cold in their service to the Company."[52] Again in the interests of candor, Desideri confessed that he was extremely scandalized that the pope had written to "an infidel king" before he answered Desideri's own letter. "Other missionaries of the Society," Desideri reminded the general, "might have the same impression if, when writing to the Society's first superior, to him who holds the place of St. Ignatius himself, they never saw a single response. I repeat that it is clear a posteriori that the fault is not with Your Very Reverend Paternity, so I ask with all warmth and urgency that you seek out those who are at fault, and apply the remedy."[53] A litany of complaints followed. Desideri—rightly, I think—noted the lack of financial support for his mission, an understandable complaint given the missionaries' loss of money during the sack of Lhasa and the inflation that followed the establishment of the Manchu protectorate. But Desideri's complaint that he had been denied the opportunity to make his final profession while in Tibet is more difficult to understand. Usually a Jesuit professed his final vows in the presence of the provincial, in this case at a Jesuit college such as at Agra or Goa. Although exceptions were often granted for missionaries, it hardly seems reasonable that Desideri would have expected to profess his final vows in Tibet, unless, of course, the general established a permanent mission there with a number of missionaries. Desideri's stated reasons for desiring the vows are less praiseworthy; noting that fellow Jesuits would one day read about him in the archives, Desideri protested that the delay in making his final profession would tarnish his reputation.[54]

On October 5, 1721, Desideri wrote a more restrained letter to Tamburini from Nyalam, again informing the general of his desire to return to Rome and letting him know that he had already written an appeal to the pope.[55] As in his previous letter to the general, Desideri hinted that he alone knew the reason why the Capuchins abandoned the mission in 1711. This time he even re-marked that he could deliver this information only in person. The Jesuit's confidence is apparent enough. He clearly savored the thought of returning to Rome to argue his case. In all likelihood he considered it as he traveled with da Montecchio from Nepal to the Capuchin hospice in Patna. Although Desideri said he enjoyed da Montecchio's "spirited conversation," some tension must have existed between two men who had sparred so energetically in their correspondence. Perhaps tensions flared only at the end of their journey, for just before parting company with the Capuchin friar, Desideri wrote him a letter on March 19, 1722, in which he expressed his feelings "with all openness" (*con tutto chiarezza*).[56] Asking da Montecchio not to imagine that "their friend-ship had ended," the Jesuit took the opportunity to complain to the friar about the "gash" (*sfreggio*) that the Society had received when he was "expelled" from Tibet, an effort he judged to impede the propagation of the faith and the salvation of souls. Desideri told da Montecchio that he felt obliged in good conscience to "complain, protest, and appeal" to the supreme tribunal of the pontiff.[57] To this end, Desideri included a summons that formally initiated canon litigation against Domenico da Fano and Felice da Montecchio along with his letter. Desideri, who identified himself as "a priest of the Society of Jesus and the former Superior of the Tibet Mission," acknowledged that he had abandoned the Tibetan mission at the behest of the Congregation for the Propagation of the Faith, but called the two Capuchins back to Rome in the name of that very bureau:

> I declare openly and clearly that right which the Society of Jesus appears lawfully to have had and to have on the Tibetan mission, until it be decided otherwise by the Sovereign Pontiff. For which reason, in the name of the Most Holy Trinity, and after calling upon the name of Jesus, I appeal to the immediate and supreme tribunal of Our Most Holy Lord Clement XI, the Sovereign Pontiff, or his successor. And to it I summon you, that you may attempt to defend yourselves, with whatever arguments you have, from the arguments that I will pronounce in judgment against your endeavor to expel me and the Society of Jesus from the entire Kingdom of Tibet.[58]

The Missionaries Before Propaganda

Desideri seems not to have realized that the Capuchins were quite skilled in canonical litigation. By the time Felice da Montecchio appeared before the Sacred Congregation in 1728, he had amassed a small cache of documents and prepared twelve separate "accounts" (*memorie*) and three summaries (*sommari*) of his case against Desideri's charges.[59] Da Montecchio began with a conciliatory tone before progressing to more overtly polemical passages. He noted that Desideri was about to publish the account of his travels and pronounced himself pleased to read the Jesuit's "erudite efforts," but he also politely reminded Desideri and the Sacred Congregation that Pope Clement X forbade the publication of any works pertaining to the missions without the approval of the Congregation in 1673 and that any missionary who did so faced the threat of excommunication. Da Montecchio acknowledged that Desideri had made progress in the common Tibetan language (*la lingua thibettana volgare*) but still made several errors while composing his first work in Tibetan. The Capuchin emphasized, however, that both Desideri and Orazio della Penna had begun to study the literary language (*la lingua litterale*) together at Sera. He rightly credited Desideri for being the leading hand in the translation of *The Great Stages of the Path* (*Lam rim chen mo*), a work quite useful for missionaries (*che utile a' missionarij*) but did not belabor this point.[60] Rather, he stressed that Desideri did not open a new mission field and that the Jesuits simply followed the Capuchins, whose mission from 1704 was permanent, even if it was not always occupied. Da Montecchio explained that the aim of this first Capuchin mission, after it had been delegated by de Tournon, was to establish a more reliable transportation of correspondence between China and Rome. He hammered the accusations that the Capuchins did not have a reliable guide in the Tibetan language, listing among their teachers the names of several Armenian merchants in Lhasa, including Khwaja Dawith, who had lived in Lhasa for thirty years. He also mentioned several Russians and alluded to a few Chinese Christians from whom the Capuchins learned Tibetan. Against Desideri's allegations that the Capuchins used the highly inappropriate term *sangyé könchok* (*sangs rgyas dkon mchog*), or "Buddha jewel," for God, da Montecchio noted simply that this was the term preferred by António de Andrade.[61]

The documents provided by da Montecchio displayed no small amount of juridical bravura. He followed a copy of Desideri's strongly worded letter from Patna on March 19, 1722, with a letter written by Tamburini to da Montecchio on April 30, 1710, thanking the Capuchin for the services that his order rendered to the Jesuits in Puducherry and Bengal and promising him the kindness and respect that Jesuits owed him. More important, da Montecchio's first summary of the case included a series of five decrees from the Sacred Congregation itself, including the original decree of 1656, a confirmation of that decree in 1698, and its official commissioning of him as an apostolic missionary to Tibet in 1704. More surprising to Desideri, perhaps, were two rescripts dated March 1, 1717, and December 12, 1718, in which the Congregation affirmed its previous decrees, even before the heated exchange with Felice da Montecchio about the alleged deportation to Beijing. These dates indicate that Rome had already taken action based upon the *quid agendum* that Domenico da Fano sent from Kathmandu when he met Manoel Freyre returning from Lhasa in late March or early April 1716. The swiftness with which the Congregation decided this case shows how weak it thought the Jesuit claim to be; presuming that the decision was not sparked from an earlier meeting of Jesuits and Capuchins at Surat, only under ideal circumstances could a letter from Kathmandu have arrived in Rome before the Congregation decided the case against the Society of Jesus. The Tibetan mission must have been opened and shut in a matter of days, if not minutes, and Desideri's removal from the mission was decreed before the quarrel had even begun. The more damning charge, and one that Desideri made some effort to refute, was that Tamburini had renounced the Jesuit claims on the mission before the pope in 1703 and had thereby acted in bad faith when he sent Desideri to Tibet.

Desideri was not a man to give up easily, though. Unlike his first reports to Tamburini and Pope Clement XI, Desideri now argued the Jesuit claim based on the previous mission of Andrade in Tsaparang, surely a more mature tactic than claiming that he had occupied the mission himself for more than a year. But Desideri's attempts to deflect some of the Capuchins' charges were less successful. He again related his composition of *The Dawn That Dispels Darkness* and his audience with Lhazang Khan without mentioning the Capuchins. Following his own script, he argued that the Capuchins had abandoned the mission, thereby invalidating the decrees of 1656 and 1698. He also tried to argue, in a particularly unconvincing manner, that the commissioning of the Capuchins in 1704 and 1714 did not exclude missionaries from other orders. Attempting to answer the Capuchins' charge that Tamburini had sent Desideri into the mission knowingly against the wishes of the pope, Desideri appealed to an audience he had had with Pope Clement XI in September 1712. "I reflected I clearly told His Holiness that I was going to Tibet, and His Holiness approved, he gave it, etc."[62] Desideri seems to have had a very hard time letting go of this argument; as his case worsened before the Sacred Congregation and within his own order, he repeatedly resorted to it. Rome was still a bureaucracy, and without official documentation, even the pope's word meant little to the Sacred Congregation.

Desideri's second *difesa* rebutted the charges made against him personally. He answered the accusation that he wished to sow dissension among the Capuchin ranks and, somewhat disingenuously, informed the Congregation that he had no desire to begin litigation against the friars. Echoing St. Paul, Desideri exclaimed:

Could you imagine how many treks, how many sufferings, and how
horrible they were, and how many threats I endured to reach the third
Tibet? I will say nothing of the storms I braved in the Mediterranean
Sea or on the ocean; or of the discomfort of the long sea journey to
Goa; or from Goa to Surat; having to cross the entire Mughal Empire,
south to north in the intolerable heat from Surat; having to cross
torrents, frozen wastes, the Caucasus Mountains, freezings, and the
most horrible things; gravely ill during these journeys for many
months in changing climes without doctors, medicine, or comfort;
blinded by the dazzling stretches of snow; two months of hiking,
between terrible, unimaginable cliffs; crossing the harshest desert,
with storms of snow and ice, treacherous mountain paths, and
intolerable cold from the ninth of October until the fourth of January;
suffering constant hunger and thirst for ten months during the
journey from Kashmir to Lhasa, sleeping on the ground in the open
air, amid the snow, and ice, and other discomforts that would horrify
anyone who read about them. In sum, enduring a hell of unspeakable
sufferings.[63]

No one doubted Desideri's sufferings; their harshness may have stored him
treasures in heaven, but it did little to move the more mundane hearts of the
fathers of the Sacred Congregation. But Desideri was not the only missionary
to have suffered—da Montecchio had practically been driven insane by his
trials in the Himalayas—and any appeal to the amount of suffering endured as
proof of one's good intentions would surely render the point moot. Desideri
also ardently wished to squash any notion that he had not hastily complied
with the decrees of the Congregation. Here, too, though, the Jesuit's arguments
were not entirely convincing. He first claimed that the Capuchins had not
shown him proper canonical documentation of their rights to the mission until
April 16, 1721. However true this may have been, Desideri thereby revealed that
he knew nothing of the Congregation's previous decrees when he entered
Tibet. The second *difesa* again attacked the linguistic abilities of the Capuchins,
noting that their catechism was "full of errors *in substantialibus*," especially in
its Trinitarian theology. As he ridiculed the Capuchins' use of the term *sangyé
könchok* to refer to God, Desideri strategically omitted mentioning that Domenico da Fano had composed the catechism that used this term before Desideri
arrived in Tibet. He even accused his Capuchin rival of learning Tibetan from
his cook, a man from north India named Uday Cand (Sanskrit: *Udayacandra*),
and filling the catechism with errors as a result of the cook's idolatry. Desideri
failed to mention that learning Tibetan from a lama presumably posed the

THE FIGHT WITH THE FRIARS   149

same risk and again neglected to inform the tribunal that this was during Domenico da Fano's first visit to Tibet. Desideri's third *difesa* largely amplified the claims he made in his first two but took advantage of some of da Montecchio's mistakes about Tibetan geography to strengthen his claims. His language became even more vehement during his final arguments, especially when compared to some of the strangely dispassionate language of the first *difesa*. The abuse Desideri heaped upon the Capuchins looks remarkably similar to the language he used to describe Tibetan religion. Their catechism was nothing but "a collection of errors in essential points and a tangle of sad and idolatrous superstitions" (*un gruppo di sostanziali errori e una matassa di pessime e idolatriche superstizioni*).[64]

Reports of these proceedings enraged the Franciscans in Tibet, whose letters from this period display a special vehemence. A series of three letters written in 1731 by Gioacchino da Sant'Anatolia in particular show a mounting exasperation with Desideri and soon boiled into outright hatred. In a letter written from Lhasa on July 20, 1731, the friar complained that Desideri had reneged on his promise to plead on their behalf to the Congregation for the Doctrine of the Faith for a more generous annuity after having taken advantage of the Capuchins' hospitality in Dakpo, Patna, and Agra. Were he to meet the Jesuit, the friar exclaimed, he would cry, "*Ah sem ngakpo* [*sems nag po*]," "Ah, black heart!" which "is said in Tibetan to hypocrites [*uomini bugiardi*]."[65] A letter written on August 2 increased the charges against Desideri. Gioacchino was most incensed by Desideri's report about the Capuchins themselves, and his letter repeatedly speaks of Desideri "stripping the vines without gathering fruit" (*spampanamento di foglie non curandosi de' frutti*), a euphemism for boasting. "Ah, evil fig [*Ah fico maledetto*]," the friar exclaims. "What law did you confute? Vines, vines of French *cabarrette*, stripped of fronds and tendrils, but without grapes!"[66] Of the Jesuit's supposed fluency in Tibetan, he says, "He claims to have debated lamas and professors. His conversations went like this: 'Are you Kashmiri?' 'No.' 'Do you like mutton?' 'No, I prefer lamb.' 'Do you like our tea? Do you eat pork?' And so on. These conversations happen every day!"[67]

Gioacchino's reconstruction of their friars' early Tibetan instruction is particularly interesting. According to Gioacchino, the same cook who had taught Domenico da Fano when the Capuchin friar had been in Tibet earlier taught Desideri for the six months before the Capuchins arrived in October. Only then, the friar related, did Domenico da Fano secure "a *ranjampa* [*rab 'byams pa*] of middling skill" from Lhazang Khan to teach them all Tibetan. Desideri, the friar insisted, never went before Lhazang Khan without the friars' assistance, and only appeared before him because the khan summoned Domenico da Fano. The final insult, though, was Desideri's claim to have taught Orazio della Penna Tibetan. "Oh, that surpasses all!" (*questa sì che trapassa tutte*). The Capuchins, Gioacchino claimed, did not learn their Tibetan from a cook after that, but rather found a teacher at Zhidé (*bzhi sde*) and were given the same instruction as Desideri himself. As proof, Gioacchino noted, he found translations of a small catechism, a life of the Buddha Śākyamuni, Tsongkhapa's *The Great Stages of the Path*, and a "most copious" dictionary when he arrived. Another letter of August 23, 1731, railed against "the Jesuits, with all of their little political manifestos, letters, and the contradictions of their general, procurator, provincial, Desideri, etc."[68] In this letter, Gioacchino was especially concerned with refuting Desideri's claim that the Capuchins had never even attempted to preach the Gospel in Tibet, and he again questioned Desideri's claim to have catechized Lhazang and the grandees of his court. Decrying the Jesuit's "braggings of his own invention" (*millantazioni da lui ideate*), the friar says, "I cannot believe that the Holy Catholic Church of Rome could produce men of this sort." In Gioacchino's opinion, the Jesuit was not only a "showoff" (*spicco*) but a devilish one at that, and the entire affair in Rome was nothing but a sad "joke" (*barzelletta*) caused by "the Devil and the Jesuits with their evil lawsuits [*maledetta lite*]."[69]

Gioacchino's accusations may very well have been un-Christian, but they were not much different from Desideri's own accusations. They may have even contained a grain of truth. In any event, Desideri stood little chance in the battle before the Sacred Congregation. Da Montecchio provided a flood of documents in his third and final *summario* for the Congregation, including a series of witnesses that attested that da Fano did not abandon the mission willingly but left for medical reasons.[70] Among these witnesses, da Montecchio even included the Jesuit superior of Bengal. He also included a web of *relationes* and letters, many between Jesuits and Franciscans, that stretched from Mailapur to Beijing. While these letters could not demonstrate that Tamburini knowingly violated the decrees of the Congregation, they did make it quite difficult to argue that the Society knew nothing of the Capuchin presence in Tibet. Desideri's own arguments were also faulty, and da Montecchio backed him into a corner as the case wore on. Desideri insinuated that the Capuchins knew no Tibetan, only to admit grudgingly that Orazio della Penna had progressed in the language. The Jesuit's arguments about Domenico da Fano's catechism broke on the same shore, when da Montecchio forced Desideri to admit that the Capuchins had replaced it with della Penna's translation of the great Jesuit Bellarmine's *Dottrina cristiana*. Ultimately, though, the legal battle was one of canonical jurisdiction. While Desideri's argument about the need for missionaries with better linguistic abilities was sound enough, its validity presumed the success of his previous arguments, namely, that the Capuchins' alleged abandonment of the mission invalidated the decrees of 1656 and 1698, and that the decrees of 1704 and 1714 that awarded the missions to the Capuchins did not exclude other missionaries. Perhaps this argument was a bit too sly, and the Sacred Congregation apparently saw right through it. The only way that the latter two decrees did not exclude the Jesuits was if the former, which did in fact exclude them, had been invalidated. Even if da Montecchio had not established a convincing case against the first charge, Desideri made an egregious error in his reasoning: no Capuchin had abandoned the mission after the 1714 decree that Domenico da Fano had secured when he returned to Rome as procurator of the mission. When he and his Franciscan brothers arrived on October 1, 1716, they were simply following the Sacred Congregation's own orders.

Desideri must have become aware of the hopelessness of his case at some point. By the close of his third *difesa*, the loquacious Jesuit was at a loss for words; having been buried under da Montecchio's documentation, Desideri now asked to be excused from the proceedings, judging it ridiculous that two missionaries should have to travel from the world's farthest reaches only to waste time in "accusing, defending, attacking, and evading" one another, while failing to mention, or even to recall, that he had initiated the lawsuit.[71] Even the Society of Jesus seems to have grown weary of its wayward son. Eventually, the father general gave up all claims to the Tibetan mission and forbade Desideri from bothering the ministers of the Sacred Congregation any further.[72] On Saturday, November 29, 1732, the Sacred Congregation of the Propagation of the Faith decided in favor of the Capuchins and reaffirmed their exclusive rights to the Tibetan mission.

Jesuits and Friars, Again

Desideri's loss of the Tibetan mission had little to do with the controversies over missionary methods. Although Gioacchino complained about the sad state of Christians under Jesuit care in Malabar and China in one of his letters, his lament stands out as an exception to the general rule, except for a squabble about the appropriateness of offering ceremonial scarves.[73] Desideri's own works show little interest in the Chinese Rites or Malabar Rites controversies. None of his extant letters mentions the condemnation, nor do any of the surviving letters from Tamburini to the Italian missionary. It is difficult to imagine that a young Jesuit just chosen to be a missionary to the Indies would have been ignorant of the official censure of the Jesuits' position on October 11, 1711, or of Tamburini's heated submission to the pope on November 20 of the same year—two highly publicized events that happened almost an entire year before Desideri departed from Rome and eighteen months before he left Lisbon. It is doubly difficult to imagine that he remained ignorant of them during his stay in Puducherry. The controversy was very much alive when Desideri entered his legal battle with the Capuchins, and very much alive as he wrote the account of his travels in Tibet. This silence presents some of the most difficult problems in Desideri studies. Were Desideri a supporter of Jesuit accommodation, we could surmise that his reluctance to discuss the controversies was a deliberate attempt to avoid jeopardizing the Jesuits' legal claim on the Tibetan mission.[74]

If we have a difficult time demonstrating that Desideri practiced accommodation, it is because no single Jesuit training manual existed for the Asian missions, and all concerned hotly debated the manuals that were written for specific missions, including those of Matteo Ricci and Alessandro Valignano. Niccolò Longobardo, the man chosen by Ricci himself to be the next superior of the mission, did not agree with Ricci's methods. Francisco Cabral preferred his own missionary methods to those of Valignano.[75] Jesuits did not merely argue among themselves about how one might accommodate the truths of Christianity to local customs; they also argued whether the principle was worthwhile at all.[76] Luis da Gama, the Jesuit visitor for China and Japan, was "a narrow-minded Portuguese" who made the friars look "recklessly lax" by comparison.[77] João Rodríguez, who had lived in Asia since he was sixteen and whose fluency in Chinese earned him the nickname "the Interpreter," was a fierce critic of Jesuit accommodation, and Juan Valat prohibited his converts from participating in the rites altogether. Reducing the members of other religious orders to preconceived positions is similarly difficult. Jesuits praised those friars, such as the Dominican Domenico Maria Sarpeti, who agreed with their methods in China.[78] Such a list can be expanded to cover the entire history of the Jesuit mission in China, despite efforts by the Society of Jesus to provide a united front on this issue. Even after de Tournon's visit, the Jesuits had no unified view on the question of the rites.[79]

It is similarly mistaken to imagine that other religious orders had not reflected on their own missionary endeavors. The Franciscans, for example, looked to St. Francis as the preeminent missionary and saw themselves as the missionary order par excellence.[80] Their rule had a special chapter on missions, and friars sent on missions were exempted from their usual monastic observances. In their first missions to Mongolia, they were permitted to carry money, wear clothes other than their habits, and grow their beards—all things that have been praised as hallmarks of Jesuit flexibility in China. They celebrated the sacrifice of the Mass in Mongolian and set up schools for missionaries as early as the fourteenth century. Nor would the Franciscans have forgotten that they were the first Roman Catholic visitors to China or that one of their own was the first archbishop of Beijing. One could hardly accuse friars such as Bernardino de Sahagún of lacking intellectual curiosity, or Bartolomé de las Casas of having the spirit of a conquistador.[81] Franciscans enthusiastically promoted Erasmus in the New World, and some of their catechisms, such as Constantino Ponce de la Fuente's *Summa de doctrina cristiana* (1543) or Bishop Zumárraga's *Doctrina breve* (1544), look not unlike Ricci's famously pared-down catechism.[82] Friars could also be expected to show refined scientific interests; the Augustinian Martín de Rada was an early Copernican, and one of his confreres, Diego de Zúñiga, was responsible for introducing Copernicus into the syllabus at Salamanca—only to be attacked by Jesuit rivals. All missionaries tiptoed around the issue of the salvation of non-Christians, especially when asked whether Confucius or other ancient sages had been saved, but Jesuits were no more delicate than Franciscans on this score.[83] Indeed, none of the accommodative methods allegedly pioneered by the Jesuits were alien to the friars of the New World.[84] Franciscans used music and drama just as the Jesuits did, and even opened fencing schools to attract converts in Kyoto.[85] Franciscan friars in Mexico developed new artistic forms of the Cross rather than display crucifixes in places where they might be desecrated, and also wrestled with the question of how to translate theological terms for three full generations before the Chinese rites and terms controversies erupted.[86] One very important difference, however, is that Franciscans, Dominicans, and Augustinians often had pastoral experience in the Americas or the Philippines before arriving in Asia, whereas Jesuits were chosen for the missions before they had professed their final vows.[87] As a result, friars arrived in Asia with a greater practical understanding of the pitfalls involved in accommodating Christianity to new cultures.

If recent studies of the Asian missions eschew the all-too-common contrast between Jesuit and friar in terms of liberal accommodation and dogmatic orthodoxy, we might pause before casting Ippolito Desideri as a progressive Jesuit battling retrogressive forces. After all, it hardly seems fair to contrast Desideri's sympathy for the Tibetans with the Capuchins' alleged abuse when we catalogue the Jesuit's own deprecations. The Jesuit did not hesitate to characterize Tibetan religion as "vain" (*vana*) or "depraved" (*viziata*), nor did he refrain from telling his readers that he felt "full of joy and triumph" when the Zünghar-Geluk coalition destroyed the statues and books of Padmasambhava, who had "deceived these blind people most wretchedly and for such a long time."[88] Translating the Jesuit's characterizations of Tibetan religious practitioners requires a thesaurus: he repeatedly calls them "magicians" (*maghi*), "sorcerers" (*fattucchieri*), and "warlocks" (*stregoni*). Of course, we have already seen the Jesuit's rather strong language about reincarnation and the Dalai Lama. If the modern historian recoils in horror at the emphatic preaching of slogans, Desideri must be judged as repulsive as any of the Capuchins. The Jesuit entertained some rather ambitious hopes about the imminent conversion of Tibet; clearly Snellgrove and Richardson have not read the ample reflections on the missions that de Filippi omitted from his translation of the *Notizie istoriche*. It is equally strange that these eminent Tibetologists look down their noses at the Capuchins, who "even wrote with satisfaction how they had proved to several reincarnating lamas that such a kind of rebirth was impossible, and that the lamas expressed 'great interest.'" Ippolito Desideri was the one who wrote a massive refutation of the doctrine and who boasted of the great interest it engendered in Lhasa, especially among "learned men and professors, who came from the monasteries and universities, especially from Sera and Drepung, to gain permission to see and read my book"—an excitement that no Tibetan texts record.

Nor were the Capuchins as ignorant as Snellgrove and Richardson insinuate. François-Marie de Tours and Giuseppe da Ascoli composed a small catechism in 1707–8, which was translated into Tibetan by Khwaja Dawith, and Orazio della Penna translated Robert Bellarmine's *Dottrina cristiana* into Tibetan. While the Capuchin's work might very well be a simple catechism—as Snellgrove and Richardson have it—Bellarmine's famous catechism did not contain merely moral maxims with which the Tibetans would be in perfect agreement. If either writing a simple catechism or feeling that Christians and Buddhists shared a general agreement on moral issues is a sin, then Desideri, too, must be judged guilty. In any case, della Penna composed a dictionary of thirty-five thousand entries, translated at least nine Tibetan works into Italian, and translated Nicolas Turlot's massive *Thesaurus doctrinae christianae* into Tibetan, a feat that required more than nine hundred folios.[89] Nor could the Capuchins' apologetic works differ that much in tone from Desideri's own. Because they have been lost, we cannot know if they match the brilliance of the Jesuit's own compositions, but a glance at their titles and subjects indicates that the Jesuits and Capuchins shared almost identical preoccupations. Like the Jesuit, they too wrote polemical works that attempted to establish the existence of a first cause, to deny the Tibetan insistence upon reincarnation, and to refute the claims of the Dalai Lama. Although it is doubtful that any of the Capuchins' lost Tibetan works matched the sophistication of Desideri's own, any purported difference in religious sensibilities is entirely inadequate to explain the tensions between Desideri and the Capuchin fathers—even less some alleged intuition or sympathy for Tibetan religion and culture.

If it cannot be proved that Desideri displayed a greater sympathy than the Capuchins, might there still be a difference in their missionary methods? At first glance, it would appear that there was little difference. Desideri seemed eager to distinguish the rituals of Tibetan religion from those of Roman Catholicism, and he tended to ascribe parallels to demonic imitation. He apparently felt no need to incorporate Tibetan rituals into Christian worship, celebrate the Mass in Tibetan, or dress in the red robes of a Tibetan monk. He even ridiculed those who said that Tibetans venerated the Cross of Christ because they dyed their clothing with the pattern. Tibetans, he says, repeatedly show their contempt for the Cross.[90] On the other hand, Desideri did flirt with the Khoshud court and the Tibetan literati, namely, the "masters and doctors" of Tibetan colleges like those at Sera. And just as Ricci and the editors of the *Confucius Sinarum philosophus* chose to concentrate their efforts of accommodation on the Chinese classics because the civil examination system was founded upon them, Desideri concentrated his efforts on the philosophical teachings of Madhyamaka, the most difficult topic to be mastered in the examinations that allowed one to progress in the monastic hierarchy. Desideri selected a classic of Tibetan philosophical literature, Tsongkhapa's *Great Stages of the Path*, to study with the Capuchin fathers, and his works on Madhyamaka look quite a bit like Ricci's *Tianzhu shiyi* or Aleni's *Wanwu zhenyuan*, that is, like what we might now call natural theology, a philosophical apology based on certain principles that are common to all men and women. But Desideri knew well enough that Tibetans, or at least the Mādhyamikas he read, did not share such principles as he understood them. Nor, after he learned a small amount of Madhyamaka, did Desideri imagine that Tibetans had worshiped God in the past, such that he might exhort them to return to the religious sentiments expressed by their ancestors. Although he allowed that Tibetans might worship God implicitly in their actions, he remained ambivalent about the resemblances to Christianity he saw in the *Testimonial Record of Padmasambhava*. Desideri excluded the historical assumptions of both Ricci's genealogical accommodation and the figurists' mythic speculations from his own apology for Christianity. For Desideri, Tibetans had never practiced a true faith, even before the coming of Christ. Whatever implicit faith they had was not recovered from a distant past, but was to be established through philosophical controversy with his contemporaries.

It is also difficult to maintain that Desideri was committed to interreligious dialogue in the usual academic sense of the term. Although Desideri's *The Essence of Christian Doctrine* is often adduced as evidence of his dialogical concerns, it is really little more than a typical catechism, and the model Desideri followed, namely, Francis Xavier's *Doctrina christiana*, was written before any more complicated method of accommodation.[91] Like the *Catechismus romanus* promoted after the Council of Trent, Desideri's catechism discussed the Creed, the sacraments, the Ten Commandments, and the main prayers of the Christian faith, the Lord's Prayer especially. In this regard, Desideri's *The Essence of Christian Doctrine* is quite similar to the two famous Jesuit catechisms of Peter Canisius and Robert Bellarmine.[92] Similarly, the dialogue that takes up a great amount of *The Essence of Christian Doctrine* is probably meant to train future missionaries in the answers that they would give to typical Tibetan questions, rather than represent a "dialogue" between Christian and Buddhist philosophers. Catechists chose dialogues both to help priests anticipate questions and to help parishioners remember the proper answers, and so this does not indicate any especially accommodative interests on Desideri's part. The Jesuit himself describes the work as one of simple answers for those unlettered in the faith, and in any event the dialogue form was not unique to the Jesuits.[93] Nor can its composition be said to reveal an interest in accommodation. Athanasius Kircher published a bilingual Latin-Chinese catechism, the *Divinae legis compendium*, in his *China illustrata*, although he himself was no supporter of Jesuit accommodation.[94]

If Desideri did not actively engage in the practices that we commonly associate with Jesuit accommodation, he was still forced to translate Christian concepts into the language of the people he evangelized, and in this minimal sense we can speak of his "accommodation" of Christianity to Tibetan Buddhism. Although I would not characterize Desideri's Tibetan as "very nearly flawless in its polished classical style," the Jesuit's linguistic achievements are quite impressive given the adverse conditions he endured.[95] His compositions are excellent for someone who spent only six years in Tibetan-speaking regions. He was quite adept at using the vigorous confrontational phrases of Buddhist polemical literature, frequently comparing Tibetan religion to poison (*dug ngan pa*) or fool's gold (*gser brdzun*) and bemoaning his opponents' "wrong view" (*log blta*) and "senseless babble" (*bab jol*).[96] At the same time, he sometimes uses terms from Tibetan polemical literature in interesting ways, as when he compares himself to a "babbling child" (*brda la ma byang ba'i byis pa*) when speaking about the mystery of the Holy Trinity.[97] Despite his criticism of the Capuchins, Desideri was not so worried about the use of the term *könchok* to outlaw it altogether. As we have seen, the Jesuit chose *könchok chik* (single jewel) rather than *sangyé könchok* (Buddha jewel) to translate "God," often glossing the name with various philosophical qualifiers, such as "self-established" (*rang grub*) and "spontaneous" (*lhun grub*).[98] He did not mind describing the Trinity and Christ in terms that might suggest Avalokiteśvara, such as "great compassion" (*rnying rje chen po*) or "measureless compassion"

(*mtha' med par thugs rje*), or that might suggest the Primordial Buddha Samantab-
hadra (*kun tu bzang po*), such as "thoroughly good" (*kun tu bzang pa*), but he drew
no analogies between the Trinity and any number of well-known Buddhist triads.
He did not, for example, compare the Trinity to the three bodies of the Buddha.

Some of Desideri's most thoughtful Tibetan occurs in the twelve folio
sides of *The Essence of Christian Doctrine* in which he explains the Christian
doctrine of the Trinity. He describes God, the "self-established jewel" (*rang grub
dkon mchog*), as a "mystery" (*ya mtshan*) of three unsurpassable persons (*bla
med bdag nyid*) and one undifferentiated essence (*ngo bo tha dad med par gcig*) or
undivided nature or continuum (*rgyud dbyer med*).[99] Desideri's Trinitarian
theology is generally Augustinian in character, rather than Greek or Victorine,
inasmuch as he makes use of the bishop of Hippo's so-called psychological
analogy, but the missionary, probably anticipating Tibetan objections to Augustine's Neoplatonic psychology, avoided explicitly comparing the Father,
Son, and Holy Spirit to memory, intellect, and will.[100] At a deeper level,
Desideri also tried to respect the two dominant biblical traditions of Christology: the Logos Christology of the Gospel of John and the imago Christology of
the Pauline epistles, taking special note that the Son is both an explication
(*bshad*) of the Father and His "image" or "reflection" (*gzugs brnyan*). Although
the Son is generated or "begotten" (*bskrun*) by the Father, and the Spirit
proceeds from the Father and the Son, the three persons (*bdag nyid*) are not
three gods (*rang grub dkon mchog*), but rather one God established as three
persons, free of the three confines of past, present, and future. The missionary
clearly chose his words carefully; in his discussion of the Holy Trinity, he used
the term *daknyi* (*bdag nyid*) for "person" rather than the usual philosophical
term *gangzak* (*gang zag*) to avoid the inference that the three persons of the
Trinity were merely imputed. Ironically, the very terms Desideri chose in his
struggle to develop a philosophical vocabulary to describe the mysteries of
Christianity—*rang bzhin, bdag nyid, ngo bo*—mimic the ambiguities of the
Greek and Latin terms *hypostasis, prosopon, ousia, natura*, and *persona* that led
to the great Christological and Trinitarian controversies of the fourth and fifth
centuries. If such terms were hardly applied consistently in the West—even
after their conciliar definitions—we can hardly wonder why missionaries
struggled to find equivalent expressions in Asian languages.

Desideri's deliberation is not restricted to his Trinitarian theology. He
translated "grace" with some suppleness, as *kudrin* (*sku drin*), *kadrin* (*bka'
drin*), or *jinlap* (*byin rlabs*), as the context merited.[101] His Christology also
demonstrates a vocabulary capable of drawing nuanced comparisons between
Catholic and Tibetan Buddhist concepts. In Desideri's telling, Christ appears
like a practitioner of the "yoga of entering death" (*grongs 'jug gi rnal 'byor*).[102] He

travels in the hell realms (*dmyal ba'i khams su byon*), rises in a body that neither suffers nor disintegrates, and departs into the sky (*nam mkha'i zhing khams*).[103] Although Desideri shied away from his earlier use of the term "Buddha" (*sangs rgyas*) to describe Christian illumination, he later still spoke of Christ's mind and body having ornaments (*brgyan*) and signs (*mtshan rnams*), which his interlocutors surely would have associated with the Buddha.[104] Some of the odder results of Desideri's accommodative Tibetan are applied to the Virgin Mary. She intercedes for the faithful, for example, like a "government official" (*drung 'khor*).[105] I blush to think that Desideri, in describing the Virgin Mary as "thoroughly pure" (*kun tu bzang ma*), might have suggested that she was like the female deity Kuntuzangmo (*kun tu bzang mo*), who is depicted *in flagrante delicto*.[106]

The Jesuit also adopted etymologically creative spellings, a tradition among Tibetan scholars that allegedly dates back to the invention of the Tibetan alphabet during the first propagation of Buddhist doctrine in Tibet. His rendering of the Italian *Gesù* (*g.yas gzu*), for example, consists of the word "right," as in "sits at the right hand of the Father," and a term that connotes mediation and, in a more archaic sense, sacrifice. By rendering the Italian word for "church" (*chiesa*) by the Tibetan *gyeza* (*rgyas za*), Desideri constructed a word whose first syllable is the same syllable, meaning "expansion," that one sees in the word for "Buddha" (*sangs rgyas*). Another well-known difficulty in Desideri's Tibetan is whether he intended a neologism when he identified himself as *mgo skar* (literally, "star head") instead of *mgo dkar* (literally, "white head"), the term used to describe people from Western regions generally, including both Armenians and Muslims. Since both words are pronounced "*gokar*," I am inclined to think that Desideri self-consciously coined a homophonic term meant to evoke the original, but which would ultimately distinguish him and other Christians from the general mass of Westerners.[107] It is difficult to determine whether Desideri himself intended such etymological significance when he transliterated these basic terms. We know that Desideri was familiar with the practice, since he mentions it with regard to the words *könchok* (*dkon mchog*) and *Urgyen* (*u rgyan*) in his *Notizie istoriche*, but no smoking gun exists that would make us think he wittingly manipulated such etymologies.[108] Lacking an explicit admission, we can only wonder. Perhaps Tibetans saw some occult significance pulsating in Desideri's choices. If one wishes to attribute a certain deliberation to the Italian missionary, he might very well have intended to evoke such resonances. He then would have needed to show Tibetans how to discriminate between the true and false religions after having evoked resemblances between them.

Desideri may have laid a trap for himself. His explanations could easily serve to identify the Tibetan and Christian rituals further rather than to distinguish them. One might even wonder whether Tibetans, despite protests from Desideri, saw the Jesuit as anything other than a lama with a different lineage. The Eucharist, after all, might look like little more than a *tsok (tshogs)* offering in the eyes of the Tibetans who visited Desideri in his chapel. If left to resemblances alone, the Tibetans might have made the same mistake as the early Christian missionaries, marveling that these strange *gokar* lamas knew about the Three Jewels. If friars and Jesuits debated about how long to delay teaching about the passion in order to avoid scandalizing potential Chinese converts, one can imagine the opposite problem in Tibet: how does one distinguish the Crucifixion from the skulls, flayed skin, and hanging entrails that decorated Tibetan chapels? Jesus Christ might very well appear to Tibetans as a *chöpa (gcod pa)*, a yogi who gives his body as a ritual offering, or, as Desideri himself implied, a practitioner of the yoga of entering death.[109]

None of this should take away from the genius of *il gran pistoiese*. Always passionate, sometimes hotheaded, certainly argumentative, both his Tibetan and Italian writings reveal Desideri to have had a keenly analytical mind. They also reveal a man entirely convinced, almost mesmerized, by his own powers of persuasion. Whether the Jesuit was the progressive saint of late twentieth-century Jesuit hagiographies or the conniving litigator of the Capuchin letters, Desideri was just the sort of man to spend hours writing a brilliant, but overwrought, refutation of reincarnation. He was also just the sort of man to pay backhanded compliments if a hard-earned mission was at stake. The Jesuit's polemical brilliance, however, may have come at the expense of more practical wisdom. Although he could not have known it at the time, what had initially appeared to Desideri as tentativeness on the part of the Capuchins was but a desire to follow the procedures already established by the Congregation for the Propagation of the Faith. By sending Rome the *quid agendum* before proceeding to Tibet, Domenico da Fano showed himself to be a seasoned political operator who documented his compliance with the rules of the Sacred Congregation at every turn. Knowing full well the political power that the Capuchins had at the Congregation, he confidently laid down a paper trail that he could follow all the way back to Rome. He was prepared for the ensuing legal battle before he had even met Desideri; he may have even relished it as the culmination of twenty long years of political maneuvering. Whatever virtues Ippolito Desideri possessed, he lacked the one virtue necessary for political success in Rome, namely, discernment, the lack of which cost him his mission, his book, and—if I may adopt the romantic tone of some more popular accounts of the Jesuit missionary—his very life.

6

Compositio Loci: Tibet

So full of shapes is fancy that it alone is high fantastical.
— Shakespeare, *Twelfth Night, or What You Will*

A great silence blanketed the land of snows when Desideri wrote his account of Tibet, which remained unknown, "except as a name."[1] The Jesuit resolved to publish his recollections and "with one stroke when Desideri wrote his account of Tibet, satisfy the lively curiosity that so many "scholars, gentlemen, and eminent persons" had shown in Tibet. He seems to have written hastily; it is possible that Desideri began his account, at the behest of Jean Bouchet, before leaving India. He also seems to have finished several, and perhaps all, of the known drafts of his account when Felice da Montecchio invoked Clement X's strictures on missionary writings in their case before the Sacred Congregation. On the face of things, the Jesuit presented his account as a correction of previous scholarly literature on Tibet, addressing Athanasius Kircher's *China illustrata,* António de Andrade's *Novo descobrimento do Gram Cathayo,*[2] Louis Moréri's *Le grand dictionnaire historique,*[3] Jean-Baptiste Tavernier's *Les six voyages,*[4] Antonio Franco's *Imagem da virtude em o noviciado da Companhia de Jesu na corte de Lisboa,*[5] and the collection of Giovanni Battista Ramusio, which included the travels of Marco Polo.[6] Desideri singled out Moréri for making several mistakes— including the claims that Tibetans recognize the Holy Trinity and that they believe the Dalai Lama is invisible, immortal, and unchanging like God the Father. He chided Kircher more gently and, after granting all due

respect to Tavernier, frankly accused the famous Frenchman of fanciful invention.[7] But we would be mistaken to see Desideri's account merely as an anticipa-
tion of the more enlightened geographical and historical accounts of the
nineteenth and twentieth centuries. From his opening *salutatio* to his final
conclusio, Desideri self-consciously followed stylistic conventions that are alien to
the canons of modern historiography, and his account is saturated with the
conventions of ancient rhetoric, especially as the Society of Jesus understood
them. Tragically, the Jesuit's rhetorical prowess went unnoticed. He could not
seek the Congregation's permission to publish the account of his travels, because
Michelangelo Tamburini, most likely embarrassed by the whole affair, ordered
Desideri not to have any more dealings with its representatives. The general
passed away in 1730, and the Society's bureaucratic powers may have been too
overwhelmed in the transition between generals to take further action. We do not
know whether Desideri alienated other Jesuits, but the Society's curia did not seek
permission on his behalf. Had Desideri lived longer, weathered the change of
administrations, and found new allies in the Society, the account of his travels in
Tibet might have seen the light of day.

Rhetoric in the *Notizie Istoriche*

The full title of Desideri's account is *Notizie istoriche del Thibet e memorie
de' viaggi e missione ivi fatta dal P. Ippolito Desiderj della Compagnia di Gesù
dal medesimo scritte e dedicate*, which might be rendered literally as "Historical notices of Tibet and recollections of the voyages and mission made
there by Fr. Ippolito Desideri of the Society of Jesus, written and dedicated
by the same."[8] Scholars usually abbreviate this typically baroque title to its
first two words, *Notizie istoriche*, which are by no means easy to translate.
Notizie is roughly equivalent to the modern English "news," meaning any
knowledge that might be profitably reported to a large number of people.
An early eighteenth-century English translator would have probably rendered it "tidings." The word *istoriche* is trickier, since early modern Romance languages did not draw a sharp distinction between "history" and
"story," as modern English does. An *istoria* can be any narrative, fictional
or otherwise, that relates events worth telling. The word typically connoted
adventure on a grand scale, whether romantic, political, or comic. Works
such as Shakespeare's *King Lear* and Cervantes's *Don Quixote* were styled
"true histories" much in the way that we might today watch a film that is
"based on a true story."[9]

Desideri's title and repeated characterization of his account as a collection of *notizie* and *memorie*—tidings and recollections—identify it as a quintessential work of baroque rhetoric. Like other works of the era, it is Janus-faced, looking forward and backward simultaneously as it confronts the reader in a somewhat ambiguous present. Its evocation of novelty—"news"—marks its modernity; its evocation of memory—the fourth of Cicero's five canons of rhetoric—ties it back to the rhetorical and meditative practices of antiquity. In this respect, Desideri's journey from Rome to Lhasa, his account of Tibet's civil and religious institutions, and his return to Europe together form one great *topographia*, the rhetorical description of a place. His *istoria* is a formal *narratio*, a presentation of essential facts in a judicial argument, and he favors rhetorical practices that were common in such arguments, such as *enumeratio*, the listing of details, and *accumulatio*, the emphasis of points previously made. If we were to describe Desideri's *compositio loci* in terms of ancient rhetoric, we might say that his *memorie* assist in the formal *inventio* of an *istoria* meant to persuade his readers of his superiority as a Tibetologist and his rightful share of the Tibetan mission.

One can get a sense of the importance with which Desideri and his readers imbued these rhetorical conventions by looking at the formal address to the reader that opens the *Notizie istoriche*:

> I did not intend these narrative tidings of Tibet or the recollections of my travels and missions to see the light of day; I assembled them during my return to Europe for my own relief as reminders of and testimonies to the suffering I had undergone and kept them so that I might enjoy reading about the dangers I once risked with such readiness in the safety of my own study. I had seen, too, more than one *relatio* of the peoples and things of the Indies whose accounts I found so incredible and exaggerated and so far distant from my own experience of fifteen years that I feared being accused of their lies should I publish my own account. After all, the manners, customs, laws, houses, foodstuffs, and peoples of the Orient are so different from our own that they bewilder the imaginations of those who are unaccustomed to them, and anyone who wishes to say anything at all about the Indies risks being thought a liar, even if such a charge is undeserved.[10]

An appeal to the truthfulness of its narration runs through the *Notizie* like a red thread. Desideri appeals to his own virtues, which are plentiful, and levels an extended *argumentum ad hominem* against his rivals. These appeals need not worry us; on closer inspection, they are entirely consistent with the rhetorical practices of Desideri's day. Any work composed by a Jesuit who taught *humaniora* that did not appeal to the emotions and morals of his readers in addition to their reason—the three forms of argument enumerated in Aristotle's *Rhetoric*—would be thought a rhetorical failure. It would be akin to writing a book for a modern academic audience that contained no acknowledgments, no review of the scholarly literature, no citations, no bibliography, and no critical apparatus. It was common to warn readers of impending attacks by one's enemies and, given the stinging polemic of the early modern era—recall Gioacchino's tirades against Desideri—quite prudent.

Desideri wrote for scholars, to be sure, but he also wrote for missionaries. He compares his account to an old Roman military banner that depicted the empire's triumphs with brightly painted fortresses, the most recent military technology, and "savage and scarcely seen" styles of war. Just as these painted banners instructed Romans in the military arts and incited them to greater acts of heroism in the service of the empire, so Desideri's own account, by recounting the spiritual triumphs of the Society of Jesus in Tibet, would instruct missionaries in spiritual combat and incite them to acts of heroic virtue in the service of the Church. Extending the martial metaphor, Desideri says, "A shot is always more accurately and surely landed when the target has been properly sighted and the attack well planned."[11] The missionary's target, of course, was Tibetan religion:

> The religious sect that reigns here, which is so entirely different from all others, is founded on the Pythagorean system, and deserves to be better known, that it be better impugned. I flatter myself to think that these pages, besides sating a hunger for novelty, might also rouse the talents of learned men to confute this novel mix of superstitious errors and to move many to charity and so bring assistance to this blind people.[12]

Being mindful of proper etiquette, just as he had once been in the court of Lhazang Khan, Desideri assures the reader "with all of the gravitas and candor fitting his character and profession" as a priest and a member of the Society of Jesus that he need not fear his narrative's faithfulness to the events. There is nothing in the book, he promises, that he himself has not witnessed or examined thoroughly.

> I ask only that you not read these pages with that malign prejudice that believes everything extraordinary must be false for the mere reason that it is extraordinary. Even our ancestors, from whom we descend, would not recognize us today, nor would we recognize them, given the changes and fickleness of fashion, comportment, and custom. Neither

they nor we are made up or make-believe. If you strip yourself of the false opinion that everything extraordinary is false, I have no doubt that you will recognize the note of sincerity in these pages.[13]

With a bit of a flourish, Desideri refuses to apologize for his "rough and unadorned" style. A person who gives someone a gift of the first fruits of the year, or fruits from a strange land, or fruits that had never been grown in one's own climate need not make excuses for their imperfect flavor or if he presents them honestly in a little rustic basket:

> The nature of such gifts is their excuse, and their rarity is their beauty. My notes are valuable only because they are honest and noteworthy; this is the whole of their beauty. An overly elegant and artful choice of words can be considered a vice, since it may give rise to the suspicion that an elegant and cultivated delivery was employed, not to beautify the truth that one makes public, but rather to hide some fraud and falsify those things one fears might be exposed.[14]

Anyone familiar with ancient rhetoric will notice several common tropes in these passages. Desideri's appeal to his status as an eyewitness, for example, is a rhetorical figure known as *autopsy*.[15] His apology for a plain, frank style, whose rustic quality serves as a guarantee of truthfulness, is another classic rhetorical device known as the *captatio benevolentiae*.[16] The comparison of persuasion to warfare, which Desideri liked so much that he later put it in the mouth of Lhazang Khan, is a stock metaphor from Cicero's *Philippic Orations*. Amid this blizzard of rhetorical devices, probably the one most readily associated with the baroque age, and the Society of Jesus itself, was the appeal to *curiositas*. For many medieval authors, *curiositas* was the chief bane of mnemonic practice. Such mental "wantonness" (*fornicatio*) made the monk a "dilettante" (*palpator*, literally "flatterer") or a "nibbler" (*degustator*), unable to take nourishment from Scripture. Curiosity, in other words, inhibited the *affectus* necessary to strengthen one's *phantasmata* in single-pointed meditation.[17] When Desideri speaks of "curious" readers and "curious" tales, he uses the word in a different sense.[18] Ignatius Loyola emphasized a positive understanding of *curiositas*, understood as the care, attentiveness, and skill necessary for rigorous study, which earlier Christian authors like Peter of Celle and Hugh of St. Victor valued in the reader of Scripture.[19] Ignatius instructed missionaries to encourage this very quality in readers:

> Some leading figures of the city read have read the letters from India to their great edification, desire, and indeed ask me repeatedly, that

something should be written about the cosmography of those regions where Ours live. They want to know, for example, how long the days are in summer and winter, and whether the shadows move to the left or to the right. Finally, if there are things that seem extraordinary, let them be noted, for example, details about animals and plants that are either unknown or not normally found in such a size, etc. And this news—a salsa for the taste of a certain curiosity that is not evil and we wish to be found among men—may come in the these very letters or with others.[20]

Ignatius Loyola's own spirituality informed these instructions to Gaspar Barzaeus. Ultimately, Jesuits promoted curiosity because their saintly founder was curious himself:

We often saw how even the smallest things could make the spirit of Ignatius soar upward to God, who even in the smallest things is Greatest. At the sight of a little sprout, a leaf, a flower, or a fruit, even at the sight of a useless worm or a tiny bug, he could soar free above the heavens and penetrate such things as lie beyond the senses of men and women.[21]

After the example of Ignatius, Jesuits treated the world as a manuscript illustrated by the divine hand.[22] New lands were like new chapters, new flora and fauna like new words of an ancient tongue. A curious beast like an elephant or a rhinoceros required careful study; in the mind of an early modern missionary and his readers, its interpretation cast new, emblematic light on the whole.[23]

The ultimate aim of curiosity, though, was missionary success. Desideri encouraged curiosity, as he says in his prologue, to "rouse the talents of learned men to confute this novel mix of superstitious errors," so that Tibetans themselves could soar free above the heavens and penetrate things that lie beyond the senses. Desideri wrote, in short, to effect their conversion to Roman Catholicism, and he carefully modulated his style to appeal to the different constituencies that might contribute to this effort. Like works written by other Jesuit missionaries, especially the procurators of the China missions, his style was ornamental, prolix, and melodramatic. More often than not, he used well-worn but easily recognizable images from other missionaries' letters, the travels of Marco Polo, and the bogus Egyptology of the Renaissance. In this regard, Desideri's portrayals of Lhazang Khan, the sixth Dalai Lama, Padmasaṃbhava, and even ordinary Tibetans are animated as much by the spirit of the Society of Jesus as their own. His *compositio loci* owes as much to European fantasies about other peoples, Tartars and Egyptians especially, as it does to some particular fascination with Tibet itself.

Curiosity and *Topographia*

The successful *topographia*, like the successful construction of mnemonic *phantasmata* and *superaedificationes*, required an accumulation of details. Each book of the *Notizie istoriche* is accordingly brimming with facts, digressions, consolations, desolations, and a healthy dose of adventure. The impetus for such multifaceted *enumerationes* can be found in the instructions for *dictamen*, the art of writing letters, given by Ignatius Loyola to his missionaries, and their primary stylistic models are the letters and *relationes* of the Society of Jesus. The publication of missionaries' letters was a thriving industry by Desideri's day, perhaps best exemplified by the monumental *Lettres édifiantes et curieuses*, the thirty-four-volume collection of "curious and edifying" letters published in Paris between 1703 and 1776.[24] With such letters in hand, the educated European reader could become an armchair antiquarian, ethnographer, or mystic as his mood demanded. The industry was so successful that publishers translated letters with a rather loose hand, often edited them to suit the tastes of their readers, and rushed them into print. Not surprisingly, many missionaries, Desideri included, lamented that their letters were published without their permission or in a highly corrupted form.[25] Letters from Jesuit missionaries in Japan such as Organtino Gnecci-Soldi lingered so long on their descriptions of cedar paneling, gold leaf, and gleaming mirrors that censors occasionally felt it necessary to edit them.[26]

These letters sold well because they promised news of "curious" peoples and things; the very term served as an advertisement in Jesuit titles of the period, being applied not only to collections like the *Lettres édifiantes et curieuses* but also to news of the most recent technological advances, as in Gaspar Schott's *Technica curiosa, sive mirabilia artis*.[27] The title page of the English translation of Louis le Comte's *Nouveaux memoires sur l'état présent de la Chine*—note le Comte's twin evocation of novelty and memory—promises a typical list of curious things:

> Memoirs and Remarks GEOGRAPHICAL, HISTORICAL, TOPOGRAPHICAL, PHYSICAL, NATURAL, ASTRONOMICAL, MECHANICAL, MILITARY, MERCANTILE, POLITICAL, and ECCLESIASTICAL, made in above Ten Years Travels through the Empire of CHINA: Particularly, upon Their Pottery and Varnishing Silk and other Manufactures, Pearl-fishing, the History of Plants and

Animals, with a Description of their Cities and Publick Works, Number of People, Manners, Language, and Customs, Coin, and Commerce, their Habits, Oeconomy, and Government, the Philosophy of the Famous CONFUCIUS. With many curious Particulars; being, in general, the most authentick Account of the COUNTRY.[28]

China was thought the most curious land during Desideri's day, and writings such as le Comte's dominated the curiosities market.[29] Kircher's *China illustrata*, which we have already seen many times in these pages, is perhaps the best-known example of this *chinoiserie*. Figure 6.1 shows Kircher's enticing image of Chinese flora, which has a nice detail that displays how publishers creatively evoked curiosity in their readers. The small child whom Kircher placed in the center of the composition would have reminded readers of Moses abandoned among the reeds. This clever ploy allows the Jesuit scholar to promote his own speculations about the Egyptian origins of Chinese reli-

FIGURE 6.1. Exotic Plants, from Athanasius Kircher, *China illustrata* (Amsterdam: Joannem Janssonium à Waesberge & Elizeum Weyerstraet, 1667). Courtesy of Special Collections, Georgetown University Library.

gions visually, but it also hints that the Chinese might discover Moses in their own land and so be led to the true law.

Desideri's *Notizie istoriche* fits squarely into this tradition. Its first book carries the Jesuit from Rome to Lisbon, describes his maritime adventures, and lingers on the exotica of Mozambique, Goa, Delhi, Agra, Kashmir, Ladakh, and eventually Lhasa. Its story line culminates with Desideri meeting Lhazang Khan and Targum Trashi, gaining entry into the Mongol court, and healing the chieftain and his vassal from a mysterious poisoning. Desideri skillfully marks the geographical boundaries of the land of snows in the second book and describes its climate, crops, animals, rivers, boats, bridges, cities, and capital. He teaches the reader about Tibetan politics, writing, clothes, culinary habits, games, marriages, and funeral customs. The third book contains rather lengthy arguments meant to convince the reader that the office of the Dalai Lama was the work of the Devil alongside descriptions of several other lesser lamas, monks, nuns, oracles, monasteries, convents, music, and religious customs. He explains Tibetans' ethics, cosmology, and notions of the afterlife, enumerating the multileveled Tibetan conception of hell with some gusto. He also summarizes the stories of Śākyamuni Buddha, Trisong Detsen, and Padmasaṃbhava, and narrates important events in the religious history of Tibet such as the "curious tale" of their mythic origins from Avalokiteśvara and the construction of the temple at Samyé. The fourth book of the *Notizie istoriche* recalls Desideri's departure from Lhasa and the no less exciting adventures of his return journey by sea. He adds Kathmandu, Bhaktapur, Patna, Varanasi, and Allahabad to his travelogue, describes the austerity of the Jesuits in Puducherry, and adds further details about the political strife of the Mughal Empire.

Desideri seemed particularly intent upon detailing all manner of political intrigue; not content to narrate the events that led to the Tibetan civil war, Desideri notes that the ship upon which he sailed was one of a fleet of several men-of-war, commanded by Dom Lopo de Almeida and preparing to leave Goa and sail toward Surat against the Arabs of Mascati, who had captured a Portuguese vessel from Macao. This slight flourish gives the missionary reason to digress for a few pages about the atrocities committed during the internecine strife in the Mughal Empire. His hagiographic interlude on Dona Giuliana Diaz da Costa allows him to mention that she fled as a young child from Cochin as the Dutch captured it from the Portuguese in 1663.[30] We can only suppose that, apart from a personal predilection for such stories, Desideri knew his audience—perhaps even his market—and intended to give it what it wanted.[31] Much the same might be said about his references to Asian trade. His narrative lingers on exotic commodities of every kind: the elephant tusks, amber, and slaves of Mozambique; the fruits, flowers, and shawls of Kashmir;

the opium, tobacco, and sugar found in Patna. Although Goa was the center-piece of the Portuguese Empire in Asia, Desideri reserved his highest praise for Agra, which boasted splendid buildings, beautiful gardens, and sumptuous mausoleums, all made in a fashion to rival "Roman magnificence."[32] His enthusiasm for Tibet, if somewhat muted in comparison, is still vigorous. Its western deserts have large sheep with tasty meat and fine wool; gold and butter are plentiful; monasteries abound with riches.[33] None of these remarks should seem out of the ordinary, nor should Desideri's missionary efforts seem insincere on account of them. Missionary undertakings of such scope de-pended as much upon the revenue generated from their own trade as they did upon royal and ecclesiastical patronage.

Nor does the Jesuit omit detailed descriptions of exotic flora and fauna. He found his own curiosity piqued by the great variety of herbs in Mozambique and showed a similar enthusiasm for Tibetan herbs. He was evidently satisfied to confirm claims about the herb *zodoria* advanced by Avicenna and to correct the claims of Sarapion. He describes the effects of various liquors and intoxicants, including exotic brews such as bhang, the potent mixture of milk and hashish from Northern India, which the Jesuit missionary found "very refreshing, but apt to make men drunk and stupid." Desideri also devoted considerable time to correcting Mattioli's description of the musk deer, provides instructions for properly extracting its musk, and reports the costs and qualities of Tibet's cattle and horses, its eagles and ravens, and its "uncommon and extraordinary" dogs. He delights to tell his reader then the rhinoceros really is as Tavernier depicts it—at least in the French edition of his work.[34] Desideri's descriptions of people and races follow similar stylistic norms, most notably those laid down in classical sources such as Herodotus.[35] The inhabitants of Rajaput are "a gentile sect and people, bold by nature, tall, most warlike, and renowned for their military prowess. A part of these people are subjects of a great and powerful gentile king, called a Rana, who has his residence and holds his court in the city of Udaipur, which he rules with admirable rigor and most just laws."[36] Desideri describes Tibetans with the same classical contours: "Tibetans are of ordinary height, of fair and rosy complexion, and not without an olive hue. They are rather well built and bare of face, for their beards do not grow."[37] Their minds are "lively," "ingenious," and "able"; they show great devotion, enjoy modest fash-ions, and neither divorce their spouses nor succumb to rowdiness—even at festivals and marriages.[38] Although the missionary would fairly rail about the sexual peccadilloes of the sixth Dalai Lama, he worried little about the ordinary Tibetans who celebrated Tsangyang Gyatso's exploits and discusses their sexual practices in a rather matter-of-fact manner. Owing to salubrious climate, he says, illness is rare except in large towns such as Lhasa and Zhikatsé, where the "free rein of the vices" (*libertà de' vizj*) causes many to contract venereal diseases.[39]

A modern reader might find these passages overly stereotyped. When compared with the general European view of any number of other peoples, they seem remarkably generous. Despite the horrors he had witnessed during the Zünghar invasion, the Jesuit can still say that Tibetans abhorred cruelty. Except for his tales about the *lhowa* to the south—tales he would have heard from Tibetans themselves—Desideri did not believe that Tibetans were cannibals.[40] In this, he marks a significant advance over the stories other Europeans had invented about Tibet.[41] Neither are Tibetans divided by feelings of caste like Hindus, for they deal, eat, and congregate with anyone regardless of religion or nationality. Nor do they have superstitions about food or prejudices about ablutions.[42] Tibetans have no aversion to Christians and, most important of all, display a real "curiosity" for the faith.[43] Tibetans have the greatest respect for their priests and monks, a devotion that Desideri believes exceeds that shown by Europeans.

Jansenist protests aside, it was common for European authors to appeal to the ardent religiosity of non-Christians in order to criticize the moral failings of their own nations. The primary difference between the virtuous sages of Jesuit missionary literature and the noble pagans of Dryden, Voltaire, Diderot, and Rousseau is that the ancient pagan sages of the Jesuits criticized the dearth of devotion in modern Europe, while the *bon sauvage* of the *philosophes* criticized its Jesuitical excesses.[44] Figurists such as Joachim Bouvet and Jean-François Fouquet, for example, acknowledged that the ancient worship of the Chinese was closer in fact to biblical religion than to religion's present European form, and missionaries such as Bartolomé de las Casas imbued the oppressed with revolutionary voices that criticized the conquistadores. Portuguese Jesuits including António Vieira denounced the slave trade, and Antonio Ruiz de Montoya obtained permission to supply Amerindians with firearms against kidnappers.[45] Nor can we forget that Catholic religious orders generally saw Europe itself as their primary mission field, and the rural Christians as their most stubborn and morally deficient "converts."[46] Andrea Pozzo's *Allegory of the Missionary Work of the Society of Jesus*, which appeared in the first chapter, depicted Europe as one of the four continents upon which the Society worked, and the methods of *accommodatio* ascribed to St. Francis Xavier or José de Anchieta, such as teaching catechism by setting it to popular melodies, were first pioneered in missions to rural Spaniards. The trope of the virtuous pagan served as a spur to increase the fervor of educational reforms and what were called "internal missions" to these rural Christians, who were thought far more barbarous than any Chinese, Japanese, or Tibetan.[47] On the whole, Desideri's view of Tibetans is positive, without the undue romanticism of later twentieth-century accounts. The same cannot be said for his view of Mongols.

A Note on the True and Tragic History of Lhazang Khan

Viewed as a work of history, Desideri's *narratio* is a curious mélange of hard-nosed reporting, breezy innuendo, and simple mistakes. The missionary shows some real historical flair in noting the material conditions of the war in Ü and Dakpo, but his overall narrative is meant to demonstrate God's handiwork in Tibetan affairs.[48] Ironically, the broad outlines of Desideri's story mirror the stele erected in Lhasa in 1721 to mark the victory of the Qing over the Zünghar. The stele condemns the regent Sangyé Gyatso for concealing the death of the fifth Dalai Lama; credits Lhazang Khan for reviving Buddhism in Tibet; celebrates the Manchu, Mongol, and Han forces for braving malarial jungles and recapturing Lhasa; and finally praises Kangxi for pacifying Tibet and reviving Buddhist teachings.[49] The stele's mention of Buddhism provides the only contrasting note; in the missionary's view, Tibetan Buddhism—especially in its political manifestations—was the primary force that oppressed Tibetans. The positive comparisons, however, are instructive. Desideri vilified the regent and the sixth Dalai Lama; recounted the clash of various Tibetan, Mongol, and Chinese forces in a highly romantic strain; and presented Lhazang Khan and Kangxi as paragons of natural virtue.

Ignatius Loyola instructed missionaries to give an account of a nation's rulers, and Jesuits often concentrated their missionary efforts on the nobility.[50] Desideri's marked emphasis on Lhazang Khan, however, exceeds these mandates and betrays a greater European fascination with Tartary, especially the khans.[51] The dream of an oriental Christian king, whether the fabled monarch Prester John or a new Tartar convert, was a long-standing fantasy of medieval Christians. Those Christians who hoped that an eastern monarch would come to their aid against the expanding Muslim dynasties vastly overestimated the extent to which their religion had spread in Asia. The Franciscan and Dominican embassies to the Mongols in the thirteenth and fourteenth centuries discovered that Asia boasted no thriving Christian monarchy. At best, the Mongols tolerated remnants of Nestorian and Jacobite expressions of Christian dogmas in a largely syncretic milieu.[52] Johannes de Plano Carpini felt that Güyüg, the khan commanded by Pope Innocent IV to submit to his divine authority, was on the verge of becoming Christian, at least before the khan issued his famous threat to destroy the pope. Guillelmus of Rubruc believed that Sartaq, the son of Batu, the khan of the Golden Horde, had become a Christian. Jesuit missionaries—not unlike Tibetans—framed their encounters with Lhazang Khan and Kangxi with past hopes of Qubilai Khan, who dispatched Marco Polo and his entourage with a message to the pope and an invitation to send "a hundred men learned in the Christian religion, learned in the seven liberal arts, and capable of demonstrating the superiority of their own faith."[53] Even Desideri's appearance before Lhazang Khan on Epiphany day was but one of several similar encounters that had found their way into missionary lore. The Great Khan Möngke had Guillelmus of Rubruc debate Nestorians and Muslims. Akbar, the Mughal emperor who reigned from Kabul to Bengal, sent an embassy to India to request that Jesuits come to his court to debate with various Brahmin, Persian, and Muslim theologians. The great Mughal, religiously inclined, open to discussion, and tolerant of missionaries, excited such hopes of conversion among the Jesuits that the wise and generous pagan king became an obligatory trope in missionary literature.[54]

In this regard, Desideri's *Notizie istoriche* owes a great deal to the theatrical Tartar fantasies of the previous century, most notably Martino Martini's *De bello tartarico historia*.[55]Along with his more scholarly works, the *Novus atlas sinensis*[56] and the *Sinicae historiae decas prima*,[57] Martini's account of the "Tartar War" was a vastly popular work that combined adventure and exhortation in equal measure. Stylistically indebted to the travels of Marco Polo, especially after the embellishments of Giambattista Ramusio and Rustichello of Pisa, such accounts took advantage of the early modern taste for military exploits to generate interest in the missions and promote the world-spanning efforts of the Society of Jesus.[58] Jesuit writings on Kangxi were equally melodramatic.[59] Figure 6.2, the title page from a bootleg edition of Martini's work—with the snappier title *A Narration of the Tartar's Devastation of the Kingdom of China*—gives a good sense of the appeal of these Poloesque Tartar fantasies.[60] Indeed, there is hardly a single detail in early modern travel literature that had not been pioneered by Polo, including shipwreck, piracy, extortion, wild and dangerous animals, and abundant treasures; he even admired the Buddha's sanctity and the austerity of Hindu "idolaters." Humanists generally decried the fantastic elements of Polo's narrative, but he found fervent defenders among Catholic missionaries in Asia, such as the Augustinians Martín de Rada and Juan González de Mendoza and Jesuits such as Matteo Ricci, Martino Martini, and Gabriel de Megalhães. Athanasius Kircher, basing himself on Martini, frequently cited the "clear-eyed observer Marco Polo of Venice" (*oculatus inspector Paulus Marcus Venetus*).[61] None of Rustichello's embellishments prevent Polo—or Rustichello's Polo—from appealing to his own status as an eyewitness or protesting that no one would believe the wonders he witnessed, even as

REGNI SINENSIS
a
TARTARIS
devastati
ENARRATIO,
Authore Martino Martinii.
AMSTELÆDAMI,
Apud Ægidium Lanßonium Valckenier: Aᵒ 1661.

FIGURE 6.2. Title page of Martino Martini's *Regni Sinensis a Tartaris devastati enarratio* (Amsterdam: Aegidius Janssonius, 1661). Courtesy of Special Collections, The Sheridan Libraries, The John Hopkins University.

he emphasized every marvel and minor piece of exotica imaginable, or as he based his telling of Marco Polo's tales on the exploits of Alexander the Great or on King Arthur and the Knights of Round Table.[62]

It is difficult not to think that Desideri shaped his account of the Zünghar invasion to better accommodate aficionados of this literature, especially in his descriptions of its major players, such as the sixth Dalai Lama and Taktsepa. Often the features of Desideri's most prominent heroes and villains do not find corroboration in the rather expansive Tibetan historical works of the period. This somewhat disturbing fact—at least from the perspective of more modern historiographical methods—is nowhere more apparent than in his treatment of the various Mongols who populate his tale. Consider Desideri's first meeting with Targum Trashi:

> On April 28, 1716, I went to the palace to meet Targum Trashi as we had planned, but found that he was with the king in his private apartments. Hearing that I had arrived, Targum Trashi left for his own apartment, where he greeted me with extraordinary expressions of affection and honor, vowed his strong and enduring friendship in the most obliging terms, and asked me to do the same. These mutual demonstrations of affection astonished everyone, and they could speak of nothing else. They marveled that two people could enjoy such intense familiarity at their very first meeting.[63]

Tibetan records do not speak of a *darqan* Trashi who served as a minister under Lhazang Khan, and some of the greatest scholars of Tibetan history have been flummoxed in their attempts to locate the figure who plays such a sympathetic role in Desideri's account. That the missionary and his protagonist were so affectionate only compounds the difficulty, for it seems highly unlikely that Desideri would have forgotten the name of one of his closest friends. Several of the singular events narrated by Desideri, such as the ambush of Zünghar troops as they retreated through Ngari, prompted Luciano Petech to identify Desideri's friend with Kangchené, although Petech later retracted this identification because several of the deeds ascribed to Desideri's friend could not have been plausibly performed by Lhazang Khan's minister. Of course, the other possibility, which would justify some of the Capuchin's carping, was that Desideri simply exaggerated his access to Lhazang Khan's court. I do not mean to suggest that Desideri merely invented a tale, but only that it was common in the histories of his day to sacrifice historical detail for overall dramatic effect. If Jesuits found such literature especially well suited for their own purposes, it only makes sense that they did not alter its conventions. They added a few, to be sure, generally fusing the conventions of travel literature and medieval hagiography into an action-packed whole, but the primary purpose of the *relationes* was closer in spirit to hagiography. They were, in sum, meant to edify and inspire Jesuit novices. Desideri's *Notizie istoriche* is no exception.

Desideri did not set out to deceive his readers; in all likelihood, he exaggerated his friendship with Kangchené and mistook rumors of Polhané's exploits during the sack of Lhasa for his friend's own. Whatever the extent of Desideri's friendship with various Mongols, Targum Trashi is a literary amalgam of Kangchené and Polhané. Given the difficulty of identifying Desideri's friend and his close resemblance to these two, who were both loyal to Lhazang Khan and who both played dramatic roles defending Lhasa during the Zünghar invasion, Desideri's encounter with Targum Trashi seems a bit of a set piece. The inexplicable friendship between two men of different races had such a long and healthy run that Herman Melville could parody it in the famous meeting of Ishmael and Queequeg at the Spouter-Inn in *Moby-Dick*.[64]

Still, it is difficult not to wonder about Desideri's literary ambitions when one reads his description of the commander of the Zünghar army:

> Tsering Döndrup was lively and skilled, rebellious and passionate, intrepid and warlike. He was insensible to discomfort or travails. His favorite seat, even when there was no war, was a saddle, his bed and couch a horse-rug, his softest pillow a shield, a sword, a quiver and arrows. What he trusted most was vigilance, which suggested to his mind continually diverse stratagems; his principal and most faithful adjutants in all he undertook were secrecy and simulation, so that he outwardly concealed his plots and resolutions. In sum, he largely resembled Alexander the Great and, like him, showed the world that the great victors in the camp of Mars are those who have been educated in the school of liberal arts and the lyceum of science, and that to govern troops it is best first to submit to the rigors of Aristotle.[65]

This tone was not all that unusual for its day. Mongols had enjoyed a long reign as characters in European literature and would continue to do so for some time. Hearing that Lhazang Khan had been killed in battle, Tsering Döndrup threw himself on the corpse and "bathed its wounds with tears, loudly praising the many virtues and admirable qualities of the king he infamously betrayed and unjustly persecuted."[66] Touched up with a little Martial, this "tender and heart-wrenching scene" would have made a fine vignette recited by young Jesuit charges.[67] One of the wealthier Jesuit schools in Rome, Cologne, or Paris could have staged *The True and Tragic History of Lhazang Khan* with a full array of mechanical props depicting roiling seas and falling snow. I suspect that the missionary sustains such a tone not so much out of loyalty to his own patron—although that too may be true enough—but to emphasize the many virtues and admirable qualities of the people he evangelized. If Desideri took a few dramatic liberties when he wrote about the final days of Lhazang Khan, it was because he hoped to paint a florid and sentimental portrait of the Mongol chieftain without giving the impression that he sympathized unduly with the religion of his subjects. Quite the opposite, in fact; in Desideri's telling, the Tibetan civil wars led to the murder of a great khan who was on the verge of converting to the Catholic Church.

Humanism and the Gods of Old

The description of Tibetan religion that constitutes the third book of the *Notizie istoriche* careens from intense polemic to surprising sensitivity, often in the space of a single chapter or paragraph. Here, too, Desideri's theological style is indebted to previous sources, and he sometimes sacrifices historical accuracy for the well-placed literary allusion. When Desideri notes, for example, that the only virtue that Buddhist texts do not describe is humility—a rather outlandish claim for a man who translated Tsongkhapa's massive *Great Stages of the Path*—his readers would have immediately caught his allusion to the eighth book of Augustine's *Confessions*, where the celebrated bishop says the same of the books of the Neoplatonists. Just as the writings of Plotinus served as a bridge for Augustine's conversion from a crude Manichean mythology to the proper Catholic doctrine of God, Desideri hints that Buddhism might play a similar role in combating Hindu polytheism and bringing Asia into the fold of the Catholic Church. Desideri probably intended his extended description of the Buddhist hells to serve a similar literary purpose. In more refined circles, it would have garnered comparisons to Dante's *Inferno*. Such exacting descriptions of the torments of hell would have been the single feature that everyone who had made the *Spiritual Exercises*, from the most refined Jesuit to the simple layman, would have identified with the first stages of Christian meditation.[68] The Jesuit's robust description of the Buddhist hells would have thus served to validate Buddhist asceticism, which Desideri described using terms reminiscent of the Principle and Foundation of the *Spiritual Exercises*, and to justify the positive connotations in the Buddhist notion of *bodhicitta*, the compassionate attitude of the bodhisattva for all sentient beings. Of course, the ultimate end of all this hellfire was to show that Tibetans genuinely believed that bad deeds were punished and that

FIGURE 6.3. The similarity of American, Asian, and Egyptian deities, from Joseph-François Lafitau, *Moeurs des sauvages ameriquains, comparées aux moeurs des premiers temps* (Paris: Charles Estienne Hochereau, 1724). Courtesy of Special Collections, Georgetown University Library.

they thus admitted divine providence implicitly even as their philosophers denied it.

Desideri's treatment of paganism also boasts a literary pedigree; even its polemical aspects would have recalled earlier heights of Italian literature. Boccaccio's *Ninfale fiesolano* speaks of the "false creed of the wicked, corrupt, and lying gods" (*la falsa credenza degl'iddii rei, bugiardi e viziosi*), a phrase that echoes Dante's "time of the false and lying gods" (*al tempo delli dei falsi e bugiardi*).[69] Although a modern reader might be put off by such phrases, we would do well to keep in mind that a Jesuit theologian who comfortably assumed that these gods were the products of poets' fables could just as comfortably adopt them for his own literary ends.[70] The ancient gods and goddesses, properly understood, could be enjoyed just like a riddle, a butterfly, or a well-crafted piece of silk. The Jesuit emblematist Herman Hugo, for example, thought nothing of illustrating his own meditations on the torments of hell with the story of Diana and Actaeon.[71] Nor did Athanasius Kircher hesitate to compare himself to Hermes in his *Obeliscus Pamphilius* or style himself the Oedipus Aegyptiacus in his book of that title. By Desideri's day, the old gods and goddesses had become the tutelary spirits of the age, compelled into the service of the Church much as Padmasaṃbhava compelled the indigenous spirits of Tibet into the service of Buddhism.

In the sixteenth and seventeenth centuries, the gods and goddesses of Asia were generally compelled into service as doubles for better-known Greek or Egyptian deities. More often than not, missionaries treated all non-Christian religions as a single system of deities based on ancient European and Near-Eastern models. Figure 6.3 shows that Desideri's contemporary, the French Jesuit Joseph-François Lafitau, believed he could discern iconographic similarities between ancient Near Eastern myths and the Amerindians of North America by appealing to the rather fantastic renderings of Chinese iconography that we saw in the third chapter. Desideri's description of Tibetan religion took part in this larger trend of domestication, and he consistently traced elements of Tibetan religion to Western models. The cosmology of the land of snows, he argued, was derived from the system propounded by Cosmas Indicopleustes, and Tibetans' description of their land as a prone demoness was a faint hint of the ancient myth of Prometheus.[72] Desideri's readers would have snapped to attention at the description of a Tibetan image of the Wheel possessive of Life as a "hieroglyphic," much as they readily gobbled up other missionaries' references to the "pyramids"—whether Hindu temples or Buddhist stūpas—found in South India and Tibet.[73] Indeed, by Desideri's day, the very word "hieroglyphic" was largely synonymous with "emblem," and the missionary explicitly compared the Wheel of Life, which we can see in figure

FIGURE 6.4. Wheel of Life, Eastern Tibetan, eighteenth-century. Ground Mineral Pigment, Fine Gold Line on Cotton, 23.75 x 16.63 in. Collection of Rubin Museum of Art (HA 591).

FIGURE 6.5. Title page of Giovanni Pinamonti's *L'Inferno aperto* (Milan, 1693). Courtesy of the Bayerische Staatsbibliothek, Munich.

6.4, with the title page of *L'inferno aperto*, Giovanni Pinamonti's book of hellfire mnemonics, which we see in figure 6.5. Desideri's readers would have also found his description of the Samyé oracle reading hieroglyphics in the sky exceedingly Egyptian, and most likely associated the smoking censers, beating drums, and outbreaks of religious violence that occasionally attended the processions of the Nechung oracle with the ancient Greco-Roman mystery cults.[74]

Desideri's reduction of Tibetan religion to European models is nowhere more apparent than when he claims that Tibetan religion was "based on the Pythagorean system," an allusion to Xenophanes's attribution of the doctrine of metempsychosis to Pythagoras and the often-cited—and often-parodied—testimony that Pythagoras had remembered four of his own previous reincarnations.[75] It is difficult to convey the complex range of associations that Desideri would have evoked from his learned readers when he called Tibetans Pythagoreans. Christian humanists of Desideri's day would have been familiar with Pythagoras from a number of sources, since his influence was ubiquitous in the classical world. Desideri's most likely source, given its prominent role in Jesuit education and the Chinese missions, was Aristotle's *De Anima* and its voluminous scholastic commentaries.[76] Matteo Ricci, who shared the same classical curriculum as his Jesuit confrere, dismissed Chinese Buddhist beliefs in similar tones.[77] By identifying Tibet with the sage from Samos, Desideri placed the land of snows in a genealogy that any humanist would have recognized: Plato was taught by Philolaus, the student of Pythagoras, who was taught by Aglaophemus, who was initiated by Orpheus into the ancient theology founded by the Egyptian priest Hermes Trismegistus.[78] Pythagoras bridged ancient Egyptian and classical Greek culture—no mean feat among Renaissance humanists—but was also Italian, at least by adoption, since the ancient sage left Samos and settled in Calabria. Renaissance humanists would have noted proudly that philosophy was first practiced with a religious purpose on Italian soil, and that one of their own could boast of being the first to understand the principles of music as well as the source of the philosophical speculations on number that—through Vitruvius—ruled Italian Renaissance architecture.[79]

Desideri's descriptions of Tibetan architecture take on an otherworldly air when considered in this light. On the surface, the Jesuit simply played the baroque aesthete; he described various Tibetan buildings with his typical meticulousness and noted their strength of construction or slight stylistic flaws. After effusing about the magnificence of the Potala—paying much attention to the higher artistic conceptions displayed by its colonnades and façade—he could not resist stating that its two wings do not quite correspond.[80] In Renaissance architectural treatises, the true architect could manipulate the invisible forces, fantasies, and anxieties called forth by a skillfully crafted building. The *rationes* he created with the interaction of architectural lines and volumes had the power to invoke ideal men, women, or, if a patron's taste so inclined, monsters. Desideri's allusion to Pythagoras, then, would have suggested to his architecturally savvy readers that Tibetans were skilled magicians, not merely able to call down the power of the stars into their idols, but able to raise magical buildings for their own protection. If this speculation seems strange, we should note that Tibetans described their hidden sanctuaries (*sbas yul*) in similar terms, and although Desideri does not mention this particular genre of Tibetan literature, he knew some of its proponents and was well acquainted with Tibetan treasures (*gter ma*) and prophecies, its sister genres. The visualization practices associated with various maṇḍala employed by all Tibetan schools played upon similar tropes. If the Jesuit's interlocutors explained the relationship of the representation he saw—in sand or in paint—to the temple imagined in its visualization, I see no more likely analogue in Desideri's neo-Pythagorean world. In such a reading, Tibetan mystical architecture would be a demonic parody of the *superaedificationes* of the Jesuits' own mnemonic practices.

Desideri's identification of Tibetan religion with Pythagoreanism also allowed him to hint that Tibetan religion had even earlier roots, since his readers would have assumed, like Athanasius Kircher, that all pagan civilizations descended from Egypt.[81] This suggestion, too, is not without positive connotations. The land's status as the birthplace of idolatry seems not to have lessened the vogue for all things Egyptian in early modern Europe: pyramids were common accoutrements to tombs across the continent; obelisks dominated the urban planning of papal Rome; and hieroglyphics served as the inspiration of humanist emblems for two centuries.[82] Arguably, the single most important element of the neo-Egyptian renaissance, however, was the rediscovery of the literature associated with Hermes Trismegistus.[83] Although Hermeticism faced the twin onslaught of Martín del Rio's voluminous refutation and Isaac Causabon's text-critical demythologization of the Hermetic literature, interest in this pseudo-Egyptian sorcery continued well into the eighteenth century.[84] The Society of Jesus tolerated moderate expressions of Christian Hermeticism. Diego Laínez and Jerónimo Nadal had Llullist sympathies, even as figures of no less stature than Francisco Suárez and Robert Bellarmine opposed Llull's doctrines. Joachim Bouvet, inspired by Huet's *Demonstratio evangelica*, felt that the "hieroglyphic" faith of the ancient Chinese demonstrated the invisible things of God in a natural manner, as indeed all creation does, but also with numerical manifestations (*rationes numericas*) after the manner of Pythagorean philosophy and the Kabbalah, which hid the mysteries of the faith in "obscure enigmas."[85] Athanasius Kircher, arguably the chief authority in the baroque age on all things Egyptian, was among the admirers of Jerónimo de Prado and Juan Bautista Villalpando, two Jesuits who

FIGURE 6.6. An Egyptian labyrinth from Athanasius Kircher, *Turris Babel, sive Archontologia* (Amsterdam: Chez Jean Janssons à Waesberge, 1679). Courtesy of Special Collections, The Sheridan Libraries, The John Hopkins University.

specialized in Pythagorean architectural theory.[86] The Jesuit polymath believed that Hermes Trismegistus was a contemporary not of Moses but of Abraham and, more strikingly, that the Egyptian sage taught the hieroglyphs to Fuxi, the mythical inventor of Chinese writing, after Ham and his descendents had migrated eastward from Egypt to China.[87] Despite its ancient pedigree, Kircher still condemned Hermeticism as the "impious teaching of Trismegistus" (*Trismegisti impia doctrina*), citing the great Jesuit debunker Martín del Rio with approval.[88] He also omitted all references to the purity of ancient Chinese religions when he borrowed from missionary accounts; the source of Chinese religion was neither the natural theology of Enoch nor the ancient covenant between God and Noah, but the "idols of the Egyptians."[89]

Such ideas informed Kircher's depiction of the Dalai Lama. Truth be told, the Jesuit polymath's description could hardly have been more sensationalistic. Invisible to all but his closest followers, the Dalai Lama was more malignant force than man in his telling.[90] If Desideri corrected a few of the details in Kircher's portrait, he did nothing to alter its overall effect; like Kircher, he presented the Dalai Lama as an antipope and repeated the scandalous claim of coprophagy.[91] Desideri's readers would have most likely taken his comparison of reincarnation to a labyrinth for an allusion to Egypt, again with Kircher as the forerunner, as we see in figure 6.6.[92]

I do not think that Desideri self-consciously manipulated these tropes to the extent that he encouraged curiosity about Tartars, but the missionary could not have found a more perfect embodiment of European anxieties than the sixth Dalai Lama, a man who was, for all intents and purposes, a living embodiment of pagan Egypt. Blind to his own origins and unaware of his fate, the lecherous pagan pope of Desideri's account used reincarnation to convince his followers of his divinity and ruled from an immense Pythagorean palace whose foundation lay not on the sacred Red Mountain but on the darkest sands of Egypt itself. The Dalai Lama passed upon his people a distillate of the purest paganism, equal parts Egyptian magic and scholastic disputation, swallowed by the credulous to their own ruination. It probably mattered little whether Desideri intended his readers to associate Tibet and Egypt: they could not have missed the similarities. It is hard to imagine how else they would have interpreted his description of the Samyé oracle reading hieroglyphs in the sky, or his repeated references to subterranean caverns, to which the followers of Padmasaṃbhava fled during their persecutions. Indeed, it would not have been thought odd had Desideri identified the sorcerer from Oḍḍiyāna with Pythagoras himself, for the founder of the Tibetan religion curiously found himself in a literary landscape that Europeans associated wholly with Egypt, its phantasmagoric gods, and its cursed treasures.[93]

The Ideal Missionary

Desideri's account of the harrowing events that shook Tibet in the early eighteenth century—whether the fruit of deliberate distortion or wishful thinking—portrayed the fate of a people hanging in the balance between a virtuous Tartar prince and a licentious pagan pope. The one thing necessary to round out this composition was a missionary, especially one who "knew well the arms of the enemy." In this respect, the *Notizie* is also an autobiography: in its pages, the Jesuit presents himself as an ethnographer, a historian, and a theologian, but each of these roles is subsumed into a larger presentation of Desideri as an ideal missionary and Jesuit. It displays a consistent tone of exception: Desideri never fails to mention the talents required to be a success-ful missionary (talents his enemies did not possess), records the patience with which he endured his trials, outlines his many accomplishments, and always stresses his own readiness to comply with orders, whether from his superiors, the father general, the Sacred Congregation for the Propagation of the Faith, or the pope himself. The *Notizie istoriche* consistently defends Desideri's status as a Jesuit as much as it argues for his rights to the mission. Its juridical *narratio* was intended to win the battle with da Montecchio, but also to absolve Ippolito Desideri of any wrongdoing in his often-troubled relations with his superiors.

In retrospect, Desideri appears to have been something of a free agent from the moment he arrived in Goa. His letters from Goa to Leh form a litany of insinuations against the entire hierarchical structure of the Society in India, as though the young Tuscan saw his provincial and other superiors not merely as hurdles to be leapt on the fast track to Tibet—or brushed aside by a patent from the general—but as agents actively seeking his own delay and the consequent delay of the Tibetan mission. As we have seen, Desideri cast Freyre in the same accusatory light, although probably for good reason.[94] But if Desideri so eagerly sought Tamburini's direct supervision—and freedom from his superiors in India—before he set off for Tibet, he seems to have taken the opposite course of action after Tamburini ordered him to leave Tibet. To silence insinuations— real or imagined—that he had not complied with the orders of the Sacred Congregation, Desideri maintained that he undertook the mission to Tibet only in obedience to his superiors.[95] He even protested—somewhat weakly— that his return to Europe would arouse the suspicion that he had been dismissed from the mission. If Desideri imagined that he could appeal to the pope against the wishes of the general, he acted too hastily, for the infamous fourth vow of the Jesuits, which placed them under the direct orders of the supreme pontiff, applied only to the professed. Desideri was not yet among that elite group when he wrote Tamburini, and antagonizing the general was probably not the best *modus procendi*.[96] We have also seen that Desideri defied the order to return to a Jesuit house in the Portuguese Assistancy and sought refuge with Jean Bouchet in the French-run Puducherry, where he finally finagled an opportunity to return to Rome to protest the ruling of the Sacred Congregation.

The discrepancies between the missionary's epistolary self-presentation and his self-presentation in the *Notizie istoriche* are subtle, but noteworthy, indications of his rhetorical skill. Desideri's letters are refreshingly frank; he expresses his doubts, suspicions, hope, and anger with particular vehemence, as Ignatius Loyola had instructed missionaries. The *Notizie*, on the other hand, is a polished rhetorical work. One of its salient strategies—and one his Jesuit readers would have picked up immediately—is a near constant recourse to the language of the *Spiritual Exercises*. The opening sentence invokes the prompt service the *Exercises* meant to inculcate in young Jesuits, and Desideri ascribes his mission to the "inner impulse" that he successfully discerned.[97] He always notes his ready compliance.[98] Desideri also makes repeated reference to his submission to the divine will from his initial trials at sea to the loss of his mission, echoing both the *Exercises* and the spirituality of abandonment to divine Providence of Jesuit theologians such as Jean-Pierre de Caussade. The *Notizie* repeatedly insists that Desideri was chosen to open the Tibetan mission before he left Rome, whether by Tamburini or by Pope Clement XI.[99] The Jesuit's account starts off with the father general ordering Desideri to open the mission to Tibet that had been begun by António de Andrade in 1624. Next we find Desideri at the feet of Pope Clement XI being blessed to undertake this very mission.[100] It is difficult not to think that the juxtaposition of these two benedictions is meant to absolve the young missionary from any wrongdoing in the Tibetan mission, if not continue his controversy with Tamburini himself. Desideri's appeal to Pope Clement XI fortified his claim to being a model of obedience, since it echoed the primary sense of mission given in the Society's Constitutions. It also allowed him a sarcastic aside about his superiors. When told that the Jesuit was destined for the Tibetan mission, Desideri has the pope exclaim, "How far!" (*tanto lontano*), and upon hearing that Desideri was a Jesuit, the pope mutters, "*Dabit panem arctum et acquam brevem.*" The grammar of Desideri's allusion to Isaiah 30:20 is ambiguous; it is not clear whether the mission would give Desideri "the bread of adversity and the water of affliction" or whether the Society of Jesus would do the honors. Most likely, the disaffected Jesuit intended this ambiguity. Tellingly, Desideri's account of his meeting with Clement XI is found only in his later writings, long after the pontiff had passed away.

The *Notizie istoriche* glides similarly over Desideri's differences with Freyre. As we saw in the second chapter, Desideri was incensed by Freyre's refusal to stay in Leh, and he did not hesitate to write a seething letter reporting Freyre's actions to Tamburini. In the *Notizie*, Desideri makes no mention of his reluctance to leave Leh for Lhasa, but rather claims that Lhasa was his destination all along. He never refers to Freyre as his superior, but always as his "companion," and does his best to give the impression that the two fathers conferred and made decisions as equals.[101] At the end of the day, Desideri even adopted Freyre's own story of wanting to return to the warmer climate of India to suit his own purpose. Similarly, in recounting one of his first interviews in Lhazang Khan's court, Desideri's original letter says that he told the court he intended to stay in Tibet until he died—a sentiment especially worthy of being read for the edification of Jesuit novices back home. In his later account, the Jesuit says that he told the court he intended to stay until his death unless prevented by the king or "by orders from my superior."[102] While it makes perfect sense to acknowledge Lhazang Khan's jurisdiction in such circumstances, it seems quite unnecessary to mention the Jesuit vow of obedience to a Mongol chieftain and his court. Most likely, this aside was meant for his European readers. Obedience, after all, is better than sacrifices.

Desideri's self-presentation aims a few barbs at the Capuchins, too. Presumably the Jesuit meant to argue his case for the Tibetan mission in the press, and Felice da Montecchio was prudent to block its publication. In Desideri's surprisingly curt account, Father da Ascoli rushes away immediately after Domenico da Fano arrives in 1710. When Giovanni da Fano arrives a year later, Desideri tells his readers that the Capuchin father convinced the lone Capuchin present to abandon the mission altogether.[103] Desideri also contrasted his linguistic ability with the Capuchins'. No matter where we find the young Jesuit in his account, he takes care enough to note that he learned the language and composed books and sermons. We find him learning Persian in Kashmir before he entered Tibet and Tamil in Puducherry after he left.[104] When Desideri mentioned the great effort it took to learn these languages, he certainly had in mind the failure of the Capuchin fathers to do so. The Jesuit never resorted to outright slander and always gave the Capuchin fathers credit where it was due. When discussing Tibetan medicine, Desideri remarked that the Capuchin fathers displayed great charity by distributing medicine freely among the Tibetans and by curing their sick while refusing any money. In doing so, he acknowledged that the Capuchin fathers secured the salvation of many souls.[105] Even so, he could not refrain from leveling many of the charges that would later come up before the tribunal of the Sacred Congregation, including his claim the Capuchins did not understand the word *könchok* (*dkon mchog*) and thus identified the Buddhist Three Jewels with the Holy Trinity.

The *dispositio* of Desideri's chapters is especially effective in undermining competing Capuchin claims. In the first book of the *Notizie*, Desideri describes his journey to Lhasa, enumerates his complete Tibetan writings, recounts the history of the Jesuit missions of which he was a part from Jerónimo Xavier to the present, and only then resumes his narrative with the imminent arrival of the Capuchins in October 1716. This clever prolepsis allows Desideri to give the impression that he was fully formed as a missionary, both linguistically and spiritually, before the Capuchins arrived, and fortifies his claim that he introduced the Capuchins to Lhazang Khan and instructed them in Tibetan. In order to dispel any suspicion that he wrote his account to criticize the Capuchins, Desideri recounted his own misunderstanding of the word *könchok* and admitted that he, too, had thought that it meant "God" and had drawn a number of false conclusions about Tibetans and their religion because of his mistake. He admitted that he thought the people of Ladakh and western Tibet did not believe in reincarnation and even believed that they had some knowledge of God and the Holy Trinity because they used the phrases *könchok chik*, "one jewel," and *könchok sum*, "three jewels." He justified his mistake by noting that all who travel in these regions, whether European, Armenian, Russian, or Muslim, fall into the error of assuming that the word *könchok* signifies "God."[106] Desideri's earnestness, however genuine, did not entirely conceal a more subtle insinuation. If Desideri cloaked his pleas in mock self-effacement, he still aimed straight at the most vulnerable failures of the Capuchin mission. Not only did he implicitly criticize their lack of Tibetan language skills, he accused them of unwittingly accommodating Christianity to Tibetan religion as a result. By admitting his own mistake, Desideri highlighted the possibility that the same could happen again to other missionaries unless he returned to Tibet to instruct them.

Desideri's Theology of the Missions

If Desideri's prologue serves as a *captatio benevolentiae* and the four books of the *Notizie istoriche* as a formal *narratio*, the four chapters with which Desideri ends his account are an *exhortatio* to the missions. Overtly theological—and most likely omitted from Filippi's translation for that reason—these chapters are perhaps the most passionate pages in an already passionate oeuvre. Replete with quotations from the Bible, the Fathers of the Church, and the *Summa theologiae*—as well as frequent exclamations—these chapters give us the clearest sense of how Desideri understood his own undertaking. This theology of the missions, which he himself characterized as "ample and sublime," defies easy summation.[107] It is composed of a series of moral *exempla* taken from the lives of the men and women of the Old and New Testament, a biblical theology of idolatry, and a Thomistic account of the moral imperative of "spiritual" almsgiving. It offers a cosmic counterpoint to the more mundane political aspects of Desideri's self-presentation that we have just seen, for in these last four chapters the Jesuit outlines the qualities of the ideal missionary and expresses his eschatological hopes for the conversion of all people to Catholicism. Desideri's theology of mission also serves as a mirror of sorts, in which we can see some of his most fervent hopes echoed in the Tibetan stories he read while on the roof of the world.

Desideri's *conclusio* is a theological recapitulation of the entire *Notizie*. It begins, like the prologue, with an appeal to curiosity and the need to study the minutiae of another culture; having satisfied the curiosity of the scholars and eminent persons, however, the Jesuit now appealed to the missionary as the paragon of curiosity in the specific sense in which Ignatius Loyola used the term. The ideal missionary, Desideri says, should have a natural excellence and a superior intellect. He should show an aptitude for the mechanical arts, for the sciences, and for teaching, which is to say, for logic, natural philosophy, metaphysics, medicine, astronomy, theology, and whatever intellectual ornaments a man might attain while a pilgrim in this world.[108] The missionary must possess nerve and vigor to combat idolatry, confute false systems, and persuade his charges. Above all, such a missionary must manifest a "magnanimous heart" in the face of insults, threats, torture, and death. He must, in sum, be subtle as a serpent and gentle as a dove. Aside from the appeal to martyrdom, it is difficult to escape the conclusion that the ideal missionary should come from a patrician family and be educated according to the norms of the Ratio Studiorum; in other words, the model for the ideal missionary might very well appear to be none other than Desideri himself.

To be fair, though, Desideri probably adopted a high style because he intended his work to be read for the edification of Jesuit novices. Like the tone he adopted when describing Tsering Döndrup or the Dalai Lama, no one would have thought it out of the ordinary given the conventions of such literature. Condemning commonness and mediocrity as incompatible with the profound teaching and sublime wisdom necessary for the "grand undertaking" of the missions, Desideri appealed to the preaching of St. Stephen, the first martyr, and to the travels of St. Paul, the first and greatest of all missionaries to the gentiles.[109] Like many treatises on missiology, Desideri's treats the story of St. Paul in the Areopagus from the seventeenth chapter of the Acts of the Apostles as a model for the ideal missionary. Unlike most modern theologies of interreligious dialogue, however, Desideri does not appeal to the Apostle's famous invocation of the "unknown God" (Acts 17:23) to justify non-Christian religious sensibilities, but rather treats St. Paul as an *exemplum* illustrating the intellectual and moral capacities necessary to learn "abstruse" philosophical systems. The Jesuit emphasizes the Apostle's difficulties and the Athenians' incredulity. Ippolito Desideri's Paul is the apostle who was violently hauled before the crowd at the Areopagus and accused of proclaiming new divinities (*alij vero, novorum daemoniorum videtur annunciator esse*) and teaching strange things (*nova enim quaedam infers auribus nostris*) (Acts 17:18–19). Desideri's Paul is the apostle who disputed Greeks (or Hellenists) in Jerusalem (Acts 9:29) and disputed his fellow Jews in the synagogue at Corinth (Acts 18:4). Desideri's Paul is reviled and mocked, but ultimately sustained by God (Acts 13:45).

Confrontation is the dominant metaphor of these pages, and the next chapter—ostensibly about the "nerve and vigor" necessary to refute intricate philosophical systems—reads like a series of biblical variations on Cicero's comparison of persuasion to military victory. Not one to beat around the bush, the Jesuit took his first illustration from the story of Judith and Holofernes in medias res:

> And she struck his neck twice with all her might and severed his head from his body. Then she pushed his body off the bed, pulled the canopy from its posts, and after a moment went out, giving Holofernes' head to her attendant, who placed it in her purse. (Jud 13:8)

Given the Ciceronian metaphor, it makes sense that Desideri encourages missionaries to imitate Judith's ingenuity. At first glance, it seems strange—at least to this reader—to urge them to imitate her natural charm (*natural bellezza*), but Desideri is simply developing his theme of the need for subtlety in missionaries; later he will turn to the patriarch Jacob, who was also famous for his cunning. Following a predominantly visual logic of the sort favored by Renaissance mnemonics, Desideri moves from Judith's triumph to a series of other biblical tableaux that feature scenes of decapitation. He naturally turns to David's victory over Goliath (1 Sam 17:51) and then to the more mysterious fate of the idol Dagon, which was found with its head and hands broken off after the Philistines offered it the Ark of the Covenant in tribute (1 Sam 5:1–5). Desideri draws his subsequent lessons from two stories that close the Vulgate text of the Book of Daniel. In both, a king asks the prophet to worship an idol, but Daniel stands firm in his faith in the God of Israel, and later exposes the folly of the idolatry. In the first, wicked priests have fooled the Babylonians into thinking that the idol Bel is a living god by staging his daily consumption of twelve bushels of fine flour, forty sheep, and fifty gallons of wine. When Daniel uncovers their ruse, the king abruptly puts the priests to death and gives the statue of Bel to Daniel, who promptly destroys it and the surrounding temple (Dan 14:21). In the second, Daniel refuses to worship a dragon, which he promises to slay without using a sword or a club. Mixing pitch, fat, and hair into cakes, Daniel feeds the dragon, which promptly bursts asunder. After mocking the Babylonians for worshiping a mere creature, the prophet is cast into a den of lions by jealous idolaters. When the king discovers Daniel unharmed after seven days, he orders the men who plotted against him to be fed to the lions, which immediately devour them before the onlookers' eyes (Dan 14:41).

One could multiply such violent references indefinitely. Just as Desideri's vocabulary for Tibetan religion strained to find ever-new synonyms for witchcraft, these final four chapters run the gamut when describing the destructive acts meted out against idols. In one of his more shocking texts, Desideri offers an extended spiritual exegesis of the fifth chapter of the first book of Maccabees, in which Judas Maccabeus attacks the cities of Bozrah and Carnaim. Desideri picks up the story when a "large army" of gentiles has gathered to attack the Jews (1 Macc 5:38). Judas Maccabeus emerges victorious over this army only because he exhorted every man to enter the fight, and Desideri quickly seizes upon this injunction to urge Catholics to give themselves for the spiritual battle of the missions. The Jesuit also follows this story to its bloody conclusion. Judas Maccabeus crosses the stream and leads the entire force of Jews against the gentile army:

> All the gentiles were defeated before him, and they cast their weapons aside and fled to the temple that was in Carnaim. But he took the city and the temple he burnt with fire, together with all who were in it. Thus Carnaim was conquered, and could not stand before the face of Judas. (1 Macc 5:43–44)

Warming to his theme, Desideri imagines the enemies of the Church conquered, exclaiming:

> The repentant peoples, long of heart and vomiting forth their superstitious laws, will renounce their false opinions and detest their monstrous dogmas: *they cast their weapons aside.* Triumphant missionaries will be able to destroy the vain mosques and

superstitious temples freely with fire, and be able to smash with iron bars obscure idols and sacrilegious altars: *the temple he burnt with fire, together with all who were in it.* Infidelity conquered and falling, unable to sustain its errors any longer before the Gospel; faith triumphant, glorious in every kingdom, and in every corner of the world: *Carnaim was conquered and could not stand before the face of Judas.*[110]

This admittedly purple passage is followed—incredibly—by a dispassionate reiteration of Tibetan errors, a brief discussion of *The Great Stages of the Path*, and another list of the books that Desideri composed in Tibetan.

But one can almost turn to any page in the final four chapters of the *Notizie istoriche* to find similarly passionate passages:

> Let all join together in Guinea and Ethiopia and Monopotapa and Socotra and Maranhão and Malabar and the Mughal Empire and China and Japan and a hundred other most afflicted kingdoms and empires of Africa, Asia, and America, to confute errors, to abolish superstitions, to smash infernal idols by the millions, to tear down countless sacrilegious temples, to baptize kings and to convert people, to build churches and institute Christianity with sweat, with toil, with fervor, with blood, with the martyrdom of the most zealous and upright missionaries in every part of the world and among innumerable nations, magnificent trophies and splendid triumphs of the holy Catholic faith! Ah! The martyrs still cry out! Ah![111]

For the record, I do not believe that Ippolito Desideri actually advocated razing mosques or smashing idols "by the millions." He certainly never raised a hand against any Tibetan statue or temple and, as far as we can tell, was nothing but courteous and respectful to Tibetans. While the Jesuit was probably a bit too vigorous in the application of his extended metaphor, such confrontations were a staple of missionary lore, hearkening to the confrontations between Moses and the pharaoh's magicians (Ex 7:8–13), between Elijah and the priests of Baal (1 Kings 18: 20–40), between St. Peter and Simon Magus (cf. Acts 8:9–24), even between Christ and Satan himself (Mt 4:1–11; Mk 1:12–13; Lk 4:1–13). Desideri's description of his encounter with Padmasaṃbhava on Mount Kailash earlier in the *Notizie* is a wonderful variation on this theme:

> On the ninth of November, we arrived at the highest point of our journey, in fact the highest point that we reached in all of our wandering. This place—a bleak desert indeed—is greatly respected

and venerated on account of a certain Urgyen, who established the
religion or sect that one finds in Tibet. Away from the road is a
mountain of excessive height, quite large in circumference, its
summit enveloped in cloud and perpetually encased in snow and ice,
which remains quite horrible and austere, for it is most bitterly cold.
Urgyen lived for some time in complete solitude and continuous
contemplation in a cave carved from the living rock of this
mountain.[112]

This description may seem dry enough to us today, but to his readers, it would
have bristled with tension. Windswept deserts and lonely mountain peaks were
common settings in Christian literature, portending epic temptations and
terrible battles. Just as Matteo Ricci's readers would have caught the biblical
allusions when he spoke of China as *un deserto si lontano* or its people as *questa
remotissima gente*, Desideri's readers would have shivered with fear when he
referred to the Himalayas as "the very picture of desolation, horror, and death
itself."[113] Since scientists of Desideri's day still believed that the irregularities
on the earth's surface, such as mountain ranges and deep river gorges, formed
only as the waters of Noah's flood subsided, it is no exaggeration to say that
Desideri most likely thought that the very existence of the Himalayas, including the mountain upon which the missionary confronted Padmasaṃbhava,
spoke of the most ancient sins of the human race.[114] His Jesuit readers would
have recalled the many times they composed mental images of the desolate
plains around Babylon in dark rooms set aside for their meditation on the Two
Standards from the *Spiritual Exercises*. The bitter cold, piercing winds, and
terrifying ice would have caused his erudite Tuscan readers to think of the
lowest realms of the Inferno, where Dante saw "a thousand faces made doglike
by the cold."[115]

No stranger to spiritual combat, the Catholic Church deployed its own
thaumaturges in the war for souls and took evident delight in the miracles they
performed. Desideri unabashedly described the miracles of the saints who
preceded him in the Asian missions and treated his readers to several
anecdotes calculated to instill in them the faith that the Holy Spirit still
performed miracles in the Church. Agra was the site of several Christian
miracles, including many that had occurred at the tomb of the Jesuit missionary Jerónimo Xavier through the intercession of Marc'Antonio Santucci. Desideri did not fail to notice that Muslims and Hindus also came to pray at Xavier's
tomb, nor that they believed that its dust "cured every malady." Desideri
himself believed that the intercession of St. Venantius had saved him from
an avalanche between Srinagar and Ladakh, and that João de Brito, a martyr of

the Jesuit missions whose canonization documents Desideri carried to Rome, had healed him of illness as he passed Mozambique on his return journey. His letters ask that Masses be offered for the success of his mission, and his final exhortation appeals to the Catholic mystics St. Gertrude the Great, St. Catherine of Siena, St. Teresa of Avila, and St. Maria Maddalena deï Pazzi, whose "tears, wails, fasts, mortifications, and fervent daily prayers" at home assisted apostolic missionaries abroad.[116] Writings on the missions went hand in hand with larger mystical, even eschatological aspirations. The Jesuit missionary António Vieira, in his wonderfully titled *História do futuro*, asserted that the activities of the Society in Brazil had been foretold by Daniel's prophecy of a fifth and final monarchy that preceded the final judgment—a prophecy that justified more than a few political revolutions in the early modern world.[117] Catholics and Protestants alike associated the conversion of Asians and Americans with the final events in world history.[118] Although opposition to the Protestant Reformation played a minuscule and indirect role in the Asia missions, Jesuits sometimes depicted other religions in terms of Protestantism, just as later Protestant missionaries decried the "papist" rituals of Buddhists and Hindus.[119] Often the success or failure of a Protestant missionary was judged more in terms of his confrontation with Catholicism than with the indigenous followers of another religion.[120] Desideri worried little about Protestants—he seems to have enjoyed an urbane friendship with at least one, the Dutch traveler Samuel van de Putte—but the eschatological tone of his own missionary aspirations marks him as a Jesuit of the pre-Suppression Society to the end.

The images of Tibet in Desideri's writings vary—some are sharp, some distorted; few are monstrous, none divine—but in one instance in the third book of the *Notizie*, after turning mirror against mirror, we can see Desideri's missionary aspirations reflected in a Tibetan tale. In a paradox of the sort beloved by Jorge Luis Borges, Desideri tells his readers about Trisong Detsen, an ancient Tibetan king of "sublime genius" (*ingegno sublime*), "extraordinary prudence" (*straordinaria prudenza*), and "a magnanimous heart" (*un cuor magnanimo*)—all qualities that Desideri extols in the ideal missionary.[121] As an expression of his magnanimity, Trisong Detsen wished for nothing more than a true religion for his subjects. He gathered the best and brightest Tibetans, fired their passion for adventure, and sent them on a long journey, where they suffered indignation at the hands of barbarians, crossed rugged mountains, and, after arriving in India, struggled to master a foreign tongue, only to have wicked ministers and black magicians sully the faith the king's apostolic missionaries brought home. The teachings corrupted, the wise and sublime king Trisong Detsen called upon an uncommonly strong thaumaturge. With this final note, Desideri can turn an ornate Tibetan mirror upon himself. Called to Tibet for the greater glory of God, the Jesuit missionary met a magnanimous king, wicked ministers, and all manners of black magic. In doing so, he found his mission not merely confirmed in the teachings of the Catholic Church but prophesied in the Tibetan tales themselves. I like to imagine that as he followed an ancient sorcerer's footsteps across Tibet, Ippolito Desideri came to think of himself as a second Padmasaṃbhava, locked in battle with demons for the land of snows, and intending to repeat his rival's great feats for the Roman Catholic Church.

Epilogue

Ippolito Desideri died in 1733, leaving the *Notizie istoriche* unpublished. It is customary to end scholarly accounts of his work by lamenting his loss of the Tibetan mission and the subsequent oblivion of his account. Such lamentations generally identify the missionary's loss of the Tibetan mission as a loss for Buddhist Studies, even though an early eighteenth-century Jesuit missionary would have recognized neither the academic field of study nor the modern institutions in which it is taught. The modern Tibetologist's lament allows him to adopt one of the dominant tropes of Desideri's own account while implicating the Jesuit in a progressive narrative that Desideri himself would have rejected. For the sake of historical precision, we must admit that had Ippolito Desideri's own wishes been fulfilled, Tibetans would have deposed the Dalai Lama, cast aside their idols, and become Roman Catholics of the most fervent Tridentine variety. Indeed, the people of the land of snows would not be Buddhists at all, and their infinite bodhisattvas—Avalokiteśvara and Padmasaṃbhava included—would cavort, like so many nymphs and satyrs, across the erudite canvases of the late baroque era. For Desideri, the loss of the Tibetan mission was a loss for the Society of Jesus but, what is more important, also meant the eternal perdition of countless Tibetans. For Desideri, the threat of idolatry was real. He likened the man who ignored it to Nero, who strummed a guitar "while Rome and the surrounding towns perished in hungry flames."[122] No doubt the missionary was deeply moved by the extended meditations on hell he read in Tsongkhapa's *The Great Stages of the Path*, for he could not have but associated them with the meditations that make up the first and second weeks of the *Spiritual Exercises*, meditations that in all likelihood spurred his first fantasies of being a missionary. If his concern for the damnation of Tibetans measures the distance between him and his more modern readers, it draws the Jesuit closer to the concerns of the Tibetans themselves. Ippolito Desideri felt Tibetans' suffering—if I may borrow a metaphor—not like a hair in his hand but like a hair in his eye, and he responded as any bodhisattva would in such circumstances. He did everything in his power to save them; indeed, his own salvation depended upon it. "One who saves a sinner from the error of his ways," Desideri reminded readers on the last page of the *Notizie istoriche*, "saves his own soul from death, and covers a multitude of sins" (James 5:20).[123]

Had Desideri not lost his mission to the Capuchins, he would have witnessed even greater bloodshed in Tibet. In September 1723 the Kökenuur Khoshud revolted against Manchu rule and were crushed into submission, thereby ending their dreams of restoring the glory once enjoyed by their ancestor Güüshi Khan. After weakening the Tibetans' economy and exhausting their granaries, the Manchu military garrison left the Tibetans to fight among themselves, and fight they did. As tensions grew between the various Tibetan factions that survived the wars of 1717–20, the Geluk in Yongzheng's court pressured him to issue an edict outlawing sorcery, which led to another series of persecutions of the Nyingma. Tibetan factions were again polarized, with Kangchené and Polhané from Ngari and Tsang on the one side and the Geluk from central Tibet and Amdo on the other. Desideri's old friend Kangchené, in an attempt to court favor with the opposing party, encouraged the persecutions. Government officials stabbed him to death during a cabinet meeting on August 5, 1727. The next morning his wife and sister were hacked to pieces. On July 3, 1728, Polhané and a coalition of Tsangpa Geluk emerged victorious over the Lhasa triumvirate of Ngapöpa, Lumpané, and Jarawa. A Manchu force arrived shortly thereafter, carrying an imperial edict granting temporal power to the Panchen Lama—a move that strengthened Polhané at the expense of the seventh Dalai Lama, who was effectively banished from central Tibet from 1728 to 1735. The Capuchin fathers meanwhile continued to evangelize Tibet without success. They abandoned their mission in 1733 and reestablished it in 1741. The following year, Benedict XIV ended all discussion on the issue of accommodation in the missions, siding against the Jesuits. Polhané, under pressure from the Tibetan ecclesiastical authorities, ordered all foreigners out of Tibet on April 20, 1745, beginning its political isolation and sowing the seeds of Europe's fascination with the mythical land of Shangri-la. After Kelzang Gyatso's death in 1757, Mongol delegates of the Manchu court chose the candidates for his office, thereby preventing the headaches that the Dalai Lamas had caused the Qing Dynasty during the reign of Kangxi. As a result, the office of the Dalai Lama would remain powerless until the collapse of the Manchu dynasty. Only then would the thirteenth and fourteenth Dalai Lamas attempt to unify Tibet in the face of greater dangers, and only then would they look to the West.

Abbreviations Used in Notes

A. TIBETAN WRITINGS OF IPPOLITO DESIDERI

Tho rangs	*Tho rangs mun sel nyi ma shar ba'i brda*
Sems can dang chos	*Sems can dang chos la sogs pa rnams kyi 'byung khungs*
Chos lugs	*Ke ri se ste aṇ kyi chos lugs kyi snying po*
Skye ba snga ma	*Mgo skar bla ma i po li do shes bya ba yis phul ba'i bod*
	kyi mkhas pa rnams la skye ba snga ma dang stong pa
	nyid kyi lta ba'i sgo nes zhu ba

B. MISSIONARY WRITINGS

CL	Cappuccini, Lettere
CR	Cappuccini, Relazioni
DD	Desideri, Difese
DL	Desideri, Lettere
DR	Desideri, Relazione
MITN	*I Missionari italiani nel Tibet e nel Nepal*
OT	*Opere Tibetane di Ippolito Desideri, S.J.*

C. OTHER COLLECTIONS AND ARCHIVES

APF	Archivio della S. Congregazione de Propaganda Fide
AHSI	*Archivum Historicum Societatis Iesu*
ARSI	Archivum Romanum Societatis Iesu
CLE	*Corpus Librorum Emblematum*

DI   Documenta Indica
DS   Denzinger-Schönmetzer, *Enchiridion Symbolorum* (36th ed.)
IHSI   Institutum Historicum Societatis Iesu
IJS   Institute of Jesuit Sources
IsIAO   Istituto italiano per l'Africa e l'Oriente
IsMEO   Istituto italiano per il Medio ed Estremo Oriente
MI   Monumenta Ignatiana
MHSI   Monumenta Historica Societatis Iesu
PG   Patrologiae cursus completa, series Graeca
PL   Patrologiae cursus completa, series Latina
SF   Sinica Franciscana
Somm.   Sommervogel, *Bibliotheque de la Compagnie de Jesus*

Notes

INTRODUCTION

   1. For a bibliography of Desideri's writings, see Giuseppe Toscano, S.X., *Opere Tibetane di Ippolito Desideri, S.J.* (Rome: IsMEO, 1981), 3, pp. 31–63; Enzo Gualtiero Bargiacchi, *Ippolito Desideri S.J. Opere e Bibliografia*, Subsidia ad Historiam Societatis Iesu 15 (Rome: IHSI, 2007). Cf. Pietro Angelini, *Leggere il Tibet: bibliografia italiana del paese delle nevi, 1624–1993* (Bologna: Il Nove, 1994). For the textual history of Desideri's Italian manuscripts, see Enzo Gualtiero Bargiacchi, "La *Relazione* di Ippolito Desideri fra storia locale e vicende internazionali," *Storialocale: Quaderni pistoiesi di cultura moderna e contemporanea* 2 (Pistoia, 2003), pp. 4–103, especially 14–50. The same author's other works also represent the most advanced surveys of Desideri's travels. Cf. Enzo Gualtiero Bargiacchi, *Ippolito Desideri S.J. alla scoperta del Tibet e del buddhismo* (Pistoia: Edizioni Brigata del Leoncino, 2006); "Il contributo di Ippolito Desideri alla conoscenza geografica," *L'Universo* 84 (Florence: Istituto Geografico Militare, 2005), pp. 788–807. For a general survey with some newly discovered information, see Bargiacchi, *A Bridge Across Two Cultures: Ippolito Desideri, S.J. (1684–1733), a Brief Biography* (Florence: Istituto Geografico Militare, 2008).

   2. Of these manuscripts, the first, commonly referred to as the "Florentine manuscript," or Ms. F, bears the title *Breve e succinto Ragguaglio del Viaggio alle Indie Orientali del Padre Ippolito Desideri della Compagnia di Gesù.* It is a quarto volume of 316 folios, written consecutively, without division into parts or chapters, except for the odd appearance of chapters numbered 13, 14, and 15 at the end of the volume. This was the manuscript discovered by Carlo Puini in a private collection in Pistoia in 1875 and passed to the National Library in Florence. It shows obvious signs of being dictated, but

the possibility remains that it was only partially dictated, since it bears the writing of three different hands. Another manuscript, Ms. C, which totals 159 pages, is identical to the first 112 folios of the Florentine manuscript, save orthographical mistakes. A second version of his travels, Ms. A, which is held in the Archivum Romanum Societatis Iesu, is a slightly smaller volume, written in a pleasant hand for 222 folios, with a preface, three books, and a table of contents. There has been some debate about whether the writing is Desideri's own. Its title is the one most generally known today, *Notizie istoriche del Thibet e Memorie de' viaggi e Missione ivi fatta dal Padre Ippolito Desiderj della Compagnia di Giesù, dal medesimo scritte e dedicate.* The table of contents shows four books, including a missing third book on Tibetan religion in twenty-two chapters. Its colophon bears the invocation "Laus Deo, Beatissimae Virgini Mariae ac Sto Francisco Xaverio, Indiarum Apostolo" and the date June 22, 1728, although the title page says 1712–1733, which indicates that the manuscript was prepared shortly before the missionary's death. Attached to this manuscript are printed appendices entitled *Alla Sacra Congregazione di Propaganda Fide*, which are the printed "defenses" of Desideri's case before the bureaucratic office that coordinated the missions. A fourth version of his travels exists in two manuscripts, Mss. B1 and B2. The original, which bears the title *Relazione de' viaggi all'Indie del P. Ippolito Desiderj della Compagnia di Gesù. Distinta relazione de Regni del Thibet: del governo, costumi e setta di quei popoli, scritta dal medesimo e dedicate*, is a quarto volume of 296 folios and appears to stand midway between the Florentine manuscript and Ms. A, as if it were a heavily elided and expanded version of Ms. F, divided into books and chapters so that Desideri could prepare for the writing of Ms. A. The corrected version, incidentally, bears the same title as Ms. A, the *Notizie istoriche.* Ms. B is the only manuscript that contains what we now know as the third book on Tibetan religion. Cornelius Wessels believed the writing of Ms. A to be that of an amanuensis. P. Tacchi Venturi and G. Vacca believed it to be written by Desideri himself. Cornelius Wessels, *Early Jesuit Travellers in Central Asia 1603–1721* (The Hague: Martinus Nijhoff, 1924); P. Tacchi Venturi, "Desideri," *Enciclopedia Italiana*, vol. 12 (1931), pp. 678–79; G. Vacca, "Manoscritti del Padre Ippolito Desideri," *Bollettino della R. Societa Geografica Italiana*, series VI, vol. 9 (1932), p. 524. Petech's critical redaction comprises the first two books of Ms. A, includes the book on Tibetan religion from B$_2$ for its third book, and adds the third book of Ms. A for its fourth and final book. These are gathered in Luciano Petech, *I Missionari italiani nel Tibet e nel Nepal*, 7 vols. (Rome, 1954). Petech's critical edition restores the portions on Tibetan religion and culture that were mysteriously omitted from Ms. A, although it honors its multiple elisions of political and historical matters. I have followed Petech for my own work here, but future studies of Desideri will do well to explain the motives behind his changes, especially in light of the rather drastic elisions of the juicier, political details and the entire section on Tibetan religion. A partial translation of Desideri's account exists in English, which unfortunately leaves out much of value for an understanding of Desideri's own conception of his mission: Filippo de Filippi, *An Account of Tibet: The Travels of Ippolito Desideri of Postoia S.J., 1712–1727*, rev. ed. (London: George Routledge & Sons, 1937). Translations of most, but not all, of Desideri's letters, can also be found in

H. Hosten, "Letters and Other Papers of Fr. Ippolito Desideri, S.J., a Missionary in Tibet 1713–1721," *Journal of the Asiatic Society of Bengal* (1938), pp. 567–767. For an annotated bibliography, see Enzo Gualtiero Bargiacchi, *Ippolito Desideri S.J. Opere e Bibliografia*, Subsidia ad Historiam S.I. 15 (Rome: IHSI, 2007), pp. 1–20.

3. Carlo Puini, "Di alcune lettere inedite o ignorate del P. Ippolito Desideri d.C.d. g., missionario nel Tibet," in *Al Professore Giovanni Marinelli nel 25° anniversario delle sue nozze* (Florence: M. Ricci, 1895), pp. 5–8; "Lhasa secondo la descrizione che ne fa Ippolito Desideri nella Relazione inedita del suo viaggio nel Tibet," *La Cultura geografica* 6–7 (1899), pp. 71–74; "Il P. Ippolito Desideri e i suoi viaggi nell'India e nel Tibet (1712–1727)," *Studi Italiani di Filologia Indo-Iranica* 3 (1899), pp. i–xxxii; "Il Buddhismo nel Tibet secondo la Relazione inedita del P. Ippolito Desideri," *Studi Italiani di Filologia Indo-Iranica* 3 (Florence, 1899), pp. 1–61; "Il matrimonio nel Tibet," *Rivista Italiana di Sociologia* 4, fasc. II (Rome, 1900), pp. 149–68; "Viaggio nel Tibet del P. Ippolito Desideri," *Rivista Geografica Italiana* 7, fasc. X (Florence, 1900), pp. 565–82; *Il Tibet (Geografica, Storia, Religione, Costumi); secondo la Relazione del Viaggio di Ippolito Desideri 1715–1721* (Rome: Società Geografica Italiana, 1904). At the same time, Alberto Magnaghi published his "La Relazione inedita di un viaggio nel Tibet del Padre Cassiano Beligatti da Macerata," *Rivista Geografica Italiana* 11, fasc. III (1904), pp. 96–108.

4. Clements Robert Markham, "Discovery of Father Desideri's Journal in Tibet," *The Geographical Magazine* 3 (1876), p. 20; Hermann von Schlagintweit, *Reisen in Indiën und Hochasiën*, 4 vols. (Jena: H. Costenoble, 1869–80); W. W. Rockhill, *The Land of the Lamas: Notes from a Journey Through China, Mongolia, and Tibet* (London: Longmans Green, 1891); *Diary of a Journal Through Mongolia and Tibet in 1891 and 1892* (Washington: Smithsonian, 1894); L. Austine Waddell, *The Buddhism of Tibet, or Lamaism, with Its Mystic Cults, Symbolism, and Mythology, and its Relation to Indian Buddhism* (London: W. H. Allen, 1895); Georg Wegener, *Tibet und die Englische Expedition* (Halle: Gebauer-Schwetscheke druckerei und Verlag, 1904).

5. Graham Sandberg, *The Exploration of Tibet: Its History and Particulars from 1623 to 1904* (Calcutta: Thacker and Spink, 1904), pp. 52–53; Perceval Landon, *Lhasa, an Account of the Country and People of Central Tibet and of the Progress of the Mission Sent There by the English Government in the Year 1903–1904* (London: Hurst and Blackett, 1905), 1, p. 8–9; and Thomas Holdich, *Tibet, the Mysterious* (London: F. A. Stokes, 1906), p. 78; L. Austine Waddell, *Lhasa and Its Mysteries, with a Record of the Expedition of 1903–1904* (London: J. Murray, 1905), pp. 10–11.

6. C. H. D. Ryder, "Exploration and Survey with the Tibet Frontier Commission, and from Gyangtse to Simla viâ Gartok," *Geographical Journal* 26 (1905), p. 369–91; C. G. Rawling, *The Great Plateau* (London: E. Arnold, 1905), p. 4.

7. David Macdonald, *The Land of the Lama* (London: Seeley Service & Co., 1929).

8. Charles Bell, *Tibet, Past and Present* (Oxford: Clarendon Press, 1924); *The People of Tibet* (Oxford: Clarendon Press, 1928). Bell did treat Desideri briefly in *The Religion of Tibet* (Oxford: Clarendon Press, 1931), pp. 146–49.

9. Carlos Sommervogel, S.J., *Bibliothèque de la Compagnie de Jésus* (Bruxelles and Paris, 1890–1900), 2, col. 1963–4; 9 Suppl., coll. 204–5.

10. Henri Hosten, S.J., *Jesuit Missionaries in Northern India and Inscriptions on Their Tombs, Agra (1580–1803)* (Kurseong: St. Mary's Indian Academy, 1906), p. 42; "List of Jesuit Missionaries in Mogor (1580–1803)," *Journal of the Asiatic Society of Bengal* 6 (n.s.) (1910), pp. 527–42; *Jesuit Letters and Allied Papers on Mogor, Tibet, Bengal, & Burma*, 2 vols. (Calcutta: Asiatic Society, 1914–1916); "A Letter of Fr. A. de Andrade, S.J. (Tibet, August 29th, 1627)," *Journal of the Asiatic Society of Bengal* 21 (n.s.) (1925), pp. 75–91; "The Jesuits at Agra in 1635–1637," *Journal of the Asiatic Society of Bengal* (1938), pp. 479–501: "Letters and Papers of Fr. Ippolito Desideri, S.J., a Missionary in Tibet (1716–1721)," *Journal of the Asiatic Society of Bengal* (1938), pp. 567–767; Cornelius Wessels, S.J., "Lettura inedita del P. Ippolito Desideri S.I. scritta da Agra il 21 agosto 1714 al P. Francesco Piccolomini," in *Atti e memorie del Convegno de geografi-orientalisti tenuto in Macerata il 25, 26, 27 settembre 1910* (Macerata: Tip. Giorgetti, 1911), pp. 30–39; *Early Jesuit Travellers in Central Asia 1603–1721* (The Hague: Martinus Nijhoff, 1924).

11. Sven Hedin, *Trans-Himalaya: Discoveries and Adventures in Tibet* (London: Macmillan, 1909–1913), I, p. 279. Hedin was rather generous with his praise of other missionaries as well. Of Andrade he says, "He stands like a milestone on the highroad of the centuries, a boundary cliff in the stream of time, and he marks the point from which the history of Tibetan exploration really begins." Sven Hedin, "Early European Knowledge of Tibet," *Geografiska Annaler* 1 (1919), pp. 290–339.

12. Filippo de Filippi, "Il 'Ragguaglio' e le 'Memorie de' viaggi e missione nel Tibet' di padre Ippolito Desideri da Pistoia," *Bollettino della Soceita Geographica Italiana* 6 (1929), pp. 295–301; *An Account of Tibet: The Travels of Ippolito Desideri 1712–1727* (London: George Routledge & Sons, 1931), p. 37; *La spedizione nel Karakorum e nell'I-malia occidentale, 1909*, 2 vols. (Bologna: Zanichelli, 1912); *Storia della spedizione scientifica italiana nel Himàlaia, Caracorùm e Turchestàn cinese (1913–1914)* (Bologna: Zanichelli, 1924).

13. Giuseppe Tucci, "L'Italia e gli studi tibetani," *Civiltà* (quoted by Toscano, OT 2, p. 26): "Col Desideri nascono gli studi tibetani." Compare the following judgment, from "Le missioni Cattoliche e il Tibet," *Le Missioni Cattoliche e la cultura dell'Oriente* (Rome: IsMEO, 1943), p. 227: "Dopo questo che ho detto non vi meravigliate se aggiungo che l'opera del Desideri fu in anticipo sui tempi: i segreti delle speculazioni del Buddhismo *mahāyāna*, che cominciarono ad essere rivelati dall'erudizione orientalistica degli ultimi anni del secolo scorso, sono già chiari nelle scolastiche architetture logiche della sua relazione."

14. Giuseppe Tucci, *To Lhasa and Beyond: Diary of the Expedition to Tibet in the Year MCMXLVIII* (Rome: Istituto Poligrafico dello Stato, 1956), p. 5. Cf. *Italia e Oriente* (Milan: Garzanti, 1949), pp. 201–4; *Tibet paese delle nevi* (Novara, 1967), p. 67. *Italia e Oriente* has been reissued with a new introduction by Prof. Gherardo Gnoli and a name index compiled by Francesco D'Arelli (Rome: IsIAO, 2005).

15. Giuseppe Tucci, "L'Italia e l'esplorazione del Tibet," *Asiatica* 6 (1938), p. 441: "l'arrivo del Desideri a Lhasa segna una data memorabile nella storia degli studi tibetani perché egli fu il primo a rivelare all'occidente il Tibet, non dico nei suoi caratteri etnografici o nei suoi confini geografici, quanto piuttosto nella sua profonda e intima realtà spirituale." Compare p. 442, where Tucci says of Desideri's writings, "anche oggi,

a due secoli di distanza, è per profondità e chiarezza una delle più sicure esposizioni delle credenze religiose del Tibet." In Italia e Oriente (p. 25), he says that Desideri "per la sua larghezza di mente e per la simpatia con la quale avvicinò il popolo di cui era ospite e la sua cultura."

16. Robert Fazy, "Le P. Ippolito Desideri à Lhasa, 1716–1721 et son exposé de la religion tibétaine," *Bulletin de la Société Suisse des Amis de l'Extrème Orient* 6 (1944), p. 19 n. 18: "Avec l'humilité qui caractérise ses écrits, Desideri ne dit rien de sa vocation." Hosten judges Desideri to be "pluckier" than Freyre, and more patient. Cf. "Letters and Papers of Fr. Ippolito Desideri," pp. 56, 68.

17. Luciano Petech, MITN 5, p. xv: "nel viaggio meraviglioso da lui intrapreso con entusiasmo giovanile, ma con completa maturità spirituale e con uno zelo apostolico quale pochi missionari mai esplicarono." Cf. "Ippolito Desideri, S.J., 1684–1733," *Indica* 23 (1986), p. 112: "egli fu il primo tibetologo nella storia, anche se la sua opera non ebbe diffusione e rimase sepolta negli archivi per secoli."

18. Luciano Petech, *China and Tibet in the Eighteenth Century*, 2nd ed. (Leiden: E. J. Brill, 1972).

19. In addition to his various editorial comments in the four volumes of *Opere Tibetane di Ippolito Desideri, S.J.*, see Giuseppe Toscano, S.X., *La prima missione cattolica nel Tibet* (Parma: Istituto missioni estere, 1951); "Pensiero buddhista e pensiero cristiano," *Fede e Civiltà* 60 (Parma: Istituto Saveriano Missioni Estere, 1962), pp. 641–741; *Alla scoperta del Tibet. Relazioni dei missionari del sec. XVII* (Bologna: E.M.I., 1977); "The Death of Lha-bzang Khan According to the Writings of Fr. Desideri, S.J.," *Tibet Journal* 7 (1982), pp. 87–92; "The King Lha-bzang Khan and the Jesuit Priest Father Desideri," *Tibet Journal* 7 (1982), pp. 58–62; "Contributo del Desideri alla conoscenza dell'Asia nel sec. XVIII," in *La conoscenza dell'Asia e dell'africa in Italia nei sec. XVIII e XIX* (Naples: Istituto Universitario Orientale, 1984), pp. 293–302; G. Gispert-Sauch, S.J., "Tibetan Christian Literature," *Ignis Studies* 9 (1985), pp. 26–34; Richard Sherburne, S.J., "A Buddhist-Christian Dialog? Some Notes on Desideri's Tibetan Manuscripts," in *Reflections on Tibetan Culture: Essays in Memory of Turrell V. Wylie*, ed. Lawrence Epstein and Richard F. Sherburne (Lewiston: Edwin Mellen Press, 1990), pp. 295–305; Philip Caraman, S.J., *Tibet: The Jesuit Century* (St. Louis: IJS, 1997).

20. OT 2, pp. 7–8. Father Arrupe links Desideri to the twentieth-century Jesuit theologian Henri de Lubac, who also wrote of Desideri. Cf. Henri de Lubac, S.J., *La recontre du bouddhisme et de l'Occident* (Paris: Aubier, 1952), p. 137.

21. Giuseppe Toscano, S.X., "Il concetto di śūnyatā nel Desideri," in *Orientale Iosephi Tucci Memoriae Dicata*, ed. G. Gnoli and L. Lanciotti (Rome: IsMEO, 1988), pp. 1465–92; Robert E. Goss, "The First Meeting of Catholic Scholasticism with dGe lugs pa Scholasticism," in *Scholasticism: Cross-cultural and Comparative Perspectives*, ed. José Cabezon (Albany: State University of New York Press, 1997), pp. 65–90.

22. Along with Enzo Bargiacchi, Michael Sweet is currently producing the best scholarly writing on Ippolito Desideri. "Desperately Seeking Capuchins: Manoel Freyre's 'Report on the Tibets and their Routes (*Tibetorum ac Eorum Relatio Viarum*)' and the Desideri Mission to Tibet," *Journal of the International Association of Tibetan Studies* 2 (2005), pp. 1–33. As of this writing, a revised Italian version of this wonderful

article is set to appear in *Storialocale: Quaderni pistoiesi di cultura moderna e contemporanea*. A great deal of fascinating scene-setting can also be found in his "Jesus as World-Protector: Eighteenth-Century Gelukpa Historians View Christianity," *Buddhist-Christian Studies* 26 (2006), pp. 173–78. Sweet is working on a much-anticipated English translation of the entire *Notizie istoriche* and kindly provided me drafts of his translations of its first three books.

23. Donald S. Lopez Jr., *Prisoners of Shangri-la: Tibetan Buddhism and the West* (Chicago: University of Chicago Press, 1998), p. 3. Cf. Rudolph Kaschewsky, "Das Tibetbild im Westen vor dem 20. Jahrhundert," *Mythos Tibet* (Köln: Dumont, 1997), pp. 16–30.

24. Lopez, *Prisoners*, p. 4.

25. Donald S. Lopez Jr., "Foreigner at the Lama's Feet," in *Curators of the Buddha: The Study of Buddhism Under Colonialism*, ed. Donald S. Lopez Jr. (Chicago: University of Chicago Press, 1995), pp. 251–52.

26. John W. O'Malley, S.J., "The Historiography of the Society of Jesus: Where Does It Stand Today?" in *The Jesuits: Cultures, Sciences, and the Arts, 1540–1773*, ed. John W. O'Malley, S.J., Gauvin Alexander Bailey, Steven J. Harris, and T. Frank Kennedy, S.J. (Toronto: University of Toronto Press, 1999–2004), 1, pp. 3–37. See the same author's *The First Jesuits* (Cambridge: Harvard University Press, 1993), pp. 1–22. In fact, the term "Jesuit" (from *Jesu ita*, "like Jesus"), which was never used by Ignatius Loyola himself, was a derogatory term applied to those who called upon the name of Christ too frequently. In this regard it is not unlike *hīnayāna*, although the Jesuits eventually adopted the slur.

27. Many of these sources are featured in the chapter "'Rhapsodies of Calumny': The Creation of the Anti-Jesuit Myth," in Jonathan Wright's popular history of the Jesuits, *God's Soldiers* (New York: Doubleday, 2004), pp. 133–71. Cf. Michael Niemetz, *Antijesuitische Bildpublizistik in der Frühen Neuzeit. Geschichte, Ikonographie und Ikonologie* (Regensburg: Schnell und Steiner, 2008); Mario Rosso, "Gesuitismo e antigesuitismo nell'Italia del Sei-Settecento," *Revista di Storia e Letteratura Religiosa* 42 (2006), pp. 247–81.

28. Sabine Pavone, *The Wily Jesuits and the Monita Secreta* (St. Louis: IJS, 2006).

29. Even the old *Catholic Encyclopedia* entry on the Society of Jesus notes how much of Michelet's fantasy rested on a mistranslation. He read *obligatio ad peccandum* for *obligationem ad peccatum* in the famous passage of the Jesuit Constitutions, making the text say that a Jesuit was under obedience even to the point of having to commit mortal sins if so commanded. The obvious meaning of the text, however, is that the Constitutions do not oblige one to commit sin.

30. R. Po-Chia Hsia, *The World of Catholic Renewal 1540–1770* (Cambridge: Cambridge University Press, 1998), p. 2. Sommervogel has a long list of anti-Jesuit works. Cf. O'Malley, "The Historiography of the Society of Jesus," p. 29 n. 1, which includes more citations of anti-Jesuit works.

31. John W. O'Malley, S.J., *Trent and All That: Renaming Catholicism in the Early Modern Era* (Cambridge: Harvard University Press, 2000). Another useful survey, in addition to O'Malley and Hsia, is John C. Olin, *Catholic Reform: From Cardinal Ximenes*

to the Council of Trent 1495–1563 (New York: Fordham University Press, 1990), pp. 1–43. Partisans of O'Malley may have noticed that Hsia begins his book with the Council of Trent and his chronology with the foundation of the Society of Jesus.

32. Hubert Jedin, *Katholische Reformation oder Gegenreformation? Ein Versuch zur Klärung der Begriff nebst einer Jubiläumsbetrachtung über das trienter Konzil* (Lucerne: Josef Stocker, 1946). Leopold von Ranke, *Deutsche Geschicte im Zeitalter der Reformation*, 6 vols. (Berlin: Duneker und Humblot, 1842–47); *The History of the Popes*, trans. E. Foster (London: Henry G. Bohn, 1853), I, pp. 135–78. Jedin's terms invited a great deal of debate. O'Malley, "The Historiography of the Society of Jesus," pp. 21–22. For a larger summary of these debates, see Henry Outram Evennett, *The Spirit of the Counter-Reformation* (Cambridge: Cambridge University Press, 1968).

33. Benedetto Croce, *Storia dell'età barocca in Italia: Pensiero, poesia e letteratura, vita morale* (Bari: G. Laterza, 1929), pp. 3–51. For a review of the voluminous literature on this association, see Gauvin Alexander Bailey, "'Le style jésuite n'existe pas': Jesuit Corporate Culture and the Visual Arts," *The Jesuits: Cultures, Sciences, and the Arts*, I, pp. 38–89. For Bailey's extended counterformulation, see *Between Renaissance and Baroque: Jesuit Art in Rome, 1565–1610* (Toronto: University of Toronto Press, 2003).

34. O'Malley, "The Historiography of the Society of Jesus," p. 24.

35. The bibliography on Jesuit missions is immense, but few works highlight the intercultural cooperation that was necessary for the success of many Jesuit enterprises, or the multicultural artifacts that were often produced as a result. A notable exception is Gauvin Alexander Bailey, *Art on the Jesuit Missions in Asia and Latin America, 1542–1773* (Toronto: University of Toronto Press, 1999).

36. Pierre Janelle, *The Catholic Reformation* (Milwaukee: Bruce Publications, 1963); Wolfgang Reinhard, "'Gegenreformation als Modernisierung?' Prolegomena zu einer Theorie des konfessionellen Zeitalters," *Archiv für Reformationgeschichte* 68 (1977), pp. 226–52; John Bossy, *Christianity in the West 1400–1700* (Oxford: Oxford University Press, 1985). Jean Delumeau has provocatively argued that, as a popular phenomenon, Christianity itself was largely an invention of modernity. Jean Delumeau, *Le catholicisme entre Luther et Voltaire* (Paris: Presses Universitaires de France, 1971).

37. Most notably, John W. Witek, S.J., *Controversial Ideas in China and in Europe: A Biography of Jean-François Foucquet, S.J. (1665–1741)* (Rome: IHSI, 1982); and Jonathan Spence, *The Memory Palace of Matteo Ricci* (New York: Viking Penguin, 1984).

38. Liam Brockey, in what is surely the most important work on the Jesuit missions to China in the last decade, still contrasts the "religious dynamism" of the Jesuits with the "repressive force of the institutional church." Brockey, *Journey to the East: The Jesuit Mission to China 1579–1724* (Cambridge: Belknap Press, 2007), p. 6.

39. The massive two-volume collection of essays edited by O'Malley, Bailey, Harris, and Kennedy under the title *Jesuits: Cultures, Sciences, and the Arts, 1540–1773*—a superb collection that covers almost every conceivable aspect of the Society, even gardening and clockmaking—contains not a single essay on Jesuit theology in Europe. The closest thing one gets is James F. Keenan's essay on the Jesuit roots of the practical divinity of the British Puritans.

40. Studies of the Jesuit contribution to international law are exceptions that prove this rule, as they are simultaneously scholastic and "modern." Cf. Bernice Hamilton, *Political Thought in Sixteenth-Century Spain* (Oxford: Clarendon Press, 1963); Frank Bartholomew Costello, *The Political Philosophy of Luis de Molina, S.J. (1535–1600)* (Rome: IHSI, 1974); and recently Harro Höpfl, *Jesuit Political Thought: The Society of Jesus and the State, c. 1540–1640* (New York: Cambridge University Press, 2004).

CHAPTER 1: JESUIT *PHANTASIA*

1. I owe this comparison to a wonderful story related by Matthew Kapstein. When asked about his impressions of the Apollo moon landing, the Ladakhi lama Stokden Rinpoché told Kapstein, "We Ladakhis have never been motivated to visit the surface of the moon because we had it here all along." Matthew T. Kapstein, *The Tibetans* (Oxford: Blackwell Publishing, 2006), p. 5.

2. Manoel Freyre, *Tibetorum ac eorum Relatio Viarum* (MITN 7, p. 203): "Altera dierum uno eius camelo inter nives pereunte etiam equus meu, quo sedebam, fame intrinsecus ustulante e naribus sanguinem emittens nequaquam progredi ulterius valuit, ad noctem tandem cecidit supra nives, mecum servo uno tantum Mauro manete. Sol autem deficiente, simul et antecedentium vestigia defecerunt. Quid facerem nesciens, supra nives prosternens, me equi, ut mihi ejus attraheram, calorem, pectori accubui, alterum denique expectarem diem." Cf. DR 1.10 (MITN 5, p. 181n): "In un battar d'occhio furono a cavallo i Tartari; vanno, corrono, gridano, e doppo ben lungo tratto di cammino trovano il padre in mezzo alla neve e l'interprete mezzo intirizzito dal freddo, a causa che, non avendo potuto, come speravano, far rilevare il cavallo, ed essendo passata tutta la gente, per non esser possibile di ritrovare il cammino, si trovarono costretti di quivi rimanere."

3. Two articles are essential for work in these archival materials: Edmond Lamalle, "La documentation d'histoire missionaire dans le 'Fondo Gesuitico' aux Archives Romaines de la Compagnie de Jesus," *Euntes docete* 21 (1968), pp. 131–76; "L'Archivo Generale di un grande ordine religioso: quello della Compagnia di Gesù," *Archiva ecclesiae* 24–25 (1981–82), pp. 89–120.

4. Joseph de Guibert, S.J., *The Jesuits: Their Spiritual Doctrine and Practice* (Chicago: Loyola University Press, 1964), p. 287; G. C. Roscioni, *Il desiderio delle Indie. Storia, sogni e fughe di giovani gesuiti italianai* (Turin: G. Einaudi, 2001).

5. N. Rauty, "Notizie inedite su Ippolito Desideri e sulla sua famiglia tratte dagli archivi pistoiesi," *Bullettino Storico Pistoiese* 86 (1984), pp. 3–31; Bargiacchi, *Ippolito Desideri, S.J., alla scoperta del Tibet e del buddhismo*, p. 1; *A Bridge Across Two Cultures*, pp. 7–9.

6. Cristina Acidini Luchinat, *La Cattedrale di San Zeno a Pistoia* (Milan: Silvana Editoriale, 2003); Alberto Cipriani, *A Brief History of Pistoia*, trans. Miriam Kimber Barbieri (Pisa: Pacini Editore, 2004); *Storia illustrata di Pistoia* (Florence: Edizioni Firenze, 2005). I am grateful to Enzo Gualtiero Bargiacchi and Ivani Paci for their kind gift of these books.

7. Philip Caraman, *Tibet: The Jesuit Century* (St. Louis: IJS, 1997).

8. William V. Bangert, S.J., *A History of the Society of Jesus*, 2nd ed. (St. Louis: IJS, 1986), pp. 273–74.

9. MI III, 1, p. 26: "Quicunque in Societate nostra, quam Iesu nomine insigniri cupimus, vult sub crucis vexillo Deo militare, et soli Domino atque romano Pontifici, eius in terris Vicario, seruire, post solenne perpetuae Castitatis uotum, proponat sibi in animo se partem esse Societatis, ad hoc potissimum institutae, ut ad profectum animarum in uita et doctrina Christiana, et ad fidei propagationem."

10. For a discussion of the phrase "to serve as a soldier of God" (*militare Deo*), see Antonio M. de Aldama, *The Formula of the Institute: Notes for a Commentary*, trans. Ignacio Echániz (St. Louis: IJS, 1990).

11. John O'Malley, S.J., "The Cultural Mission of the Society of Jesus," p. xxv; "Mission and the Early Jesuits," *The Way (Supplement)* 79 (1994), pp. 3–10. Adriano Prospero, "L'Europa cristiana e il mondo: Alle origini dell'idea di missione," *Dimensioni e problemi della ricerca storia* 2 (1992), pp. 189–220.

12. MI III, 3, p. 97: "Et quamvis nostrae vocationis sit diversa loca peragrare, et vitam agere in quavis mundi plaga, ubi maius Dei obsequium et animarum auxilium speratur."

13. John C. Olin, *The Autobiography of St. Ignatius Loyola with Related Documents* (New York: Fordham University Press, 1992), pp. 111–13, offers a fine bibliographical survey of the major works on Ignatius and the early Jesuits. On the images of Ignatius himself, including cycles of his life, see Heinrich Pfeiffer, S.J., "The Iconography of the Society of Jesus," *Jesuits and the Arts 1540–1773*, ed. John W. O'Malley and Gauvin Alexander Bailey (Philadelphia: St. Joseph's University Press, 2005), pp. 200–28. For critical supporting documents, see Cándido de Dalmases, S.J., *Fontes Documentales de S. Ignatio de Loyola: documenta de S. Ignatii familia et patria, iuventute, primis sociis* (Rome: IHSI, 1977).

14. I pray readers familiar with the literature on St. Ignatius will pardon my use of this cliché; it is simply too good not to repeat. I am not aware of its first use, but my favorite comes from Preserved Smith, *The Age of the Reformation* (New York: H. Holt, 1920), pp. 398–99: speaking of Ignatius's youthful dalliances, the Presbyterian modernist says, "Not that this prevented him from addressing less disinterested attentions to other ladies, for, if something of a Don Quixote, he was also something of a Don Juan." John C. Olin makes the comparison in a wonderful summary of Ignatius's life in his "The Idea of Pilgrimage in the Experience of Ignatius Loyola," *Church History* 48 (1979), p. 389.

15. Ludolphus de Saxonia, *Vita Iesu Christi Redemptoris Nostri* (Venice: Batholomaeus Rubinus, 1568), p. 72: "Completis autem viginti novem annis aetatis suae, quibus Dominus Iesus sic poeno se, et abjecte vixerat: dicit Iesus matri suae, quia tempus est ut vadat, et glorificet, ac manifestet patrem suum, et se mundo ostendat, qui diu latuerat, et operetur animarum salutem, pro qua pater ipsum huc miserat. Vadit ergo dominus mundi solus, pedibus nudis, per spatium tam longi itineris. Intuere eum diligenter et devote: eidem que vehementer et ex corde compatere."

16. H. Turcellinus, *Francisci Xaverii epistolarum libri quatuor* (Rome, 1596). On this edition, see Donald F. Lach, *Asia in the Making of Europe, vol. 1: The Century of Discovery* (Chicago: University of Chicago Press, 1965), 1, pp. 428–30.

17. Ines G. Županov, *Disputed Mission: Jesuit Experiments and Brahmanical Knowledge in Seventeenth-Century India* (Oxford: Oxford University Press, 1999), pp. 14–15.

18. Edmond Lamalle, S.J., "La propagande du P. Nicolas Trigault en faveur des missions de Chine,"' AHSI 9 (1940), p. 114.

19. Dominique Deslandres, "*Exemplo aeque ut verbo*: The French Jesuits' Missionary World," in *The Jesuits: Cultures, Sciences, and the Arts*, 1, pp. 258–73. Deslandres has also written a full-length work on the French missions, *Croire et faire croire: Les missions français au XVIIe siècle* (Paris: Fayard, 2003).

20. Guibert, *Spiritual Doctrine*, p. 217; John O'Malley, S.J., *Religious Culture in the Sixteenth Century: Preaching, Rhetoric, Spirituality, and Reform* (Brookfield: Variorum, 1993), p. 358.

21. Georg Schurhammer, S.J., and Joseph Wicki, S.J., eds., *Epistolae S. Francisci Xaverii aliaque eius scripta*, second edition, 2 vols. (Rome: MHSI, 1996).

22. D. Ferroli, S.J., *The Jesuits in Mysore* (Kozhikode: s.n., 1955), pp. 57–58.

23. Conti published a prolix and rhetorically charged commentary on the *Spiritual Exercises* while Desideri was still in Rome. Since Desideri mentions Conti by name, his work most likely served as the guide for the young Jesuit's meditations. See his *Iter animae ad Deum piis considerationibus et affectibus gradatim euntis. Praevia itineri antecedit Dissertatio brevis de Oratione Mentali et Spiritualibus Divi Ignatii Loyolae Exercitiis* (Rome: Antonii de Rubeis, 1709). Conti also authored a work of therapeutic philosophy entitled *Le Sette Principali Malattie dell'Animo e Loro Qualita con gli Opportuni Rimedii* (Rome: Bernabo, 1712). Other important commentaries on the *Spiritual Exercises* that circulated in Rome during Desideri's day were written by Sebastián Izquierdo (1601–1681), Giuseppe Agnelli (1621–1706), Benedetto Rogacci (1646–1719), and Ranieri Carsughi (1647–1709). On these authors, see Ignacio Iparraguirre, S.J., *Comentarios de los Ejercicios Ignacianos (siglos XVI–XVIII) Reportorio crítico* (Rome: IHSI, 1967).

24. An invaluable guide to the later practices is Ignacio Iparraguirre, S.J., *Historia de la práctica de los Ejercicios Espirituales de San Ignacio de Loyola*, 3 vols. (Rome: IHSI, 1946–73). For an account of the practice of the *Spiritual Exercises* in Rome, see vol. 3, pp. 233–65.

25. Although later authors would work diligently to show that nearly every sentence of the *Exercises* had patristic precedent, the editors of the modern critical edition are sure in their judgment that Ignatius composed the small work with the few works known to him in his early career, namely, the *Imitatio Christi*, Ludolph of Saxony, the *Flos Sanctorum*, and the *Spiritual Exercises* of Cardinal Cisneros. Cf. MI II, 1, p. 136 and P. de Leturia, "Génesis de los ejercicios de San Ignacio," *Estudios Ignacianos* 2 (1957), pp. 3–55. Jesuits of the second generation such as Achille Gagliardi, Gil Gonzáles Dávila, Francisco Suárez, Alphonsus Rodríguez, and Bernardino Rossignoli, largely accomplished the Patristic synthesis.

26. Although Ignatius himself seems to have imagined that each Jesuit would make the exercises only once, and then live apostolically after the conversion wrought through them, we know that Jesuits gradually came to practice the exercises as part of their prayer, although the form and methods that they used varied widely: both the length of time spent making exercises and the meditations chosen from among them

differed individually and regionally. Iparraguirre, *Historia* 2, pp. 257–58, 267, notes that Nadal distributed personal questionnaires during many of his formal visitations to province houses of the Society in the 1560s, of which 1,323 responses survive. Cf. *MHSI MN* 1, pp. 789–95; 2, pp. 527–89.

27. Guibert, *Spiritual Doctrine*, pp. 78–79.

28. MI II, 1, p. 212. Following general practice, I will cite the *Spiritual Exercises* from the Textus Autographus [= *A*], rather than the Versio vulgata [= *V*] or the 1541 and 1547 editions of the Versio Prima [= *P1, P2*].

29. MI II, 1, pp. 164–66: "El hombre es criado para alabar, hazer reuerencia y seruir a Dios nuestro Señor y, mediante esto, salbar su ánima; y las otras cosas sobre la haz de la tierra son criadas para el hombre, y para que le ayuden en la prosecución del fin para que es criado. De donde se sigue, que el hombre tanto a de vsar dellas, quanto le ayudan para su fin, y tanto deue quitarse dellas, quanto para ello le impiden. Por lo qual es menester hazernos indiferentes a todas las cosas criadas, en todo lo que es concedido a la libertad de nuestro libre albedrío, y no le está prohibido; en tal manera, que no queramos de nuestra parte más salud que enferme-dad, riqueza que pobreza, honor que dessonor, vida larga que corta, y por consiguiente en todo lo demás; solamente deseando y eligiendo lo que más nos conduçe para el fin que somos criados."

30. MI II, 1, p. 192: "Ymaginando a Xpo nuestro Señor de lante y puesto en cruz, hazer vn colloquio; cómo de Criador es venido a hazerse hombre, y de vida eterna a muerte temporal, y así a morir por mis pecados. Otro tanto, mirando a mí mismo, lo que he hecho por Xpo, lo que hago por Xpo, lo que deuo hazer por Xpo."

31. Attentive readers will notice that I have here paraphrased the theological description of the *Exercises* found in Hugo Rahner, *Ignatius the Theologian*, trans. Michael Barry (New York: Herder and Herder), p. 81.

32. H. Pinard de la Boullaye, "Sentir, sentimiento y sentido dans le style de Saint Ignace," AHSI 25 (1956), pp. 416–30, and François Marty, *Sentir et Goûter: Les sens dans les "Exercices spirituelles" de saint Ignace* (Paris: Cerf, 2005).

33. MI II, 1, pp. 200–2: "El primer puncto será ber con la vista de la ymaginación los grandes fuegos, y las ánimas como en cuerpos ygneos; oyr con las orejas llantos, alaridos, vozes, blasfemias contra Xpo nuestro Señor y contra todos sus santos; oler con el olfato humo, piedra azufre, sentina, y cosas pútridas; gustar con el gusto cosas amargas, así como lágrimas, tristeza, y el verme de la consciencia; tocar con el tacto, es a saber, cómo los fuegos tocan y abrasan las ánimas."

34. MI II, 1, p. 218: "My voluntad es de conquistar toda la tierra de infieles; por tanto, quien quisiere venir comigo, a de ser contento de comer como yo, y así de beber y vestir, etc.; asimismo ha de trabajar comigo en el día y vigilar en la noche, etc.; porque así después tenga parte comigo en la victoria, como la ha tenido en los trabajos."

35. MI II, 1, pp. 218–20: "My voluntad es de conquistar todo el mundo y todas los enemigos, y así entrar en la gloria de mi Padre; por tanto, quien quisiere venir comigo, a de trabajar comigo, porque siguiéndome en la pena, tanbién me siga en la gloria."

36. MI II, 1, p. 224: "la grande capacidad y redondez del mundo, en la qual están tantas y tan diuersas gentes."

37. MI II, 1, p. 244: "El primer puncto es ymaginar así como si se asentase el caudillo de todos los enemigos en aquel gran campo de Babilonia, como en vna grande cáthedra de fuego y humo, en figura horrible y espantosa."

38. MI II, 1, pp. 244–46: "considerar cómo haze llamamiento de inumerables demonios, y cómo los esparze a los vnos en tal ciudad y a los otros en otra, y así por todo el mundo, no dexando prouincias, lugares, estados, ny personas algunas en particular."

39. MI II, 1, p. 441: "Alterius, Christi, summi ducis ac Domini nostri, qui hic nihil iucundum aut laetum pollicetur, sed continuum bellum, omnia aspera, dura et amara, si internum conscientae gaudium excipias."

40. MI II, 1, p. 286.

41. On the *Exercises* and images, see Pierre-Antoine Fabre, "Les 'Exercises Spirituels' sont-ils illustrables?" in *Les jésuites à l'âge baroque, 1540–1640*, ed. Luce Giard and Louis de Vaucelles (Grenoble: J. Millon, 1996), pp. 197–212; Lydia Salviucci Insolera, "Le illustrazioni per gli Esercizi Spirituali intorno al 1600," AHSI 60 (1991), pp. 160–217.

42. With the common sense (*sensus communis*), the estimative or cognitive power (*aestimativa seu cognitiva*), and the memorative power (*memorativa*), *phantasia* and/or *imaginatio* comprise the human soul. Thomas Aquinas, *Summa theologiae* Ia, q. 78, art. 4 (*Opera Omnia Leon.* 5, pp. 255–57); *Summa theologiae* Ia, q. 76, art. 1 (*Opera Omnia Leon.* 5, pp. 208–9); *In Aristotelis Librum de Anima Commentarium* 1, cap. 2 (*Opera Omnia Leon.* 45/1, pp. 9–10); 2, cap. 6 (p. 92); 2, cap. 30 (pp. 197–200).

43. Pierre-Antoine Fabre, *Ignace de Loyola: Le Lieu de l'Image: Le problème de la composition de lieu dans les practiques spirituelles et artistiques jésuites de la seconde moitié du XVIe siècle* (Paris: Vrin, 1992). Discussing the composition of place in the *Spiritual Exercises*, John W. O'Malley writes, "Ignatius borrowed this tradition from late medieval sources. It did not originate with him. In the *Exercises*, however, he gave it a powerfully codified form and sent it on its way into modern Catholicism. By means of it, he predisposed the members of the Society to an appreciation of the power of images, to which the broad and long tradition of Catholicism regarding images would already have made them sensitive." John W. O'Malley, S.J., "St. Ignatius and the Cultural Mission of the Society of Jesus," *The Jesuits and the Arts 1540–1773*, p. 26.

44. MI II, 1, p. 142. This point has been made to great effect by Mary J. Carruthers, *The Book of Memory: A Study of Memory in Medieval Culture* (Cambridge: Cambridge University Press, 1990). The earliest guides written for Jesuit spiritual directors often appealed to a statement attributed to St. Bonaventure: "Tu, inquit, si fructum ex his sumere cupis, ita te praesentem exhibeas his, quae per Dominum Iesum Christum dicta et facta narrantur, ac si tuis oculis ea videres et tuis auribus toto mentis affectu diligenter, delectabiliter et morose, omnibus aliis curis et solicitudinibus tuis omissis" (MI II, 2, p. 653). This text is taken from the Pseudo-Bonaventure's *Meditationes vitae Domini Jesu Christi*.

45. Pierre Hadot, *Exercices spirituels et philosophie antique* (Paris: Etudes augustiniennes, 1981).

46. Whether Ignatius developed the ancient mnemonic arts consciously or unconsciously in the *Exercises*, the two were frequently connected in the seventeenth century, especially among Jesuits, such as Athanasius Kircher (1602–1680) and Sebastian Izquierdo (1601–1681). Izquierdo, who authored a commentary on the *Spiritual Exercises* that was popular in Desideri's day, also wrote on mnemonic arts. Sebastian Izquierdo, *Pharus Scientiarum ubi quidquid ad cognitionem humanam humanitus acquisibilem pertinet* (Leiden: Sumptibus C. Bourgeat & M. Lietard, 1659). On Izquierdo, see Frances Yates, *Art of Memory* (Chicago: University of Chicago Press, 1966), pp. 378–82; Iparraguirre, *Comentarios de los Ejercicios Ignacianos*, pp. 251–52.

47. Mary Carruthers, *The Craft of Thought: Meditation, Rhetoric, and the Making of Images 400–1200* (Cambridge: Cambridge University Press, 1998). For wonderful reproductions of images constructed in medieval memory practice, see Mary Carruthers and Jan M. Ziolkowski, eds., *The Medieval Craft of Memory: An Anthology of Texts and Pictures* (Philadelphia: University of Pennsylvania Press, 2002).

48. A detailed account of the role and production of images in Jesuit thought and culture can be found in Jeffrey Chipps Smith, *Sensuous Worship: Jesuits and the Art of the Early Catholic Reformation in Germany* (Princeton, NJ: Princeton University Press, 2002), especially pp. 29–56. My own account is closely modeled on Smith's, although I try to highlight the role of Jesuit emblematics more than he does. For a thorough survey of the literature on Jesuit art, see Gauvin Alexander Bailey, "'Le style jésuite n'existe pas': Jesuit Corporate Culture and the Visual Arts," *Jesuits: Cultures, Sciences, and the Arts*, 1, pp. 38–89. Cf. *Between Renaissance and Baroque*, pp. 3–37. Important works on Jesuit emblematics include Jakob Bosch, *Symbolographia sive de arte symbolica* (Augsburg and Dillingen: Johann Kaspar Bencard, 1701) [= CLE J.53]; Willem van Hees, *Emblemata sacra de fide, spe, charitate* (Antwerp: Balthasar Moretus, 1636) [= CLE J.611]; Jakob Masen, *Speculum imaginum veritatis occultae* (Cologne: Johann Anton Kinchius, 1664) [= CLE J.961]; Claude-François Menestrier, *L'art des emblèmes* (Lyons: Benoit Coral, 1662) [= CLE J.986]; *La philosophie des images* (Paris: Robert J. B. de la Calle, 1682) [= CLE J.1027]; Silvestro Pietrasanta, *De symbolis heroicis libri IX* (Antwerp: Balthasar Moretus, 1634) [= CLE J.1129]. For modern studies, see Agnes Guiderdoni and Ralph Dekoninck, eds., *Emblemata sacra: Rhétorique et herméneutique du discours sacré dans la littérature en images* (Turnhout: Brepols, 2007); Richard Dimler, *Studies in the Jesuit Emblem* (New York: AMS, 2007); Anne-Élisabeth Spica, *Symbolique et emblématique humaniste: L'évolution et les genres (1580–1700)* (Paris: Champion, 1996); Peter M. Daly, *Literature in the Light of the Emblem: Structural Parallels Between Emblem and Literature in the Sixteenth and Seventeenth Centuries* (Toronto: University of Toronto Press, 1979). Jesuit "symbology" also found its way into the academic culture. Cf. Louis Rice, "Jesuit Thesis Prints and the Festive Academic Defense at the Collegio Romano," *The Jesuits: Cultures, Sciences, and the Arts*, 1, pp. 148–69.

49. In addition to the work of Jonathan Spence, see Nicholas Standaert, *An Illustrated Life of Christ Presented to the Chinese Emperor: The History of the Jincheng shuxiang (1640)* (Nettetal: Steyler Verlag, 2007); Adrian Dudink, "Lubelli's *Wanmin simo tu* (Picture of the Four Last Things of All People), ca. 1683," *Sino-Western Cultural Relations Journal* 18 (2006), pp. 1–19; Hui-hung Chen, "The Human Body as a

Universe: Understanding Heaven by Visualization and Sensibility in Jesuit Cartography in China," *Catholic Historical Review* 93 (2007), pp. 517–52.

50. Jerónimo Nadal's *Adnotationes et meditations in Evangelia* (Antwerp: Martinus, Nutius, 1595).

51. James Joyce, *A Portrait of the Artist as a Young Man* (Penguin, 1956), p. 121. Joyce has the boys begin their retreat on the feast day of Francis Xavier. Fr. Arnall even makes an appeal for the missions. "Time has gone on and brought with it its changes. Even in the last few years what changes can most of you not remember? Many of the boys who sat in those front benches a few years ago are perhaps now in distant lands, in the burning tropics or immersed in professional duties or in seminaries or voyaging over the vast expanse of the deep or, it may be, already called by the great God to another life and the rendering up of their stewardship."

52. Kevin Sullivan, *Joyce Among the Jesuits* (New York: Columbia University Press, 1958), pp. 36–37, 128–30, 138, 141–42; James R. Thrane, "Joyce's Sermon on Hell: Its Source and Its Backgrounds," *Modern Philology* 57 (1960), pp. 172–98; Elizabeth F. Boyd, "James Joyce's Hell-Fire Sermons," *Modern Language Notes* 75 (1960), pp. 561–71; James Doherty, "Joyce and *Hell Opened to Christians*: The Edition He Used for His 'Hell Sermons,'" *Modern Philology* 61 (1963), pp. 110–19.

53. Such sermons routinely found their application in "spiritual exercises" of various sorts beyond the *Exercises* of Loyola himself. In this respect, Pinamonti's *L'Inferno Aperto* is similar to the *Quattro massime di Christiana filosofia* of Giovanni Battista Manni (1606–1682), which contains four famous "considerations of eternity," or the *Manna animae* of Segneri himself. Cf. Giovanni Battista Manni, *Quattro massime di Christiana filosofia* (Rome: Madama da Francesco Leone, 1676); Paolo Segneri, *Manna animae seu Exercitium facile simul et fructuosum illis* (Dilingae: J. C. Bencard, 1723). Paolo Segneri the Younger (1673–1713) also wrote a commentary on the *Exercises* that Muratori edited: *Esercizi Spirituali esposti secondo il metodo del Padre Paolo Segneri* (Modena: Bartolomeo Soliani, 1720).

54. On Segneri, see Rocco Paternoster and Andrea Fedi, eds., *Paolo Segneri: Un Classico della Tradizione Cristiana: atti del Convegno internazionali di studi su Paolo Segneri, nel 3000 anniversario della morte (1694–1994)* (Stony Brook, NY: Forum Italicum, 1999). On Baldinucci, see Bernadette Majorana, "La pauvreté visible: réflexions sur la style missionaire jésuite dans les Avvertimenti de Antonio Baldinucci (vers 1705)," in *Missions religieuses modernes: "Notre lieu est le monde,"* ed. Pierre-Antoine Fabre and Bernard Vincent (Rome: École française de Rome, 2007).

55. I have used three editions. The first is an undated edition published in Venice in the late seventeenth century: *L'Inferno Aperto al Christiano perche no v' entri, overo Considerazioni delle Pene Infernali* (Venice: Giovanni Antonio Remondini, n.d.). The second is a contemporary English translation, *Hell Opened to Christians; to Caution them from entering into it: or, Considerations of the Infernal Pains* (London: s.n., 1715). For the images, I have used the 1693 edition from Milan.

56. Considerations of eternity, such as those in Paulo Segneri and Giovanni Pietro Pinamonti, were a favorite topic of Jesuit emblematics. Cf. Jeremias Drexel, *Infernus damnatorum* (Douai: Balthasar Bellère, 1631) [= CLE J.377]; Jan David, *Veridicus*

Christianus (Antwerp: Jan Moretus, 1601) [= CLE J.152]; Jeremias Drexel, *De Aeternitate Considerationes* (Cologne: Peter Henning, 1629) [= CLE J.176].

57. DR 3.22 (MITN 6, p. 307).

58. Desideri's application is found in OT 2, pp. 271–73. Compare the detailed account that Desideri's contemporary, the Jesuit missionary Jean-François Foucquet, left in his diary about his own attraction to the overseas missions. John W. Witek, S.J., *Controversial Ideas in China and in Europe: A Biography of Jean-François Foucquet, S.J. (1665–1741)* (Rome: IHSI, 1982), pp. 80–83. On Tamburini, see Fabrizio Martelli, *Michelangelo Tamburini XIV Generale dei Gesuiti* (Modena: Golinelli Editore, 1994).

59. Desideri's knowledge of history is quite good in this case; although the official edict on the expulsion of the *Bateren* was not promulgated until early 1614, the Bakufu issued the first decrees prohibiting Christianity and began to take steps against the Jesuit mission in 1612. These decrees led to the "Great Martyrdoms" in Nagasaki in 1622 and Edo in 1623, the apostasy of Christovão Ferreira in 1633, and the Shimabara Rebellion in 1637. For these events, see C. R. Boxer, *The Christian Century in Japan 1549–1650* (Berkeley: University of California Press, 1967), pp. 308–61; George Elison, *Deus Destroyed: The Image of Christianity in Early Modern Japan* (Cambridge: Harvard University Press, 1991), pp. 185–211; Hubert Cieslik, "The Case of Christovão Ferreira," *Monumenta Nipponica* 29 (1974), pp. 1–54.

60. DR 1.1 (MITN 5, p. 122). This passage appears in ms. B_1, but not in the final redaction in ms. A.

61. Thomas DaCosta Kaufmann, "East and West: Jesuit Art and Artists in Central Europe, and Central European Art in the Americas," *The Jesuits: Cultures, Sciences, and the Arts*, 1, pp. 274–304. St. Francis Xavier takes pride of place in Pozzo's masterpiece as well, leading a number of Asian converts in their ascent into the clouds toward Ignatius and, eventually, God Himself. Gavin Alexander Bailey, "Italian Renaissance and Baroque Painting Under the Jesuits and Its Legacy Throughout Catholic Europe 1565–1773," in *The Jesuits and the Arts*, pp. 189–95.

62. Haskell, *Patrons and Painters: A Study in the Relations Between Italian Art and Society in the Age of the Baroque* (New Haven, CT: Yale University Press, 1980), pp. 90–93. Bernard Kerber, *Andrea Pozzo* (Berlin and New York: de Gruyter, 1971); Vittorio de Feo and Valentino Martinelli, eds., *Andrea Pozzo* (Milan: Electra, 1996).

63. Cesare D'Onofrio, *Gli obelischi di Roma* (Rome: Bulzoni, 1967); Giovanni Cipriani, *Gli obelischi egizi: politica e cultura nella Roma barocca* (Florence: Olschki, 1993); Anthony Grafton, ed., *Rome Reborn: The Vatican Library and Renaissance Culture* (Vatican City: Biblioteca Apostolica Vaticana, 1993).

64. Walter Weibel, *Jesuitismus und Barockskulptur in Rom* (Strasbourg: J. H. E. Heitz, 1909); Irving Lavin, *Bernini and the Unity of the Visual Arts* (New York: Oxford University Press, 1980), p. 4; Irving Lavin, "Bernini's Death," *The Art Bulletin* 54 (1972), pp. 158–86; Maarten Delbeke, Steven F. Ostrow, and Evonne Levy, eds., *Bernini's Biographies: Critical Essays* (University Park: Penn State University Press, 2006).

65. Joseph Connors, "Bernini's S. Andrea al Quirinale: Payments and Planning," *Journal of the Society of Architectural Historians* 41 (1982), pp. 15–37; Bailey, *Between Renaissance and Baroque*, pp. 38–73.

66. Although I find her comparison of Jesuit and Nazi art heavy-handed in the extreme, much of interest can be found in Evonne Levy, *Propaganda and the Jesuit Baroque* (Berkeley: University of California Press, 2004).

67. Gauvin Alexander Bailey, "Italian Renaissance and Baroque Painting," pp. 142–54.

68. The classic popular work on Jesuit martyrs is Joseph N. Tylenda, S.J., *Jesuit Saints & Martyrs* (Chicago: Loyola University Press, 1984). For iconographic resources, see Bailey, *Between Renaissance and Baroque*.

69. This cycle served as a model for several iconographic cycles of St. Francis Xavier in Portugal. An illuminating discussion and several beautiful reproductions can be found in Gauvin Alexander Bailey, "Italian Renaissance and Baroque Painting Under the Jesuits and Its Legacy Throughout Catholic Europe 1565–1773." Ines Županov also discusses this cycle of paintings in her *Missionary Tropics: The Catholic Frontier in India (16th–17th Centuries)* (Ann Arbor: University of Michigan Press, 2005), pp. 154–55. For an analysis and reproductions of the entire cycle, see Vítor Serrão, *A Lenda de São Francisco Xavier pelo pintor André Reinoso*, 2nd ed. (Lisbon: Quetzal Editores, 2006).

CHAPTER 2: FROM ROME TO LHASA

1. On this problem, see Wessels, *Early Jesuit Travellers*, pp. 207–9; Hosten, "Letters and Papers," pp. 15, 33.

2. R. Hennig, *Terrae Incognitae*, 4 vols. (Leiden: E. J. Brill, 1936–39); A. Herrmann, *Das Land der Seide und Tibet im Licht der Antike* (Leipzig: K. F. Koehlers Antiquarium, 1938); Helmut Hoffmann, "Tibets Eintritt in die Universalgeschichte," *Saeculum* 2 (1950), pp. 258–79.

3. Cosmas Indicopleustes, *Topographie chrétienne*, 3 vols. [= *Sources chrétiennes* 141, 159, 174], ed. and trans. Wanda Wolska-Conus (Paris: Éditions du Cerf, 1968–); *La topographie chrétienne de Cosmas Indicopleustes: théologie et sciences au VIe siècle* (Paris: Presses Universitaires de France, 1962).

4. I. Hallberg, *L'Extrême Orient dans la littérature et la cartographie de l'Occident des XIIIe, XIVe et XVe siècles. Etude sur l'histoire de la géographie* (Göteborg: Zachrisson, 1907).

5. Benjamin of Tudela, *Itinerarium Beniamini Tudelensis, in quo res memorabiles, quas ante quadringentos annos totum fere terrarum orbem notatis itineribus dimensus vel ipse vidit vel a fide dignis suae aetatis hominibus accepit, breviter atque dilucide describuntur* (Antwerp: Ex Officina C. Plantini, 1575). Cf. *The Itinerary of Benjamin of Tudela: Critical Text, Translation, and Commentary*, ed. and trans. Marcus Nathan Adler (London: H. Frowde, 1907), pp. 45, 49, 53.

6. Luciano Petech, "Il Tibet nella Geografia Musulmana," *Academia Nazionale dei Lincei, Rendiconti, Classe di Scienze Morali*, ser. VIII, vol. 2 (Rome, 1947), pp. 55–70.

7. Iohannes de Plano Carpini, *Ystoria Mongalorum quos nos Tartaros appellamus* 5.14 (SF 1, pp. 60–61): "Et dum reverteretur exercitus ille, videlicet Mongalorum, venit ad terram Burithabet quam bello vicerunt, qui sunt pagani, qui consuetudinem mirabilem immo potius miserabilem habent, quia cum alicuius pater humane nature debitum solvit,

omnem congregant parentelam et comedunt eum, sicut nobis dicebatur pro certo." For the record, Pelliot did not believe that Büri-Tübät was Tibet. Cf. SF I, p. 89.

8. Guillemis de Rubruc, *Itinerarium fratris Willielmi de Rubruquis de ordine fratrum Minorum, Galli, anno grat. 1253 ad partes orientales* 26.3 (SF I, p. 234): "Post istos sunt Tebec, homines solentes comedere parentes suos defunctos, ut causa pietatis non facerent aliud sepulcrum eis nisi viscera sua. Modo tamen hoc dimiserunt, quia abhominabiles erant omni nationi. Tamen adhuc faciunt pulchros cifos de capitibus parentum, ut in illis bibentes habeant memoriam eorum in iocunditate sua." Cf. *Itinerarium* 29.50 (SF I, p. 271): "Thebec scribunt sicut nos et habent figuras valde similes nostris."

9. Rubruc, *Itinerarium* 25.2 (SF I, p. 230): "Habent etiam quocumque vadunt semper in manibus quamdam cestam c vel ducentorum nucleorum sicut nos portamus pater noster, et dicunt semper hec verba, on man baccam, hoc est: Deus tu nosti; secundum quod quidam eorum interpretatus est michi, et totiens expectat renumerationem a Deo quotiens hoc dicendo memoratur Dei."

10. Odoricus de Portu Naonis, *Relatio* 33 (SF I, p. 484): "De provincia Tibor magni Canis, ubi mulieres habent dentes aprinos; et de honore quem filius facit patri in morte, nam carnes eius incidit et eas dat aquilis et vultoribus ad manducandum, et credit eas aquilas esse angelos Dei qui portant eum in celum."

11. *Libro del Conosçimiento de todos los reynos & tierras & señoríos que son por el mundo* 14 (SF I, p. 572): "En el imperio de Catayo ay un reynado que dizen Sçim que confina con el reyno de Sarmagant y con el reyno de Bocarin y con el reyno de Trimic."

12. For a list of the various editions of Marco Polo, see John Larner, *Marco Polo and the Discovery of the World* (New Haven, CT: Yale University Press, 2001), p. 224.

13. *The Travels of John Mandeville*, ed. M. Letts (London: Hakluyt Society, 1953); Anastaas van den Wyngaert, O.F.M., *Jean de Mont Corvin, O.F.M.: premier évêque de Khanbaliq (Pe-king), 1247–1328* (Lille: Societé Saint-Augustin, Desclée de Brouwer, 1924).

14. R. W. Shirley, *The Mapping of the World: Early Printed World Maps 1472–1700* (London: Holland Press, 1983); Braham Norwick, "Locating Tibet: The Maps," in *Studia Tibetica: Quellen und Studien zur tibetischen Lexikographie*, ed. Herbert Franke (Munich: Kommission für zentralasiatische Studien bayerische Akademie der Wissenschaften, 1988), 2, pp. 301–20.

15. Matteo Ricci, *Lettere (1580–1609)*, ed. Francesco D'Arelli (Macerata: Quodlibet, 2001), p. 327. Compare the letter that Ricci wrote to de Góis on January 18, 1580 (*Lettere*, p. 83).

16. The relevant primary sources are *Historia relatio de potentissimi regis Mogor* (Mogantia: Ex Officina typographica H. Breem, 1598); *Lettere de P. Nicolo Pimenta Visitore dell'Compagnia di Giesu nell'India Orientale* (Venice: G. B. Ciotti, 1602); and *Missione al Gran Mogor del P. Ridolfo Aquaviva della Compagnia di Giesu* (Bologna: Per l'Erede del Benacci, 1672). Cf. Henri Hosten, S.J., *Jesuit Letters and Allied Papers on Mogor, Tibet, Bengal, & Burma*, 2 vols. (Calcutta: Asiatic Society, 1914–1916); E. Mac-Lagan, *The Jesuits and the Great Mogul* (London, 1932), pp. 38, 366. A. Monserrate, *The Commentary of Father Monserrate, S.J., on His Journey to the Court of Akbar*, trans. J. S. Hoyland (London, 1922), pp. 106, 215; John Correia-Afonso, S.J., *Letters from the Mughal*

Court: The First Jesuit Mission to Akbar 1580–1583 (St. Louis: IJS, 1981). Gauvin Alexander Bailey has done a great amount of recent work on the Jesuits missions in Mughal India. Gauvin Alexander Bailey, *Art on the Jesuit Missions in Asia and Latin America*, pp. 112–43; "The Truth-Showing Mirror: Jesuit Catechism and the Arts in Mughal India," *The Jesuits: Cultures, Sciences, and the Arts*, 1, pp. 380–401; "Jesuit Art and Architecture in Asia," *Jesuits and the Arts 1540–1773*, pp. 311–60.

17. For a summary of early Jesuit knowledge of Tibet, see Giuseppe Toscano, S.X., *La prima missione cattolica nel Tibet* (Parma: Istituto Missioni Estere, 1951).

18. While these passages are sometimes cited as evidence of the persistence of the myth of Prester John, it should be noted that Monserrate himself expressed no small amount of skepticism about such claims, noting that they come from yogis, who are "untrustworthy witnesses, telling many outright lies, and mixing a dab of truth with a great deal of story." He also ends his report by noting that he and the other missionaries were unable to carefully examine the claims since the end of the mission frustrated their plans. For Monserrate's use of the term Himalaya (*Imao*), see his *Relatio de Rebus Mongolensibus* of November 26, 1582 (DI 12, p. 654). Compare his letter to Father General Everhard Mercurian of October 26, 1579 (DI 11, p. 648) and Matteo Ricci's letter to Bento de Góis of January 18, 1580 (DI 11, p. 838).

19. The classic study is Arnulf Camps, O.F.M., *Jerome Xavier S.J. and the Muslims of the Mogul Empire: Controversial Works and Missionary Activity* (Schöneck-Beckenried: Nouvelle Revue de Science Missionaire Suisse, 1957).

20. On de Góis, see Wessels, pp. 1–41; Henri Bernard, S.J., *Le frère Bento de Goes chez les Musulmans de la Haute Asie (1603–1607)* (Tientsin: Hautes études, 1934); Eduardo Brazão, *Em demanda do Cataio* (Lisbon: Agência-Geral do Ultramar, 1969); Hughes Didier, *Fantômes d'Islam & de Chine: Le voyage de Bento de Góis, S.J. (1603–1607)* (Paris: Fundação Calouste Gulbenkian, 2003). A number of popular portraits exist. Cf. Charles Herbert Payne, ed., *Jahangir and the Jesuits, with an Account of the Travels of Benedict Goes* (London: G. Routledge & Sons, 1930); Wilfred P. Schoenberg, *Garlic for Pegasus: The Life of Brother Benito de Goes of the Society of Jesus* (Westminster, MD: Newman Press, 1955); and more recently, George D. Bishop, *In Search of Cathay: The Travels of Bento de Goes, S.J., 1562–1607* (Anand, India: Gujarat Sahitya Prakash, 1998). For a theological study, see Miguel Anselmo Bernard, *Five Great Missionary Experiments and Cultural Issues in Asia* (Manila: Anteneo de Manila University, 1991).

21. António de Andrade, *Novo descobrimento do gram Cathayo, ou Reinos de Tibet* (Lisbon: Mattheus Pinheiro, 1626). Cf. Václav Pantaleon Kirwitzer, ed., *Lettere annuae del Tibet del MDCXXVI scritte al M. R. P. Mutio Vitellschi, generale della Compagnia di Giesu* (Rome: Francesco Corbelletti, 1628); L. B. Barrett, "António de Andrade and the Discovery of Tibet," *Journal of Indian History* 2 (1922/23), pp. 241–46; August Hermann Francke, "Die Jesuitenmission von Tsaparang im Lichte der tibetischen Urkunden,"- *Zeitschrift für Missionswissenschaft* 15 (1925), pp. 269–76; Jürgen Aschoff, *Tsaparang-Königsstadt in Westtibet: Die vollständigen Berichte des Jesuitenpaters António de Andrade und eine Beschreibung vom heutigen Zustand der Klöster* (Munich: MC Verlag, 1989); Hughes Didier, *Les Portugais au Tibet: Les premières relations jésuites (1624–1635)* (Paris: Editions Chandeigne, 1996). On Godinho, see Henri Hosten, S.J., "A Letter of Father

Francisco Godinho, S.J., from Western Tibet," *Journal and Proceedings of the Asiatic Society of Bengal*, n.s., 21 (1925), pp. 49–73.

22. The apologists for the Younghusband expedition maligned Andrade as fiercely as they did Desideri. Thomas Holdich judged his account "scanty and confused" and the man himself "but a doubtful authority" (Holdich, *Tibet, the Mysterious*, p. 70). Sandberg felt that one might reasonably charge Andrade with "fraud" and only grudgingly admitted that there was "beneath the bungling account printed and the manifest attempt to exaggerate the importance of the achievement, a certain substratum of correctness in two or three topographical points, which makes it extremely unlikely that the whole exploit was a fiction" (Sandberg, *Exploration*, p. 24).

23. António de Andrade, *O descobrimento do Tibet*, ed. Francisco Maria Esteves Pereira (Coimbra: Imprensa da Universidade, 1921), pp. 71–72, 83, 93.

24. Ibid., pp. 70, 86–87.

25. Ibid., p. 83: "Pintão aos Anjos, a que chamão Lâs, de uarias manejras; huns muito fermosos como mancebos; outros em figuras horrendas pelejando contra os demonios; e dizem, que os representão nesta forma, não porque a tenhão; mas pera exprimir os uarios effeitos que tem contra os Espiritos malignos."

26. Hosten, "Fr. Francisco Godinho," pp. 71–72: "Il ne se peut dire combien ils cherissent et reuerent la Croix: comme c'est la plus belle marque de leur ancienne religion."

27. Giuseppe de Castro noted in a letter from August 28, 1632 that there were five Jesuit fathers in Tibet and two more in Agra who were destined for the mission. Since he mentioned in a previous letter written from Agra on August 8 that he was staying with Morando, we may presume that the other missionary destined for the Tibetan mission was Capece. De Castro's letters may not be reliable, however; from a letter of November 20, 1631, written from Bengal, Wessels notes that the five missionaries who were present at the time of the catastrophe were dos Anjos, de Oliveira, de Azevedo, da Fonseca, and Marques. Azevedo, however, was not present. In later letters, of August 28, 1632, and February 6, 1633, de Castro mentions again five Jesuits in Tibet, but by this time neither Azevedo nor de Oliveira was still in Tibet. If both had arrived in Agra in January 1632, it seems strange that de Castro would not have known about it, since he himself was stationed there with Capece and Morando in August that very year.

28. Luiza Maria Baillie, "Father Estevao Cacella's Report on Bhutan in 1627," *Journal of Bhutan Studies* 1 (2007), pp. 1–35.

29. Michael Aris, *Bhutan: The Early History of a Himalayan Kingdom* (Warminster: Aris and Philips Ltd, 1979).

30. In light of Donald Lopez's work on the mythical healthiness of Tibet, we might note that Cacella himself remarked that the climate of Bhutan was exceedingly healthy: "Never in India did I enjoy such good health, and this so with everyone. We scarcely met a sick man, and there are a great number of elderly people who remain hale and hearty" (in Luiza Maria Baillie's translation).

31. Nancy Moore Gettelman, "Karma-Bstan-skyong and the Jesuits," *Reflections on Tibetan Culture: Essays in Memory of Turrell V. Wylie*, ed. Lawrence Epstein and Richard Sherburne (Lewiston: Edwin Mellen Press, 1990), pp. 269–77.

32. Here I have used the text and translation from the *litterae annuae* found in Wessels, *Early Jesuit Travellers*, pp. 160–61.

33. I have not been able to read the 1646 edition that bears this wonderful image. The quotation is from the 1671 edition (Amsterdam: Joannem Janssonium à Waesberge & Elizeum Weyerstraet), p. 415: "Actionibus Societatis Iesu sol nunquam occumbit."

34. Grueber and D'Orville counted as acquaintances some of the most prominent Jesuits in the history of the missions. Grueber was originally sent from Macao to the China mission to assist Adam Schall von Bell at the Imperial Observatory in Beijing and was one of Athanasius Kircher's sources for *China illustrata* after returning to Europe. D'Orville met Martino Martini during his lectures on China at the University of Louvain. Among their traveling companions when they left for China was Ferdinand Verbiest, who would become Schall's successor at the Imperial Observatory.

35. On Grueber and D'Orville, see Franz Braumann, *Ritt nach Barantola: die Abenteuer des tibetreisenden Johannes Grueber* (Vienna: Herder, 1958); A. Pinsker, S.J., "Mitteilungen des Jesuiten Johann Grueber über Tibet," in *Contributions on Tibetan Language, History, and Culture: Proceedings of the Csomo de Kőrös Symposium Held at Velm-Vienna, Austria, 13–19 September 1981*, ed. Ernst Steinkellner and Helmut Tauscher (Vienna: Arbietskreis für tibetische und buddhistische Studien Universität Wien, 1983), pp. 289–302; and Gerhard Strasser, "Tibet im 17. Jahrhundert: Johannes Grueber, S.J., seine Reisebeschreibungen und die Frage inrer Veröffenlichung," *Daphnis: Zeitschrift für Mittlere Deutsche Literatur* 24 (1995), pp. 375–400. Cf. "Grueber and Dorville's Journey Across Tibet," *The Geographical Journal* 24 (1904), pp. 663–70. This is a summary of Tronnier's monograph in *Zeitschrift der Gesellschaft für Erdkunde* 5 (1904).

36. Athanasius Kircher, *China monumentis qua sacris qua profanis nec non variis naturae & artis spectaculis aliarumque rerum memorabilium argumentis illustrata* (Amsterdam: Jacobus van Meurs, 1667). According to Somm. 4, 1064, the edition by Jacobus van Meurs is a counterfeit edition of the original edition by Johannes Janssonius van Waesberge. The Meurs edition has some changes on pp. 132–33. Unless otherwise noted, my citations are from the Meurs edition of 1667. The French edition contains valuable additional material on Johannes Grueber. Cf. *La Chine d'Athanase Kirchere de la Compagnie de Jesus, illustrée de plusieurs monuments tant sacrés que profanes et de quantité de recherchés de la nature et de l'art. A quoy on à adjousté de nouveau les questions curieuses que le Serenissime Grand Duc de Toscane a fait depuis peu au P. Jean Grubere touchant ce grand Empire. Avec un Dictionaire Chinois et Français, lequel est très rare, et que n'à pas encores paru au jour* (Amsterdam: Chez Jean Janssons à Waesberge, 1670).

37. For more detailed accounts of the various provinces and assistancies, see L. Carrez, S.J., *Atlas Geographicus Societatis Jesu* (Paris: G. Colombier, 1900); A. Coemans, S.J., "De Assistentiis in quas Societatis Jesu dividebatur saeculis XVI–XVIII," AHSI 9 (1940), pp. 303–10; and J. B. Goetstouwers, S.J., and C. Van de Vorst, S.J., eds., *Synopsis Historiae Societatis Jesu* (Louvain: Typis Sancti Alphonsi, 1950). On the role of the visitor to Asian provinces, see Witek, *Controversial Ideas*, p. 20.

38. Wessels, *Early Jesuit Travellers*, p. 206 n. 3: "He is registered in the Catalogue of November 1705 as being there *ad Thibetanam missionem investigandum*."

39. Martinetti's fact-finding mission ended in April 1713 at Surat, where he stayed at the Capuchin hospice. There he learned that the mission no longer belonged to the Society of Jesus but had been awarded by the Congregation for the Propagation of the Faith to the rival order. Hosten notes that Martinetti's information was sound but outdated, for the Capuchins had withdrawn from Lhasa two years previously; in fact, by the time Martinetti arrived at their hospice Domenico da Fano had returned to Rome to inform the Congregation for the Propagation of the Faith of the dire financial straits of the Lhasa mission. Martinetti wrote to Tamburini from Daman to declare the Jesuit mission to Tibet void as Desideri was traveling from Goa to Bassein in late November 1713. If Desideri did not meet Martinetti in either Daman or Surat, he must have met one of the other Jesuit fathers who had known him in Agra. If Desideri obtained his information about the various routes to Lhasa from Martinetti, he does not credit his informant by name.

40. Hosten published this letter and a translation in his "Letters and Papers," pp. 21–27. The original can be found in ARSI Goa 9.

41. See, for example, the letter of Diogo da Cunha to Acquaviva (DI 15, pp. 225–27).

42. Stephen Niell, *A History of Christianity in India: The Beginnings to AD 1707* (Cambridge: Cambridge University Press, 1984), pp. 111–65. For a comprehensive account of the role of the Jesuits in the Portuguese empire, see Dauril Alden, *The Making of an Enterprise: The Society of Jesus in Portugal, Its Empire, and Beyond 1540–1750* (Stanford: Stanford University Press, 1996). For Goa as a Jesuit hub, see pp. 44–54.

43. The other, more serious, perils of sea travel were well known from missionary accounts. Of the eighteen companions who sailed with Albert D'Orville and Martino Martini from Lisbon to Goa in 1657, two died, one was paralyzed, and one suffered a permanent mental breakdown. Prospero Intorcetta, the Jesuit author of the *Sinarum scientia politco-moralis*, sailed from Lisbon in 1673 with twelve recruits for the China missions; when they reached Macao, only one survived. Philippe Couplet, who trans-lated the Confucian classics first published in the *Confucius Sinarum philosophus*, drowned in 1693. Nine years earlier he had told a fellow Jesuit Philippe Avril—who would also die at sea—that only about one hundred of the six hundred Jesuits chosen for the missions in China arrived safely on its shores. Bangert (*History*, p. 345) notes that Couplet's figures might need to be checked, but believes them to be fairly accurate, since in 1687 the Jesuit published a catalogue of the Society's priests in China that included the curriculum vitae of each since 1581. Compare these calculations to those of John Witek, who judges that seventeen of the eighty-two missionaries sent from Portugal to the Indies via Lisbon from 1668 to 1678 died on the way. Of these, only seven entered the Vice-Province of China (Witek, *Controversial Ideas*, pp. 21–22). Ronnie Po-Chia Hsia estimates that one-third of the Jesuits destined for China died *en route*. *The World of Catholic Renewal*, p. 189.

44. DR 1.3 (MITN V, pp. 130–31): "con mio rammarico farsi traffico della vita e libertà degl'uomini ... E una compassione il veder la gran facilità con cui, purchè si dia la detta tassa, si battezzano tali Cafri, ancorchè non abbiano alcuna instruzzione, e non intendan la lingua." Jesuits themselves were forbidden to own slaves, although

Jesuits in Goa had to be reminded of this rule, as the procurator Jerónimo Cardoso noted to Acquaviva (DI 14, pp. 335–36).

45. DR 1.2 (MITN 5, pp. 127–28).

46. DR 1.2 (MITN 5, p. 126). Jonathan Spence has some wonderful pages on the nautical adventures of Matteo Ricci. Cf. *Memory Palace*, pp. 65–81.

47. I have followed the dating offered by Enzo Gualtiero Bargiacchi, "Il contributo di Ippolio Desideri alla conoscenza geografica," *L'Universo* (2005), p. 797. Cf. Hosten, "Letters and Papers," p. 146.

48. DR (MITN 5, p. 138).

49. The *Exercises* were regularly practiced in Asia. Francis Xavier's letters are saturated with references to them. He explicitly remarks that he gave them in India, instructs Gaspar Barzaeus and Antonio Gomes to give them, and recommends them to prisoners, sinners, tax collectors, penitents, procurators, secretaries, clergy, novices, and neophytes. Jerónimo Xavier thanks Father General Claudio Acquaviva for a new edition of the *Exercises* sent to India in 1586, most likely sent on the Jubilee granted by Sixtus V to mark the opening of the Chinese mission (DI 15, pp. 202–3, 207–8). Pedro Martins, the provincial at Goa, reports on them in his annual letters of 1590 (DI 15, p. 525), and 1591 (DI 15, p, 644). The annual letter of Francisco Cabral for 1595 notes that they were made in Cochin (DI 17, p. 404); a letter from Jorge de Castro to Acquaviva mentions exercises made at Vaipikotta (DI 18, p. 472); and the annual letter of Simão de Sá from 1598 reports on their practice in the professed house at Goa (DI 18, p. 871). On the requirements of tertianship in India, see Acquaviva's instructions to the Procurator Francisco de Monclaro (DI 15, p. 57); and to the provincial Pedro Martins (DI 15, p. 816).

50. DL 1 (MITN 5, p. 3).

51. DL 1 (MITN 5, p. 4): "Padre Nostro, Dio mi chiama al Tibet, e se non giungo là, non proverrà certamente da me; onde quando S. D. M. nel Giudizio mi dicesse: perchè non andasti? che cosa gl'ho da rispondere? Non avevo l'autorità di ciò fare, mentre gli uomini me l'impedivano. Ma perchè sarebbe mia colpa l'istesso non procurare tal'autorità, per questo gliela dimando."

52. DL 1 (MITN 5, pp. 3–4): "L'altra sorte d'impedimenti, i quali l'esperienza di ciò che in altri succedè altre volte m'insegna essere i più gagliardi, e perciò più da temersi, e perciò da meglio precautelarsi contro d'essi, sono le volontà de' Nostri medesimi, che incatenano chi corre, tagliano le ali a chi vola, in una parola, a spada tratta si oppongono a' voleri dello zelo di Sua Paternità, e perciò a' manifesti voleri di Dio."

53. DL 2 (MITN5, p. 5): "Nec deterreant ullae difficultates; *Nam causa Dei est.* Ah, Padre Nostro, io non posso qui esprimerle che animo, che vigore mi diano quelle belle parole: *Causa Dei est.*" Jesuits' letters necessarily passed through their superiors; see, for example, the exchange between the procurator Francisco de Monclaro and Claudio Acquaviva (DI 15, p. 59). A letter normally took between one and a half and two years to be delivered to Europe, depending on when ships left from India and whether they wintered in Mozambique (DI 15, p. 262), although much longer delays occasionally occurred. A letter written by Alessandro Valignano to Acquaviva in 1589 did not arrive in Rome until 1606 (DI 15, p. 381).

54. The importance of this patent can be seen in the endorsement of the letter itself: "Explicat desideria quibus flagrat, ingrediendi Missionem Tibet tensem, vel moriendi in ipsamet expeditione, et ne ab aliquo nostrorum, impediatur, petit ut P. V.a illi mittat Patentes litteras, quibus independenter abaliis posit progredi in hac determinatione, etc." Hosten, "*Letters and Papers*," p. 21.

55. DL 2 (MITN 5, p. 6).

56. Rome granted the rights to the Capuchins in 1703, at the same time that it awarded them with the rights to evangelize Tibet. A letter Desideri later wrote to Tamburini from Leh (DL 6, MITN 5, pp. 31–32) hints at some tension. Desideri could not help remarking on a curious rumor that the "king" of the third Tibet had sent a delegation to the Mughal Empire sometime between 1705 and 1707 in search of the Jesuits. This delegation, the Jesuit argued, not knowing that members of his own company could be found at Delhi and Agra, went instead to Surat, where they discovered the Capuchins, who—note how Desideri glides from speculation to reportage—quieted the matter and stealthily went to Tibet instead. Hosten speculates that the Capuchins at Surat invented this story to explain how their order came to be in Tibet, but such an interpretation presumes that they needed to justify their presence against previous Jesuit claims. If the Capuchins invented the story, why did they not simply say that the king of Tibet sought Christians or, better yet, Capuchins?

57. DL 6 (MITN 5, p. 22).

58. DL 3 (MITN 5, p. 7). This letter gives no hint that the Jesuit visitor José da Silva made any suggestion about possible companions for a journey to Tibet. In fact, it did not mention Tamburini's representative at all, giving one reason to think that Desideri wrote the letter before he met da Silva and that he only mailed it after arriving in Surat.

59. Hosten, "Letters and Papers," p. 28, believes the detainees to be Monteiro, Carvalho, Gill, Torres, Martinetti, and Koch. Desideri probably meant Carvalho and Torres, whom Sarayva had commissioned to open the Tibetan mission at Amaral's insistence, but who were sent to Mysuru instead. Desideri might have also referred to Peter Gill since he had originally petitioned Tamburini with Carvalho. We have no evidence that other Jesuits were actively detained; in most cases, it appears that they were limited either by personal shortcomings, understandable exhaustion, or circumstances beyond their control.

60. DL 3 (MITN 5, p. 8). In all likelihood, Desideri feared that he would have to stop to make the studies for his own tertianship, the final period in a Jesuit's training before he makes his "fourth vow" of obedience to the pope, and enters the rank of the "professed." Following the normal course of Jesuit studies, he had been ordained to the priesthood after twelve years of study on August 28, 1712, but did not have sufficient time to complete his tertianship in Europe, since he departed from Rome on September 27, or in India, since he remained in perpetual motion after departing from Goa. In this regard, his request for Tamburini's patent mirrors his request for the general's rescript for Freyre. Both the patent and the rescript would prevent their superiors from delaying the mission to Tibet.

61. DL 3 (MITN 5, p. 9): "*Ecce ego, mitte me*; son pronto ad andar senza verun sussidio, senza viatico, senza cosa veruna. Bastami solo la fiducia nell'assistenza divina,

giacchè tengo scolpite nel cuore le parole di V. P. scritte a' Superiori di questa Provincia in una sua lettera, nella quale, ordinandogli che trattino di aprir nuove Missioni, e che trattino con maggior impegno *de reditu ad Thibetum.*"

62. On this date, see Bargiacchi, "Il contributo di Ippolito Desideri," p. 797, and Hosten, "Letters and Papers," p. 27.

63. DL 4 (MITN 5, p. 11). Hosten, "Letters and Papers," p. 38 n. 3: "Sanganer is 7 m. S.W. of Jaipur; hence *Amir* must not be identified with Ajmer, but with Amber or Amer, alias Jaipur. Amber was thus a few miles further ahead [*piu avanti*]." Petech repeats Hosten, MITN 5, p. 227 n. 9.

64. DL 3 (MITN 5, p. 7); DR 1.5 (MITN 5, p. 148): "sostegno e decoro della nostra S. Fede in quell'Imperio." On Giuliana, see Henri Hosten, *Journal of the Punjab Historical Society* 7 (1917), pp. 1–11.

65. DL 4 (MITN 5, p. 12): "Sta quivi all cura di quei trecento più o meno Cristiani, che quivi si ritrovano, un nostro Padre, da cui fui accolto e ricevuto con molta cortesia e carità."

66. DL 4 (MITN 5, p. 12): "Convien sapere, come, avendo in Goa ottenuto d'andar a procurar d'aprire una nuova Missione nel Thibet, fui destinato sì, ma solo senza verun compagno in un impresa molto argua ed in luoghi tanto remoti e da' Nostri e da qualunque Cristiano."

67. On Freyre, see Sweet, "Desperately Seeking Capuchins."

68. Hosten provides a running commentary on Desideri and Freyre's early journey in his footnotes, which are worth reading in order. Cf. Hosten, "Letters and Papers," pp. 35 n. 4; 40 n. 1; 41 n. 1; 49 n. 1; 55 nn. 1–2; 59 n. 9; 73 n. 7.

69. As noted in Alessandro Valignano's summary of the rules for the India province (DI 14, p. 871), a Jesuit was subject to superiors even while traveling.

70. DL 4 (MITN 5, p. 13): "che sono i due condimenti, che rendono agevole tutto l'aspro e fanno dolce tutto l'amaro."

71. DL 4 (MITN 5, pp. 13–14): "la pena più sensibile è il veder davanti agl'occhi di continuo tanta ruina d'anime preziose e tante e tanto grandi offese che si fanno contro l'Infinito Bene, e non poter nè pur dar un passo per ovviare a sì lagrimevole scon-certo.... Si compiace S.D.M. *in vinculis charitatis* con dolce amorosa violenza di tirarmi con tutto il cuore là dove è grande la perdita dell'anime e più oltraggiata è la di lui amabilissima bontà; e nel tempo medesimo con durissimi legami mi sono stretti e stirati in altra parte i piedi, senz'altro poter fare se non mandar sole e scompagnate le potenze dell'animo, dove non può il corpo far loro compagnia. Ma ben presto ritornano elle a me sconsolate; come cani che, scoperta la preda bramata, non potendola essi afferrare, tornano al cacciatore e lo stimolano ad andar egli più avanti a trafiggerla con le sue armi."

72. DL 4 (MITN 5, p. 14): "Faccia il Demonio e l'Inferno tutto quanto vuole, ponga in contrario tutte le sue forze; non per questo mi atterrisce, perchè *scio cui credidi.*" Desideri alludes to 2 Timothy 1:12.

73. DL 4 (MITN 5, p. 19): "P. Piccolomini mio carissimo, la riverisco con tutto l'affetto, e la supplico a pregar di continuo per me.... Il Signore si degni per sua misericordia di riempre V.R. e tutti gl'altri del suo santo amore, d'un grande e constante

fervore nel suo santo servizio e nel zelo della salute dell'anime, e d'ogni consolazione, finchè ci dia grazia di rivederci nel Santo Paradiso. Vale, vale, vale."

74. DL 3 (MITN 5, pp. 8–9): "*Ecce ego, mitte me.* Ancorchè mi sia necessario camminar per le fiamme, e ancorchè mi fosse necessario passare per tutto l'Inferno a fine di arrivare a dar la notizie di Dio e della Santa Fede Cattolica a quelle povere genti del Thibet, per le fiamme camminerò, e per tutto l'Inferno passerò, confidato in Dio, purchè la Compagnia non resti punto aggravata, purchè si promova la gloria di Dio, purchè si procuri la salute eterna di quell'anime."

75. While Županov is right to say that missionaries' letters "closely follow" the structure of the medieval *dictamen*, it is a bit of an exaggeration to say that missionaries studiously avoided refined style as a form of active asceticism and obedience. I am more inclined to think that their rough and ready quality owes more to the occasional nature of their composition than a self-consciously ascetic style. *Disputed Mission*, p. 6.

76. MI I, pp. 539–47.

77. Consider a letter written by the Italian missionary Organtino Gnecci-Soldi: "Any Jesuit who comes to Japan and does not foster a love for this bride of wondrous beauty, not caring to learn her language at the first opportunity, not conforming to her customs, deserves to be deported to Europe as an inept and unprofitable worker in the Lord's vineyard." A reader of postcolonialist studies might read into this passage any number of sinister connotations; seventeenth-century readers would have noticed a range of associations in this passage now largely forgotten. It evokes the allegorical interpretation of the beautiful captive (Deut 21:10–13), St. Paul's exhortation on a husband's duties to his wife (Eph 5:1–33), chief of which is that he willingly lay down his life for his bride, and the eschatological vision of the bride of the Lamb (Rev 21:1–4). I have used the translation quoted by Andrew C. Ross, "Alessandro Valignano and Culture in the East," in *The Jesuits: Cultures, Sciences, and the Arts* 1, p. 344. On the theology of the beautiful captive and non-Christian religions, see Henri de Lubac, S.J., *Medieval Exegesis*, trans. Marc Sebanc (Grand Rapids: Wm. B. Eerdmans, 1998), 1, pp. 211–24.

78. DL 5 (MITN 5, p. 20).

79. This would place Freyre at approximately the same place in the four-stage progression as a Jesuit as Desideri himself. All Jesuits begin as novices, whether they aspire to the priesthood or are received as lay brothers; they then become formed scholastics after taking simple vows and remain so for two to fifteen years of study. A formed coadjutor makes perpetual vows, whether he is a lay brother or priest, and the professed make the three solemn vows of religion plus the famous "fourth vow" of the Society. In practice, those who are ordained as formed scholastics progress immediately from perpetual to solemn vows.

80. DR 1.7 (MITN 5, p. 159): "Questi monti son come una scala di continuate e l'un'all'altra sopraposte montagne, che arrivano alla più alta, che si chiama Pir-Pangiàl, così denominata dal nome d'un gran genio da quelle genti molto riverito, e a cui intuito tal luogo è altresì da esse molto rispettato. Una tal montagna è molto alta e molto scabrosa, in varj mesi dell'anno ricoperta d'altissime nevi, e in alcune sue parti più concave occupata da perpetui ghiacci, che sembrano emulare la durezza e fermezza de' marmi."

81. DR 1.7 (MITN 5, p. 160): "dissenteria accompagnata da flusso di sangue." Hosten, "Letters and Papers," p. 60, identifies this "dissenteria" with the gastrointestinal disorder well known to travelers in India; Wessels, *Early Jesuit Travellers*, p. 211, identifies it with the pulmonary hemorrhages associated with altitude sickness.

82. DR 1.8 (MITN 5, p. 160). It is difficult to translate *favoloso*, which implies an imaginary creation based on fables. Both of the English words "fantastic" and "fabulous" have taken on positive connotations that are quite at odds with their etymological meanings.

83. DR 1.8 (MITN 5, p. 163): "Dalle radici di questo monte sin a tutta l'estensione di circa nove mesi di cammino, quanto son necessarj per arrivar alla Cina, finisce affatto la fertilità e l'amenità della terra, e altro non s'incontra che sterilità e infecondi orrori de' Monti Caucasi più settentrionali sin là continuati, che da' geografi si chiamano Dorsum Orbis."

84. DL 6 (MITN 5, p. 24): "Ma che? cammino sì angusto, che nè pure è capace molte volte di porsi in esso un sol piede drittamente, ma un sol piede doppo l'altro difficoltosamente e travagliosamente sospeso di maniera, che se erra alcun poco il piede conviene andare a precipizio cadendo tra pietre, ed ire a perdersi ne' furiosi torrenti che giù nel basso stanno posti, e quando si scappi per buona sorte la morte, conviene almeno restare o mezzo sfraggellato o miserabilmente stroppiato, come in alcuni infelici n'abbiamo veduto l'esempio." Cf. DR 1.8 (MITN 5, p. 167): "Col moto di chi passa s'agita il detto ponte da destra a sinistra e da sinistra a destra, e perciò non può passarsi se non da un solo alla volta. Oltre di ciò, essendo molto sollevato sopra del fiume ed essendo in basso e da ogni banda tutto scoperta, il moto precipitoso dell'acque che corrono nel fondo offende notabilmente la vista e causa notabil giramento di testa."

85. DL 7 (MITN 5, p. 35): "Je vous avoue que je frémis encore au seul souvenir de ces affreux passages."

86. On Desideri's knowledge of Ladakh, see Enzo Gualtiero Bargiacchi, "Ippolito Desideri's first remarks on Ladakh," a paper presented at the Thirteenth International Association of Ladakh Studies (IALS) Colloquium in Rome (September 7–11, 2007) (manuscript kindly provided by the author).

87. Freyre, *Tibetorum ac eorum Relatio Viarum* (MITN 7, p. 197): "Tunc temporis portatores, posis sarcinis, frontem fluviali aqua et pedes humectando, ocularem retinere conabant humorem. Nos vero frigoribus parum assueti vultum solum aqua conspersimus."

88. DL 6 (MITN 5, p. 27).

89. DL 6 (MITN 5, p. 28): "Appena arrivammo in vista di questo Leh o Lades, il P. Superiore, oppresso da tanti travagli e patimenti di viaggio sì lungo cominciò a pensare di ritornare al Mogor, dimandando e facendo diligenza per sapere se vi era altro camino diverso da quello, che havevamo fatto, per tornare al Mogor."

90. DL 6 (MITN 5, p. 29).

91. DL 6 (MITN 5, p. 29): "desiderando anzi di restar qui immobile qual pietra, o incontrar mille volte la morte; ma *melior est oboedientia quam victimae*." Desideri quotes Samuel's admonition of Saul in 1 Samuel 15:22.

92. I cannot do justice to this difficult historical puzzle. Enzo Gualtiero Bargiacchi, Michael Sweet, and Leonard Zwilling have each contributed important elements toward its solution, and I must defer to their collective expertise. It seems amazing that neither Desideri nor Freyre had learned the most rudimentary facts about Tibetan geography from other Jesuits that they may have encountered in their travels, even if they kept their intentions to go to Tibet secret. Hosten plausibly suggests that Desideri and Freyre knew that Andrade had traveled to Tibet by way of Srinagar, but mistook the Srinagar of Kashmir for the Srinagar of Garhwal. If either Freyre or Desideri knew that the Capuchins had gone to Tibet by way of Bengal and Patna, they may have simply wished to avoid them by taking the alternative route. Sweet, in the introduction to his English translation of Freyre's *Relatio*, suggests that Freyre, following the orders of his Jesuit superiors, took advantage of Desideri's desire to reopen the Tibetan mission in order to gather information on their Capuchin rivals, and brought Desideri to Lhasa as he sought them out. In personal conversation, Sweet tells me that he now thinks that Freyre and Desideri took the route they did to avoid the Capuchins, rushing ahead to Lhasa in order to establish Jesuit priority after the Capuchins abandoned the mission. Both of these interpretations are entirely plausible. I think we need to leave open the possibility that Desideri himself shared some unspoken understanding with Tamburini, or that Tamburini manipulated both Desideri and Freyre, but at present I do not believe that we have enough information to judge the motives of our protagonists. For important pieces of this puzzle see Enzo Gualtiero Bargiacchi, *A Bridge Across Two Cultures*, pp. 41–61; Michael Sweet, "Desperately Seeking Capuchins"; "An Unpublished Letter in Portuguese by Fr. Ippolito Desideri" (AHSI, forthcoming); Leonard Zwilling, "Fr. Manoel Freyre S.J. and 'La Causa del Tibet,'" a paper given at the Fifteenth Congress of the International Association of Buddhist Studies.

93. DL 6 (MITN 5, pp. 30–31).

94. DR 1.9 (MITN 5, p. 172). Wessels concludes from the absence of sulfur springs on the usual valley road that Desideri probably traveled to Tankse over the Ke pass and around the southern shore of the Pangong Lake.

95. Freyre, *Tibetorum ac eorum Relatio Viarum* (MITN 7, p. 199): "Proindeque renuntiavit, defuncti uxorem istius territorii gubernatoris, quam et apud se vocat Regulus Lassae, mense Octobris modo profecturam, atque ad me primo venturam benedictionis causa. Rogabo, ut vos commode in Lassam portet. Vobis autem consulo et commoneo, ut cum venerit huc Caçal, domina scilicet gubernatrix, vestris affectam muneribus visitetis."

96. Freyre, *Tibetorum ac eorum Relatio Viarum* (MITN 7, p. 200): "Verum tantis noctu nivibus pluit, ut Pater Hipolytus, quasi orbem videret mutatem, nihil praeter fugam arripiens, vel baculi oblitus, ad Mauri fugeret coquinam, qui missis famulis suis ut nostra portarent, omnes in eadem recepit coquina, relicto tentorio, quod nivium pondere pressum, quae sequenti nocte ceciderunt, ultimo stare non potuit."

97. DR 1.10 (MITN 5, p. 177). I have paraphrased Desideri here. The full passage is: "L'allogio della notte altro non è che la terra, da cui molte volte convien levar via la neve, e per tetto il cielo, d'onde o cadono nevi, o scendono brine."

98. DR 1.10 (MITN 5, p. 179): "La notte era più tosto un cessamento dal travaglio che un prender riposo."

99. DR 1.10 (MITN 5, p. 180): "In mezzo poi a tutti questi disagi e patimenti che ho raccontato, sperimentammo sensibilmente gli effetti della paterna amorevolissima assistenza di Dio, per cui amor unicamente avevamo tutto ciò intrapreso, e c'eravamo di buon cuore esposti a tutto quello che potesse accaderci. Con sì buona disposizione di sanità, con sì costante contentezza di cuore, con sì tranquilla conversazione tra di noi e con gli altri, e con tal soddisfazione a alacrità passammo quel deserto come se facessemo un viaggio di divertimento e di ricreazione."

100. DR 1.10 (MITN 5, p. 182): "Così avessi io saputa fondatamente la lingua, mentre con lei viaggiavo, per procurar di tirarla alla S. Fede, com'allora vivamente desideravo, et era ella inclinatissima al ben fare. Prego ora instantissimamente Iddio d'illuminarla e di guidarla all'eterna salute."

101. Françoise Pommaret, "Foreword," in Lhasa in the Seventeenth Century: The Capital of the Dalai Lamas, trans. Howard Solverson (Leiden: Brill, 2003), pp. xiv–xv.

102. DR 1.11 (MITN 5, p. 183): "e con ciò restai io tutto solo per qualche tempo, senz'esservi in tutt'affatto l'immensa estensione de' tre Thibet."

103. Desideri's letter to Ildebrando Grassi gives a cursory account of these first few events in Tibet. The letter makes no reference to Freyre. I am inclined to think that it is pre-dated, like his earlier letter from Surat.

104. In the first edition of China and Tibet in the Early XVIIIth Century, Petech identifies this figure with the minister Kangchené. In the second edition, he retracts his identification and concludes that Desideri must have confused some of the basic aspects of his narrative. Although Desideri often confuses historical details, it seems unlikely that he would have been so confused as to forget the name or station of one of his best Tibetan friends, unless Desideri is exaggerating the friendship. I will take up this problem in my final chapter.

105. DR 1.11 (MITN 5, p. 185): "Trovavasi egli allora insieme col re nel di lui segreto gabinetto, dove avendo intesa la mia venuta prontamente n'uscì, e venuto al suo appartamento, con molto speciali dimostrazioni e d'amor e d'onore m'accolse, e senza frametter dimora mi promise con obbligantissime espressioni una molto stretta e per sempre costante amicizia; e volle ch'io altresì per parte mia gli promettessi una simigliante amichevol corrispondenza. Furono poi sì palesi queste nostre reciproche dimostrazioni d'affetto, che attoniti tutti sembrava che non sapessero saziarsi di parlarne, nè potevano a bastanza maravigliarsi, che tra due persone non più vedutesi nel prim'incontro si fosse contratta una sì stretta e sì intensa familiarità."

106. DL 7 (MITN 5, p. 39): "Le présent du Lama estoit considerable, & le mien de très-peu d'importance; cependant celuy du Lama resta à la porte selon l'usage, & le Roy se fit apporter le mien; & pour témoigner combien il en estoit content, il le garda auprès de luy; ce qui est en cette cour une marque singulière de distinction."

107. DR 2.9 (MITN 6, p. 40): "Il di lui naturale era molto ilare ed affabile. Verso tutti si mostrava amante, facile in dar udienza e consolare, e di genio ancora liberale. Professava un amore straordinario a' forestieri, e quanto questi erano di paesi più lontani."

108. There seems to be some tension between Desideri's repeated assertions that he was lacking resources and his ability to purchase a house in Lhasa. This apparent discrepancy was pointed out to me independently by both Michael Sweet and Matthew Kapstein.

109. DR 1.11 (MITN 5, p. 188): "Ma io, date le dovute grazie a Dio di sì felice successo e di sì buon principio della mia missione, è incredibile l'ardor che concepij per applicarmi con tutto lo sforzo all'esercizio del mio impiego, e specialmente a uno studio ben fondato di quella lingua. Per tal fine, dal seguente sin all'ultimo giorno della mia dimora in quel regno, presi questo tenore, che continuai per lo spazio di quasi sei anni, cioè di studiar da mattina a sera; e per farlo più comodamente, differivo il pranzo a notte, sostenendomi fra giorno (eccettuati i dì solenni e di qualche convenienza), col bever del cià, che manipolato a quell'usanza, è di grand'alimento."

110. DR 1.11 (MITN 5, p. 190). Witek mentions that the Jesuits supplied Kangxi with one bottle of teriaca (*te li ya er ka*) after the emperor requested European drugs and wine for the court in 1709, after Giuseppe Baudino (1657–1718), the court pharmacist in Beijing, effected a cure for the emperor's heart palpitations (Witek, *Controversial Ideas*, p. 167).

111. Hosten is undecided: his chronology accepts the August 9 date as the meeting with the general, even as he notes that it must be mistaken. Desideri might have transferred much of the subject matter of later meetings of the summer to the first.

112. DR 1.11 (MITN 5, p. 184): "Risposi esser io venuto da remoti paesi che son di là segregati, non solo da vaste terre, ma ancora da immensi tratti di mare; dall'occidente essermi portato a quelle estremità dell'oriente, dall'Europa al Thibet. Quant'alla mia qualità e professione, esser io christiano e religioso ed esser Lamà, cioè sacerdote, in obbligo e in uffizio di guidar altri per il diritto sentiero della salute; e attualmente in esercizio di procurar con tutte le mie forze di ritirar quelli che fossero in errore da' loro traviamenti e di condurli alla nostra S. Legge, come a unicamente vera e legittima strada, fuori di cui non v'è altra per arrivar al cielo e al conseguimento dell'eterna felicità. E questo appunto esser il fine e l'affare per cui ero venuto in que' paesi. Constarmi di certo che tutti essi erano in sommo errore, che in sì misero stato non avevano alcuno che facesse loro conoscere i lacci da' quali erano avvinti e i precipizj tra i quali andavano in rovina con una irrimediabil perdizione."

113. DL 10 (MITN 5, p. 47): "non voler io nessun loro onore, nessuna loro grandezza, nessuna loro ricchezza; in somma nessun mio vantaggio temporale; ma unicamente la gloria di Dio e la loro eterna salute. Molto in questo punto mi combatterono; ma l'amoroso Giesù tenne molto saldo il mio cuore."

CHAPTER 3: TIBETAN RELIGION IN THEOLOGICAL PERSPECTIVE

1. DL 10 (MITN 5, p. 48): "Là passiamo con esemplare uniformità in tutto e con carità scambievole più che da fratelli."

2. Missionaries were particularly interested to discover whether Asian cultures believed in reincarnation, largely because it allowed them to relate Asian cultures to their own European antiquity through the analogous notion of metempsychosis, or the

"transmigration of souls," associated with Pythagoras. Nicolaus Lancillottus reported on the belief in a letter to Ignatius Loyola as early as December 1550 (DI 2, p. 128).

3. DL 7 (MITN 5, p. 36): "Ils appellent dieu Konciok, & ils semblent avoir quelque idée de l'adorable Trinité; car tantost ils nomment Konciok-cik, Dieu un; & tantost Konciok-Sum, Dieu trin. Ils se servent d'une espèce de chapellet, sur lequel ils prononcent ces paroles: *Om, ha, hum*. Lorsqu'on leur en demande l'explication, ils répondent que *Om* signifie intelligence ou bras, c'est-à-dire, puissance; que *ha* est la parole; que *hum* est le coeur ou l'amour; & que ce trois mots signifient Dieu. Ils adorent encore un nommé Urghien, qui naquit, à ce qu'ils disent, il ya a sept cens ans. Quand on leur demande s'il est dieu ou homme, quelques-un d'eux répondent qu'il est tout ensemble dieu & homme, qu'il n'a eu ny père ny mère, mais qu'il est né d'une fleur. Néanmoins leur statues représentent une femme qui a une fleur à la main, & ils disent que c'est la mère d'Urghien. Ils adorent plusieurs autres personnes qu'ils regardent comme des saints. Dans leurs églises on voit un autel couvert d'une nappe avec un parement: au milieu de l'autel est une espèce de tabernacle, où, selon eux, Urghien reside, quoyque d'ailleurs ils assurent qu'il est dans le ciel."

4. DR 2.14 (MITN 6, p. 90); 2:17 (MITN 6, p. 102); DR 3.17 (MITN 6, pp. 253–24); DR 3.20 (MITN 6, pp. 291–92); DR 4.2 (MITN 7, p. 11).

5. DR 3.13 (MITN 6, p. 228).

6. Matthew Kapstein, *The Tibetan Assimilation of Buddhism* (Oxford: Oxford University Press, 2000).

7. DR 3.18 (MITN 6, pp. 265–66): "Convien dunque sapere che tra molti libri che da antico tempo corrono nel Thibet per le mani di tutti due specialmente son molto notabili al presente proposito. Uno è intitolato Lung-tèn, cioè Profezie d'Urghien, e fu questo appunto il primo libro che mi capitò alle mani e che parola per parola mi feci con molta diligenza spiegare nel primo mettermi a studiare i libri di quella gentilità poco dopo il mio arrivo a Lhasà. L'altro contiene la vita d'Urghien, la sua andata al Thibet e sua dimora in esso; e fu questo il secondo libro che in quella lingua studiai, e che parimenti parola per parola mi fece molto accuratamente interpretare. Or in tutto quel primo libro e in alcuni capitoli del secondo, in forma di dialogo tra il re del Thibet e tra Urghien, si riferisce una lunga serie di profezie da questi fatte circa le cose che in quel regno per lunga serie di secoli erano per succedere."

8. See Luciano Petech's editorial remarks in MITN 6, pp. 346–49, nn. 141–63; OT 1, pp. 77–82. On Desideri's use of the *gter rtags*, see OT 1, p. 157 n. 2. On his vocabulary, see pp. 161 n. 15 and 209 n. 8. On his style, see pp. 187 n. 7 and 200 n. 2.

9. The *Tho rangs* was begun as a Tibetan translation of an Italian draft, and was accompanied by another Italian work refuting reincarnation that presumably served Desideri as a guide of sorts when he composed the *Skye ba snga ma*. The Italian draft of the first seven chapters of the *Tho rangs* can be found in OT 1, pp. 283–315. The draft on reincarnation has not yet been published; it is held in ARSI Goa 73, fol. 285–308.

10. DR 3.12 (MITN 6, p. 220); DR 3.22 (MITN 6, pp. 296–97). Desideri is not alone in asking such historical questions. Nor are they as implausible as one might think. Contemporary Tibetologists such as Paul Pelliot, Giuseppe Tucci, and Per Kvaerne also considered the possibility of Jewish or Christian influence on Tibetan

religion. Paul Pelliot, *Chrétiens d'Asie Centrale et d'Extrême Orient* (Leiden: E. J. Brill, 1914); Giuseppe Tucci, *The Religions of Tibet*, trans. Geoffrey Samuel (Berkeley: University of California Press, 1980); Rolf Stein, "Une mention du Manichéisme dans le choix du Bouddhisme comme religion d'état par le roi tibétain Khri-srong lde-bcen," in *Indianism et Bouddhisme: Mélanges offerts à Mgr Étienne Lamotte* (Louvain: Institut Orientaliste, 1980), pp. 329–37; Géza Uray, "Tibet's Connections with Nestorianism and Manichaeism in the 8th–10th Centuries," in *Contributions on Tibetan Buddhist Religion and Philosophy*, ed. Ernst Steinkellner and Helmut Tascher (Vienna: Arbeitskreis für Tibetische und Buddhistische Studien Universität Wien, 1983), pp.399–429; Per Kvaerne, "A Preliminary Study of Chp. VI of the Gzer-mig," in *Tibetan Studies in Honour of Hugh Richardson*, ed. Michael Aris and Aung San Suu Kyi (Warminster: Aris and Phillips, 1980), pp. 185–91. See the same author's "Dualism in Tibetan Cosmogonic Myths and the Question of Iranian Influence," *Silver on Lapis: Tibetan Literary Culture and History*, ed. C. I. Beckwith (Bloomington: Tibet Society, 1987), pp. 163–74. Matthew Kapstein treats his readers to an enlightening variation on this theme in a recent work, suggesting that the *Dba' bzhed*, like the first book of Kings, opens with a maternity dispute, recounts the construction of a temple complex that serves as an architectural *axis mundi*, and reaches its denouement with the ideological division of the Buddhist kingdom. If Kapstein's detour is not sufficiently provocative, he also lists some truly curious similarities between the *Yar lung jo bo'i chos 'byung* and the Christian Gospels: the birth of a boy is accompanied by a new star, which Chinese court astrologers take as an evil omen, and is followed by the slaughter of male infants. Matthew Kapstein, *The Tibetan Assimilation of Buddhism*, pp. 30–32.

11. DR 1.6 (MITN 5, pp. 154–55).

12. Augustine had no small amount of trouble with these verses, interpreting them to mean that God will save all classes of men. Cf. *De Spiritu et Littera*, c. 33, n. 58 (PL 44, c. 238); *Contra Iulianum*, IV, 8, 42 (PL 44, c. 759). Aquinas's discussion of these verses is found in *Summa theologiae* Ia, q. 19, art. 6, ad 1 (*Opera Omnia Leon.* 4, p. 241). The Council of Orange declared that God predestined no man to perdition: "Aliquos vero ad malum divina potestate praedestinatos esse, non solum non credimus, sed etiam, si sunt, qui tantum mali credere velint, cum omni detestatione illis anathema dicimus." (DS 397). In Desideri's day, Popes Alexander VIII and Clement XI combated the rigorist interpretation of these verses which attempted to interpret "all" to mean all classes of men—butchers, bakers, and candlestick makers but not all butchers, all bakers, nor all candlestick makers. Cf. DS 2005; 2426; 2429.

13. Thomas Aquinas, *Summa theologiae* IIa, IIae, q. 2, aa. 7–8 (*Opera Omnia Leon.* 8, pp. 33–35).

14. Augustine, *In Johannem*, tr. CVI, n. 4 (PL 35, c. 1910).

15. Thomas Aquinas, *De Veritate*, q. 14, a. 11 (*Opera Omnia Leon.* 22/2, pp. 469–72).

16. Suárez, *De praedestinatione et reprobatione* IV, c. 3, n. 19 (*Opera Omnia* I, p. 495).

17. Juan Martínez de Ripalda (1594–1648), for example, argued that a broad faith in God's existence and providence was possible based upon metaphysical knowledge of created things. In such a case, God himself would elevate the unbeliever's natural knowledge of His existence and confer upon it the status of a supernatural act of faith.

Ripalda, *De Ente Supernaturali*, disp. 20, sect. 23 (vol. 1, pp. 190–92). Juan de Lugo (1583–1660) felt that wherever even the faintest idea of a just God survived, there remained a vestige of the revelation God gave to Adam and Eve that would suffice for the salvation of those who sincerely wished to do God's will. Lugo even felt that God would, in exceptional circumstances, confer miracles upon non-Christians in order to preserve what remained of this primitive revelation. De Lugo, *De Virtute Fidei Divinae*, disp. 12, n. 51 (*Disputationes scholasticae et morales*, 1, p. 405): "Quod idem dicendum puto de philosophis antiquis, si qui fuerunt, qui verum Deum crediderint super omnia: neque enim ipsi ignorarunt fidem, quae apud illos erat de uno Deo derivata, vel per Scripturas, vel per traditionem parentum ad posteros. Quam fidem amplecti et ipsi potuerunt, sicut et filii eam a parentibus sibi traditam amplectuntur. Notitia vero illa de uno Deo, quam ex ratiocinatione philosophica assequebantur, numquam fuit in ipsis adeo efficax, ut firmissimo assensu et super omnia assentirentur illa conclusioni." A slightly different text can be found in Lugo, *Opera Omnia Theologica* (Paris: Martin-Beaupré Fratres, 1868), 1, p. 628.

18. DR 3.21 (MITN 6, p. 295): "Il secondo e forse più ben fondato dubbio può essere il ricercar se in quelle parti vi sia alcuna volta stata anticamente fondata la cristianità, o vi sia colà giunto alcun Apostolo. Tal dubbio molto ragionevolmente si fonda in moltissime cose, che nella setta e religion thibetana sembrano aver grand-issima somiglianza o co' misterj della nostra S. Fede, o con le cerimonie, instituzioni e gerarchie ecclesiastiche, o con le massime e principj della morale della nostra S. Legge, o con le regole e direzioni dell'istessa perfezion cristiana."

19. DR 3.21 (MITN 6, p. 297): "Conchiudo infine che quantunque non vi sia alcun indizio di credere che abbiano Thibetani in alcun tempo avuto notizia della cristianità e della nostra S. Fede, è molto credibile che l'abbian avuta gli antichi gentili dell'Hen-dustan, da' quali riconosce il Thibet la sua religione e la sua falsa credenza."

20. DR 3.7 (MITN 6, pp. 165–66).

21. DR 3.19 (MITN 6, p. 279).

22. Missionaries in India commonly attributed Hindu idolatry and other misfor-tunes to demons. See Valignano's instructions from 1575 (DI 11, pp. 10–12) or Andreas Fernandes's letter of December 13, 1577 (DI 11, p 41). Much the same might be said about Chinese religions; see the Franciscan Martin Ignatius de Loyola's discussion of Chinese religion in his *Ytinerario* (SF 2, pp. 206–10).

23. Johannes Nieuhof, *An Embassy from the East India Company of the United Provinces to the Grand Tartar Cham Emperor of China* (1669), pp. 42–43. The Latin reads, "ad quem advenae capitibus humi prostratis advoluti, non secus ac Summo Pontifici pedes incredibili, veneratione osculantur; ut vel indè Daemonis fraudulentia luculenter appareat, qua venerationem soli Vicario Christi in terris Romano Pontifici debitam, ad superstitionum barbararum gentium cultum, uti omnia caetera Christianae Religionis mysteria, insitâ sibi malignitate, in abusum transtulit; Unde uti Patrum patrem Pontificem Romanum Christiani, ita Barbari hunc Deastrum Magnum Lamam, id est, sacerdotem Magnum, & Lamam Lamarum, id est, Sacerdotem Sacerdotum appellant, eò quod ab eo, ceu à fonte quodam tota religionis, seu potiùs *eidolomanias* ratio profluat, unde & eundem Patrem quoque Aeternum vocant."

24. See, for example, Matteo Ricci's praise of ancient Chinese religion in *Della Entrata della Compagnia di Giesù e Christianità nella Cina* (*Fonti Ricciane* 1.10, n. 170), p. 108: "Di tutte le gentilità venute a notitia della nostra Europa non so di nessuna che avesse manco errori intorno alle cose della religione di quello che ebbe la Cina nella sua prima antichità." The parallel Latin passage can be found in Nicolaus Trigault, *De Christiana Expeditione apud Sinas* (Christoph Mangium, 1615), p 104.

25. Neither were Jesuit professors immune to the pagan gaiety of such festivities. A visitor to the Museum Kircherianum, the curiosities collected by the Jesuit polymath Athanasius Kircher, would be greeted in the antechamber by a large statue called the "Delphic Oracle." When one asked the oracle a question, Kircher answered in a mock prophetic tone through a speaking tube connected to his apartment upstairs, while causing the oracle's eyes to roll back and forth by means of a hidden mechanical device. It is hardly a censorious world in which a Jesuit such as Kircher could emblazon a mechanical dragon with the title *The Wrath of God*. Johannes Stephanus Kestlerus, *Physiologia Kircheriana Experimentalis* (Amsterdam: Jansonnius-Waesbergius, 1680), p. 118.

26. Pico della Mirandola could remark that the one who comprehended the unity of Venus and the trinity of the graces knows the *modus procendi* of "Orphic" theology. Franciscans such as Arcangelo da Borgonuova followed Pico in their own speculations on the pre-Christian knowledge of the Trinity, and the Dominican Antoninus of Florence quoted pagan authors favorably under the rubric *testimonia Trinitatis in doctrinis ethnicorum*. Another Franciscan, Francesco Giorgi, declared the Chaldean trinity Ohrmazd-Mithra-Ahriman to be *superexcelsae trinitatis vestigium*. Marsilio Ficino believed that Orpheus, Plato, and Zoroaster had foreknowledge of the Trinity, and Gyraldus hailed Hermes Trismegistus and Orpheus as "prophets" of the Trinity, much in the same way that Augustine celebrated the Sybil's prophecy of the Incarnation. This Neoplatonic mania for sacred triads so inspired the philosophers of the Renaissance that they discovered (or invented) unheard-of triads in Christian history, such as the infamous *trinubium Annae*, the belief that three Marys mentioned in the New Testament were daughters of Anne by three different husbands, Joachim, Cleophas, and Salomas. Indeed, it is hard to find a Renaissance philosopher who did not find traces of the trinity in the religions of antiquity. The hegemony of the biblical chronology also led Renaissance writers to identify figures from classical myths with characters from the ancient biblical narratives. Thus Giles of Viterbo and Sir Thomas Browne, among others, identified the Roman god Janus with Noah on the basis of their shared penchant for seafaring. E. Wind, *Pagan Mysteries in the Renaissance*, rev. ed. (New York: W. W. Norton, 1968).

27. *Della Entrata della Compagnia di Giesù e Christianità nella Cina* (*Fonti Ricciane* 1.10, n. 193), p. 128: "Ambedue queste sette [i.e., Buddhism and Daoism] finsero il suo ternario, acciocchè si vegga chiaro esser il padre della bugia autore di tutte queste, il quale non ha anco lasciato la superba pretensione di voler essere simile al suo Creatore." For the discussion of the Buddhist "Trinity" see *Fonti Ricciane* 1.10, n. 183, pp. 123–24.

28. Athanasius Kircher, *China illustrata* (Amsterdam: Jacobus van Meurs, 1667), p. 133: "Porque en la Provincia de *Paquin* entre los otros Idolos, que alli tienen, ay una

figura del hombre, que tiene tres cabezas, y se miran la una à la otra, y dizen los *Chinas*, que significa aquello, que todos tres non tienen mas de un solo querer y voluntad." Kircher adds: "*P. Martinus Martinus* in Provincia *Fokien* imagines varias Christianae fidei olim introductae vestigia se vidisse recenset, Cruces pervetustas, Beatae Virginis filium suum benedictum inter brachia stringentis imagines detectas asserit, quae & etiamnum in Ecclesia nostra spectandae exhibentur, tum ad confirmandos Neophytorum animos, tum ad devotionem concitandam opportunae." Kircher also discussed whether the Egyptians had a knowledge of the Trinity in *Qedipus Aegyptiacus* (Rome: Vitalis Mascardi, 1654), 2 (2), pp. 506–10; 2 (3), pp. 575–77.

29. Joachim Bouvet was perplexed about similarities to the Holy Trinity, the Incarnation, the Virgin Birth, the creation and redemption of the world, and the sacrifice of the Mass. Joseph Henri Marie de Prémare was similarly concerned by the miraculous birth of Hou Ji and tried to establish the necessary conditions for the survival of the primitive revelation made to Adam among the Chinese. On Bouvet, see Mungello, *Curious Land*, pp. 300–28. On Prémare, see Knud Lundbaek, *Joseph de Prémare (1666–1736), S.J.—Chinese Philology and Figurism* (Aarhus: Aarhus University Press, 1991) and "Joseph de Prémare and the Name of God in China," *The Chinese Rites Controversy: Its History and Meaning*, ed. David Mungello (Nettetal: Steyler Verlag, 1994), pp. 129–45. Also see David E. Mungello, "The Reconciliation of Neo-Confucianism with Christianity in the Writings of Joseph de Prémare, S.J.," *Philosophy East and West* 26 (1976), pp. 389–410; and "Sinological Torque: The Influence of Cultural Preoccupations on Seventeenth-Century Missionary Interpretations of Confucius," *Philosophy East and West* 28 (1978), pp. 123–42. For Foucquet, see John W. Witek, S.J., *Controversial Ideas in China and in Europe: A Biography of Jean-François Foucquet, S.J. (1665–1741)* (Rome: Institutum Historicum Societatis Iesu, 1982).

30. Sabine MacCormack, *Religion in the Andes: Vision and Imagination in Early Colonial Peru* (Princeton, NJ: Princeton University Press, 1991), p. 312. In light of the persistent association of demons and celestial troubles in the seventeenth century, it is worth noting that Desideri judged Samyé to be situated in a "quite horrible place" (*il sito molt'orrido*) that is "continually beset by the fiercest winds" (*continuamente dominata da rigidissimi venti*). One can only imagine how he would have felt about the various forms of weather magic in Tibet.

31. Missionaries in India consistently remarked on the Hindu "Trinity." Gaspar Barzaeus seemed particularly fascinated by the subject (DI 1, pp. 505, 629, 698; DI 2, p. 254); Melchior Gonçalves mentions it in a letter from January 1551 (DI 2, p. 184); Melchior Diaz remarks on the *trimūrti* again in 1565 (DI 6, p. 579); and Pedro Páez Xamarillo alludes to it in his description of the idol with three heads in the Great Cave at Elephanta (Ghārāpuri) (DI 15, pp. 263–64).

32. Hosten, "Fr. Francisco Godinho," p. 66: "Les peuples de ce grand Thibeth ne sont pas idolatres: car nous avons trouvé qu'ils recognoissent l'Unité & Trinité adorable du vray Dieu, ils sçavent qu'il y a trois Hierarchies d'Esprits Angeliques, divisés en neuf choeurs, selon les differences de leurs excellences & dignitez, Qu'il ya un Enfer qui attend les meschans, & un Paradis pour la recompense des bons. Mais parmy ces

veritez, il s'est meslé tant de nuages d'erreur, que le voisinage des Payens leur a faict prendre par contagion."

33. On de Nobili, see Wilhelm Halbfass, *India and Europe: An Essay in Understanding* (Albany: State University of New York Press, 1988), pp. 38–43; Niell, *History of Christianity in India*, pp. 279–309; Županov, *Disputed Mission*, p. 3; Francis X. Clooney, S.J., "Roberto de Nobili's *Dialogue on Eternal Life* and an Early Jesuit Evaluation of Religion in South India," in *The Jesuits: Cultures, Sciences, and the Arts*, 1, pp. 402–17.

34. Abraham Roger, *Offene Thür zu dem verborgenen Heydenthum* (Nürnberg: Endter & Wolfgang, 1663); Thomas Burnet, *Archaeologiae philosophicae* (London: G. Kettilby, 1692). These and a great many similar sources are described in the classic work of Frank Manuel, *The Eighteenth Century Confronts the Gods* (Cambridge: Harvard University Press, 1959).

35. Bartholomäus Ziegenbalg, *Beschreibung der Religion und heiligen Gebräuche der malabarischen Hindous [Genealogie der malabarischen Götten]* (Berlin: Verl. der Königl. Preussischen Akad. Kunst- und Buchh., 1791). Cf. Daniel Jeyaraj, ed. and trans., *Genealogy of the South Indian Deities* (London: Routledge Curzon, 2005). On Ziegenbalg, see Briraj Singh, *The First Protestant Missionary to India* (New Delhi: Oxford University Press, 1999).

36. I have used the translation found in *The Travels of Several Learned Missionaries of the Society of Jesus into Divers Parts of the Archipelago, India, China, and America* (London: R. Gosling, 1714), pp. 21–22. Bouchet's letter to Huet is a digest of missionary theology: the Jesuit denies that Hindus are atheists, describes the Hindu Trinity, explains the errors of Hinduism in terms of pagan fables, and defends the primogeniture of Moses.

37. See the triple-sun motif on the title page of Paul Aler, *Annus secularis Archi-Episcopatus Coloniensis* (Cologne: Peter Wilhelm Alstorff, 1683) [= CLE J.2]; Claude-François Menestrier, *La philosophie des images* (Paris: Robert J. B. de la Calle, 1682) [= CLE J.1027]. For an eye in the triangle, see the *ubique centrum* emblem from Paulus Baranyal, *Viaticum spirituale peregrinationis animae* (Claudiopolis, 1695) [= CLE J.32]. Drexel's work with the Janus-faced title page was published in several editions, including an Italian edition published in Rome: *Il trismegisto christiano ouere Tre sorti di culto della conscienza de santi del corpo* (Rome: H. Scheus, 1643).

38. Leo Steinberg, *The Sexuality of Christ in Renaissance Art and in Modern Oblivion*, 2nd ed. (Chicago: University of Chicago Press, 1996), pp. 333–40.

39. Philip Johan Tabbert von Stralenberg compared the three-headed Guhyasamāja on the *tsha tsha* he published in *Das Nord- und Östliche Theil von Europa und Asia* (Stockholm, 1730) with the Amida Buddha (or "idol Pussae") depicted by Kircher in both *Oedipus Aegyptiacus* and *China illustrata*. The point of comparison seems to have been their shared floral iconography, since Kircher's deity did not have three heads but was seated on a lotus, as in the two examples from Maximilianus Sandaeus. On Stralenberg, see Braham Norwick, "The First *Tsha-Tsha* Published in Europe," in *Soundings in Tibetan Civilization: Proceedings of the 1982 Seminar of the International Association for Tibetan Studies Held at Columbia University*, ed. Barbara Aziz and Matthew Kapstein (New Delhi: Manohar, 1985), p. 77.

40. DR 3.21 (MITN 6, p. 295n): "Così per esempio, ancorchè que' tre complessi d'oggetti d'adorazione, cioè i loro Santi primarij e supremi, i libbri o leggi da' medesimi dati al mondo, e de' fedeli più perfetti osservatori di tali leggi, ancorchè, dico, siano totalmente e separate e opposte alle tre Persone della SS. Trinità: Padre, Figlio e Spirito Santo; con tutto ciò, se ben si considerino da una parte gli attributi principali della tre Divine Persone della Santissima Trinità e dall'altra parte le qualità che ne' detti tre complessi d'oggetti d'adorazione... parmi potersi dubitare se la trinità di quei complessi sia un oscuro simbolo e cieco favoleggiamento della vera augustissima e Divina Trinità."

41. *Summa theologiae* IIa, IIae, q. 94, a. 1 (*Opera Omnia Leon.* 9, pp. 304–5).

42. DR 2.1 (MITN 6, pp. 3–4): "E cosa in vero curiosa ciò che in quella lingua medesima hanno lasciato scritto ne' loro libri alcuni autori e che da quelle genti vien asserito e creduto, come cosa confermata da lunga e costante tradizione, circa l'origine di quella nazione. Dicono che dalla banda di mezzogiorno... una donna tra que' monti, venne a perdersi tra essi, senza poter più rinvenire la strada. Mentre afflitta e inconsolabile girava deplorando la sua disgrazie, accorse un grande scimiotto, di quei che nella lingua portoghese si chiamono monos, con molte dimonstrazioni di festa e d'allegrezze; e addimesticatosi con essa le portò frutti salvatichi per sostentarla, finchè s'avanzò tanto la familiarità, che concepì di lui e partorì varj figliuoli. Nell'errar poi ch'ella fece per quelle balze, arrivò a un piccol monte di pietra che fu denominato Potalà, molto vicino al luogo in cui dopo fu fondata la città di Lhasa: e ivi trovò un certo Cen-ree-szi (idolo favoloso), che disse esser custode di quei luoghi e tutelare del paese. Da esso le furono portati alcuni grani di frumento, di riso, d'orzo e di qualche legume, e per comandamento di lui la donna, e poscia i suoi figliuoli già cresciuti, gettarono nella terra que' grani, i quali rinascendo si moltiplicarono poi tanto che servirono per loro sostentamento e n'avanzò per nuova semenza, andandosi così d'anno in anno sempre più aumentando.... In tal opinione è fondato l'essere in varj loro libri i Thibetani da' loro medesimi autori chiamati col titolo di pronipoti dello scimmiotto."

43. DR 3.14 (MITN 6, p. 232): "Le particolari doti e perfezioni che ricercò in quella che doveva scegliere per sua madre, sono quasi un'altra copia che la detta scimmia infernale prese a far di ciò che i nostri ascetici e contemplativi costumano dire dell'elezione fatta dal Verbo Divino della Santissima Vergine per esser ella sollevata alla gran dignità di Madre d'un Dio Incarnato." Cf. DR 3.14 (MITN 6, p. 231): "e che avessa pigliata l'impresa di far (come si suol dire) la scimmia, e d'imitar interamente quel tanto che costumano o possono esprimere i nostri asceti e i nostri contemplativi per farci concepir il decreto che la Santissima Trintà formò della reparazion del genere umano e che il Verbo Divino accettò di venir in terra."

44. From this period of Desideri's studies, we have notes with citations from the *Bka' 'gyur* dated March 25, 1717, as well as drafted Tibetan versions of the Our Father, the Hail Mary, the Creed, and the Sign of the Cross. Desideri also took notes for various logical exercises dated July 1, 1717, and began to copy passages from the *Great Stages of the Path to Enlightenment* (*Lam rim chen mo*), the summa of Buddhist doctrine written by Tsongkhapa. These various fragments can be found in ARSI Goa 74. On them see OT 1, pp. 53–59.

45. DR 3.5 (MITN 6, p. 155).

46. DR 1.14 (MITN 5, p. 197): "Convien ancora sapere che hanno i Thibetani la dialettica, la spiegazion de' termini, le definizioni, divisioni e argomentazioni, che tutte son a forza di semplici entimemi; la maniera di promuovere gli argomenti, di convincere d'implicanza, di negare, di concedere, di negar il supposto, di ritorcer l'argomento, e così del resto."

47. DR 2.15 (MITN 6, p. 95).

48. Such texts are the bread and butter of any philosophical training in Tibet. It is tempting to think that some of the Jesuit's peculiar ideas about Madhyamaka show signs of influence from an institution that placed more emphasis on commentary (*bshad*) than debate (*rtsod*). The missionary's favorite texts, which he cites in abundance, are Nāgārjuna's *Treatise on the Middle Way*, Āryadeva's *Four Hundred Stanzas*, and Candrakīrti's *Introduction to the Middle Way*. When one adds his citations from the *Abhidharmakośa*, Desideri's studies do look quite similar to the study of the thirteen great texts (*gzhung chen bcu gsum*) of a modern-day Nyingma monastery such as Namdröling. Indeed, the three years that Desideri would soon spend in Dakpo correspond almost exactly to the three years that one would spend in such a study on the lower exoteric course at a modern commentarial institution. This apparent correspondence might also explain the surprising lack of citations from Dharmakīrti's *Pramanavarttikakārikā* or the five treatises attributed to Maitreya. Still, I think we should resist the temptation to think that Desideri had any formal training at the Nyingma or Kagyü institutions. Points at which one might expect clear indications of Nyingma influence, such as when he discusses the intermediate state between death and birth, follow the lines developed by the Geluk approaches to these topics. Although more detailed research must be done, I am inclined to think that Desideri's knowledge of Madhyamaka texts came primarily from his brief five-month stay at Sera. There is also the larger question of whether he actually read these individual works or culled quotations from the *Lam rim chen mo*. This question could be answered fairly easily with a detailed analysis of his quotations, but such an analysis is beyond the scope of this study.

49. For a full list, see OT 3, pp. 18–23; OT 4, pp. 13–18.

50. DR (MITN 5, pp. 198–99, 199n–200): "Essendo arrivato a studiar questi trattati, il dottor che era stato assegnato per mio maestro, si protestò di non sapermeli spiegare nè dar a intendere. Giudicando io esser ciò un pretesto per impedirmi la cognizione di tali materie, lo pregai e scongiurai più volte a volermele dichiarare; e vedendo egli non restar io in modo alcuno capace ch'egli, com'affermava, non fosse a ciò sufficiente, e che appena alcun de' più cospicui Lamà m'averebbe potuto in ciò contentare, affin di rendermi convinto, si esibì di condurmi altri dottori, e ancor io ne ricercai degli altri; ma tutti unitamente s'accordarono a confessar quel che egli m'aveva detto, esser cosa troppo più che da loro lo spiegarmi sì reconditi e sì implessi trattati.... assister qualche volta alle loro dispute e publiche conclusioni; e sopra tutto procurar di saper e penetrar a fondo i trattati più astrusi e più intrigati che chiamano del Tongbà-gnì, cioè del Vacuo, non già preso in senso materiale e filosofico, ma in senso allegorico, il di cui scopo è di escluder finalmente l'existenza d'alcun Ente che da se stesso abbia il suo essere e che sia increato e independente, e con ciò chiuder affato la porta alla cognizion di Dio Risoluto nulladimeno io di voler penetrare quel che in essi si

conteneva, e vedendomi mancar ogn'altro mezzo umano, mi raccomandai caldamente a Dio, che è Padre de' lumi e per la di cui sola gloria m'ero accinto a quell'impressa. Indi mi posi da me stesso con tutta l'intenzione e posatezza a legger più volte e ripassar da capo que' libri; ma sempre senza frutto; tanto eglino con oscuri. Non mi perdei d'animo, un'altra volta molto attentamente li rilessi. Nè pur questa volta mi riuscì di fare una benchè minima discoperta. Persuaso tuttavia, che *Labor improbus omnia vincit* [Steady work conquers all], fattomi nuovo coraggio, tornai a riscorrer tutto intieramente da capo a piedi, ma senza niente di profitto. In poche parole non lasciai giammai di continuare l'incominciata impresa, sinchè doppo oscure tenebre cominciò a spuntar un qualche piccol barlume di luce. Con ciò eccitatasi nel mio core una viva speranza di poter giugnere a veder finalmente spuntar il sole e a rimirar ancora la più bella chiarezza del mezzo giorno, senza punto diminuir giammai, anzi aggiungendo sempre nuovo e più attivo vigore, e cento volte tornai a leggere e rileggere, a scrutinare e a profondare; finchè grazie a Dio arrivai non solamente ad intendare ma sì intieramente possedere (siana tutta la gloria a Dio) e magistralmente comprendere tutte quelle materie sì sottili, sì sofistiche, sì astruse, e al mio intento sommamente importanti e necessarie." Many contemporary readers may wonder at Desideri's use of the word "vacuum." He denies that the word is to be understood in a material or philosophical sense to avoid associations with the infamous "vacuum" debate among late seventeenth-century Jesuits. On this debate, see Michael John Gorman, *The Scientific Counter Revolution: Mathematics, Natural Philosophy, and Experimentalism in Jesuit Culture, 1580–c.1670*, a dissertation submitted to the European University Institute (Florence, 1998), pp. 174–214.

51. DR 3.10 (MITN 6, p. 194): "L'errore primario della setta de' Thibettani e la scaturigine di tutti gli altri falsi dogmi che credono è il negare positivamente, direttamente e expressamente l'existenza d'alcun ente a sè, increato, indipendente, e d'alcuna causa primaria e universale di tutte le cose. La malizia dell'infernal nemico tal finezza e sottil artifizio ha saputo inventare, che non solamente ha ricoperto con bella inorpellatura l'estrema mostruosità .... e quasi riparandosi dietro a ben ricamate e dorate cortine, tra la vaghezza e lustro di queste ha fatto travedere gli occhi de' suoi spettatori e gli è riuscito d'acciecarne a forza d'artificiosa e mendicata luce gl'incauti intendimenti."

52. DR 3.9 (MITN 6, p. 184): "Non ammenttono i Thibettani alcun giudice supremo che distribuisca il premio ai buoni e condanni i malvagi e prescriva loro le pene e i meritati castighi. Vogliono dunque che senza veruna sentenza d'alcun giudice e senza la disposizione d'alcun supremo regolator del mondo, in vigor del puro loro merito trovino i buoni il premio e dovuto e proporzionato alle loro virtù; e in vigor del proprio demerito trovino i cattavi il castigo dovuto e proporzionato a i loro peccati."

53. *Summa theologiae* Ia, q. 2, a. 2 (*Opera Omnia Leon.* 4, p. 30).

54. Suárez noted that the absolutely simple God makes Himself known through a diverse array of concepts, among which "one opinion about God may be true even when another is false, and so the true God may in some way be known even if mistaken judgments are held about some of his attributes." *De Fide*, disp. 12, sect. 3, n. 3 (*Opera Omnia* 12, p. 345).

55. An important assumption in this view is that motives with absolute objective validity are easily within the reach of all, whether through the common consent of tradition or the metaphysical knowledge of creation. It is for this reason that Pope Innocent XI condemned the proposition "Assensus fidei supernaturalis et utilis ad salutem stat cum notitia solum probabili revelationis" (DS 2121).

56. DR 3.11 (MITN 6, p. 206).

57. DR 3.11 (MITN 6, p. 207): "Che se taluno così mi replicasse: dunque voi venite a dir che i Thibetani son atei? Ciò pare una proposizione molto capricciosa, sì perchè pare non potervi esser nel mondo alcuna intera nazione che faccia espressamente professione d'ateismo, sì perchè un tal asserto verrebbe a contradire manifestamente all'assunto che di sopra vi siete proposto di dar notizia della loro religione."

58. DR 3.11 (MITN 6, p. 207): "Rispondo . . . che se per ateo voglia intendersi persona o gente che nè *signate et riflexe* (per sequitar a parlar con la scuola) nè *implicite et confuse*, e di più nè teoricamente nè praticamente in modo veruno riconoscano una qualque o vera o falsa divinità; in tal caso dico non meritarsi, a mio giudizio, i Thibetani l'obbrobrioso titolo di atei,"

59. DR 1.13 (MITN 5, pp. 193–94): "Toccati di già e penetrati dalla forza della grazia divina, che assai più di quel che io parlassi a' loro orecchi faceva sentir la sua voce a' loro cuori, continuamente mi dimandavano se vi fosse gran differenza fra la nostra santa legge e la loro setta. In riposto spiegai loro più volte che in qualsivoglia legge due cose si ritrovano, cioè, primo alcuni principj, massime o dogmi da credersi; e secondo varj precetti e direzioni circa quello che deve o farsi o tralasciarsi. Quant'alla prima parte, la nostra e la loro legge esser totalmente opposte ed esser assolutamente necessaria una total mutazione di credenza. In ordine poi alla seconda parte, non esservi tra loro e noi tanta differenza che non potessimo, quando avesser voluto, accordarci. Da tale spiegazione si mostravano grandemente consolati e incoraggiati, dando sempre a divedere nel lor esterno l'impulso interno e l'operazione della grazia divina che segretamente gli animava e gli'incitava."

60. For an overview, see Ilaria Morali, "Gratia ed infidelitas. Nella Teologia di Francisco de Toledo e Francisco Suarez al tempo delle grandi missioni gesuitiche," *Studia Missionalia* 55 (2006), pp. 99–150.

61. For Casal, see DR 1.10 (MITN 5, p. 182); For Lhazang, DR 1.12 (MITN 5, p. 192).

62. A partial translation exists: Luis de Molina, *On Divine Foreknowledge (Part IV of the Concordia)*, trans. Alfred Freddoso (Ithaca, NY: Cornell University Press, 1988).

63. *Concordia Liberi Arbitrii cum Gratiae Donis*, qu. 14, art. 13, disp. 40 (pp. 230–31): "Asserimus auxilia praevenientis atque adiuvantis gratiae, quae lege ordinaria viatoribus conferuntur, quod efficacia aut inefficacia ad conversionem seu justificatione sint, pendere a libero consensu et cooperatione arbitrii nostri cum illis, atque adeo in libera potestate nostra esse, vel illa efficacia reddere consentiendo et cooperando cum illis ad actus, quibus ad iustificationem disponimur, vel inefficacia illa reddere, continendo consensum et cooperationem nostram, aut etiam eliciendo contrarium dissensum." Cf. *Animadversio V* on this passge, p. 601. Other key passages include qu. 14, art. 13, disp. 12 (p. 51): "Quare fieri potest, ut duorum qui aequali auxilio interius a Deo vocantur, unus pro libertate sui arbitrii convertatur et alter infidelitate permaneat"; and qu. 14, art 13,

disp. 41 (p. 239): "Auxilium gratiae praevenientis est influxus Dei in liberum arbitrium, quo illud movet et excitat, potensque reddit, ut eo pacto motum, tamquam habens jam in seipso principium efficiens actuum supernaturalium, simul influendo ulterius eos producat."

64. Bellarmine, *De Gratia et Libero Arbitrio*, 1, c. 12 (*Opera Omnia* 5, p. 527): "Prima opinio eorum est, qui gratiam efficacem constituunt in assensu et cooperatione humana, ita ut ab eventu dicatur gratia efficax, quia videlicet sortitur effectum, et ideo sortitur effectum, quia voluntas humana cooperatur. Itaque existimant hi auctores, in potestate hominis esse, ut gratiam faciat esse efficacem, quae alioquin, ex se non esset nisi sufficiens." He then opposes to this opinion the words of Augustine and scripture: "Haec opinio aliena est omnino a sententia B. Augustini, et quantam ego existimo, a sententia etiam Scripturarum divinarum."

65. Jesuit theologians happily found the distinction between *gratia congrua* and *gratia incongrua* in Augustine himself. *Ad Simplicianum*, I, qu. 2, n. 13 (PL 40, cc. 118–19): "Si vellet [Deus] etiam ipsorum misereri, posset ita vocare, quomodo illis aptum esset, ut et moverentur et intelligerent et sequerentur. Verum est ergo: Multi vocati, pauci electi. Illi enim electi, qui congruenter vocati illi autem qui non congruebant neque contemperabantur vocationi, non electi, quia non secuti, quamvis vocati. Item verum est: Neque volentis neque currentis, sed miserentis est Dei, quia etiamsi multos vocet, eorum tamen miseretur, quos ita vocat, quomodo iis vocari aptum est ut sequantur. Falsum est autem, si quis dicit: Igitur non miserentis Dei, sed volentis atque currentis est hominis, quia nullius Deus frustra misereretur. Cuius atem miseretur, sic eum vocat quomodo scit ei congruere, ut vocantem non respuat."

66. Clement XI, *Constitutio "Unigenitus Dei Filius"* (September 8, 1713), prop. 41: "Omnis cognitio Dei etiam naturalis, etiam in philosophis ethnicis, non potest venire nisi a Deo; et sine gratia non producit nisi praesumptionem, vanitatem et oppositionem ad ipsum Deum loco affectuum adorationis, gratitudinis et amoris" (DS 2441).

67. Pius V, *Bulla "Ex Omnibus afflictionibus"* (October 1, 1567), prop. 25: "Omnia opera infidelium sunt peccata et philosophorum virtutes sunt vitia" (DS 1925).

68. *De Spiritu et Littera*, c. 3, n. 5 (PL 44, c. 203): "Nam neque liberum arbitrium quidquam nisi ad peccandum valet, si lateat veritatis via." *Contra Duas Epistulas Pelagianorum* II, c. 9, n. 21 (PL 44, c. 536): "Quapropter multa Deus facit in homine bona, quae non facit homo; nulla vero facit homo, quae non facit Deus, ut faciat homo." Prosper of Aquitaine, *Sententiae ex Augustino delibatae*, n. 106 (PL 51, c. 441): "Omnis vita infidelium peccatum est et nihil est bonum sine summo bono. Ubi enim deest agnitio summae et incommutabilis veritatis, falsa virtus est etiam in optimis moribus."

69. Jesuits claimed that faith here cannot mean the theological habit, but rather refers to conscience, as the context demands. See 1 Cor 8:10–13. Indeed, most modern translations follow the Jesuit reading.

70. Alexander VIII, *Decretum* (December 7, 1690), prop. 5: "Pagani, Iudaei, haeretici aliique huius generis nullum omnino accipiunt a Iesu Christo influxum: adeoque hinc recte inferes, in illis esse voluntatem nudam et inermem sine omni gratia sufficienti" (DS 2305).

71. Alexander VIII, *Decretum* (December 7, 1690), prop. 8: "Necesse est infidelem in omni opere peccare" (DS 2308).

72. Jansen's doctrine was summarized in the infamous five propositions condemned by Innocent X, "Cum Occasione" (May 31, 1653) (DS 2001–2007). These five propositions asserted that (1) man is unable to keep some of God's commandments for want of grace; (2) in the state of fallen nature no one ever resists interior grace; (3) to gain merits in the state of fallen nature, freedom from external constraint is sufficient; (4) the Semipelagian heresy consisted in assuming the existence of a grace that man might either obey or resist; and (5) Christ did not die for all men, but only the predestined.

73. Jansen, *Augustinus*, tom. III (4), 10, c. 435: "ita inefficax, ex qua operatio ne quidem posit sequi, nisi ejus inefficacia per aliam suppleatur." Cf. III (3), 3, c. 258: "Illud a recentioribus prolatum gratiae sufficientis genus, quo adjuvante nullum unquam opus factum est, aut fiet unquam, si est verum distictumque a gratia efficace membrum, videtur monstrum quoddam singulare gratiae, solummodo peccatis faciendis majorique damnationi accersendae serviens."

74. *De Natura et Gratia*, c. 43, n. 50 (PL 44, c. 271): "Non igitur Deus impossibilia jubet, sed iubendo monet, et facere quod possis, et petere quod non possis." *De Spiritu et Littera*, c. 34, n. 60 (PL 44, c. 240): "Consentire vocationi Dei, vel ab ea dissentire . . . propriae voluntatis est." *De Peccatorum Meritis et Remissione* II, c. 17, n. (PL 44, c. 167): "Gratia Dei est, quae hominum adiuvat voluntates: qua ut non adiuventur, in ipsis itidem causa est, non in Deo." *Epistula* 157, 2, 10 (PL 33, c. 677): "Neque enim voluntatis arbitrium ideo tollitur, quia iuvatur; sed ideo iuvatur, quia non tollitur."

75. *Summa theologiae* IIa, IIae, q. 10, a. 4 (*Opera Omnia Leon.* 8, p. 82).

76. Even Molina, who is sometimes accused of arguing that men and women could dispose themselves positively for the reception of grace, rightly noted that that any such positive disposition would have to be dependent upon God's universal salvific will. Aquinas is sometimes said to favor such a position in his earlier works. *In Sent. II*, d. 28, q. 1, a. 4 (*Opera Omnia Parm.* 6, pp. 642–43). Gabriel Vásquez went to the other extreme, denying that men and women could prepare themselves negatively. Vásquez, *Comment. In Summam Theol.* 1a, d. 91, c. 10–11. For a convenient list of sources for this debate, see Ripalda, *De Ente Supernaturali*, disp. 17, sect. 1 (vol. 1, pp. 118–20).

77. Vásquez felt that such acts were accompanied by supernatural assistance in the form of a "congruous thought" (*cogitatio congrua*) that was itself entitatively natural, but directed to God as its end by a secondary, supernatural impulse. *Comment. In Summam Theol. S. Thomae* 1a, 2ae, disp. 189. Vásquez might be accused of pseudo-Baianism, in which naturally good acts are impossible in the present order, but he avoids the charge by accepting the Scotist dictum that morally indifferent acts of the will are possible, and maintains that it is impossible to conceive such acts apart from the *cogitatio congrua* that orients them to God. Juan Martínez de Ripalda felt that naturally good actions were invariably accompanied by prevenient grace in the present economy of salvation. For Ripalda, God provided all naturally good actions with "intrinsically supernatural graces" of illumination and confirmation precisely as a merciful dispensation of grace to those

who had not had a chance to hear the Gospel. Ripalda, *De Ente Supernaturali*, disp. 20 (vol. 1, pp. 150–92).

78. Texts often cited to explain this division are Phil 2:13; Eph 5:14; 2 Tim 1:9; Rom 8:26 sqq; and Rev 3:20. Cf. Augustine, *De Grat. et Lib. Arbitr.*, c. 17, 33 (PL 44, c. 901): "Quoniam ipse ut velimus, operatur incipiens, qui volentibus cooperatur perficiens."

79. DR 2.9 (MITN 6, p. 41n): "di sapere alle volte sospettare; per mancanza di che perdè il suo regno, la sua famiglia e la propria sua vita."

CHAPTER 4: THE ZÜNGHAR INVASION

1. DR 2.1 (MITN 6, p. 5): "la figura d'una persona che sta a giacere col petto resupino, cioè nella positura in cui i poeti si rappresentano il favoloso Prometeo legato sopra l'orride rupi de' Caucasi, che son appunto le alte e per sì lungo tratto continuate montagne del Thibet. E certamente reppresentando i poeti l'infelice Prometeo esposto a essere nel petto e nel ventre lacerato e sempre rilacerato dall'ingordo insanziabile uccello, in che altra figura vengono a reppresentando se non d'una persona stesa e costretta a star a giacere colla faccia all'in su e resupina. E certamente chi legge l'epigramma di Marziale che comincia: *Qualis caucasea religatus rupe Prometheus, adsiduam nimio pectore pascit avem* [As Prometheus bound to a Caucasian cliff, upon whose breast a bird greedily feeds]." Michael Sweet informs me that this quotation is from *De Spectaculis* 7, although the original begins *qualiter in Scythia*. I am grateful to Michael for this reference.

2. Most notably Luciano Petech, *China and Tibet in the Eighteenth Century*, 2nd ed. (Leiden: E. J. Brill, 1972). Petech's "Notes on Tibetan History of the 18th Century," *T'oung Pao* 52 (1965–66), pp. 261–92, still contains valuable insights, especially into Desideri's limitations as an historian. As a work of general history, Petech's *China and Tibet* is still unsurpassed, and I have depended upon it heavily in this chapter.

3. Turrell Wylie, "Reincarnation: A Political Innovation in Tibetan Buddhism," in *Proceedings of the Csoma de Kőrös Memorial Symposium Held at Mátrafüred, Hungary 24–30 September 1976*, ed. Louis Ligeti (Budapest: Akadémiai Kiadó, 1978), pp. 579–86.

4. Giuseppe Tucci, *Tibetan Painted Scrolls* (Rome: La Libreria dello Stato, 1949), 1, pp. 3–93. For an investigation of Mongol contact with other orders during the same time period, see Eliot Sperling, "Notes on References to 'Bri-Gung-pa—Mongol Contact in the Late Sixteenth and Early Seventeenth Centuries," in *Tibetan Studies: Proceedings of the 6th Seminar of the International Association for Tibetan Studies, Narita, 1989*, ed. Ihara Shōren and Yamaguchi Zuihō (Tokyo: Naritasan Shinshoji, 1992), 2, pp. 741–50.

5. Pedro Carasco, *Land and Polity in Tibet* (Seattle: University of Washington Press, 1959). One can find great help in Luciano Petech, *Aristocracy and Government in Tibet 1728–1959* (Rome: IsMEO, 1973).

6. Yumiko Ishihama, "A Study of the Seals and Titles Conferred by the Dalai Lamas," in *Tibetan Studies*, ed. Ihara Shōren and Yamaguchi Zuihō, 2, pp. 501–14; "On the Dissemination of the Belief in the Dalai Lama as a Manifestation of the Bodhisattva Avalokiteshvara," *Acta Asiatica* 64 (1993), pp. 38–58.

7. The regent presented the fifth Dalai Lama as the very embodiment of the five perfections: place, teacher, retinue, time, and teaching. Thus, in Desi Sangyé Gyatso's reckoning the perfect place was the Potala; the perfect teacher was the fifth Dalai Lama; the perfect retinue was Güüshi Khan and the Khoshud Mongols, the perfect time was the year that the Dalai Lama's remains were placed in the Single Ornament Stupa, and the perfect teaching was Ngawang Gyatso's collected works. Cf. Kurtis Schaeffer, "Ritual, Festival, and Authority Under the Fifth Dalai Lama," in *Power, Politics, and the Invention of Tradition: Tibet in the Seventeenth and Eighteenth Centuries*, ed. Bryan J. Cuevas and Kurtis R. Schaeffer (Leiden: Brill, 2006), pp. 188–89.

8. Ahmad Zahiruddin, *Sino-Tibetan Relations in the Seventeenth-Century* (Rome: IsMEO, 1970), pp. 140–43.

9. Zhva sgab pa Dbang phyug lde ldan (Tsepon Shakabpa), *Bod kyi srid don rgyal rabs* (Delhi, 1976), I, pp. 428, 432–33. I owe this reference to my friend Derek Maher. See his "The Lives and Time of 'Jam dbyangs bzhad pa," in *Power, Politics, and the Invention of Tradition*, ed. Bryan J. Cuevas and Kurtis R. Schaeffer, pp. 129–44.

10. Bryan J. Cuevas, "Preliminary Remarks on the History of Mindröling: The Founding and Organization of a Tibetan Monastery in the Seventeenth Century," in *Places of Practice: Monasteries and Monasticism in Asian Religions*, ed. James Benn, Lori Meeks, and James Robson (Honolulu: University of Hawai'i Press, forthcoming); Jake Dalton, "Recreating the Rnying ma School: The *Mdo dbang* Tradition of Smin grol gling," in *Power, Politics, and the Invention of Tradition*, ed. Bryan J. Cuevas and Kurtis R. Schaeffer, pp. 91–101.

11. In the early seventeenth century, the Mongols consisted of various tribes in a state of extreme political flux. Usually these tribes were first divided into the Western Mongols, or the *derben Oirat* ("four Oirat"), which included the Khoshud, Zünghar, Dörböd, and Torghud (Kalmyk) Mongols who lived near Lake Balkash and Lake Zaisan north of Tianshan and the Tarim Basin. The Eastern Mongols, which included the Khalkha, the Buriat, the Jurchens, and the Chakhars, roamed from the Altai Mountains to Manchuria. For Mongol views of the Qing, see Johan Elverskog, *Our Great Qing: The Mongols, Buddhism, and the State in Late Imperial China* (Honolulu: University of Hawai'i Press, 2006).

12. Pamela Crossley insists that we should not refer to the Qing as a "merely a dynasty," but properly as an "empire." I myself do not have strong opinions about the use of the term "dynasty," but I have adopted Crossley's usage because I do think that it points to the vast multi-ethnic panorama that was the Qing. On that point, however, I am not sure that we can properly call the Qing multinational, as Tsyrempilov does, if only because it is difficult to find all, or even many, of the characterizations of the modern nation-state among the various Qing tributaries. Certainly it would be difficult to find them among the various Mongol factions, although the admittedly odd example of Tibet during the seventeenth and eighteenth centuries might be the exception that proves the rule. Cf. P. K. Crossley, *The Manchus* (Oxford: Basil Blackwell, 1997), p. 8, and Nicolay Tsyrempilov, "Dge lugs pa Divided: Some Aspects of the Political Role of Tibetan Buddhism in the Expansion of the Qing Dynasty," in *Power, Politics, and the Invention of Tradition*, ed. Bryan J. Cuevas and Kurtis R. Schaeffer, p. 47.

13. Joseph Sebes, S.J., *The Jesuits and the Sino-Russian Treaty of Nerchinsk* (Rome: IHSI, 1961).

14. Peter C. Perdue, *China Marches West: The Qing Conquest of Central Eurasia* (Cambridge: Belknap Press, 2005). Cf. Laura Hostetler, *Qing Colonial Enterprise: Ethnography and Cartography in Early Modern China* (Chicago: University of Chicago Press, 2001); Pamela Kyle Crossley, Helen F. Siu, and Donald S. Sutton, eds., *Empire at the Margins: Culture, Ethnicity, and Frontier in Early Modern China* (Berkeley: University of California Press, 2006).

15. Important information on the sixth Dalai Lama can be found in Piotr Klafkowski, *The Secret Deliverance of the Sixth Dala Lama* (Vienna: Arbeitskreis für Tibetische und Buddhistische Studien, 1979); Helmut Hoffman's introduction to G. W. Houston, *Wings of the White Crane: Poems of Tshangs dbyangs rgya mtsho (1683–1706)* (Delhi: Motilal Banarsidass, 1982); Michael Aris, *Hidden Treasures and Secret Lives* (London: Kegan Paul International, 1989); Per K. Sørensen, *Divinity Secularized: An Inquiry into the Nature and Forms of the Songs Ascribed to the Sixth Dalai Lama* (Vienna: Arbeitskreis für Tibetische und Buddhistische Studien, 1990); and Paul Williams, *Songs of Love, Poems of Sadness: The Erotic Verse of the Sixth Dalai Lama* (London: I. B. Tauris, 2004).

16. Michael Aris, *Hidden Treasures.*, pp. 160–62. Matthew Kapstein has cautioned me against repeating the anecdotes found in Aris, who often reprises Shakabpa's account of these events without evidence from the previous historical record. Upon some consideration, I have decided to keep them, if only because these anecdotes represent oral traditions from Lhasa with which Desideri seems to have been familiar. If we cannot say which anecdotes the Jesuit missionary knew, apart from his remarks about the Dalai Lama's sexual exploits, I do think that the reports agree in their general tone.

17. Desideri confuses these events mightily, conflating the events of the 1640s with the early 1700s in his account, but he does mention the poisoning and cure of Lhazang Khan. DR 2.9 (MITN 6, pp. 38–39).

18. Petech, *China and Tibet*, pp. 10–11, suggests that the oracle ordered Lhazang Khan to reteat. If so, the central Tibetan monasteries could have avoided an armed clash and gotten rid of Lhazang Khan by greasing the palm of the oracle. Perhaps, but only if the Geluk factions from central Tibet and Tsang overcame their difference. Cf. Shakabpa, *A Political History of Tibet* (New Haven, CT: Yale University Press, 1967), pp. 131–32. Petech insists, incidentally, that the proper name for this oracle is the *La mo*, not *Lha mo*, oracle, but he seems to be a distinct minority in this.

19. As with the Jamyang Zhepa's previous intervention, we here see a politician trying desperately to order his relations; if the Panchen had little desire to sever ties with the central Tibetan Geluk, he had even less desire to sever his ties with their enemies. Lhasa oral tradition suggests that a forged letter from the Dalai Lama ordered the Khan to attack the regent, a tradition that has some support from Desideri. Cf. Aris, *Hidden Treasures*, p. 163.

20. Zhva sgab pa Dbang phyug lde ldan (Tsepon Shakabpa), *Bod kyi srid don rgyal rabs* (Delhi, 1976), p. 483: "*sgar du rgyal mo tshe ring bkra shis sar phebs te sde srid gang na*

yod gsungs par/ med zer ba la. khyod tsho 'di 'dra ma zer. nga tsho de ring jis kyang mjal 'phrad dgos yod gsungs pas/ bkrongs nas med zer/ phel cher sku pur la drod ma yal tsam red jes gleng/ [. . .] sgo mang mkhan po thugs 'tshigs nas/ khyod tsho las ma rabs pa mi 'dug." Except for the final grisly note, this account is taken almost word for word from Gönchok Jikmé Wangpo's biography of Jamyang Zhepa. Cf. Kun mkhyen 'Jigs med dbang po, *Kun mkhyen 'Jam dbyangs bzhad pa'i rnam thar* (Lanzhou: Kan suu mi rigs dpe skrun khang, 1987), p. 118.

21. Although Petech remarks that the conclusion of the Manchu Emperor had been "forced chiefly by the general opinion of his court" (Petech, *China and Tibet*, p. 15), he neither identifies the members of the court nor does he determine how or why they themselves came to this conclusion. Petech's judgment suggests that he has been too influenced by Tibetan accounts of Kangxi. For contrasting views of Manchu involvement in Tibetan Buddhism, see Evelyn S. Rawski, *The Last Emperors: A Social History of Qing Imperial Insitutions* (Berkeley: University of California Press, 1998), pp. 231–63; Patricia Berger, *Empire of Emptiness: Buddhist Art and Political Authority in Qing China* (Honolulu: University of Hawaï'i Press, 2003).

22. Petech, *China and Tibet*, p. 20: "Although the sixth Dalai Lama had not enjoyed much personal respect, the Tibetans, and above all the clergy, strongly resented any interference with the consecrated mode of succession. Tshangs-dbyangs rgya-mtsho, however unworthy, had still been the rightful Dalai Lama. Lhajang Khan could impose his puppet on the lamas by force, but they would not accept him in their hearts as the true incarnation of Avalokiteśvara." Here, Petech seems to overgeneralize the Tibetan support for the "true" Dalai Lama. He even effects a somewhat romantic tone to heighten the tension. The problem with this account is that it does not really address the Geluk factions from Tsang who supported the puppet Dalai Lama.

23. Okada Hidehiro, "The Third Dalai Lama and the Altan Khan of the Tümed," *Tibetan Studies*, ed. Ihara Shōren and Yamaguchi Zuihō, 2, pp. 645–52.

24. Giuseppe Tucci, *Tibetan Painted Scrolls*, 1, pp. 27, 57–58, 609–10; Giuseppe Tucci, *Indo-Tibetica*, vol. 1 (Rome, 1941), pp. 49, 54–56, 78–84.

25. DR 2.10 (MITN 6, p. 50n): "Appena comparvero queste squadre, che con alte grida di festa, di acclamazioni e di non esplicabile contentezza uscirono da' sopradetti conventi li religiosi e li Lama ad accoglier i Tartari con affettuosi ringraziamente, a portar loro e vettovaglie e armi, e munizioni da guerra."

26. DR 2.10 (MITN 6, p. 50n): "La notte de' 30 di Novembre dopo la mezzanotte con fiero assalto attaccarono i nemici da tutte le parti le mure di Lhasa, e conforme alle già premesse intelligenze, essendo loro in varij luoghi somministrate le scale per salire sopra le mura, ed essendo loro aperte le porte sì della banda di Nort come de quella dell'Est, entrarono nella infelice città, e dopo un combattimento sanguinolento di poche ore allo schiarire dell'aurora restarono padroni di tutta la città."

27. DR 2.10 (MITN 6, pp. 50n–51n): "e con più sordida avidità li religiosi, che da' sopradetti conventi in qualità di soldati si erano al medesimo congiunti, si sparsero impetuosamente con le armi nude alle mani per tutte le case a dare il sacco, senza perdonar a veruno, neppure a' quelli medesimi, che con occulte intelligenze si erano con essi confederati. Non si contentò la loro cupidigia di tutto ciò che ritrovarono nelle

case, ma andarono a ricercar tutto ciò che ne' conventi de' religiosi e ne' templi de' loro idoli era stato conservato e riposto. Neppur con questo si appagò la loro incontentabile e inexpleta avidità, e perciò tornando più e più volte per tutte le case, senza perdonare nè a età nè a sesso nè a qualità di persona alcuna, altri ferivano con puntate di spade, altri miserabilmente piagavano per tutto il corpo con spietate battiture di sciabocchi, altri con le mani legate dietro alle spalle gli sospendevano alle travi del soffitto, e repetutamente gli flagellavano, altri finalmente in altre barbare maniere e con intollerabili insulti inumanamente tormentavano fin che confessassero dove si trovavano le loro nascoste ricchezze. In tal modo continuarono per due interi giorni e due notti, sin che ebbero rapito, dissotterrato e radunato tutto ciò che o di prezioso o di alcun valore poterono ritrovare o nella città di Lhasa o nelle di lei vicinanze."

28. DR 2. 11 (MITN 6, p. 53n): "Fuggivano dunque, e accortisi della loro fuga li barbari nemici con precipitoso furore non molto da lungi gl'inseguivano, quando arrivati li fuggitivi a un fosso munito di duplicata palizzata, s'intimorì il cavallo del Re, e nella perturbazione del timore offeso dalla palizzata, invece di passare il fosso cadde in esso e con la sua caduta seco trasse l'infelice Cinghes-Khang. Arrivarono intanto i Tartari inumani e con le armi alla mano assalirono il caduto Re, che con generosa resistenza avendo e ferito e ucciso varij degli spietati assalitori, e con magnanimo sforza avendo in un colpo reciso intieramente a un di essi il destro braccio, se morì infelice, non lasciò però di rendere e appresso del mondo e appresso de' nemici medesimi molto gloriosi e molto memorabili gl'ultimi momenti della sua vita."

29. Petech, *China and Tibet*, p. 52. Petech rightly interprets this departure as a disavowal of the Zünghar regime. But he wrongly implies that the Panchen Lama was disappointed that the rightful incarnation did not arrive in tow. One could hardly expect the Panchen to support the Zünghars in the first place, since he had been an active defender of Lhazang Khan and had consecrated his puppet Dalai Lama. More likely, he left for Tsang to consult his oracle and various nobles about the possibility of supporting the Amdo reincarnation.

30. Paltul Jampal Lodoe (Dpal yul rdzong nang 'jam dpal blo gros), *Bod na bzhugs pa'i rnying ma'i dgon deb; Record of Nyingma Monasteries in Tibet* (Dalhousie, 1965). For a decidedly Nyingma perspective on the Zünghar invasion up to the murder of Kang-chené, see Khyung po ras pa, *Rje btsun mi 'gyur dpal gyi sgron ma'i rnam thar* (Thimpu, Bhutan: The National Library of Bhutan, 1984), fols. 74–98. Scattered information can also be found in Gu ru Bkra' shis, *Gu bkra'i chos 'byung* (Beijing: Krung go'i bod kyi shes rig dpe skrun khang, 1990), esp. pp. 582, 660, 708–12, 735–36.

31. DR 3.6 (MITN 6, pp. 161–62): "Confiscarono tutte le loro ricchezze, si appro-priarono i loro feudi, saccheggiarono i loro palazzi, distrussero gran parte de' loro conventi e de' loro tempij, parte ne diroccarono, parte ne convertirono in stalla, e parte affatto ne spogliarono. Spezzarono le statue e bruciarono le figure e i libbri d'Urghien, quanti ne poterono con minuta ricerca trovare. Proibirono sotto pena della vita mede-sima pena rigorosamente proibirono a tutt'i Thibettani il recitar alcuna preghiera al medesimo Urghien, l'invocarlo in alcun modo e il precisamente pigliar il di lui nome." Cf. DR 3.19 (MITN 6, p. 273n): "ne criticano i libri, ne censurano in alcuni passi la vita, ne tacciano non assolutamente ma come in alcune particolarità eccessiva la

venerazione." Desideri echoes debates about the biographies of Padmasaṃbhava discussed by Anne-Marie Blondeau, "Analysis of the Biographies of Padmasambhava According to Tibetan Tradition: Classification of Sources," in *Tibetan Studies in Honour of Hugh Richardson*, ed. Michael Aris and Aung San Suu Kyi (Warminster: Aris and Phillips Ltd., 1980), pp. 45–52. Compare her "Une polémique sur l'authenticité des Bka'-thang au 17e siècle," in *Silver on Lapis: Tibetan Literary Culture and History*, ed. Christopher Beckwith (Bloomington: Tibet Society, 1987), pp. 125–62.

32. DR 3.6 (MITN 6, p. 159): "Finalmente, con aperta e dichiarata persecuzione dal primo giorno che s'impadronirono del Thibet sin all'ultima loro disfatta, cioè dal 1° di dicembre del 1717 sin a verso il fin d'ottobre del 1720 altro quasi non facero, che con ispietate carneficine sfogar la detta loro invidia contro i religiosi della seconda classe [i. e., the Nyingma] e contro tutto ciò che potesse aver alcun rapporto e attinenza a i medesimi. Quanti loro conventi saccheggiarono? Quanti ne distrussero e abbatterono? I più ricchi e più stimati Lama parte furono presi e miseramente ammazzati; e parte con la fuga salvarono bensì la vita, ma si videro raminghi, spogliati di tutto e quasi sepolti in oscure caverne."

33. DR 2.8 (MITN 6, p. 34).

34. DR 3.6 (MITN 6, pp. 159–60): "Aveva egli stretto con me una grandissima amicizia e un'intima familiarità. . . . Frequentemente m'invitava ad andar da lui a passar ora due e ora tre giorni in sua compagnia; e come era di genio molto liberale, m'aveva più e più volte fatto copiose offerte, specialmente d'oro in quantità."

35. DR 3.6 (MITN 6, p. 159): "Non senza compassione e non senza lacrime soccorsi io nella sua fuga il Lama di Lungar, miseramente fuggitivo e con gran pena scappato dalle mani de' barbari persecutori." This passage precedes Desideri's description of the lama: "Come sopra ho detto, è questi uno de' Lama che son maritati. Era egli di complessione molto grasso, di genio molto affabile e cortese, d'ottima indole, signore d'un gran feudo, abbondante di ricchezze, potente per la parentela di grosse e molto cospicue famiglie e universalmente molto amato e rispettato."

36. Khyung po ras pa, *Rje btsun mi 'gyur dpal gyi gron ma'i rnam thar dad pa'i gdung sel*, p. 96.

37. For an overview of *gter ma* literature, see Janet Gyatso, "Drawn from the Tibetan Treasury: The gTer ma Literature," in *Tibetan Literature: Studies in Genre*, ed. José Cabezon and Roger R. Jackson (Ithaca, NY: Snow Lion Publications, 1996), pp. 147–69; Samten Karmay, *The Great Perfection* (London: E. J. Brill, 1988). Important studies include Janet Gyatso, "Signs, Memory, and History: A Tantric Buddhist Theory of Scriptural Transmission," *Journal of the International Association of Buddhist Studies* 9 (1986), pp. 73–135; "The Logic of Legitimation in the Tibetan Treasure Tradition," *History of Religions* 33 (1993), pp. 97–134; David Germano, "Architecture and Absence in the Secret Tantric History of rDzogs Chen," *Journal of the International Association of Buddhist Studies* 17 (1994), pp. 203–335.

38. I depend heavily on the work of Geoffrey Childs and Franz-Karl Ehrhard for my discussion of *sbas yul*. Geoffrey Childs, "Refuge and Revitalization: Hidden Himalayan Sanctuaries (*Sbas-yul*) and the Preservation of Tibet's Imperial Lineage," *Acta Orientalia* 60 (1999), p. 132. Compare Franz-Karl Ehrhard, "The Role of 'Treasure

Discoverers' and Their Writings in the Search for Himalayan Sacred Lands," in *Sacred Spaces and Powerful Places in Tibetan Culture*, ed. Toni Huber (Dharamsala: Library of Tibetan Works and Archives, 1999), pp. 227–39.

39. E. Gene Smith, "Introduction," *The Autobiography of the First Panchen Lama Blo-bzang-chos-kyi-rgyal-mtshan* (New Delhi: Ngawang Gelek Demo, 1969), p. 2: "Tibetan sectarian and political rivalries were increasingly aired to Mongol patrons; and, in turn, these princes implored manifestations of the magical powers of their favored lamas, sometimes against their enemies, more often against their closest kin."

40. *Rje btsun mi 'gyur dpal gyi sgron ma'i rnam thar*, fols. 88, 97–98. Cf. Gu ru Bkra' shis, *Gu bkra'i chos 'byung*, pp. 248–49; 287–89, 292, 301, 641, 784. For Rindzin Nyima Drakpa, one of the most feared Nyingma sorcerers of the time, see Bryan J. Cuevas, *The Hidden History of the Tibetan Book of the Dead* (Oxford: Oxford University Press, 2003), pp. 179–204.

41. Dan Martin, "Bonpo Canons and Jesuit Cannons," *Tibet Journal* 15 (1990), pp. 3–28.

42. Bryan J. Cuevas, "On the Politics of Magical Warfare in 17th-Century Tibet," (manuscript kindly provided by the author). Interested readers should also keep an eye out for the same author's "The 'Calf's Nipple' (*Be'u bum*) of Ju Mipam ('Ju Mi pham): A Handbook of Tibetan Ritual Magic," in *Tibetan Ritual*, ed. José I. Cabezón (Oxford: Oxford University Press, forthcoming).

43. Samten Karmay, *Secret Visions of the Fifth Dalai Lama: The Gold Manuscript in the Fournier Collection* (London: Serindia Publications, 1988), p. 30. Much of the anxiety between the rigorists and the more syncretic Geluk in central Tibet was expressed in terms of the ritual daggers or pegs (*phur pa*) used in Nyingma sorcery and black magic.

44. Gu ru Bkra' shis, *Gu bkra'i chos 'byung*, p. 162.

45. O rgyan gling pa, *Padma bka' thang U rgyen gu ru padma 'byung gnas kyi skyes rabs rnam par thar pa* (Chengdu: Si khron mi rigs dpe skrun khang, 1987), pp. 558–74. I suspect that Desideri thought the sixth Dalai Lama was the "heretical leader" prophesied in the *Shel brag ma*. Given his cast of mind, the missionary might even have imagined that he himself was Rashak, the revealer who was knowledgeable about the magic cross (*mdos*) and who would ripen the "heart" (*snying po*) in Dakpo. *Padma bka' thang*, p. 563: "*dwags sgom snying po'i don bsgom khyu gcig 'byung: mchims bu kho mthing sbas pa'i gter ka 'di: mi bzhag 'don pa'i rtag der bstan nas byung: ra shag gter ston mdos la mkhas pa 'byung.*".

46. Kah thog Tshe dbang nor bu, *Bod rje gdung rabs* (1745).

47. Athansius Kircher believed that he could understand Chinese by a *lectio idealis*, a "reading" of God's own ideas that were mystically represented by Chinese "hiero-glyphics." Whether Kircher might legitimately have possessed a *dgongs gter*—or merely a *rkup gter*—is a question that I will leave for theologians.

48. DR 3.18 (MITN 6, p. 265): "Un sol genere di sì fatte cose mi giova qui il riferire, che al puro intenderle e ritrovarle parte scritte e parte stampate ne' libri, ne' primi principj della mia dimora in quel regno, mi diedero occasione di far beffe e di ben grasse risate, ma dipoi nel progresso del tempo m'obbligarono e mi costrinsero a inchinar milioni di volte e batter per terra riverente la testa profondamente adorando la

suprema, giustissima, santissima, imperscrutabile Provvidenza di Dio, e col S. Profeta David mille e mille volte ripetendo quelle parole: *Iustus es Domine, et rectum judicium tuum.*" Desideri quotes Psalm 119.137: "Righteous art thou, O Lord, and right are thy judgments."

49. I must credit my friend Bryan Cuevas for first identifying this lama, as he beat me in our race through the *Gu bkra'i chos 'byung.* I have provided the following confirmatory texts in the footnotes that follow.

50. Gu ru Bkra' shis, *Gu bkra'i chos 'byung*, pp. 415–18.

51. Kun bzang nges don klong yangs, *Bod du byung ba'i gsang sngags snga 'gyur gyi bstan 'dzin skyes mchog rim byon gyi rnam thar nor bu'i do shal* (Dalhousie: Damchoe Sangpo, 1976), p. 324.

52. Chojé Lingpa and Mingyur Peldrönma seem to have been in Kongpo at the same time. *Rje btsun mi 'gyur dpal gyi gron ma'i rnam thar dad pa'i gdung sel*, p. 104.

53. *Rig pa 'dzin pa blo bzang 'phrin las kyi rtogs brjod skel bzang dga' ston (The Collected Works of Sle lung Rje drung Bzhad pa'i rdo rje, vol. 1)* (Leh: T. Sonam, 1983), pp. 12, 368, and 454. Franz-Karl Ehrhard has briefly touched on the relationship of Polhané to Lelung Zhepé Dorjé, especially after the Imperial Edict forbidding Nyingma practices in 1726. He says, "For bSod-nams stobs-rgyas himself, Sle-lung bZhad-pa'i rdo-rje came forward with some advice that obviously must be seen as relating to his strong reaction against the edict of the Manchu ruler Yung-chen. The tradition of the dGe-lugs-pa was thereby characterized as something the ruler could place confidence in (*zhwa ser cod pan 'chang ba'i rings lugs 'di ni yid brton rung ba'o*), the reason for this being the purity and continuity of the teachings of Padmasambhava, Atisha, and Tshong-kha-pa. What we witness here, is in my opinion, the effort on the part of the priest from rNam-grol gling to add some critical perspective to the standpoint of bSod-nams stobs- rgyas with the aim of dissolving the polarization between the dGe-lugs-pa and the rNying-ma schools." Franz-Karl Ehrhard, "Political and Ritual Aspects of the Search for Himalayan Sacred Lands," in *Sacred Spaces and Powerful Places in Tibetan Culture*, ed. Toni Huber (Dharamsala: LTWA, 1999), pp. 240–57. Although Ehrhard is right to highlight the political prominence of figures such as Lelung, his explanation tells us little. Polhané had already shown great support for the Nyingma and had, in fact, been educated at one of their most prominent monasteries, Mindröling. There would have been little reason for Lelung to convince Polhané of the legitimacy of Nyingma teachings. Any reconciliation Lelung would have wished to effect would have been between Geluk parties. If Petech favors the meeting with Mingyur Peldrönma, it is only because it is all the more extraordinary.

54. *Mi dbang bsod nams stobs rgyas rnam grol gling du byon pa'i lo rgyus ngo mtshar 'bum snang* in *The Collected Works of Sle lung Rje drung Bzhad pa'i rdo rje* (Leh: T. Sonam, 1984), 9, pp. 279–359.

55. Chos rje rling pa, *Khrag 'thung mā ha gu ru padma drag po'i chos skor and Other Revelations* (Darjeeling: Kargyud Sungrab Nyamso Khang, 1985).

56. Although Desideri mentions that several lamas copied portions of his writings, his manuscripts give no evidence of having been printed. In any event, they do not appear in the survey of printing blocks in central Tibet. *Gangs can gyi ljongs su bka' dang*

bstan bcos sogs kyi glegs bam spar gzhi ji ltar yod pa rnam nas dkar chag in *Three Karchaks*,
ed. E. Gene Smith (New Delhi: Ngawang Gelek Demo, 1970), pp. 169–243.

57. DR 3.1 (MITN 6. pp. 115–16); 3.15 (MITN 6, pp. 235–36).

58. DR 2.3 (MITN 6, pp. 12–13); 2.18 (MITN 6, pp. 108–14).

59. DR 3.7 (MITN 6, p. 166); 3.10 (MITN 6, pp. 195, 201).

60. DR 2.6 (MITN 6, p. 24).

61. DR 2.10 (MITN 6, p. 41n–42n): "Contro il costume inviolabile de' Lama
e Religiosi del Thibet cominciò con nutrire e coltivare la capelliera; passò a bere
cose che possino ubriacare; s'accostumò al giuoco; si diede in preda all'ubriachezza;
in fine talmente si lasciò trasportare dalla libidine, che non vi erano zittelle o
maritate, nè vi era bellezza dell'uno o dell'altro sesso, che scappassero dalla sua
sfrenata licenza."

62. DR 3.4 (MITN 6, p. 143): "Finalmente a tale eccesso arriva l'adorazione di
quelle cieche e illuse gente verso il Gran Lama del Thibet, che i medesimi suoi
escrementi, ridotti in piccole pillole, li dimandano come una molto gran reliquia. Tali
pillole l'inghiottiscono con molta devozione e le conservano con molto rispetto in alcuni
reliquiarj, che portano addossa, e nelle malattie o simili occorrenze prendono con molta
fede di tali pillole, come potente rimedio a' loro mali e come sicuro preservativo da
ogn'infortunio."

63. DR 3.1 (MITN 6, p. 115): "Per dar ragguaglio di quella setta di religione
particolarissima, o per dir meglio, di quel miscuglio di dogmi stranissimi che com-
pongono un mostro di religione, a cui non so se n'habbia simile in tutto il mondo,
è conveniente dar principio dal capo di essa, che è il Gran Lama, o sia Papa di quelle
genti."

64. For this section I have been greatly assisted by Michael Sweet's "Human Fraud
or the Devil's Work? Ippolito Desideri on the Reincarnate Succession of the Dalai
Lama," a paper given at the XV Congress of the International Association of Buddhist
Studies, Atlanta, June 23–28, 2008.

65. DR 3.2 (MITN 6, pp. 121–22). Desideri seems to have let his argument get away
when he adduced the inexplicable ease with which the Dalai Lama is selected as a proof
of demonic tampering.

66. DR 3.2 (MITN 6, p. 125): "Il demonio sí che ha tutto il fondamento da
potersi credere esser egli il motore e l'agente immediato dell'inganno di cui si
tratta. Perchè, conoscendo egli molto bene gl'uomini, il temperamento, la complessione e fisica disposizione di ciascuno, può di proposito e crear e apposta
eleggere per ministro del suo inganno più tosto il tal fanciullo in particolare che in
tal altro a quello uguale negl'anni; perchè prevede che quello per la sua migliore
attitudine e organizazione probabilmente camperà più. Può in oltre guardarlo da'
pericoli, difenderlo dalle cascate, curarlo nelle malattie e in mille maniere con-
currere alla sua conservazione, operando appostatamente per rendere più credibile
l'errore che quello sia il Lama morto tornato a rivivere." Scholastic theologians
would have noted that in this passage Desideri presents the Devil as parodying
God's threefold work of creating, conserving, and concurring in the actions of all
things in his possession of the child Dalai Lama.

67. DR 3.3 (MITN 6, p. 134): "Che anzi s'ingrandisce più la maestà di questa divina vittoria coll'affermare, che anch'oggi si trovano popoli dominati dall'infernale tirannide e in pena de' lor peccati stranamente avvolti in superstizioni inaudite, che aspettano un ministro evangelico che spieghi contro al maligno nemico la bandiera della Croce, e messolo in fuga, continui fra di loro in quelle remote parti il trionfo di Xpo sopra i demonij, tanti secoli prima cominciato nell'Europa e sì felicemente portato attorno a quasi tutto il resto del mondo." This is but a small part of a much larger threefold argument *ex convenientia* about God's permission of evil in this section of the *Notizie istoriche*, which has been expertly summarized by Michael Sweet in "Human Fraud or the Devil's Work." Desideri assumes two very important things in this argument that most, if not all, of his expected readers would have accepted. First, he assumes that demons, being fallen angels, have intellects vastly superior to those of any humans. The Devil, being the chief of the fallen angels, would necessarily have one of the keenest of angelic intellects, and would thus be able to take in the whole of creation in a glance as well as see very hidden phenomena such as the relations of effects to their causes. So, too, the Devil would be able to predict future effects with uncanny accuracy. In light of the theological positions outlined in the last chapter, Desideri here argues that human beings, however intelligent, are simply no match for demons, and thus must depend on God's grace to confound them. Second, Desideri would have assumed, basing himself on the "Rules for the Discernment of Spirits" found in the *Spiritual Exercises*, that the action of demons becomes sweeter and less violent the longer one is under their influence. The peaceful election of the Dalai Lama, strangely enough, would then show just how formidable the Devil's influence had become in Tibet. Similarly, any Jesuit would have rejected the idea that "Providence confirms Tibetans in their false religion" as a Calvinist or Jansenist heresy, because such a formulation implies that God had not given Tibetans grace sufficient for their salvation. All orthodox Catholic theologians rejected the idea that God abandoned people to error by commanding the impossible; if Desideri did not finish this part of the *Notizie istoriche*, I think it is because he wished to compose an airtight refutation of these subtly coded Jansenist positions.

68. DR 2.10 (MITN 6, p. 43): "E queste furono le prime faville, che dopo lunghe e coperte insidie di più anni, partorirono poi quell'incendio che tolse al re e vita e regno."

69. DR 2.10 (MITN 6, p. 42n).

70. DR 2.9 (MITN 6, p. 39). In addition to the Tibetan works listed above, accounts of the tensions between the sixth Dalai Lama, Lhazang Khan, and Sangyé Gyatso can also be found in Blo bzang ye shes dpal bzang po, *Shākya'i dge slong blo bzang ye shes kyi spyod tshul gsal bar byed pa ngor dkar can kyi phreng ba*, in *The Collected Works (gsung-'bum) of the Second Panchen Blo-bzan-ye-śes* (New Delhi: Bkra sis lhun po Monastery, 1981–85), 1, p. 447; and Mdo mkhar Tshe ring dbang rgyal, *Dpal mi'i dbang po'i rtogs pa brjod 'jig rten kun tu dga' ba'i gtam shes bya ba* (Chengdu: Khron mi rigs dpe skrun khang, 1981), p. 119.

71. Petech, *China and Tibet*, p. 12.

72. Shakabpa, *Bod kyi srid don rgyal rabs*, p. 482.

73. Georges Dreyfus, "The Shuk-den Affair: History and Nature of a Quarrel," *Journal of the International Association of Buddhist Studies* 21 (1998). pp. 236–37, where

he describes Jamyang Zhepa as "one of the leading Ge-luk lamas opposing the Fifth and his third prime minister (sde srid) Sang-gye Gya-tso. . . . This opposition had come to the fore when the prime minister tried to entice the Lo-sel-ling college of Dre-bung monastery to adopt the fifth Dalai-Lama's works as its textbooks in place of Panchen Sö-nam-drak-pa's works. After the college's refusal, Sang-gye Gya-tso asked Jam-yang-shay-ba to refute Panchen Sö-nam-drak-pa. This was an attempt at strengthening the government's control over the monasteries as well as a way of removing Drak-pa Gyel-tsen's posthumous influence, two goals with which Jam-yang-shay-ba had little sympathy. Hence, the latter refused to oblige."

74. Petech, *China and Tibet*, pp. 10–11.

75. Gene Smith has also pointed out the fascinating connections between Sera, Polhané, and Sumpa Khenpo. E. Gene Smith, *Collected Works of Thu'u-Bkwan Blo-bzang-chos-kyi-nyi-ma* (New Delhi: Ngawang Gelek Demo, 1969), 2, p. 26.

76. Aris, *Hidden Treasures*, p. 161.

77. Petech, "Notes on Tibetan History of the 18th Century," p. 272.

78. Sum pa mkhan po Ye shes dpal 'byor, *Mtsho sngon byi lo rgyus sogs bkod pa'i tshangs glu gsar snyan* in *The Annals of Kokonor*, trans. H. C. Yang (Bloomington: Indiana University Press, 1970), p. 44: *spus ma yin bzhin*. Yang translates this phrase as "no ordinary person." Richardson believes this text to be corrupt. Matthew Kapstein prefers to translate it as "unfit" or "unworthy."

79. Hugh Richardson, "The Fifth Dalai Lama's Decree Appointing Sangs-Rgyas Rgya-Mtsho as Regent," *Bulletin of the School of Oriental and African Studies* 43 (1980), pp. 329–44.

80. DR 3.18 (MITN 6, p. 272).

81. DR 3.6 (MITN VI, p. 158).

82. Benjamin Bogin, "Royal Blood and Political Power: Contrasting Allegiances in the Memoirs of Yol Mo Bstan'Dzin Nor Bu (1598–1644)," in *Power, Politics, and the Invention of Tradition*, ed. Bryan J. Cuevas and Kurtis R. Schaeffer, pp. 7–16.

83. Desideri does not seem to have differentiated any of the "Red Hat" sects. Although the name derives from the red ceremonial hat worn by Tibetan scholars in all traditions except the *zhwa lu* tradition of Butön, it was applied generally by Mongols, Manchus, and Geluk authors to all non-Geluk religious orders in Tibet, Bhutan, and Sikkim, including the Nyingma and the various Kagyü sects. It is clear from Desideri's descriptions that he has the Nyingma in mind, or at least Nyingma sympathizers. DR 3.6 (MITN 6, p. 158): "I religiosi del berretton rosso, quantunque venerino Sciacchia Thubba come loro legislatore universale, nondimeno sono specialmente addetti a Urghien, come a institutore e fondator della lor classe, al di cui culto e imitazione fanno professione d'essere specialmente dedicati, anche con alcuni riti speciali e non communi agli altri religiosi." I owe this last correction to Matthew Kapstein, who kindly pointed out to me in personal conversation that by Desideri's day, the Nyingma were entirely "mainstream," and so other orders widely adopted the trappings of their cult.

84. Melvyn Goldstein, "Religious Conflict in the Traditional State," in *Reflections on Tibetan Culture: Essays in Memory of Turrell V. Wylie*, ed. L. Epstein and R. F. Sherburne (Lewiston: Edwin Mellen Press, 1990), pp. 231–47.

85. Zahiruddin, *Sino-Tibetan Relations*, p. 191.

86. Georges Dreyfus, "The Shuk-den Affair," p. 232: "The resentment against the power of the fifth Dalai Lama was primarily connected to a broad and far-reaching issue, the desire of some of the more sectarian Ge-luk hierarchs to set up a purely Ge-luk rule. Some even seem to have argued for the suppression of the schools against which they fought for more than a century, particularly the Kar-ma Ka-gyu tradition."

87. Matthew Kapstein, *The Tibetan Assimilation of Buddhism*, p. 130: "The world-view of these churchmen bore a strange resemblance to that of medieval Latin Christendom, with the Manchus filling the role of imperial Rome and the Geluk [Dge-lugs-pa] hierarchy that of the Catholic Church. These were not the products of a denomination under fire but rather represented the synthesis of a peerless salvific vehicle with a universal temporal order. Not personally threatened by the Central Tibetan feuds, they could afford to regard the situation there only with equanimous compassion." Although the comparison may cause some Tibetanists to bristle, I have always found Matthew Kapstein's comments about the Amdo Geluks especially perspicacious. The multi-ethnic and, as some might argue, multinational expanse of the Geluk in the seventeenth and eighteenth centuries is precisely the way in which it most resembled the Catholic Church. This is not to say, of course, that there were not serious political tensions between Amdo Geluks and other Tibetan sects.

88. Tsyrempilov has pointed out a passage in Jamyang Zhepa's biography that seems to indicate that Lozang Puntsok was responsible for the inclusion of his master's works in the curriculum at Gomang in 1716. Tsyrempilov, "Dge lugs Divided," p. 58.

89. As Peter Perdue argues, official Chinese reports make it appear that the Khoshud and the Qing shared a seamless, almost telepathic, communication, united as brothers in their opposition to the barbarous Zünghar, but other sources, such as Yinti's suppressed memoirs, indicate that the Khoshud in Kökenuur only reluctantly opposed the Zünghars. In fact, Khoshud princes routinely refused to supply men for Qing armies during these years. Likewise, the Qing knew that Tsewang Rapten would enter Tibet after he had been expelled from Hamli; they did not know, however, whether he could gain the support of Lhazang Khan. Desideri's own account preserves some of this ambiguity. He felt, for example, that the Khoshud Khan trusted the Zünghar chieftain and that Tsewang Rapten in turn took Lhazang Khan's money to defend the Zünghar state against Russians and Kazakhs.

90. Perdue, *China Marches West*, pp. 135–38.

91. Perdue again argues that Kangxi was primarily concerned with preventing Russian penetration into northern Manchuria in the 1680s. Although he had been greatly supported by the Chakhars, Kangxi was well aware that the Oirat confederation lay beyond his power. If he decided in 1689 to launch a series of extremely risky campaigns of expansion, Kangxi was simply following the same strategy that Sangyé Gyatso had pursued when he bestowed the title on Galdan and unified the Oirat under Zünghar rule.

92. Peter Perdue's *China Marches West* is a gold mine for the military history of the Qing-Zünghar conflict. For other works on inner Asian warfare see, among others,

Joanna Waley-Cohen, *The Culture of War in China: Empire and the Military Under the Qing Dynasty* (London: I. B. Tauris, 2006); "God and Guns in Eighteenth-century China: Jesuit Missionaries and the Military Campaigns of the Qianlong Emperor (1736–96)," in *Contacts Between Cultures*, vol. 4 (Lewiston: Edwin Mellen Press, 1992), pp. 94–99; Nicola di Cosmo, *Diary of a Manchu Soldier in Seventeenth-Century China* (London: RoutledgeCurzon, 2006); *Warfare in Inner Asian History (500–1800)* (Leiden: Brill, 2002).

93. DR 2.12 (MITN 6, p. 75): "Con tal vittoria, dopo sì luttuose e sì lunghe catastrofi di circa vent'anni, nel mese d'ottobre del 1720 il domino di tutto questo terzo e principal Thibet da' Tartari passò sotto l'imperator della Cina, a cui è presentemente governato e alla di cui gran potenza resterà."

94. DR 2.12 (MITN 6, p. 74n): "Il Debà Tâzê e gli altri, avendoli legati ad alcune macchine che per tal cosa usano, gli fecero ignominiosamente tormentare e penosamente saettar con frezze, finchè miseramente spirassero. Così in questi iniqui inumani traditori si verificò e per minuto si adempi ciò che scrisse un savio poeta de' nostri tempi, cioè che Su la rota di Fortuna/ chi con fraude s'inalzò/ il feretro nella cuna/ al suo farlo riportò./ L'alma rea d'infedeltà/ mai non va senza supplizio/ e nel mar del proprio ignanno/ fassi porto il precipizio."

95. Although Petech mentions that the puppet lama had no supporters, it seems odd that the Manchus would go to such measures had he not had some supporters. Later Petech addresses the possibility that he did in fact have supporters since an incarnation was discovered in Kham (Petech, *China and Tibet*, p. 105).

96. DR 3.6 (MITN 6, p. 161). "Sono inesplicabili le lacrime e le amorevoli espressioni, con cui il buon Lama mi fece conoscere che la disgrazie e l'assenza non solamente non avevano punto in lui diminuito l'antica amicizia, ma che più tosto l'avevano resa più forte e più solida. Voleva egli non solamente restituirmi il denaro che gli avevo inviato, ma voleva aggiugnergli copiosi donativi; ma ricusando io di ricevere nè questi nè quello, prese quindi motivi di sentir più al vivo la perdita, che veniva a far con la mia partenza d'un suo più sincero amico."

CHAPTER 5: THE FIGHT WITH THE FRIARS

1. DR 4.1 (MITN 7, p. 6): "e quanto grande fu la contentezza che sperimentai nel goder la di lui giocondissima conversazione, altrettanto mi fu di pena l'essere spettator del molto che il povero Padre, in età, se non erro, di sessant'anni, per cammini sì precipitosi e per tali rompicolli e fra i sommi rigori di quella stagione soffriva."

2. I would like to thank Michael Sweet for pointing this out to me. Michael also shared a draft of his article, "An Unpublished Letter in Portuguese by Fr. Ippolito Desideri" (AHSI, forthcoming), which investigates Desideri's tensions with the authorities at Goa.

3. DR 4.10 (MITN 7, p. 61). On Bouchet, see Francis X. Clooney, S.J., *Fr. Bouchet's India: An 18th Century Jesuit's Encounter with Hinduism* (Chennai: Satya Nilayam Publications, 2005).

4. Desideri was being a bit underhanded when he titled his published arguments "defenses"; after all, it was he who had formally initiated the legal proceedings against the Capuchins.

5. Jesuits had the Franciscan missionary Pedro de Alfaro and his companions removed from China even though the Franciscans had entered China four years earlier. Not to be outdone, friars used their own political power to have exclusively Jesuit mission fields opened to other orders, as when they successfully petitioned Rome to allow them to evangelize China in 1600 and Japan in 1608. For trouble in the New World, see Andrés Pérez de Ribas, *History of the Triumphs of Our Holy Faith Amongst the Most Barbarous and Fierce Peoples of the New World*, trans. Daniel T. Reff, Maureen Ahern, and Richard K. Danford (Tuscon: University of Arizona Press, 1999), p. 29; John F. Bannon, *The Mission Frontier in Sonora, 1620–1687* (New York: Catholic Historical Society, 1955); Charles W. Polzer, S.J., "The Franciscan Entrada into Sonora, 1645–1652: A Jesuit Chronicle," *Arizona and the West* 14 (1972), pp. 253–78.

6. Bonaventura Ibañez, *Responsum quaestionibus* (SF 3, p. 74): "In nisuno delli regni circumvicini della China hano potuto intrare ministri evangelici et ancora che intorno nel regno de Tybeth o vicino a lui non potero conservarsi la, ne fare alcun fruto per essere idolatre contumaci."

7. SF 3, p. 520: "Con todo esso, mientras viviere la madre deste Emperador, no tenemos esperança que revoque dicho decreto, porque esta Reina madre nos es contrario, instigada de los vonços del reino de Lamasen, a los quales tiene en su palacio edificado templo de diablos, y ellos no se apartan de su lado y de instigarle contra nuestras cosas; mas lo bueno que tiene la cosa es que el Emperador no gusta de ellos, los consiente por no disgustar a la madre." This letter shares Matteo Ricci's distrust of the Buddha, whom Agostino refers to as "idolo pessimo en este reino" (SF 3, p. 521).

8. Giovanni Francesco Nicolai, writing to de Tournon in 1702 (SF 6, p. 272), says, "Chi anche da Surat volesse per terra passare ad Agra, regia del Gran Mogol, e di là proseguire il viaggio di terra per i regni di Tibet e Lamas o Barantola, per entrare in China dalla parte occidentale, potrebbe farlo; ma non in minor tempo di 6 mesi, e non senza gran pericoli e patimenti, quando la navigazione da Surat a China non suol essere che di 3 mesi." Nicolai also reported on the first Capuchin mission to his provincial in 1704 (SF 6, pp. 299–300), incidentally noting the Chinese Rites controversy and that the Jansenist Artus de Lionne, M.E.P., was arguing the case in Rome *con zelo*. Bernardino della Chiesa also corresponded with Giuseppe da Ascoli (SF 5, pp. 545–46).

9. Sandberg, *The Exploration of Tibet*, p. 52. These suspicions are not entirely without basis in the historical record. If Hosten could speculate on Capuchin interference with the Jesuits at Surat, it is not prima facie unreasonable to inquire about Jesuit attempts to disrupt the Capuchin missions. Hosten himself acknowledged that the Jesuits might have attempted to have François-Marie de la Tour assigned to Tibet to be rid of his meddling in the Rites controversy.

10. Holdich, *Tibet the Mysterious*, p. 78.

11. Landon, *The Opening of Lhasa*, I, p. 9.

12. Snellgrove and Richardson, *A Cultural History of Tibet*, pp. 220–21.

13. Ibid., p. 222.

14. Bangert, *History*, p. 156, is typical: "Valignano's fears were justified. The strong contrast between the Franciscan and the Jesuit approach soon became evident as the friars, imitating their successful methods in Ibero-America where the indigenous cultures were primitive, tended to brush aside the mature civilizations of Japan to which the Jesuits deferred with respect; the friars were free, but the Jesuits cautious, in the distribution of medals, rosaries, holy water; the friars concentrated on the poor, while the Jesuits worked among the influential classes." It is telling that on the following page Bangert begins his description of Valignano's missionary strategy with this: "Convinced that the Society must disassociate itself from the image of the westerner as a marauder avid only for conquest, he formulated general principles for the missionaries." By enumerating the "deep sympathy and respect," "perfect command of the language," the use of science, the emphasis on conversation, the special concern for the cultivated classes, and—note this—the "supernatural virtue" necessary for the missions, Bangert implies that friars lacked these characteristics.

15. OT 3, p. 7; OT 4, pp. 33–35; Sherburne, "A Buddhist-Christian Dialog?" pp. 299–300.

16. Ronnie Po-Chia Hsia contrasts the "gentleness" (*sauvitas*) of the Italian missionaries "in contrast to the uncompromising inflexibility of Spanish methods, a difference due no doubt to the Spanish experience of imperial conquest." The emphasis on *il modo soave* founded in the missiological directives of Valignano and Ricci probably tell us more about Italian feelings for Spaniards than about Spanish missionaries themselves, feelings that would only have been reinforced in later Italian missionaries by the Spanish sack of Rome in 1527. Hsia, *The World of Catholic Renewal*, p. 42. Cf. ibid., pp. 186–87.

17. George Minimaki, *The Chinese Rites Controversy from Its Beginnings to Modern Times* (Chicago: Loyola University Press, 1985); D. E. Mungello, ed., *The Chinese Rites Controversy: Its History and Meaning* (Nettetal: Steyler Verlag, 1994). The definitive new history of the China mission is Liam Matthew Brockey, *Journey to the East: The Jesuit Mission to China 1579–1724* (Cambridge: Belknap Press, 2007). For an account of the final days of the mission, see Ronnie Po-Chia Hsia, "Twilight in the Imperial City: The Jesuit Mission in China, 1748–60," in *The Jesuits: Cultures, Sciences, and the Arts*, 2, pp. 725–37. For bibliographic resources, see Nicolas Standaert, S.J., ed., *Handbook of Christianity in China* (Leiden: Brill, 2001).

18. G. H. Dunne, S.J., "What Happened to the Chinese Liturgy?" *Catholic Historical Review* 48 (1961), pp. 1–14.

19. S. Rajamanickam, *The First Oriental Scholar* (Tirunelveli: De Nobili Research Institute, 1972). Cf. P. Dahmen, S.J., *Un Jésuite Brahme, Roberto de Nobili, S.I., 1577–1656, missionaire à Maduré* (Bruxelles: C. Bayaert, 1924); A Rocaries, S.J., *Roberto de Nobili, S.I., ou le "sannyasi chrétien"* (Toulouse: Éditions Prière et vie, 1967); P. R. Bachmann, S.J., *Roberto Nobili 1577–1656: Ein Missionsgeschichtlicher Beitrag zum christlichen Dialog mit Hinduismus* (Rome: IHSI, 1972); N. Tornese, S.J., *Roberto de Nobili, 1577–1656: Contributo al dialogo con i non cristiani* (Cagliari: Pontificia facoltà teologica del S. Cuore, 1973).

20. Županov, *Disputed Mission*, p. 35. Although Županov contrasts de Nobili's recognition of the civilization of Brahmanism with his critic Gonçalo Fernandes's

characterization of it as a pagan "machine" (*máquina do Bramanismo*), we should note that the distinction between the civil and the religious does not "relativize" religion as she claims. Such happens only when later thinkers collapse the division or reinterpret it along the divide between public discourse and private experience.

21. Bangert, *History*, p. 237.

22. See the exchange between Antonio de Santa Maria and Martino Martini recounted by Bonaventura Ibañez, *Brevis Relatio anno 1668* (SF 3, pp. 81–84).

23. Clement X, *Creditae nobis coelitus* (April 6, 1673).

24. Pope Alexander VII founded the apostolic vicariates in 1658 at the suggestion of the famous French Jesuit missionary in Vietnam, Alexandre de Rhodes, who suggested that the Far East be organized into several difference vicariates run by secular priests at the behest of Rome and free from the encumbrance of the Portuguese ecclesiastic government. A. Perbal and Bernard de Vaulx, "La Création et les débuts des vicaires apostoliques (1626–1689)," in *Histoire universelle des missions catholiques*, ed. S. Delacrois (Paris: Grund, 1957); Fortunato Margioti, "La Cina, ginepraio di questioni secolari," in *Sacrae Congregationis De Propaganda Fide Memoria Rerum, 1622–1972*, ed. J. Metzler (Rome: Herder, 1972), I, pt. 2, pp. 612–15.

25. As Desideri left Europe, it looked as if the Jesuits had pounded the final nail in Jansen's coffin. They had already taken the initial steps toward securing yet another condemnation, and Louis XIV had razed Port-Royal, the symbolic headquarters of the Jansenists, slightly less than a year before Desideri sailed for Asia. When Pope Clement XI condemned Pasquier Quesnel and Jansenists in the bull *Unigenitus* in September 1713, Desideri was making his first contacts among the missionaries in Goa. When Louis XIV died, the Jansenists increased their polemic against the Jesuits considerably. Fourteen years later, as the Italian missionary returned to Europe, the Jansenist controversy had fully enveloped Jesuit politics. David E. Mungello, "Malebranche and Chinese Philosophy," *Journal of the History of Ideas* 41 (1980), pp. 551–78. On the poltical conflict between Jesuits and Jansenists, see Robert Kreiser, *Miracles, Convulsions, and Ecclesial Politics in Early Eighteenth-Century Paris* (Princeton, NJ: Princeton University Press, 1978); Dale K. van Kley, *The Jansenists and the Expulsion of the Jesuits from France, 1757–1765* (New Haven, CT: Yale University Press, 1975). Fascinating material on the conflict between Jesuits and Jansenists in China can also be found in the archives, including two catalogues of Jansenist works found in China (ARSI Jap-Sin 196, ff. 1–9, 21–23) and *Le Phantome du Jansenisme* (ARSI Jap-Sin 196, ff. 24–63).

26. Francis A. Rouleau, S.J., "Maillard de Tournon, Papal Legate at the Court of Beijing," AHSI 31 (1962); Antonio Sisto Rosso, O.F.M., *Apostolic Legations to China of the 18th Century* (Pasadena: P. D. & I. Perkins, 1948), pp. 149–86; Liam Matthew Brockey, *Journey to the East*, pp. 164–203; D. Kessler, *Kang-hsi and the Consolidation of Ch'ing Rule 1661–1684* (Chicago: University of Chicago Press, 1976).

27. Edward Malatesta, "A Fatal Clash of Wills: The Condemnation of the Chinese Rites by the Papal Legate Tommaso Maillard de Tournon," in *Chinese Rites Controversy*, ed. David Mungello, pp. 211–46. Cf. the anonymous *Statu Missionis Sinensis* written in 1708 (ARSI Jap-Sin 150, ff. 284–326) and the *Confutatio* of 1709 (ARSI Jap-Sin 137a, ff. 14–32).

28. Minamiki, *The Chinese Rites Controversy*, p. 54. Interesting material concerning Kangxi can be found in the anonymous *Diarium Mandarinorum* of 1720 (ARSI Jap-Sin 198, ff. 347–99) and Parrenin's notes on the emperor's questions from November 20, 1720 (ARSI Jap-Sin 137a, ff. 166–69).

29. Bangert, *History*, p. 338.

30. J. Rickaby, S.J., "Clement the Eleventh and the Chinese Rites," *The Month* 73 (1891), pp. 70–79.

31. During the last two decades of the Sun King's reign, France replaced Rome as the political and economic center of the missions. By the last decade of the seventeenth century, the Jesuit procurator for the Chinese missions was sent to Paris rather then Rome to secure funds. Mungello, *Curious Land*, p. 301.

32. Amaral to Tamburini, Macao (January 8, 1713), ARSI *Jap. Sin. 174*, 306–7. Cf. Witek, *Controversial Ideas*, p. 223.

33. Witek, *Controversial Ideas*, p. 225.

34. Isacio Rodriguez, "Alvaro de Benavente, OSA y su 'Relación' de las misiones agustinianas de China (1680–1686)," *Estudio Augustiniano* 12 (1977), pp. 731–90.

35. Sebald Reil, *Kilian Stumpf, 1655–1720. Ein Würzburger Jesuit am Kaiserhof zu Beijing* (Munster: Aschendorff, 1978), pp. 178–82.

36. Witek, *Controversial Ideas*, pp. 144–59, 307–8.

37. For documents on the Rites controversies in the 1720s see ARSI Jap-Sin 198, ff. 28–344 (*Sommario di diverse lettere e documenti dall'anno 1716 al 1722* [1725]); and ARSI Jap-Sin 200, ff. 1–664 (*Riflessioni sopra il primo paragrafo riti cinensis adversus Societatis* [1728]).

38. DL 10 (MITN 5, pp. 48–49).

39. If Desideri did know that da Fano had been in Rome, his behavior would indicate a rather headstrong character. I am inclined to think rather that da Fano did not reveal this information to Desideri, and later took advantage of the Jesuit's ignorance.

40. DL 8 (MITN 5, p. 41).

41. DL 10 (MITN 5, p. 52).

42. DL 10 (MITN 5, p. 50).

43. On the Jesuit-Manchu cartography expedition, see W. Fuchs, *Der Jesuiten Atlas der K'anghsi-Zeit*, Monumenta Serica Monograph IV (Beijing: Furen Universität, 1943).

44. When Antonio Caballero de Santa María arrived in Beijing in 1634, the Jesuit Manuel Diaz had him kidnapped. In 1637, Jesuits arranged to have Franciscans arrested and interrogated, but the friars saw through the ruse, having recognized their harassers as associates of Jesuits that they knew in Manila. The general Muzio Vitelleschi even ordered Jesuits in China to deny hospitality to friars. G. H. Dunne, S.J., *Generation of Giants* (South Bend: University of Notre Dame Press, 1962), p. 239.

45. DL 12 (MITN 5, pp. 55–60). The dating of these letters is somewhat confusing. A previous letter from Desideri to da Montecchio dated March 12, 1718 bore no such animosity. In fact, Desideri wrote the friar to ask him to assist any Jesuit missionaries from the Goa province who might be making their way to Tibet by way of Nepal. He thanked da Montecchio for the kind attention he had devoted to Jesuits in the past, presumably medical care of the Jesuits in Agra. The Jesuit even claimed that he would

meet the missionaries in Agra or Patna in the event that Rome decided in favor of the Capuchin fathers, although he coyly hinted that the only one with the power to do so was the pope himself. Desideri claimed to have received the letter that da Montecchio wrote in December only in July, but this is an uncommonly long time for mail between Patna and Dakpo at that time of year. It should have traveled fast enough for Desideri to receive da Montecchio's letter well before he wrote his letter of March 12, 1718. Even so, any letters from the Capuchins in Lhasa to Nepal would have had sufficient time to inform da Montecchio that da Fano and della Penna were not being removed to Beijing well before the Capuchin father wrote his sarcastic missive to Desideri, at least as long as we accept Desideri's assurances that the affair was settled when Lhazang Khan interceded on behalf of the missionaries in early June 1717.

46. DL 12 (MITN 5, p. 55): "ma ancora mi fo ardito di umilmente e con ogni possibile efficacia supplicare la P. V. M. R. a degnarsi di compartire a me medesimo una qualche calda raccomandazione ad alcun suo corrispondente in Pekino, giacchè assai più strettamente io che li MM. RR. PP. Cappuccini sono stato da' Cinesi importunamente assalito per esser condotto a quella metropoli contro mia volontà."

47. DL 12 (MITN 5, p. 55): "E per più efficacemente impetrare il favore di siffatta raccomandazione, mi perdonerà la P. V. M. R. se io qui con tutta verità, senza neppur alterar un minimo puntino la cosa, e senza neppur minima mistura di passione, le soggiungo un fedelissimo ragguaglio del successo."

48. DL 12 (MITN 5, p. 59): "Supplico adesso la P. V. M. R. a compatirmi, se con tutta ingenuità io le espongo confidentemente il mio sospetto. Nel leggere li sopraccennati commandi della P. V. M. R., ho sospettato che ella, non per mal'animo, no, ma per non intiere informazioni ricevute da altre bande, con tali per altro cortesi formole abbia più tosto voluto darmi la non meritata mortificazione di gentilmente e copertamente piccarmi, che di dispensarmi l'onore de' di lei desideratissimi e riveritissimi commandi."

49. DL 14 (MITN 5, pp. 61–62).

50. Hosten "Letters and Papers," pp. 98–99.

51. It is inconceivable that Tamburini did not know that the Sacred Congregation had given the mission to the Capuchins in 1703 and 1704. Even though he did not become general until 1706, he had largely run the Society during the protracted convalescence of the previous general Tirso Gonzalez, and so was almost certainly responsible for Amaral's dispatch of Monteiro to Tibet in 1704 in addition to the repeated insistences that the mission be opened in the second half of the decade. He might have assumed that the Capuchins willingly abandoned Tibet in 1711, and so commissioned Desideri during the next two years, even as Domenico da Fano appeared in Rome to ask for money and recruits for the second phase of the Capuchin mission to Tibet. Since da Fano delivered a letter of recommendation from Vautrain Baudrè, a Jesuit stationed at Chandannagar, and another letter from the Jesuit procurator at Paris to the Jesuit procurator in Rome, it is impossible that Tamburini was not aware of the Capuchin presence in Tibet by 1714. Did Desideri slip through the cracks, running just ahead of the general's orders to abandon the mission? With one lost letter or two, this scenario is possible, but unlikely.

52. DL 19 (MITN 5, p. 84): "secondo l'umano è cosa che disanima molto li Missionarij e li potrebbe far raffreddare nel servizio della Compagnia."

53. DL 19 (MITN 5, p. 85): "L'istessa impressione potrebbe fare agl'altri Missionarij della Compagnia, se scrivendo al primo Superiore della Compagnia e a chi tiene il luogo di S. Ignazio, non vedessero mai giungere nè pur una risposta. Torno a ripetere, che constat a posteriori che il difetto non è della P. V. M. R., e che perciò con tutta efficacia e calore cerchi di chi sia la colpa, e assolutamente vi ponga rimedio."

54. DL 19 (MITN 5, p. 86).

55. DL 21 (MITN 5, p. 88).

56. DL 24 (MITN 5, p. 91).

57. DR 24 (MITN 5, p. 92).

58. DL 25 (MITN 5, p. 93): "aperte dilucideque profiteor, me nullo modo juri illi cedere posse, quod Societas Iesu in Missionem Thibettensem legitime habuisse et habere videtur, donec aliter a Summo Pontifice statuatur. Hac de causa in nomine Sanctissimae Trinitatis, et invocato nomine Iesu, appello ad immediatum supremumque tribunal SS.mi D.ni Nri D.ni Clementis XI Summi Pontificis, vel ejus successoris, eoque vos advoco, ut ea omnia, quae a me contra vestrum conatum expellendi meipsum et Societatem Iesu ab omnibus Regnis Thibet in judicium deferri possint, a vobis ipsis (si rationes suppetant) avertere conemini."

59. As Bargiacchi notes, da Montecchio's accounts seem to have been edited in 1728, although they are dated 1729. *Bridge Across Two Cultures*, p. 55. Since my account will not go into the particulars of this case, I have contented myself with the selections provided by Luciano Petech (MITN 3, pp. 38–46; MITN 5, pp. 97–113). I hope another scholar follows the immense paper trail that Petech omits from his selection, especially since the great Tibetologist omitted the exact sections in which da Montecchio argued the Capuchin case or combated "various points of minor importance" in Desideri's writings. Bargiacchi makes use of three important documents in his work that have not been published in their full forms and for which he generously provided copies: "Lettera ai Cardinali di Propaganda (Lhasa 21.12.1719)" (APF, CP 84, ff. 79–84); "Lettera di un religioso non identificato sulla questione del Tibet (contesa Gesuiti- Cappuccini), da Londra 10.11.1724" (APF, CP 84, ff. 56–59); and "Lettera dalla Casa Professa della C.d.G a Propaganda Fide. Roma 16.3.1728" (APF, CP 84, f. 275).

60. CR 2 (MITN 3, p. 39).

61. CR 2 (MITN 3, p. 42).

62. DD 1 (MITN 5, p. 99).

63. DD 2.38 (MITN 5, p. 107): "Per arrivar là a quel terzo Thibet, chi potrà mai concepire quanti viaggi, quanti e quanto orribili patimenti, e quanti pericoli mi costasse? Non dirò niente delle tempeste incontrate nel Mediterraneo e nell'Oceano, e de' disagi d'una lunga navigazione sin a Goa. Da Goa a Surat, da Surat per caldi intolerabili dover attraversar tutto il Mogol da mezzogiorno a settentrione. Dover superar torrenti, ghiacci, Caucasi, freddi, orribilissimi. Per più mesi nelle mutazioni di climi cader gravemente infermo nel viaggio, senza medici, senza medicine e senza verun conforto. Perder gl'occhi tra le nevi continue. Per due mesi viaggiar a piedi tra orribilissimi precipizj, che nessun può immaginarseli. Da' 9 d'Ottobre sin a 4 di Gennaro passar un

rigidissimo deserto pieno di nevi, di ghiacci, di monti penosissimi e di freddi affatto intolerabili. Per 10 mesi di viaggio da Cascimir sin a Lhasà soffrir continua fame e sete, dormir sul suolo, a cielo scoperto, fra nevi e ghiacci, e fra altri disagi atti a metter orrore in chi li leggesse. In somma patir un inferno di patimenti da non potersi spiegare."

64. DD 3 (MITN 5, p. 110).

65. CL 50 (MITN 1, p. 137).

66. CL 52 (MITN 1, p. 148): "E qual legge ha confutata? Vite, vite della cabarrette di Francia spampanate di frondi o pampani, ma senz'uva." *Fico*, like the French *foutre* and the English "fig," was a euphemism used to describe an obscene hand gesture, as we see in *2 Henry IV*, Act 5, Scene 3, when Pistol exclaims, "When Pistol lies, do this; and fig me, like the bragging Spaniard." It was common enough that even St. Teresa of Avila could speak of giving the Devil a "fig" when he appeared as an angel of light.

67. CL 52 (MITN 1, p. 148): "Vorrei che dicesse con quali Lami o dottori. Il discorso sarrà stato 'Così siete Cassimirro? ', egli haverà risposto 'No', 'Amazzate i castrati? ', 'No, compro la carne al bazzarro', 'Bevete il nostro the? Mangiate la carne di porco?' ecc. Questi discorsi occorrono quasi ogni giorno."

68. CL 53 (MITN 1, p. 156).

69. CL 53 (MITN 1, p. 158).

70. CR 2 (MITN 3, pp. 45–46).

71. DD 3.25 (ARSI Goa 72, f. 334): "che due Missionarij, venuti dall'estremità del Mondo, debbano quì in Roma perder il tempo in accusarsi, e in difendersi, in attaccarsi, e in schermirsi."

72. S. Castello Panti "Nuovi documenti su Ippolito Desideri," in *Miscellanea di storia delle esplorazioni*, ed. Francesco Surdich (Genoa: Fratelli Bozzi, 1975), p. 171.

73. CL 52 (MITN 1, p. 152).

74. Desideri could hardly have found a worse time to argue his case. The Sacred Congregation had accused Prémare of exalting the Chinese classics above the Old Testament in 1726 and again in 1728. David E. Mungello, "The Reconciliation of Neo-Confucianism with Christianity in the Writings of Joseph de Prémare, S.J.," *Philosophy East and West* 26 (1976), p. 392. Mungello cites Dehergne, *Répertoire des Jésuites* (Rome: IHSI, 1973), pp. 209–10.

75. See, for example, his letter to João Álvarez (DI 18, pp. 607–10). On Cabral's missionary methods, see Josef Franz Schütte, *Valignano's Mission Principles for Japan*, trans. John J. Coyne (St. Louis: IJS, 1980), 1, pp. 187–247.

76. On Jesuit dissent, see Joseph Sebes, "A Comparative Study of Religious Missions in Three Civilizations: India China, and Japan," in *Colloque internationale de sinologie, III, Appréciation par l'Europe de la tradition à partir du XVIIe siècle*, Centre d'études et de recherches interdisciplinaires de Chantilly (Paris: Belles Lettres, 1983), pp. 271–90.

77. J. S. Cummins, "Two Missionary Methods in China: Mendicants and Jesuits," in *España en Extremo Oriente. Filipinas, China, Japón. Presencia Franciscana, 1578–1978*, ed. V. Sanchez and J. S. Fuertes (Madrid, 1979), p. 59.

78. Philippe Couplet, *Confucius Sinarum Philosophus* (Paris: Apud Danielem Horthemels, 1687), p. cix; P. Intorcetta, *De cultu sinesi* (Paris: Apud Nicolaum Pepie, 1700), p. 224.

79. Claude Visdelou, for example, agreed with de Tournon. Jean-François Foucquet also held the minority view, but was personally repulsed by Maigrot. He submitted to de Tournon's decree, but wished to defend the Society against Maigrot's rebuttal of Hervieu. None of this kept him, however, from asserting that ancient Chinese texts revealed the Christian mysteries. Matteo Ripa considered the controversy "a boring, hateful, and useless argument" (*un si tedioso, odioso ed inutile discorso*), but still engaged Foucquet in a lengthy discussion about it after the papal decree of 1715. Apart from the question of the rites, Jesuits also diverged widely on their theological opinions. Jartoux, Parennin, and de Tartre rejected figurism outright. Nor was there agreement even among figurists themselves: Prémare rejected both Bouvet and Foucquet. Foucquet was ambivalent, perhaps even deliberately ambiguous, about Prémare. He eventually attacked his confrere in an interrogation at the Sacred Congregation in mid-August 1723, even as he attempted to clarify mistakes made by Mezzabarba's legatine mission to Beijing.

80. A. Dudink, "*Tianzhu jiaoyao*, The Catechism (1605) published by Matteo Ricci," *Sino-Western Relations Journal* 24 (2002), pp. 38–50. The Franciscans were aware of Ricci's catechism. Cf. Giovanni Lucarelli, *Viaggo dell'Indie* (SF 2, p. 23); Francisco a Iesu de Escalona, *Relacion del Viaje* (SF 2, pp. 241–42). Trigault describes his Catechism in *Della Entrata della Compagnia di Giesù e Christianità nella Cina* (*Fonti Ricciane* 4.15, n. 626), 2, pp. 166–67.

81. E. E. Sylvest, *Motifs of Franciscan Mission Theory in Sixteenth-Century New Spain* (Washington, DC: Academy of American Franciscan History, 1975), pp. 101, 105; Munro S. Edmonson, ed., *Sixteenth-Century Mexico: The Work of Sahagún* (Albuquerque: University of New Mexico Press, 1974).

82. Cummins, "Two Missionary Methods," pp. 67–68. Cf. G. Kubler, *Mexican Architecture of the Sixteenth Century*, 2 vols. (New Haven, CT: Yale University Press, 1948); J. McAndrew, *The Open-Air Churches of Sixteenth-Century Mexico: Atrios, Posas, Open Chapels, and other Studies* (Cambridge: Harvard University Press, 1965), pp. 5–7, 30–31.

83. Cummins, "Two Missionary Methods," pp. 90–91; D. Lancashire, "Anti-Christian Polemics in Seventeenth-Century China," *Church History* 38 (1969), pp. 218–41.

84. Antonio Sisto Rosso, O.F.M., *Apostolic Legations*, p. 109. No less an authority than G. H. Dunne had to confess, somewhat grudgingly, "adaptation was not unknown in Mexico and South America." Dunne, *Generation of Giants*, p. 229.

85. Boxer, *Christian Century*, p. 235.

86. McAndrew, *Open-Air Churches*, p. 247; Cummins, "Two Missionary Methods," p. 94.

87. Cummins, "Two Missionary Methods," p. 76.

88. DR 2.14 (MITN 6, p. 85); DR 2.18 (MITN 6, p. 114); DR 3.6 (MITN 6, p. 162). Such examples could be multiplied ad nauseam.

89. For a list of these sources, see Petech, MITN 1, pp. lxxxvi–xciv.

90. DR 3.22 (MITN 6, p. 307).

91. Xavier's *Catechismus Brevis* was printed in numerous editions in Goa after 1557. MHSI FX Epp, pp. 93–116.

92. Although Desideri subsumed the second part of Canisius's division of wisdom and justice into the first, he still divided his treatise into treatments of Faith (the Creed), Hope (the Pater Noster and the Ave Maria), and Love (the Decalogue), with additional discussions of the four last things, the evangelical counsels, the seven deadly sins, and the seven sacraments. The only things that are missing from the form initiated by Canisius and followed by Bellarmine are the cardinal virtues, the gifts of the Holy Spirit, and the beatitudes. Although Desideri would not have felt that Tibetans possessed the theological virtues, at least ordinarily, the omission of the cardinal virtues makes sense given his own feelings that Tibetan morality was substantially identical to Catholic morality. Desideri also has a significant section on the sin of Adam and Eve that mimics the explanation of the Fall in the third book that Peter Canisius added to his catechism after the Council of Trent. Incidentally, I think it unfair to say that "Bellarmine's scholasticism lacked the calm speculative scholarship of the apologetic treatises of earlier scholasticism" (Robert E. Goss, "The Meeting," p. 72). Goss seems to imply that a theologian who wrote a catechism could not be calmly speculative. If so, we certainly cannot exempt Desideri from this judgment.

93. See, for instance, the Franciscan Giovanni Battista Lucarelli de Pisauro's *Viaggio dell'Indie* (SF 2, pp. 12–92).

94. Athanasius Kircher, *China illustrata*, pp. 121–29. As Mungello notes, *Curious Land*, pp. 141–42, the Jesuit missionary Michael Boym listed a "*Sinicus catechismus*" among his works in his own *relatio* of 1654, which may be the source of Kircher's *Divinae legis compendium*. Alexandre de Rhodes, the greatest Jesuit missionary in Vietnam, also wrote a catechism. Barbara Widenor Maggs, "Science, Mathematics, and Reason: The Missionary Methods of the Jesuit Alexandre de Rhodes in Seventeenth-Century Vietnam," *Catholic Historical Review* 86 (2000), pp. 439–58.

95. Sherburne, "Buddhist Christian Dialog?" p. 303.

96. *Chos lugs* 13 (OT 2, p. 77); 35v. (OT 2, p. 122).

97. *Chos lugs* 15v. (OT 2, p. 82).

98. For a long explanation, see *Chos lugs* 14v. (OT 2, pp. 80–81).

99. The terms Desideri uses for "Father" and "Son," *yab* and *sras*, are common in Tibetan Christian literature. His phrase for "Holy Spirit" is *bla med rnam bdag yid*, a phrase that is unique to Desideri. Yoseb Gergan, for example, translated "Father, Son, and Holy Spirit" as *yab dang sras dang dam pa'i thugs nyid*, but used the phrase *bla med* to translate "Most High" as in his translation of Luke 1:35: "*pho nyas lan du/ khyed la dam pa'i thugs nyid 'bab/ bla med mthu yis bsil grib pas/ khyed la bltam pa'i dam pa la/ dkon mchog nyid kyi sras gsol 'gyur.*" Desideri's vocabulary might also be fruitfully compared to that learned by Antonio Giorgi from the Capuchin fathers. Giorgi usually translates "Holy Spirit" with *sangs rgyas rnam dag* or *sangs rgyas rnam dag sems*, which certainly allow more favorable comparisons between Christianity and Buddhism, since he equates saintliness and buddhahood. In fact, Giorgi translates *sanctorum omnium*

communionem from the Apostles' Creed with *sangs rgyas thams cad kyi sngos po*. In his longer discussion of the Trinity Giorgi draws more explicit comparisons to the Three Jewels than Desideri, but then attempts to refute the Tibetan "Trinity" as a Manichaean heresy with passages from the writings of St. Augustine. *Alphabetum Tibetanum* (Rome: Typis Sacrae Congregationis de Propaganda Fide, 1762), pp. 272–79, 643, 647–48. Finally, one might also compare Desideri's vocabulary with the Tibetan translation of the Apostles' Creed discussed in Josef Kolmaš, "The Symbolum Fidei in Tibetan (Text, Translation, Glossary)," in *Studia Tibetica: Quellen und Studien zur tibetischen Lexikographie*, ed. Herbert Franke (Munich: Kommission für zentralasiatische Studien bayerische Akademie der Wissenschaften, 1988), 2, pp. 223–30.

100. Desideri seems to have intended the phrase *bla na med pa'i bdag nyid* to unite the Victorine definition of the person as an incommunicable form—a particular emphasis of the Scotist tradition—and the Boethian definition of the person as a "rational subsistence"—a particular emphasis of the Thomist tradition. Desideri is here true to the generally synthetic scholasticism of the Society of Jesus.

101. *Tho rangs* 6 (OT 1, p. 91), 19 (OT 1, p. 93), 30 (OT 1, p. 103), 43–44 (OT 1, p. 110); *Chos lugs* 13 (OT 2, p. 77), 27 (OT 2, p. 105).

102. Matthew Kapstein informs me that this is a corruption of *grong khyer la 'jug pa* ("entering the city," a euphemism for taking possession of another's body), although the error can be found in Tibetan texts, and so might not stem from Desideri's own misunderstanding.

103. *Chos lugs* 19–19v. (OT 2, pp. 89–90).

104. On *sangs rgyas*, see *Tho rangs* 5–26, especially 13–15 (OT 1, pp. 91–101); *Chos lugs* 20v.–21 (OT 2, pp. 92–93).

105. *Chos lugs* 34 (OT 2, p. 119).

106. *Chos lugs* 13 (OT 2, p. 77).

107. Desideri's use of the spelling *mgo skar* is found throughout his Tibetan writings, from the *Tho rangs*, in which the Christian priest is identified throughout as the "Christian *padre*" (*mgo skar dpa' 'dri*), to the title of his magnum opus, where he identified himself as the "Christian lama Ippolito" (*mgo skar bla ma i po li do*). Note that Desideri abandoned the phonetic transliteration of *padre* found in the *Tho rangs*— as well as his identity as a treasure revealer (*gter ston*)—and substituted the Tibetan word *lama* (*bla ma*) in the *Skye ba snga ma*, although he abandoned both in the *Chos lugs*, where he became the "pandita with an unerring force of mind that correctly separates truth from falsehood" (*bden brdzun dang legs nyes 'byed pa'i blo'i mthu ma nor ba zhig skyed par byed pa'i paṇḍita*). I think Desideri's consistency is reason enough to consider *mgo skar* a neologism. The Jesuit missionary was a good speller, which is no small accomplishment given the great number of silent letters in the written Tibetan language. In his later works, one finds no more misspellings than in works that were produced by Tibetans, and in some cases significantly fewer. Of course, one can be honestly consistent in his misspelling, but Desideri apparently circulated his works, especially the *Tho rangs* and the *Skye ba snga ma*. Had he simply been mistaken, a native Tibetan would have had every reason to correct him, and the missionary would have had ample time to correct his mistake. In fact, the final line of the *Dawn* added the omitted syllable *dkar*,

which was then excised and replaced with the syllable *skar*. Even if such a correction does not prove conclusive, it does show that Desideri made a conscious choice about which syllable to use. The Italian text of the *Tho rangs* shows that the missionary wished to identify himself as a Christian rather than a European as such, so we have reason to suspect that Desideri hoped to communicate something beyond what the term *mgo dkar* itself would allow, especially if he was afraid that it connoted Islamic tendencies. While the term *mgo dkar* did not have the strongly derogatory sense of the modern Tibetan term *goser* (*mgo gser*), "yellow head" or "blondie," it still had many of the same connotations as the mildly pejorative *farangi*, the generic term used across the Middle East and Asia to designate Christians. Missionaries often resisted the term *parague* and its cognates, *frangui, farangui, firinghee, ifranji, parangue, prangue.* Roberto de Nobili refused to be called a *parangue*. Cacella and Cabral avoided the designation in Bhutan. Even though they noted that the term *franguis*, by which the "entire Orient" understood the Portuguese, was itself unknown in Bhutan, they themselves did not use it, but rather introduced themselves as *portuguezes*. Desideri probably preferred the term *mgo dkar* to *perang* (*phe rang*), the Tibetan equivalent of *farangi*, knowing the xenophobic connotations of the latter without quite understanding the generic meaning of the former. In any event, Tibetan texts did not adopt the neologism, but referred to the missionaries as *mgo dkar* or *phe rang*. See Toscano's discussion in OT I, pp. 156–57 n. I. Petech's comments can be found at MITN I, p. 185 and MITN 4, p. 274. For discussion of the appearance of *mgo dkar* in texts contemporary with Desideri, see *The Annals of Kokonor*, p. 70 n. 83; Tucci, *Tibetan Painted Scrolls*, p. 698 n. 459; Luciano Petech, "The Missions of Bogle and Turner According to the Tibetan Texts," *T'oung Pao* 39 (1950), pp. 330–46; Isrun Engelhardt, "The Closing of the Gates: Tibetan-European Relations at the End of the Eighteenth Century," in *Religion and Secular Culture in Tibet*, ed. Henk Blezer (Leiden: Brill, 2002), pp. 229–45; "Between Tolerance and Dogmatism: Tibetan Reactions to the Capuchin Missionaries in Lhasa, 1707–1745," *Zentralasiatische Studien* 34 (2005), pp. 55–97.

108. DR 3.12 (MITN 6, p. 211); DR 3.15 (MITN 6, p. 236).

109. Although I can offer only anecdotal evidence in this regard, my own Tibetan friends have often made connections between Tibetan Buddhism and Roman Catholicism that many Western scholars seem intent upon denying. They thought it natural to compare Christ to a *gcod pa* who gave His life for others or to compare the Holy Trinity to the three bodies of the Buddha. Of course, these are only individual responses and would not preclude other Tibetans' reactions of disgust, scorn, or superiority.

CHAPTER 6: *COMPOSITION LOCI:* TIBET

1. DR I, prol. (MITN 5, p. 119): "Del Thibet trovo un gran silenzio in tutte le storie; e per quanto posso avvedermene, è un paese, o nuovo affatto appresso molti, o cognito poco più che solamente per nome."

2. António Andrade, *Novo descobrimento do Gram Cathayo, ou, Reinos de Tibet* (Lisbon: Mattheus Pinheiro, 1626). For a modern edition, see António de Andrade,

O descobrimento do Tibet, Francisco Maria Esteves Pereira, ed. (Coimbra: Imprensa da Universidade, 1921).

3. Louis Moréri, *Le Grand dictionnaire historique, ou le mélange curieux de l'histoire sacrée et profane*, 10 vols. (Paris: Les librairies associés, 1759). This work would become the basis of the great dictionaries of Pierre Bayle, Michel-Antoine Baudrand, and Voltaire. For English translations, see Lewis Morery, *An Universal, historical, geographical, chronological and poetical dictionary exactly describing the situation, extent, customs, laws, manners, commodities, &c., of all kingdoms, commonwealths, provinces, islands and cities in the known world* (London: Hartley, Turner & Hodgson, 1703); and *A supplement to the Great historical geographical genealogical and poetical dictionary… Collected from the best historians, chronologers, and lexicographers but more especially out of Lewis Morery* (London: Henry Rhodes, 1705). Another edition has been published just recently: Louis Moréri, *The Great Historical, Geographical, and Poetical Dictionary*, 2 vols. (London: Routledge, 1999).

4. Jean-Baptiste Tavernier, *Les six voyages* (Paris, 1676). Compare *The Six Voyages of John Baptista Tavernier, Baron of Aubonne, through Turkey, into Persia and the East-Indies, for the space of forty years giving an account of the present state of those countries as also a full relation of the five years war between Aureng-Zebe and his brothers in their father's life-time, about the succession. And a voyage made by the Great Mogul with his army from Delhi to Lahor, from Lahor to Bember, and from thence to the Kingdom of Kachemire, by the Mogols, call'd the paradise of the Indies*, trans. John Phillips (London: William Godbid, 1677).

5. António Franco, *Imagem da virtude em o noviciado da Companhia de Jesu na corte de Lisboa*, 2 vols. (Coimbra: No Real Collegio das Artes da Companhia de Jesu, 1714–19).

6. Giovanni Battista Ramusio, *Secondo volume delle navigationi et viaggi raccolta gia da m. Gio. Battista Ramusio, et hora in questa nuova editione accresciuto; nel quale si contengono l'historia delle cose de Tartari, & diversi fatti de' loro imperatori, descritta da m. Marco Polo gentil'huomo venetiano, & da Hayton Armeno. Varie descrittioni di diversi auttori, dell'Indie Orientali, della Tartaria, della Persia, Armenia, Mengrelia, Zorzania, & altre provincie* (Venice: Giunti, 1559). The travels of Marco Polo were also published separately. Cf. Marco Polo, *De regionibus orientalibus libri III cum codice manuscripto Bibliotheca electoralis brandenburgica collati* (Brandenburg: Georgii Schulzii, 1671).

7. DR 3.22 (MITN 6, p. 305).

8. Desideri's *Notizie* is often referred to as a Jesuit *relatio*, a report about mission fields written by missionaries to their superiors. Generally, *relationes* were of three sorts: personal letters sent either to the general, to a superior, or to a friend; annual letters intended for the Society; and *relationes* proper. While the first class were not intended for publication at all, and the *litterae annuae* intended only for circulation within the Society, the last class were meant to be published, for the renown of the Society and for the edification of its members.

9. Anthony Pagden, *European Encounters with the New World from Renaissance to Romanticism* (New Haven, CT: Yale University Press, 1993), pp. 62–63. Pagden notes that missionaries such as Gonzalo Fernández de Oviedo y Valdes complained that their readers could not distinguish between fact and fiction, because romances such as the *Amadís de Gaula* or the *Palmerí de Inglaterra* claimed to be "true" histories much as their

own accounts did. The case of Oviedo is especially noteworthy, since he published both. He was also the author of a well-known historical romance, *Libro del muy esforçado y invencible Cavallero dela fortuna propriamente llamado con claribalte*, which he claimed to have discovered in "that barbarous and inaccessible language in which I found it by means of a Tartar interpreter" and only later "rendered it into Castilian."

10. DR 1, prol. (MITN 5, p. 117): "Non era mia intenzione il dar alla luce le notizie istoriche del Thibet e le memorie de' miei viaggi e missioni, le quali nel mio ritorno in Europa m'ero io raccolte per mio privato sollievo, come ricordi e testimonj delle mie passate fatiche, e le serbavo per quel diletto che v'ha in andar rileggendo con sicurezza i cimenti corsi prima con sollecitudine. S'aggiungeva che, avendo io veduta più d'una di cotali Relazioni de' paesi e cose dell'Indie, v'ho trovato racconti così inverisimili ed esagerati, e sì lontani dell'esperienza che poi n'ho avuta in quindici anni, che averei temuto d'incontrar la taccia di fede screditata, che hanno alcuni di que' ragguagli, se mettessi fuora anche i miei. E per altra parte son tanto dissimiglianti da tutte le nostre d'Europa le maniere, l'usanze, le leggi, l'abitazioni, i cibi ed i paesi stessi degl'orientali, e sì fattamente distuonano all'immaginazione avvezza a questi oggetti nostrali, che, volendole raccontare, sempre corrette risico di non trovar fede, o la meritate o no."

11. DR 1, prol. (MITN 5, p. 120): "riuscendo sempre più giusto, e più accertato il colpo, quando avanti è ben previsto e premeditato lo scopo."

12. DR 1, prol. (MITN 5, pp. 119–20): "la setta di religione differentissima da tutte l'altre, che ivi regna, appoggiata su 'l sistema pittagorico, merita d'esser ben risaputa, per esser ben impugnata. Io mi lusingo che queste mie carte, oltre il gusto della novità, siano per aver anche l'utile di risvegliare gl'ingegni de' dotti, per confutar questo nuovo misto d'errori superstiziosi, e di muover la carità di molti, per recar giovamento a quell'acciecata Nazione."

13. DR 1, prol. (MITN 5, p. 120): "Basta solo, che non leggiate questi fogli con quel cattivo pregiudizio di tener per falsa ogni cosa, ch'esce fuori dell'ordinario, per questo solo argomento, che è fuori dell'ordinario. Anco i nostri maggiori, da cui pur discendiamo, oggi non ci riconoscerebbero, nè noi loro: tant'è mutato e diverso lo stile ne' vestiti, ne' portamenti, ne' costumi, da quel che usava a' tempi loro. E pure nè essi, nè noi siamo una cosa finta o un popolo favoloso. Se vi spoglierete di questa falsa opinione, non dubito, che non riconoscerete su questi fogli la nota della sincerità."

14. DR 1, prol. (MITN 5, p. 121): "La qualità di tali doni è la loro scusa, e il loro raro è il lor ornamento. Queste mie notizie altro non hanno di buono, se non che sono notizie, e purchè siano tali, cioè schiette e di cose che si meritino d'esser note, basta questo per tutto il lor bello. Anzi la troppa eleganza e l'artificio delle scelte parole potrebbe ascriversi a vizio, perchè sarebbe un dar sospetto, che l'eloquenza e la culta dicitura non fosse tanto abbellir la verità che si pone in pubblico, quanto per nasconder la frode e la falsità che ha paura di comparirvi."

15. On autopsy in missionary writings, see Stephen Greenblatt, *Marvelous Possessions: The Wonder of the New World* (Oxford: Oxford University Press, 1991) and Pagden, *European Encounters*, pp. 51–87.

16. The classic use of this rhetorical appeal in missionary literature is Bartolomé de las Casas's *Historia de las Indias*, where he notes that the "poverty of vocabulary,

humanity of the style, and lack of eloquence," should serve as proof of his text's accuracy and his own sincerity. Padgen, *European Encounters*, p. 78.

17. Cassian, *Conferences* 10, 13–14 (*Sources chrétiennes* 54, pp. 94–95); Bernard, *Apologia* 12, 28 (Opera Omnia 3, p. 104). Both of these works are cited by Mary Carruthers in her discussion of *curiositas* in medieval mnemonics. *The Craft of Thought*, pp. 82–91.

18. DR 1, prol. (MITN 5, p. 118). We have already seen that Desideri characterized the myth of the origins of Tibetans as "curious" at DR 2.1 (MITN 6, p. 3). For other uses, see DR 1.4 (MITN 5, p. 136), DR 2.1 (MITN 6, p. 5), DR 2.13 (MITN 6, p. 81), and, especially DR 4.17 (MITN 7, pp. 106–7). On the concept, see André Labhardt, "Curiositas; Notes sur l'histoire d'un mot et d'une notion," *Museum Helveticum* 17 (1969), pp. 206–24; D. E. Mungello, *Curious Land: Jesuit Accommodation and the Origins of Sinology* (Honolulu: University of Hawai'i Press, 1989), pp. 13–14. It has been common in postcolonialist studies to ascribe the gathering of "curious" information to colonialism. I see little need to defend Desideri from this accusation; the Papal States were hardly a colonial power, nor was the Grand Duchy of Tuscany. We have already seen that Desideri was none too happy with his Portuguese superiors in India. He was sheltered by French colonials in Puducherry, to be sure, most likely because of their shared distrust of the Portuguese, but none of Desideri's writings suggest that Tibetans should be subject to civil authorities in Europe.

19. On ancient and modern uses of the words *curiositas* and *curiosus*, see Henri-Irénée Marrou, *Saint Augustin et la fin da la culture antique* (Paris, 1938), pp. 148–57, 277–80, 350–52, 473.

20. Ignatius to Gaspar Berze (Barzaeus), February 24, 1554 (MI Epp 10:358): "Algunas personas principales, que en esta ciudad leen con mucha edificatión suya las letras de las Indias, suelen desear, y o piden diuersas uezas, que se scriuiese algo de la cosmographía de las regiones donde andan los nuestros, come sería quán luengo[s] son los díes de verano y de yuierno, quándo comença el verano, si las sombras uan sinistras, ó á la mano diestra. Finalmente, si otras cosas ay que parescan estraordinarias, se dé auiso, como de animales y plantas no conocidas, ó no in tal grandeza, etc. Y esta salsa, para el gusto de alguna curiosidad que suele hauer en los hombres, no mala, puede uenir, ó en las mesmas letras, ó en otras de aparte."

21. Pedro de Ribadeneyra, *Vita Ignatii Loyolae* (Rome: MHSI, 1965) [= MI Fontes narrativi de S. Ignatio de Loyola et de Societatis Jesu initiis4], p. 742: "Vidimus frequenter illum, ex tenuissimis rebus, ad Deum, qui in minimis etiam maximus est, ascendentem; ex plantulae, frondis, floris, fructus unius aspectu, ex vermiculi alicuius, aut bestiolae consideratione, supra coelos attollentem se, et ad ea, quae a sensibus remota sunt, penetrantem, capientemque e singulis utilissima documenta, ad totius informationem vitae."

22. A particularly beautiful example is Alard Le Roy, *La vertu enseigné par les oiseaux* (Liege: Bauduin Bronckart, 1653) [= CLE J.882]. Another is Franz Reinzer, *Meteorologia philosophica-politica* (Augsburg: Jeremias Wolf, 1698) [= CLE J.1239], which provides moral and political instruction based on the scientific study of lightning, fog, and snow.

23. For a discussion of animals in emblems, see the chapter "De Signis Brutorum" in Masen, *Speculum Imaginum*, pp. 75–82. On the rhinoceros, see Nieuhof, *An Embassy from the East-India Company of the United Provinces to the Grand Tartar Cham Emperor of China* (London: John Macock, 1669), p. 267. Le Comte provides an entertaining discussion of crocodiles and chameleons in *The Empire of China* (London: J. Hughs, 1737), p. 512. For a typical example of the phenomena of nature providing symbols of supernatural truth, see Kircher's discussion of butterflies in *Physiologia Kircheriana Experimentalis* (Amsterdam: Janssonius-Waesbergius, 1680), p. 44, or the discussion of images of the Virgin in Nicholas Caussin, *De Symbolica Aegyptiorum Sapientia* (Cologne: Johannes Kinchius, 1654), pp. 572–73.

24. A. Rétif, "Brève histoire des *Lettres édifiantes et curieuses*," *Neue Zeitschrift für Missionswissenschaft* 7 (1951), pp. 37–50.

25. See John Correia-Afonso, *Jesuit Letters and Indian History* (Bombay: India Historical Research Institute, 1955), p. 36, on Alessandro Valignano's demands in this regard, or Županov, *Disputed Mission*, p. 12, on Jerónimo Nadal's complaints about the *Epistolae Indicae de stupendos et praecaris rebus*.

26. Bangert, *History*, pp. 88–89.

27. Gaspar Schott, *Technica Curiosa, sive Mirabilia Artis* (Rome: Ex Typographia Varesii, 1663). Another good example, which combines the "curious" with Jesuit emblematics, is Claude-François Menestrier, *Bibliotheque curieuse et instructive de divers ouvrages anciens et modernes de literative et des arts* (Trevoux: Chez Estienne Ganeau, 1704).

28. Le Comte, *The Empire of China* (London: J. Hughs, 1737).

29. Mungello, *Curious Land*.

30. DR 1.4 (MITN 5, p. 135); DR 1.5 (MITN 5, p. 148).

31. Desideri's dilation on the strife of the Mughal Empire also serves to foreshadow later Tibetan events with the rhetorical doubling typical of baroque literature. Dona Giuliana anticipates the virtuous lady Casal, Bahadur Shah anticipates the virtuous "king" Lhazang Khan, and the "nefarious crimes" of Farrukh-Siyar anticipate those of the sixth Dalai Lama.

32. DR 1.6 (MITN 5, p. 153).

33. DR 1.7, 8 (MITN 5, pp. 161–65); DR 1.10 (MITN 5, p. 176); DR 2.5 (MITN 6, p. 22); DR 4.5 (MITN 7, p. 27). Strictly speaking, Jesuits were forbidden from engaging in trade. See Acquaviva's instructions to the Procurator Francisco de Monclaro (DI 15, p. 56).

34. DR 2.2, 3 (MITN 6, pp. 9–14); DR 4.2, 3 (MITN 7, pp. 14–16).

35. We should keep the retrospective emphasis of classical humanism in mind before we judge Desideri to be too progressive. The infamous quarrel of the Ancients and the Moderns, which occupied the years 1687 to 1716, was primarily a French affair. Although such ideas entered Italy through men such as Giovanni Ciampini (1633–1698), Alessandro Maffei (1653–1716), and Giovanni Cristoforo Battelli (1658–1725), the personal librarian of Pope Clement XI, they took on a particularly Roman light, at least in their published form, in their focus on the study of antiquities. Christopher M. S. Johns, *Papal Art and Cultural Politics: Rome in the Age of Clement XI* (Cambridge: Cambridge University Press, 1993), pp. 22–38.

36. DR 1.4 (MITN 5, pp. 142–43): "Sono que' popoli di setta gentili, di naturale ardito, di statura lunghi, di genio guerrieri e molto rinomati per la milizia. Una parte di tali popoli son soggetti a un grande e potente Re gentile intitolato Ranà, che ha la sua corte, e residenza nella città di Odepur, che governa i suoi sudditi con ammirabil rigore di giustissime leggi."

37. DR 2.16 (MITN 6, p. 97): "Sono i Thibetani ordinariamente di statura giusta, di carnagione bianca e rossa, ma che propende all'olivastro, d'aspetto sufficientemente buono, ma senza barba che a loro non cresce; di complessione forti, di buona memoria, d'acuto intelletto, d'indole docile e umana; di genio allegro; atti alle arti, attivi e assai tolleranti delle fatiche e del travaglio."

38. DR 2.14, 16, 17 (MITN 6, pp. 90–91, 99, 103–8); DR 3.12, 13, 20 (MITN 6, pp. 215, 228, 291–92).

39. DR 2.16 (MITN 6, p. 97). Cf. Ines Županov, "Lust, Marriage, and Free Will: Jesuit Critique of Paganism in South India," *Studies in History* 16 (2000), pp. 199–220.

40. DR 2.9 (MITN 6, p. 36): "Sono i Lhobà gente fiera e silvestre. Vivono per lo più nelle selve e capanne e sempre stanno occupati nell'esercizio della caccia d'ogni sorte d'animali, che mangiano così crudi o malamente arrostiti. Si pascono ancora alle volte di carne umana, non avendo nessuna difficoltà d'ammazzar gli uomini quando li vedono ben freschi e di buona carnagione. Vanno sempre armati di frezze, nel tirar le quali hanno una destrezza incomparabile. Vi è questo estremamente barbaro costume fra di essi, che, quando a taluno sta per morire alcun suo parente o più diletto amico, lo va consolando nella di lui morte dicendogli ch'egli andrà fuor di questo mondo, ma non per questo s'affligga, poichè, affin di non trovarsi egli colà tutto solo, gl'invierà tanti e tanti compagni (specificandone il numero), acciocchè questi con la loro conversazione lo sollevino. Morto che quegli sia, conforme alla promessa fatta, uccide tante persone quante prima n'aveva specificate, e per autentica della fedeltà delle sue promessa ne conserva una collana d'altrettanti denti, quante furono le persone da lui per tal fine ammazzate."

41. DR 3.12 (MITN 6, p. 214).

42. DR 2.13, 14 (MITN 6, pp. 82–86). Compare Desideri's descriptions of Newars, who were, among other things, "unsettled" (*instabile*), "turbulent" (*rivoltoso*), and "treacherous" (*traditore*): DR 4.2 (MITN 7, p. 10).

43. DR 2.14 (MITN 6, p. 86); DR 2.13 (MITN 6, p. 81).

44. More stylish literary examples are Pedro de Quiroga's *Coloquios de la verdad* and Baron de Lahonton's *Dialogues curieux entre l'auteur et un sauvage de bon sens qui a voyagé*, both made better known by Anthony Pagden.

45. C. R. Boxer, *A Great Luso-Brazilian Figure. Padre António Vieira, S.J., 1608–1697* (London: Hispanic & Luso-Brazilian Councils, 1957), p. 21; *The Golden Age of Brazil 1695–1750* (Berkeley: University of California Press, 1962), p. 277; J. E. Groh, "Antonio Ruíz de Montoya and the Early Reductions in the Jesuit Province of Paraguay," *Catholic Historical Review* 66 (1970), pp. 501–33.

46. Jennifer D. Selwyn, *A Paradise Inhabited by Devils: The Jesuits' Civilizing Mission in Early Modern Naples* (Rome: IHSI, 2004). Cf. Lance Gabriel Lazar, *Working in the*

Vineyard of the Lord: Jesuit Confraternities in Early Modern Italy (Toronto: University of Toronto Press, 2005).

47. Nor, if a letter from Carlo Antonio Broggia (1698–1767) to Ludovico Antonio Muratori noted by Ronnie Po-Chia Hsia is any indication, was this merely a trope. Justifying the establishment of a seminary to train native Chinese seminarians in Naples in 1732, Broggia lamented, "There is no people more barbaric and ignorant than our own. And to what do we owe this if not the insufficient number of clerics ready to teach and instruct them?" Po-Chia Hsia, *The World of Catholic Renewal*, p. 53. Compare the founding of the Collegio dei Cinesi in Naples to the work of Cardinal Innico Caracciolo, Vincenzo Maria Orsini, Giuseppe Catalani, and Carlo Maria Pianetti on p. 59 and the sources that Po-Chia-Hsia cites on p. 214.

48. As Daniel Reff has pointed out in his own work on Andrés Pérez de Ribas, such beliefs did not place an insurmountable barrier to historical accuracy. Discussing warfare among the Ahome, Zuaque, and Yaqui in Sinaloa and Sonora, Andrés Pérez de Ribas emphasized their competition over land, access to salt deposits and hunting territories, and even a rules dispute about a native game. Andrés Pérez de Ribas, *History of the Triumphs of Our Holy Faith Amongst the Most Barbarous and Fierce Peoples of the New World*, trans. Daniel T. Reff, Maureen Ahern, and Richard K. Danford (Tucson: University of Arizona Press, 1999), p. 4. Desideri also explains polyandry by means of a social analysis of poverty. DR 2.17 (MITN 6, p. 106).

49. Perdue, *China Marches West*, p. 237.

50. Ignatius asked da Câmara to record his reflections on four things: the nobility, the common people, the Society of Jesus, and his own personal experiences. MI Epp 10: 505–11. Ines Županov conveniently organizes these into four epistolary tropes. Jesuits' encounters with kings and nobility, she notes, consequently took the form of *dramatic* or *theatrical* vignettes; their lives among the common people gave rise to *ethnographic* descriptions; their various disputes and lawsuits took *dialogic* or *polemical* forms; and they expressed their individual ambitions with the rhetoric of *sainthood* and *utopianism*. To these four rhetorical tropes, Županov links four other Jesuit interests: evangelization, information gathering, institutional and internal litigation, and spirituality in general. One can quibble with this typology, of course. I, for one, do not think that Ignatius intended da Câmara to reduce a discussion of the Society to litigation, and I think utopianism more often expressed the ambitions of the Society as a whole rather than the individual Jesuit. Be that as it may, Županov's typology fits Ippolito Desideri with uncanny accuracy.

51. Ortelius's *Theatrum orbis terrarum*, the atlas that Jerónimo Xavier consulted before he sent Bento de Góis on his journey, has one map entitled *Tartariae sive magni chami regni*, "Of Tartaria, or the Kingdom of the Great Khan," that depicts the vast stretch of Asia as a single khanate. Although clearly out of date when it was published in 1573—and when Xavier looked at it in 1598—Ortelius's map placed "Thebet" in a tiny, out-of-the-way section in the lower center, hardly the place for the fantastic realm of nineteenth- and twentieth-century explorers.

52. Larner, *Marco Polo and the Discovery of the World*. Larner bases his account on J. Dauvillier, "Les provinces chaldéennes 'de l'extérieur' au Moyen Age," *Mélanges F.*

Cavallera (Toulouse: Bibliothéque de l'Institut Catholique, 1948), pp. 261–316, as well as the same author's *Histoire des institutions des églises orientales au Moyen Age* (London: Variorum Reprints, 1983).

53. Latham notes in his edition of Polo's travels that such an invitation "is wholly in keeping with the Khan's character," but wisely notes that the khan's motives in this "may be variously assessed." Ronald Latham, *The Travels of Marco Polo* (New York: Penguin, 1958), p. 13.

54. See, for example, Rudolf Acquaviva's accounts of their disputation (DI 12, pp. 36, 49, 54); Jerónimo Xavier's letters to Francisco Cabral (DI 17, p. 65; DI 18, pp. 555, 565) and to Claudio Acquaviva (DI 17, p. 70).

55. Martino Martini, *De bello tartarico historia* (Antwerp: Ex Officina Plantiniana Balthasaris Moreti, 1654). Martini's work was published in more than twenty editions between 1654 and 1706, including editions in French, German, English, Italian, Dutch, Portuguese, Spanish, Swedish, and Danish. For a discussion of Martini and other Jesuit presentations of the Mongols, see Laura Hostetler, "A Mirror for the Monarch: A Literary Portrait of China in Eighteenth-Century France," *Asia Major* 19 (2006), pp. 349–76; D. Mungello, *Curious Land*, pp. 110–16; Edwin J. Van Kley, "News from China: Seventeenth Century Notices of the Manchu Conquest," *Journal of Modern History* 45 (1973), pp. 563–68; "An Alternative Muse: The Manchu Conquest in European Literature," *European Studies Review* 6 (1976), pp. 21–24. On the first European Tartar fantasies, see Debra Higgs Strickland, *Saracens, Demons, and Jews* (Princeton, NJ: Princeton University Press, 2003), pp. 157–209. Europeans referred to all Mongols, not just the Tatar, as "Tartars," a word that evoked the hell realm of classical mythology *Tartarus*.

56. Martini's "New Atlas" was published as part of Joannis Blaeu, *Theatrum orbis terrarum sive novis atlas* (Amsterdam: Joannis Blaeu, 1655).

57. Martino Martini, *Sinicae historiae decas prima res à gentis origine ad Christum natum in extrema Asia, sive Magno Sinarum Imperio gestas complexa* (Munich: L. Straubius, 1658).

58. Scholars have noted that it is precisely in its account of historical events that Polo's narrative is most surely a mixture of fact and fable. Cf. Latham, *Travels of Marco Polo*, p. 22.

59. Joachim Bouvet, *Portrait historique de l'Empereur de la Chine* (Paris: Chez Estienne Michallet, 1697).

60. Martino Martini, *Regni Sinensis a Tartaris devastati enarratio* (Amsterdam: Aegidius Janssonius, 1661). This chapbook-sized edition omits the map included with the 1654 edition, but includes several illustrations not found there.

61. For Polo's reception among missionaries, see Larner, *Marco Polo and the Discovery of the World*, pp. 171–76.

62. Latham, *Travels of Marco Polo*, p. 33. Cf. Anthony Grafton, *Defenders of the Text: The Traditions of Scholarship in an Age of Science 1450–1800* (Cambridge: Harvard University Press, 1991).

63. DR 1.11 (MITN 5, p. 185).

64. Melville also employs several Trinitarian parodies to humorous effect in *Moby-Dick*, most notably in the noble savage harpooners, Queequeg, Dagoo, and

Tashtego, and in the crew's interpretation of Ahab's emblematic doubloon. Starbuck: "A dark valley between three mighty, heaven-abiding peaks, that almost seem the Trinity, in some faint earthly symbol."

65. DR 2.10 (MITN 6, p. 46n): "Il di lui intendimento era molto vivo, esperto e sollevato, il naturale ardito, intrepido e bellicoso. Pareva insensibile a ogni incomodo e a tutti gli travagli. Suo appoggio (anche fuora del tempo della guerra) era la sella del cavallo; suo strato e suo letto era la valdrappa del medesimo cavallo; suo capezzale e più delicato coscino erano lo scudo, la spada, il carcasso e le frezze. Il suo più intimo confidente era la vigilanza, da cui gli venivano somministrati continui e sempre diversi gli statagemmi; suo principale e molto fedele aiutante di tutte le sue impresse era la secretezza de' suoi secreti e la simulazione con cui sempre diverse comparivano nell'esterno, da quel che nel suo cuore fussero state premeditate le sue resoluzioni. Insomma, se in tutto, almeno in gran parte avea in sè copiata un ritratto del grande Alessandro, e con rinnovare in sè il di lui esempio, col mostrar al mondo che più intrepidi e più vittoriosi riescono nel campo di Marte quelli che escono dalla palestra dell'arti liberali e dal liceo delle scienze, e che al governo delle truppe e degli eserciti premettono la sommissione alla disciplina di qualche Aristotele."

66. DR 2.11 (MITN 6, p. 53n): "prostratosi ad abbracciarlo, ne lavò con dirotte lacrime le fresche piaghe, e doppo la morte rispettò, amò e con amplissimi encomij celebrò le virtù e le amabili qualità dell'estinto Re, da lui con infame tradimento sì ingiustamente perseguitato."

67. DR 2.11 (MITN 6, p. 55n): "A questi sì teneri e sì lacrimevoli spettacoli."

68. In fact, simple folks who heard the *Exercises* preached during rural missions would have probably learned little more than the first week and the examation of conscience.

69. *Inferno*, canto I, line 72. I did not think of this until Michael Sweet showed me another of Desideri's allusions to Dante in DR 1.8 (MITN 5, p. 163).

70. Masen provides lengthy instructions for how to do so. *Speculum Imaginum Veritatis Occultae*, pp. 252–341.

71. Herman Hugo, *Pia Desideria* (Antwerp: Henricus Aertssen, 1632), I, pp. 73–75.

72. DR 3.8 (MITN 6, p. 172).

73. DR 3.22 (MITN 6, p. 307). Bouchet refers to pyramids in his letter to Huet, and Godinho describes stūpas similarly. Bouchet, *The Travels of Several Learned Missioners*, p. 22; Henri Hosten, "A Letter of Father Francisco Godinho, S.J.," p. 71.

74. DR 3.19 (MITN 6, pp. 281–84). Bouchet's letter to Balthus is a lengthy explanation of the role of demons in India's "oracles," not unlike Desideri's argument that reincarnation was engineered by satanic powers. "A Letter from F. Bouchet, Missioner of the Society of Jesus in India to F. Balthus, of the Same Society," *The Travels of Several Learned Missioners of the Society of Jesus into Divers Parts of the Archipelago, India, China, and America* (London: R. Gosling, 1714), pp. 27–53.

75. Xenophanes, *Fragment*, 7. Cf. Empedocles, *Fragments*, 115, 117, 127, 146, 147; Herodotus, *History*, I.23; Lucian, *The Cockerel*, 20.

76. Qiong Zhang, "Translation as Cultural Reform: Jesuit Scholastic Psychology in the Transformation of the Confucian Discourse on Human Nature," in *The Jesuits: Culture, Sciences, and the Arts*, I, pp. 364–79.

77. *Della Entrata della Compagnia di Giesù e Christianità nella Cina* 5.2, p. 294 (*Fonti Ricciane*, n. 709).

78. There are several versions of this genealogy. This one is from Marsilio Ficino. For an outline of these genealogies, see Frances Yates, *Giordano Bruno and the Hermetic Tradition* (Chicago: University of Chicago Press, 1964).

79. R. Wittkower, *Architectural Principles in the Age of Humanism* (London: Warburg Institute, 1949); G. L. Hersey, *Pythagorean Palaces: Magic and Architecture in the Italian Renaissance* (Ithaca, NY: Cornell University Press, 1976).

80. DR 2.6 (MITN 6, p. 28).

81. Among Kircher's Egyptological work, see *Lingua aegyptiaca restituta* (Rome: Sumptibus Hermanni Scheus, 1643); *Oedipus Aegyptiacus* (Rome, Vitalis Mascardi, 1652–54); *Sphinx mystagoga* (Amsterdam: Chez Jean Janssons à Waesberge, 1676); and *Turris Babel, sive Archontologia* (Amsterdam: Chez Jean Janssons à Waesberge, 1679). *Oedipus Aegyptiacus* had a hard time with the Jesuit censors. Daniel Stolzenberg, "Utility, Edification, and Superstition: Jesuit Censorship and Athanasius Kircher's Oedipus Aegyptiacus," in *The Jesuits: Cultures: Sciences, and the Arts*, 2, pp. 336–54.

82. Nicolas Caussin, *De Symbolica Aegyptorum sapientia* (Cologne: Johann Kinchy, 1623). In a typical show of erudition, Kircher's *Oedipus Aegyptiacus* contains a discussion of emblems and the hieroglyphs: *Oedipus Aegyptiacus*, 2 (1), pp. 7–18. For more general works on the European fascination with Egypt during the baroque period, I have depended on R. Wittkower, *Selected Lectures of Rudolf Wittkower: The Impact of Non-European Civilizations on the West*, ed. Donald Martin Reynolds (Cambridge: Cambridge University Press, 1989); Erik Iversen, *Obelisks in Exile* (Copenhagen: Gad, 1968); Cesare D'Onofrio, *Gli Obelischi di Roma* (Rome: Bulzoni, 1967).

83. Yates, *Giordano Bruno and the Hermetic Tradition*; Charles Trinkhaus, *In Our Image and Likeness: Humanity and Divinity in Italian Humanist Thought*, 2 vols. (Chicago: University of Chicago Press, 1970); Daniel P. Walker, *The Ancient Theology: Studies in Christian Platonism from the Fifteenth to the Eighteenth Centuries* (Ithaca, NY: Cornell University Press, 1972). Claimed to be the very magic that Moses learned in the court of the pharaoh, the Hermetic philosophy found conflicting reception among the Church Fathers. Lactantius, for example, believed that Pythagoras's teacher prophesied the coming of Christ, while Augustine thought him a confederate of the Devil. Other early modern works in this vein include Samuel Bochart, *Geographia sacra* (Cadomi: Typis Petri Cardonelli, 1646); George Horn, *Dissertatio de vera aetate mundi* (Leiden: Lugdani Baratvorum, 1659); Bouchet's correspondent Pierre-Daniel Huet, *Demonstratio evangelica* (Paris, Apud Stephanum Michallet, 1679); and Gerardus Vossius, *De theologia gentili* (Amsterdam, 1641). This last work has been reprinted in three volumes (New York: Garland, 1976).

84. Martin del Rio, *Disquisitionum Magicarum* (Louvain: G. Rivius, 1599–1601). Jesuits sometimes got into trouble for teaching astrology and palm-reading, too. Henrique Leitão, "Entering Dangerous Ground: Jesuits Teaching Astrology and Chiromancy in Lisbon," in *The Jesuits: Cultures, Sciences, and the Arts*, 2, pp. 371–89.

85. Masen has a special section, "De Pythagorae Aenigmatis," in *Speculum Imaginum Veritatis Occultae*, pp. 716–25.

86. Jerónimo de Prado and Juan Bautista Villalpando, *In Ezechielem explanationes et apparatus urbis ac templi hierosolymitani commentariis et imaginibus illustratus* (Rome: Ex Typographia Aloysij Zanetti, 1596–1605); Jaime Lara, "God's Good Taste: The Jesuit Aesthetics of Juan Bautista Villalpando in the Sixth and Tenth Centuries B.C.E.," in *The Jesuits: Culture, Sciences, and the Arts*, 1, pp. 505–21. Kircher reproduced Villalpando's plate showing the astrological ordering of the Jerusalem Temple with complete approval in the second volume of *Oedipus Aegyptiacus*. Kircher, *Oedipus Aegyptiacus* II, p. 21. On Jesuit interpretations of the Temple of Solomon, see Piet Lombaerde, *Innovation and Experience in the Early Baroque in the Southern Netherlands* (Turnhout, Belgium: Brepols, 2008), pp. 201–11. For criticism of Kircher, see Johann Heinrich Ursinus, *De Zoroastre bactriano, Hermete Trismegisto, Sanchonianthone phoenicio eorumque scriptis et aliis contra Mosaicae Scripturae antiquitatem* (Nuremburg: Endter, 1661).

87. Kircher, *Oedipus Aegyptiacus* 2 (2), p. 506. Cf. *China illustrata*, p. 226. Arguably, the most controversial intellectual issue of the seventeenth century was the debate about the dating of the world sparked by the Jesuit publication of Chinese chronologies. Martino Martini's *Sinicae historiae decas prima*, by dating Chinese history to 2952 BC, allowed the Chinese to escape the universal patriarchy of Noah. The Jesuit missionary's dating scandalously disagreed with the most respected chronologist of his day, James Ussher, who dated the creation of the world to 4004 BC and Noah's flood to 2349 BC. Martini, following the ancient calculations of Eusebius and basing himself on the Septuagint rather than the Masoretic text of the Old Testament, dated the creation of the world to 5200 BC and the flood to 2957 BC, thereby extending the age of the world and preserving Noah's universal patriarchy. It was only a matter of time before Kircher's baroque speculations gave way to even greater excesses. Those more inclined to appreciate the natural virtues of Asian cultures, such as the Englishman John Webb, could follow the Jesuit Septuagint chronology in such a way that China was populated before the confusion of tongues at Babel. John Webb, *An historical essay endeavoring a probability that the language of the Empire of China is the Primitive Language* (London: Printed for Nathaniel Brook, 1669). These debates continued into Desideri's day and beyond. In 1726, the Jesuit Parrenin famously lamented that Copernicus caught less trouble than the Jesuits, for it was easier to remove the earth from the center of the universe than it was to subtract a year from the accepted chronology of the world. Antonio Giorgi's *Alphabetum Tibetanum* claimed that some Tibetan scholars dated the flood to 2190 BC while others opted for a more conservative estimate of 1730 BC, and thus counted 850 years from the flood to the appearance of the first man in Tibet. Turner and Bogle also tried to interpret Tibetan myths in light of biblical chronology late in the eighteenth century.

88. Even so, Schott could title the first chapter, in which Kircher offered a key to all systems of writing, "Mercurius Mono-Panglottus." Cf. *Technica Curiosa*, p. 483; Masen, *Speculum Imaginum Veritatis Occultae*, pp. 271–75; Kircher, *Oedipus Aegyptiacus* 2 (2), pp. 442–43; *Turris Babel*, pp. 177–83.

89. Kircher, *China illustrata*, p. 133: "In quo quidem Aegyptios Idolorum omnigena varietate infames imitari videntur." The full genealogical argument occupies pp. 129–34.

90. A letter of the Franciscan Basilio Brollo, written from China in 1702, sounds like Kircher (SF 6, p. 1106): "È questa una provinzia e più rimota e delle più grandi, benchè a proporzione di sua grandezza men popolata ch'altre diverse. Numera 123 città. Per passarla da levante a ponente è necessario un mese intiero, e altretanto—se non più—dall'ostro a settentrione. Confina a settentrione co' tartari, a ponente co' lamazeni, gente che riconoscono per dio un suo re vivente qual è religioso nè mai si vede; il suo sterco istesso è levato per reliquia; e il più bello è che mai muore perchè, quando essendo vecchio et al fine, quei religiosi che gl'assistono elegon un altro più simile a lui che possono ritrovare, e dicono ch'essendo vecchio s'è trasmigrato in un giovane. Pazzia creduta miserabilmente non solo de quelle sue genti, ma da tutti i tartari confinanti che, riconoscendolo pure per dio vivente, gli tributano e lasciano in testamento il meglio di sue sostanze, onde è creduto il più ricco principe del mondo tutto."

91. Kircher, *China illustrata*, pp. 72–74.

92. Kircher, *Turris Babel*, pp. 78–87. An image on pp. 104–5 shows us how Jesuits (and most Christians) traced the genealogy of nations from Noah. According to Kircher, Tibetans and their language derived from India, as we see on pp. 131–32. Kircher's chronology of the Flood can be found on pp. 216–17.

93. Such myths about Egypt continued well into the late eighteenth century. In the estimation of Rudolf Wittkower, Kircher's writings were "above question for at least a hundred years" (*Selected Lectures*, p. 122). Ironically, Kircher's severest critics, such as Montfaucon or William Warburton, detested his Neoplatonic appreciation of Egypt and interpreted its religion in even more sinister terms. Desideri's contemporary, the famous Neopolitan philosopher Giambattista Vico, believed that Kircher had elevated pagan Egypt to a status reserved only for ancient Israel. Giuseppe Mazzotta, *The New Map of the World: The Poetic Philosophy of Giambattista Vico* (Princeton, NJ: Princeton University Press, 1999).

94. Wessels, *Early Jesuit Travellers*, p. 208; Hosten, "Letters and Papers," p. 15. There is no scholarly consensus on the meaning of Desideri's early letters to Tamburini. While I think it fair to assume that Desideri entertained the idea of being a missionary to Tibet, even at the feet of Pope Clement XI, none of his extant letters show that Tamburini officially charged him with this task. In fact, his letter of November 12, 1713, seems to indicate just the opposite. As Wessels sees it, the provincial chose Desideri to open the Tibetan mission and the newly appointed missionary, then wrote to the general to confirm the appointment and place the mission under his direct supervision—so that Desideri could answer to Rome alone. Hosten disagrees with Wessels on this matter, believing rather that Tamburini recommended Desideri to the provincial at Goa for the task and that the provincial chose and commissioned Desideri on the basis of the general's recommendation. While there would be no need for Desideri to request the general's direct supervision if he had already given it, the absence of a written recommendation to that effect is suspicious, unless Tamburini secretly commissioned Desideri for a mission that he wished to hide from the authorities at Goa and Agra.

95. DL 18 (MITN 5, pp. 81–82).

96. One cannot rule out this possibility. Disaffected Jesuits had been known to turn suddenly to the pope against their own order. Although we cannot judge Desideri's

motives in this case, the spirituality of the Society emphasized the individual Jesuit's relationship with the pope to such a degree, at least among the professed, that one can well imagine how a Jesuit dissatisfied with his superiors might be tempted to appeal to the highest authority. José de Acosta, the famous missionary in Peru, appealed to Pope Clement VIII against Claudio Acquaviva after the general failed to appoint him as a provincial. Bangert, *History*, pp. 100–5, 110–13.

97. DR 1, prol. (MITN 5, p. 117); DR 1.1 (MITN 5, p. 122n); DR 1.10 (MITN 5, p. 173).

98. DR 1.16 (MITN 5, p. 215), DR 4.1 (MITN 7, p. 3).

99. DR 1.1 (MITN 5, pp. 122–23); DR 1.16 (MITN 5, p. 215).

100. DR 1.1 (MITN 5, p. 122).

101. DR 1.6 (MITN 5, p. 158); DR 1.9 (MITN 5, p. 171); DR 1.11 (MITN 5, p. 183); DR 1.16 (MITN 5, p. 215).

102. DR 1.11 (MITN 5, p. 184).

103. DR 1.17 (MITN 5, pp. 215–19).

104. DR 1.7 (MITN 5, p. 162); DR 2.16 (MITN 6, p. 102n); DR 4.6 (MITN 7, p. 32); DR 4.10 (MITN 7, p. 64).

105. DR 2.15 (MITN 6, pp. 95, 96n).

106. DR 3.22 (MITN 6, pp. 302, 308n, 308–9).

107. DR 4.17 (MITN 7, p. 107).

108. DR 4.17 (MITN 7, pp. 113–14).

109. DR 4.17 (MITN 7, p. 108).

110. DR 4.19 (MITN 7, pp. 125–26): "Rinunzieranno i ravveduti popoli le loro false opinioni, detesteranno i mostruosi dogmi, lungi dal lor cuore e dalla lor fede rigetteranno le superstiziose leggi: *et projecerunt arma sua*. Potranno liberamente e senz'alcuna resistenza i trionfanti missionarij distrugger col fuoco e demolir col ferro e le vane moschee e i superstizioni tempij e i confusi idoli e i sacrileghi altari. *Et fanum succendit igni cum omnibus qui erant in ipso*. Oppressa finalmente caderà l'infedeltà e in faccia all'Evangelio, non potendosi più sostener l'errore, gloriosa in ogni regno, in ogni parte del mondo trionferà la Fede: *oppressa est Carnaim et non potuit sustinere contra faciem Judae*."

111. DR 4.20 (MITN 7, pp. 138–39): "Là tutt'insieme affollate e la Guinea e l'Etiopia e Monopotapa e Socotra e Brasile e Maragnone e Malabàr e Mogol e Cina e Giappone e cent'altri afflittissimi regni e imperij e dell'Affrica e dell'Asia e dell'America, mostrando incessantemente a Dio e confutati errori e abolite superstizioni e infranti milioni d'idoli infernali e diroccati sacrileghi tempij senza numero e re battezzati e convertiti popoli e fabbricate chiese e instituite cristianità co' sudori, co' stenti, col fervore, col sangue, con la vita di tanti zelantissimi missionarij eretti in ogni parte e fra innumerabili nazioni trofei sontuosi e splendidissimi trionfi alla Fede Cattolica. Ahi esclamano ancor essi, ahi!"

112. DR 1.8 (MITN 5, pp. 174–75). "A' 9 di Novembre arrivammo al più alto de' luoghi, che abbiamo passato in tutto questo nostro pellegrinaggio. Tal luogo (che pur'è deserto) . . . è appresso i paesani di molto rispetto e venerazione, per riguardo a un certo Urghièn, che stabilì nel Thibet la religione o setta che in esso corre. V'è quivi fuori di strada un monte sterminatamente alto, molto largo di curcuito, nella sommità ricoperto

dalle nuvole e da perpetue nevi e ghiacci, e nel resto molto orrido e rigido per l'acerbissimo freddo, che in esso fà. In una spelonca, ch'è formata di viva pietra di questo monte, dicono che dimorò qualche tempo in un total ritiro e asprezza e in continuo contemplazioni il sopradetto Urghièn.... Oltre l'andar i Thibetani a visitar la spelonca, dove lasciano sempre qualch'offerta, vanno ancora con molt'incommodo a far il giro di tutto quel monte, che richiede alcuni giorni, e in ciò stimano di conseguir grandissime (per così dir) indulgenze."

113. DL 8 (MITN 5, p. 34): "se fait entre des montagnes qui sont une vraye image de la tristesse, de l'horreur & de la mort mesmes." Cf. Jonathan Spence, *Memory Palace*, p. 56.

114. Paolo Rossi, *The Dark Abyss of Time: The History of the Earth and the History of the Nations from Hooke to Vico*, trans. Lydia C. Cochrane (Chicago: University of Chicago Press, 1984).

115. *Inferno*, canto XXXII: "Poscia vid' io mille visi cagnazzi fatti per freddo."

116. DR 4.20 (MITN 7, pp. 152–53).

117. Tom Cohen, *The Fire of Tongues: Antonio Vieira and the Missionary Church in Brazil and Portugal* (Stanford: Stanford University Press, 1998).

118. Peter Henrici, "Mission und Mystik im Leben des seligen Peter Faber," *Studia Missionalia* 55 (2006), pp. 27–47.

119. Spence, *Memory Palace*, p. 42. Michael Root informs me that Lutheran scholastics such as Nicolai and Gerhard often decried *all* missions as Papist hubris. Cf. *Theologische Realenzyklopädie* 23, p. 46. Also see Antonio a Santa Maria Caballero's comments on Calvin in his *Relaçion de la Persecuçion* (SF 2, p. 508).

120. See, for example, Cotton Mather's open letter to the Reformed missionary Bartholomaeus Ziegenbalg, *India Christiana* (Boston: B. Green, 1721). Jonathan Edwards also thought the unholy alliance between French Jesuits and indigenous Americans a sure sign of Satan's activities in the British colonies.

121. DR 3.17 (MITN 6, pp. 255–57).

122. DR 4.20 (MITN 7, pp. 131–32).

123. DR 4.20 (MITN 7, p. 162).

Select Bibliography

I. ARCHIVAL SOURCES: ARCHIVUM ROMANUM SOCIETATIS IESU

ARSI FG 723, 8a
ARSI Goa 9; 20 + 20a; 52; 72–76a
ARSI Jap-Sin 68, 76, 79, 80, 108; 137a; 141; 150; 175, 196; 198; 200; IV, 3;
    IV (2), 5

II. PRIMARY SOURCES

A. *Tibetan*

Bdud 'jom rin po che 'jigs bral ye shes rdo rje. *Gangs ljongs rgyal bstan yongs
    rdzogs kyi phyi mo snga 'gyur rdo rje theg pa'i bstan pa rin po che'i ltar
    byung ba'i tshul dag cing gsal bar brjod pa lha dbang g.yul las rgyal ba'i rnga
    bo che'i sgra dbyangs.* In *The Collected Writings and Revelations of H.H.
    Bdud-'joms rin-po-che-'jigs-bral-ye-shes-rdo-rje,* vol. 1. Kalimpong: Dupjung
    Lama, 1979.
Chos rje rling pa. *Khrag 'thung mā ha gu ru padma drag po'i chos skor and Other
    Revelations.* Darjeeling: Kargyud Sungrab Nyamso Khang, 1985.
Dkon mchog 'jigs med dbang po. *Kun mkhyen 'Jam dbyangs bzhad pa'i rnam
    thar.* Lanzhou: Kan suu mi rigs dpe skrun khang, 1987.
Dpal yul rdzong nang 'jam dpal blo gros. *Bod na bzhugs pa'i rnying ma'i dgon
    deb; Record of Nyingma monasteries in Tibet.* Dalhousie, 1965.
*Gangs can gyi ljongs su bka' dang bstan bcos sogs kyi glegs bam spar gzhi ji ltar yod
    pa rnam nas dkar chag.* In *Three Karchaks,* ed. E. Gene Smith,
    pp. 169–243. New Delhi: Ngawang Gelek Demo, 1970.
Gu ru Bkra shis Stag sgang mkhas mchog ngag dbang blo gros. *Gu bkra'i chos
    'byung.* Beijing: Krung go'i bod kyi shes rig dpe skrun khang, 1990.

Gyur med 'od gsal khyung po ras pa. *Rje btsun mi 'gyur dpal gyi sgron ma'i rnam thar dad pa'i gdung sel.* Thimpu: National Library of Bhutan, 1984.

Kun bzang nges don klong yangs. *Bod du byung ba'i gsang sngags snga 'gyur gyi bstan 'dzin skyes mchog rim byon gyi rnam thar nor bu'i do shal.* Dalhousie: Damchoe Sangpo, 1976.

Mdo mkhar zhabs drung Tshe ring dbang rgyal. *Dpal mi'i dbang po'i rtogs brjod 'jig rten kun tu dga' ba'i gtam.* 2 vols. Darjeeling: Kargyud Sungrab Nyamso Khang, 1974.

Nyang nyi ma 'od zer. *Slob dpon padma'i rnam thar zangs gling ma.* Chengdu: Si khron mi rigs dpe skrun khang, 1987.

O rgyan gling pa. *Padma bka' thang. U rgyen gu ru padma 'byung gnas kyi skyes rabs rnam par thar pa.* Chengdu: Si khron mi rigs dpe skrun khang, 1987.

Paṇ chen Blo bzang chos kyi rgyal mtshan. *The Autobiography of the First Panchen Lama Blo-bzang-chos-kyi-rgyal-mtshan.* New Delhi: Ngawang Gelek Demo, 1969.

Paṇ chen Blo bzang ye shes. *Shākya'i dge slong blo bzang ye shes kyi spyod tshul gsal bar byed pa ngor dkar can kyi phreng ba.* In *The Collected Works (gsung-'bum) of the Second Panchen Blo-bzan-ye-śes*, vol. 1. New Delhi: Bkra-śis-lhun-po Monastery, 1981–85.

Sle lung Rje drung Bzhad pa'i rdo rje. *Rig pa 'dzin pa blo bzang 'phrin las kyi rtogs brjod skel bzang dga' ston (The Collected Works of Sle lung Rje drung Bzhad pa'i rdo rje)*, vol. 1. Leh: T. Sonam, 1983.

———. *Mi dbang bsod nams stobs rgyas rnam grol gling du byon pa'i lo rgyus ngo mtshar 'bum snang (The Collected Works of Sle lung Rje drung Bzhad pa'i rdo rje, vol. 9)*: 279–359. Leh: T. Sonam, 1984.

Sum pa mkhan po Ye shes dpal 'byor. *Dpag bsam ljon bzang.* New Delhi: Lokesh Chandra, 1959.

———. *Mtsho sngon byi lo rgyus sogs bkod pa'i tshangs glu gsar snyan.* In *The Annals of Kokonor*, trans H. C. Yang. Bloomington: Indiana University Press, 1970.

Thu'u bkwan Blo bzang chos kyi nyi ma. *Khyab bdag rdo rje sems dpa'i ngo bo dpal ldan bla ma dam pa ye shes bstan pa'i sgron me dpal bzang po'i rnam par thar pa mdo tsam brjod pa dge ldan bstan pa'i mdzes rgyan.* In *Collected Works*, vol. 1. Delhi: Ngawang Gelek Demo, 1969.

Zhva sgab pa dbang phyug lde ldan (Tsepon Shakabpa). *Bod kyi srid don rgyal rabs.* Delhi, 1976.

B. European Languages

Andrade, António de. *O descobrimento do Tibet*, ed. Francisco Maria Esteves Pereira. Coimbra: Imprensa da Universidade, 1921.

Aquinas, Thomas. *Opera omnia iussu impensaque, Leonis XIII. P.M. edita.* Rome: Ex Typographia Polyglotta S.C. de Propaganda Fide, 1882–.

———. *Opera omnia.* Parma: Typis Petri Fiaccadori, 1856.

Bellarmine, Robert. *Opera omnia.* 12 vols. Paris: Vivès, 1874.

Blaeu, Iohannis. *Theatrum orbis terrarum sive novis atlas.* Amsterdam: Iohannis Blaeu, 1655.

Bochart, Samuel. *Geographia sacra.* Cadomi: Typis Petri Cardonelli, 1646.

Bosch, Jakob. *Symbolographia sive de arte symbolica.* Augsburg and Dillingen: Johann Kaspar Bencard, 1701.

Bouvet, Joachim. *Portrait historique de l'empereur de la Chine.* Paris: Chez Estienne Michallet, 1697.

Caussin, Nicholas. *De symbolica Aegyptiorum sapientia.* Cologne: Johannes Kinchius, 1654.

Conti, Giovanni Battista. *Iter animae ad Deum piis considerationibus et affectibus gradatim euntis. Praevia itineri antecedit Dissertatio brevis de Oratione Mentali et Spiritualibus Divi Ignatii Loyolae Exercitiis.* Rome: Antonii de Rubeis, 1709.

———. *Le sette principali malattie dell'animo e loro qualita con gli opportuni rimedii.* Rome: Bernabo, 1712.

David, Jan. *Veridicus Christianus.* Antwerp: Jan Moretus, 1601.

Drexel, Jeremias. *De aeternitate considerationes.* Cologne: Peter Henning, 1629.

———. *Infernus damnatorum.* Douai: Balthasar Bellère, 1631.

———. *Trismegistus Christianus.* Cologne: Apud Cornel. Ab Edmond, 1631.

Esercitii spirituali di S. Ignatio. Rome: Nella Stamperia del Varese, 1673.

Francisco a Iesu de Escalona. *Relacion del viaje.* SF 2, pp. 224–314.

Franco, Antonio. *Imagem da virtude em o noviciado da Companhia de Jesu na corte de Lisboa.* 2 vols. Coimbra: No Real Collegio das Artes da Companhia de Jesu, 1714–19.

Freyre, Manoel. *Tibetorum ac eorum Relatio Viarum.* MITN 7, pp. 194–207.

Giorgi, Antonio Agostino. *Alphabetum Tibetanum.* Rome: Typis Sacrae Congregationis de Propaganda Fide, 1762.

Guillemis de Rubruc. *Itinerarium fratris Willielmi de Rubruquis de ordine fratrum Minorum, Galli, anno grat. 1253 ad partes orientales.* SF 1, pp. 147–332.

Hees, Willem van. *Emblemata sacra de fide, spe, charitate.* Antwerp: Balthasar Moretus, 1636.

Horn, George. *Dissertatio de vera aetate mundi.* Leiden: Lugdani Baratvorum, 1659.

Huet, Pierre Daniel. *Demonstratio evangelica.* Paris: Apud Stephanum Michallet, 1679.

Hugo, Herman. *Pia desideria.* Antwerp: Henricus Aertssens, 1632.

Ibañez, Bonaventura. *Responsum quaestionibus.* SF 3, pp. 58–74.

———. *Brevis Relatio anno 1668.* SF 3, pp. 75–94.

Iohannes de Plano Carpini. *Ystoria Mongalorum quos nos Tartaros appellamus.* SF 1, pp. 3–130.

Izquierdo, Sebastian. *Pharus Scientiarum ubi quidquid ad cognitionem humanam humanitus acquisibilem pertinet.* Leiden: Sumptibus C. Bourgeat & M. Lietard, 1659.

Jansen, Cornelius. *Augustinus.* Louvain: Iacobus Zegerus, 1640.

Kestlerus, Johannes Stephanus. *Physiologia Kircheriana experimentalis.* Amsterdam: Janssonius-Waesbergius, 1680.

Kircher, Athanasius. *Lingua aegyptiaca restituta.* Rome: Sumptibus Hermanni Scheus, 1643.

———. *Oedipus Aegyptiacus.* Rome: Vitalis Mascardi, 1652–1654.

———. *China monumentis qua sacris qua aliarumque profanis nec non variis naturae & artis spectaculis aliarumque rerum memorabilium argumentis illustrata.* Amsterdam: Joannem Janssonium à Waesberge & Elizeum Weyerstraet, 1667.

———. *China monumentis qua sacris qua profanis nec non variis naturae & artis spectaculis aliarumque rerum memorabilium argumentis illustrata.* Amsterdam: Jacobus van Meurs, 1667.

Kircher, Athanasius. *Ars Magna Lucis et Umbrae*. Amsterdam: Joannem Janssonium à Waesberge & Elizeum Weyerstraet, 1671.

———. *Sphinx mystagoga*. Amsterdam: Chez Jean Janssons à Waesberge, 1676.

———. *Turris Babel, sive Archontologia*. Amsterdam: Chez Jean Janssons à Waesberge, 1679.

Lafitau, Joseph-François. *Moeurs des sauvages ameriquains, comparées aux moeurs des premiers temps*. 2 vols. Paris: Charles Estienne Hochereau, 1724.

Le Comte, Louis. *The Empire of China*. London: J. Hughs, 1737.

Le Roy, Alard. *La vertu enseigné par les oiseaux*. Liege: Bauduin Bronckart, 1653.

Libro del Conosçimiento de todos los reynos & tierras & señoríos que son por el mundo 14. SF 1, pp. 566–75.

Lucarelli, Giovanni. *Viaggo dell'Indie*. SF 2, pp. 12–92.

Ludolphus de Saxonia. *Vita Iesu Christi Redemptoris Nostri*. Venice: Batholomaeus Rubinus, 1568.

Lugo, Juan de. *Disputationes scholasticae et morales*. 8 vols. Paris: Vivès, 1868–69.

Manni, Giovanni Battista. *Quattro massime di Christiana filosofia*. Rome: Madama da Francesco Leone, 1676.

Martini, Martino. *De bello tartarico historia*. Antwerp: Ex Officina Plantiniana Balthasaris Moreti, 1654.

———. *Sinicae historiae decas prima res à gentis origine ad Christum natum in extrema Asia, sive Magno Sinarum Imperio gestas complexa*. Munich: L. Straubius, 1658.

———. *Regni Sinensis a Tartaris devastati enarratio*. Amsterdam: Aegidius Janssonius, 1661.

Masen, Jakob. *Speculum imaginum veritatis occultae*. Cologne: Johann Anton Kinchius, 1664.

Mather, Cotton. *India Christiana*. Boston: B. Green, 1721.

Menestrier, Claude-François. *L'art des emblèmes*. Lyon: Benoît Coral, 1662.

———. *La philosophie des images*. Paris: Robert J. B. de la Calle, 1682.

Molina, Luis. *Concordia liberi arbitrii cum gratiae donis, divina praescientia, providentia, praedestinatione, et reprobatione*. Paris: P. Lethielleux, 1876.

Moréri, Louis. *Le Grand dictionnaire historique, ou le mélange curieux de l'histoire sacrée et profane*. 10 vols. Paris: Les libraires associès, 1759.

———. *An Universal, historical, geographical, chronological and poetical dictionary exactly describing the situation, extent, customs, laws, manners, commodities, &c., of all kingdoms, commonwealths, provinces, islands and cities in the known world*. London: Hartley, Turner & Hodgson, 1703.

———. *A supplement to the Great historical geographical genealogical and poetical dictionary collected from the best historians, chronologers, and lexicographers but more especially out of Lewis Morery*. London: Henry Rhodes, 1705.

Nadal, Jerónimo. *Adnotationes et meditationes in Evangelia*. Antwerp: Martinus Nutius, 1595.

Nieuhof, Jan. *An Embassy from the East-India Company of the United Provinces to the Grand Tartar Cham Emperor of China*. London: John Macock, 1669.

Odoricus de Portu Naonis. *Relatio* 33. SF 1, pp. 413–95.

Pietrasanta, Silvestro. *De symbolis heroicis libri IX*. Antwerp: Balthasar Moretus, 1634.

Pinamonti, Giovanni Battista. *L'inferno aperto al Christiano perche non v'entri, overo considerazioni delle pene infernali*. Venice: Giovanni Antonio Remondini, n.d.

———. *L'inferno aperto*. Milan: n.p., 1693.

———. *Hell Opened to Christians; to Caution them from entering into it: or, Considerations of the Infernal Pains*. London: n.p., 1715.

Polo, Marco. *De regionibus orientalibus*. Brandenburg: Georgii Schulzii, 1671.

———. *The Travels of Marco Polo*. Trans. Ronald Latham. New York: Penguin, 1958.

Pedro de Ribadeneyra. *Vita Ignatii Loyolae*. Rome: MHSI, 1965.

Ricci, Matteo. *Lettere (1580–1609)*. Ed. Francesco D'Arelli. Macerata: Quodlibet, 2001.

———. *Della entrata della Compagnia di Giesù e Christianità nella Cina*. In *Fonti Ricciane*, ed. Pasquale M. D'Elia, S.J. Rome: Libreria dello Stato, 1942.

Ramusio, Giovanni Battista. *Secondo volume delle navigationi et viaggi raccolta gia da m. Gio. Battista Ramusio, et hora in questa nuova editione accresciuto; nel quale si contengono l'historia delle cose de Tartari, & diversi fatti de' loro imperatori, descritta da m. Marco Polo gentil'huomo venetiano, & da Hayton Armeno. Varie descrittioni di diversi auttori, dell'Indie Orientali, della Tartaria, della Persia, Armenia, Mengrelia, Zorzania, & altre provincie*. Venice: Giunti, 1559.

Ripalda, Juan Martínez de. *De ente supernaturali: disputationes theologicae*. 4 vols. Paris: Palmé, 1870–71.

Reinzer, Franz. *Meteorologia philosophica-politica*. Augsburg: Jeremias Wolf, 1698.

Rio, Martin del. *Disquisitionum magicarum*. Louvain: G. Rivius, 1599–1601.

Sandaeus, Maximilianus. *Maria gemma mystica*. Moguntia: n.p., 1631.

———. *Maria flos mysticus*. Moguntia: n.p., 1639.

Schott, Gaspar. *Technica curiosa, sive mirabilia artis*. Rome: Ex Typographia Varesii, 1663.

Segneri, Paolo. *Manna Animae seu Exercitium Facile simul et fructuosum illis*. Dilingae: J. C. Bencard, 1723.

Suárez, Francisco. *Opera omnia*. 28 vols. in 30. Paris: Vivès, 1856–78.

Tavernier, Jean-Baptiste. *Les six voyages*. Paris: G. Clouzier, 1676.

———. *The Six Voyages of John Baptista Tavernier, Baron of Aubonne, through Turkey, into Persia and the East-Indies, for the space of forty years giving an account of the present state of those countries as also a full relation of the five years war between Aureng-Zebe and his brothers in their father's life-time, about the succession. And a voyage made by the Great Mogul with his army from Delhi to Lahor, from Lahor to Bember, and from thence to the Kingdom of Kachemire, by the Mogols, call'd the paradise of the Indies*. Trans. John Phillips. London: William Godbid, 1677.

The Travels of Several Learned Missioners of the Society of Jesus into Divers Parts of the Archipelago, India, China, and America. London: R. Gosling, 1714.

Ursinus, Johann Heinrich. *De Zoroastre bactriano, Hermete Trismegisto, Sanchonianthone phoenicio eorumque scriptis et aliis contra Mosaicae Scripturae antiquitatem*. Nuremburg: Endter, 1661.

Villalpando, Juan Bautista Jerónimo de Prado. *In Ezechielem explanationes et apparatus urbis ac templi hierosolymitani commentariis et imaginibus illustratus*. Rome: Ex Typographia Aloysij Zanetti, 1596–1605.

Vita beati P. Ignatii Loiolae, Societatis Iesu fundatoris. Rome, 1622.

Vossius, Gerardus. *De theologia gentili.* Amsterdam: Ioannem Blaev, 1641.

Webb, John. *An historical essay endeavoring a probability that the language of the Empire of China is the Primitive Language.* London: Nathaniel Brook, 1669.

Xavier, Francis. *Epistolae S. Francisci Xaverii aliaque eius scripta.* 2nd ed. 2 vols. Rome: MHSI, 1996.

III. SECONDARY SOURCES

Alden, Dauril. *The Making of an Enterprise: The Society of Jesus in Portugal, Its Empire, and Beyond, 1540–1750.* Stanford, CA: Stanford University Press, 1996.

Angelini, Pietro. *Leggere il Tibet: bibliografia italiana del paese delle nevi, 1624–1993.* Bologna: Il Nove, 1994.

Aris, Michael. *Bhutan: The Early History of a Himalayan Kingdom.* Warminster: Aris and Philips, 1979.

———. *Hidden Treasures and Secret Lives.* London: Kegan Paul International, 1989.

Aschoff, Jürgen. *Tsaparang-Königsstadt in Westtibet: Die vollständigen Berichte des Jesuitenpaters António de Andrade und eine Beschreibung vom heutigen Zustand der Klöster.* Munich: MC Verlag, 1989.

Bailey, Gauvin Alexander. *Art on the Jesuit Missions in Asia and Latin America, 1542–1773.* Toronto: University of Toronto Press, 1999.

———. *Between Renaissance and Baroque: Jesuit Art in Rome, 1565–1610.* Toronto: University of Toronto Press, 2003.

Baillie, Luiza Maria. "Father Estevao Cacella's Report on Bhutan in 1627." *Journal of Bhutan Studies* 1 (2007): 1–35.

Bangert, William J., S.J. *A History of the Society of Jesus.* 2nd rev. ed. St. Louis: IJS, 1986.

Bargiacchi, Enzo Gualtiero. "La *Relazione* di Ippolito Desideri fra storia locale e vicende internazionali." *Storialocale: Quaderni pistoiesi di cultura moderna e contemporanea* 2 (2003): 4–103.

———. "Il contributo di Ippolito Desideri alla conoscenza geografica." *L'Universo* 84 (2005): 788–807.

———. *Ippolito Desideri S.J alla scoperta del Tibet e del buddhismo.* Pistoia: Edizioni Brigata del Leoncino, 2006.

———. *Ippolito Desideri S.J. Opere e Bibliografia.* Subsidia ad Historiam Socitatis Iesu 15. Rome: IHSI, 2007.

———. "Ippolito Desideri's First Remarks on Ladakh." Paper presented at the Thirteenth International Association of Ladakh Studies Colloquium, Rome, September 7–11, 2007.

———. *A Bridge Across Two Cultures: Ippolito Desideri, S.J. (1684–1733): A Brief Biography.* Florence: Istituto Geografico Militare, 2008.

Bell, Charles. *Tibet, Past and Present.* Oxford: Clarendon Press, 1924.

———. *The People of Tibet.* Oxford: Clarendon Press, 1928.

———. *The Religion of Tibet.* Oxford: Clarendon Press, 1931.

Berger, Patricia. *Empire of Emptiness: Buddhist Art and Political Authority in Qing China*. Honolulu: University of Hawai'i Press, 2003.

Blondeau, Anne-Marie. "Analysis of the Biographies of Padmasambhava According to Tibetan Tradition: Classification of Sources." In *Tibetan Studies in Honour of Hugh Richardson*, ed. Michael Aris and Aung San Suu Kyi, pp. 45–52. Warminster: Aris and Phillips, 1980.

———. "Une polémique sur l'authenticité des Bka'-thang au 17ᵉ siècle." In *Silver on Lapis: Tibetan Literary Culture and History*, ed. Christopher Beckwith, pp. 125–62. Bloomington, IN: Tibet Society, 1987.

Bossy, John, *Christianity in the West 1400–1700*. Oxford: Oxford University Press, 1985.

Boxer, C. R. *The Christian Century in Japan, 1549–1650*. Berkeley: University of California Press, 1967.

Brockey, Liam. *Journey to the East: The Jesuit Mission to China 1579–1724*. Cambridge, MA: Belknap Press, 2007.

Camps, Arnulf, O.F.M. *Jerome Xavier S.J. and the Muslims of the Mogul Empire: Controversial Works and Missionary Activity*. Schöneck-Beckenried: Nouvelle Revue de Science Missionaire Suisse, 1957.

Caraman, Philip, S.J. *Tibet: The Jesuit Century*. St. Louis: IJS, 1997.

Carruthers, Mary J. *The Book of Memory: A Study of Memory in Medieval Culture*. Cambridge: Cambridge University Press, 1990.

———. *The Craft of Thought: Meditation, Rhetoric, and the Making of Images, 400–1200*. Cambridge: Cambridge University Press, 1998.

Carruthers, Mary, and Jan M. Ziolkowski, eds. *The Medieval Craft of Memory: An Anthology of Texts and Pictures*. Philadelphia: University of Pennsylvania Press, 2002.

Chen, Hui-hung. "The Human Body as a Universe: Understanding Heaven by Visualization and Sensibility in Jesuit Cartography in China." *Catholic Historical Review* 93 (2007): 517–52.

Childs, Geoffrey. "Refuge and Revitalization: Hidden Himalayan Sanctuaries. *Sbas-yul*) and the Preservation of Tibet's Imperial Lineage." *Acta Orientalia* 60 (1999): 126–58.

Clooney, Francis X., S.J. *Fr. Bouchet's India: An 18th Century Jesuit's Encounter with Hinduism*. Chennai: Satya Nilayam Publications, 2005.

Crossley, Pamela K. *The Manchus*. Oxford: Basil Blackwell, 1997.

Cuevas, Bryan J. *The Hidden History of the Tibetan Book of the Dead*. Oxford: Oxford University Press, 2003.

———. *Travels in the Netherworld: Buddhist Popular Narratives of Death and the Afterlife in Tibet*. Oxford: Oxford University Press, 2008.

———. "Preliminary Remarks on the History of Mindröling: The Founding and Organization of a Tibetan Monastery in the Seventeenth Century." In *Places of Practice: Monasteries and Monasticism in Asian Religions*, ed. James Benn, Lori Meeks, and James Robson. Honolulu: University of Hawai'i Press, forthcoming.

———. "The 'Calf's Nipple (*Be'u bum*) of Ju Mipam (Ju Mi pham): A Handbook of Tibetan Ritual Magic." In *Tibetan Ritual*, ed. José I. Cabezón. Oxford: Oxford University Press, forthcoming.

Cuevas, Bryan J. "On the Politics of Magical Warfare in 17th Century Tibet." Manuscript.
———, and Kurtis R. Schaeffer, eds. *Power, Politics, and the Reinvention of Tradition: Tibet in the Seventeenth and Eighteenth Centuries.* Leiden: Brill, 2006.
Cummins, J. S. "Two Missionary Methods in China: Mendicants and Jesuits." In *España en Extremo Oriente. Filipinas, China, Japón. Presencia Franciscana, 1578–1978,* ed. V. Sanchez and J. S. Fuertes, pp. 33–108. Madrid, 1979.
Dalmases, Cándido de, S.J. *Fontes documentales de S. Ignatio de Loyola: documenta de S. Ignatii familia et patria, iuventute, primis sociis.* Rome: IHSI, 1977.
Delumeau, Jean. *Le catholicisme entre Luther et Voltaire.* Paris: Presses Universitaires de France, 1971.
Didier, Hughes. *Les portugais au Tibet: les premières relations jésuites (1624–1635).* Paris: Editions Chandeigne, 1996.
———. *Fantômes d'Islam & de Chine: le voyage de Bento de Góis, S.J. (1603–1607).* Paris: Fundação Calouste Gulbenkian, 2003.
Dreyfus, Georges. "The Shuk-den Affair: History and Nature of a Quarrel." *Journal of the International Association of Buddhist Studies* 21 (1998): 227–70.
Dudink, Adrian. "*Tianzhu jiaoyao,* The Catechism (1605) published by Matteo Ricci." *Sino-Western Relations Journal* 24 (2002): 38–50.
———. "Lubelli's *Wanmin simo tu* (Picture of the Four Last Things of All People), ca. 1683." *Sino-Western Cultural Relations Journal* 18 (2006): 1–19.
Dunne, G. H., S.J. *Generation of Giants.* South Bend: University of Notre Dame Press, 1962.
Ehrhard, Franz-Karl. "The Role of 'Treasure Discoverers' and Their Writings in the Search for Himalayan Sacred Lands." In *Sacred Spaces and Powerful Places in Tibetan Culture,* ed. Toni Huber, pp. 227–39. Dharamsala: Library of Tibetan Works and Archives, 1999.
———. "Political and Ritual Aspects of the Search for Himalayan Sacred Lands." In *Sacred Spaces and Powerful Places in Tibetan Culture,* ed. Toni Huber, pp. 240–57. Dharamsala: Library of Tibetan Works and Archives, 1999.
Elison, George. *Deus Destroyed: The Image of Christianity in Early Modern Japan.* Cambridge, MA: Harvard University Press, 1991.
Elverskog, Johan. *Our Great Qing: The Mongols, Buddhism, and the State in Late Imperial China.* Honolulu: University of Hawai'i Press, 2006.
Engelhardt, Isrun. "The Closing of the Gates: Tibetan-European Relations at the End of the Eighteenth Century." In *Religion and Secular Culture in Tibet,* ed. Henk Blezer, pp. 229–45. Leiden: Brill, 2002.
———. "Between Tolerance and Dogmatism: Tibetan Reactions to the Capuchin Missionaries in Lhasa, 1707–1745." *Zentralasiatische Studien* 34 (2005): 55–97.
Fazy, Robert. "Le P. Ippolito Desideri à Lhasa, 1716–1721 et Son exposé de la religion tibétaine." *Bulletin de la Société Suisse des Amis de l'Extrème Orient* 6 (1944): 1–44.
Filippi, Filippo de, *La spedizione nel Karakorum e nell'Imalia occidentale, 1909.* 2 vols. Bologna: Zanichelli, 1912.
———. *Storia della spedizione scientifica italiana nel Himàlaia, Caracorùm e Turchestàn cinese (1913–1914).* Bologna: Zanichelli, 1924.

———. "Il 'Ragguaglio' e le 'Memorie de' viaggi e missione nel Tibet' di padre Ippolito Desideri da Pistoia." *Bollettino della Soceita Geographica Italiana* 6 (1929): 295–301.

———. *An Account of Tibet: The Travels of Ippolito Desideri of Postoia S.J., 1712–1727*. Rev. ed. London: George Routledge and Sons, 1937.

Francke, August Hermann. "Die Jesuitenmission von Tsaparang im Lichte der tibetischen Urkunden." *Zeitschrift für Missionswissenschaft* 15 (1925): 269–76.

Fuchs, W. *Der Jesuiten Atlas der K'anghsi-Zeit*. Monumenta Serica Monograph IV. Beijing: Furen Universität, 1943.

Gettelman, Nancy Moore. "Karma-Bstan-skyong and the Jesuits." In *Reflections on Tibetan Culture: Essays in Memory of Turrell V. Wylie*, ed. Lawrence Epstein and Richard Sherburne, pp. 269–77. Lewiston, NY: Edwin Mellen Press, 1990.

Gispert-Sauch, G., S.J. "Tibetan Christian Literature." *Ignis Studies* 9 (1985): 26–34.

Goss, Robert E. "The First Meeting of Catholic Scholasticism with dGe lugs pa Scholasticism." In *Scholasticism: Cross-cultural and Comparative Perspectives*, ed. José Cabezon, pp. 65–90. Albany: State University of New York Press, 1997.

Greenblatt, Stephen. *Marvelous Possessions: The Wonder of the New World*. Oxford: Oxford University Press, 1991.

Guibert, Joseph de, S.J. *The Jesuits, Their Spiritual Doctrine and Practice: A Historical Study*, trans. William J. Young. Chicago: IJS, 1964.

Gyatso, Janet. "Signs, Memory, and History: A Tantric Buddhist Theory of Scriptural Transmission." *Journal of the International Association of Buddhist Studies* 9 (1986): 73–135.

———. "The Logic of Legitimation in the Tibetan Treasure Tradition." *History of Religions* 33 (1993): 97–134.

———. "Drawn from the Tibetan Treasury: The gTer ma Literature." In *Tibetan Literature: Studies in Genre*, ed. José Cabezon and Roger R. Jackson, pp. 147–69. Ithaca, NY: Snow Lion Publications, 1996.

Hadot, Pierre. *Exercices spirituels et philosophie antique*. Paris: Etudes augustiniennes, 1981.

Hedin, Sven. *Trans-Himalaya: Discoveries and Adventures in Tibet*. 3 vols. London: Macmillan, 1909–13.

———. "Early European Knowledge of Tibet." *Geografiska Annaler* 1 (1919): 290–339.

Herrmann, A. *Das Land der Seide und Tibet im Licht der Antike*. Leipzig: K. F. Koehlers Antiquarium, 1938.

Hersey, G. L. *Pythagorean Palaces: Magic and Architecture in the Italian Renaissance*. Ithaca, NY: Cornell University Press, 1976.

Hidehiro, Okada. "The Third Dalai Lama and the Altan Khan of the Tümed." In *Tibetan Studies: Proceedings of the 6th Seminar of the International Association for Tibetan Studies, Narita, 1989*, eds. Ihara Shōren and Yamaguchi Zuihō, 2:645–52. Tokyo: Naritasan Shinshoji, 1992.

Hoffmann, Helmut. "Tibets Eintritt in die Universalgeschichte." *Saeculum* 2 (1950): 258–79.

Holdich, Thomas. *Tibet, the Mysterious*. London: F. A. Stokes, 1906.

Hosten, Henri, S.J. *Jesuit Missionaries in Northern India and Inscriptions on Their Tombs, Agra (1580–1803)*. Kurseong: St. Mary's Indian Academy, 1906.

Hosten, Henri, S.J. "List of Jesuit Missionaries in Mogor (1580–1803)." *Journal of the Asiatic Society of Bengal* (n.s.) 6 (1910): 527–42.

———. *Jesuit Letters and Allied Papers on Mogor, Tibet, Bengal, & Burma.* 2 vols. Calcutta: Asiatic Society, 1914–16.

———. "A Letter of Father Francisco Godinho, S.J., from Western Tibet." *Journal and Proceedings of the Asiatic Society of Bengal* (n.s.) 21 (1925): 49–73.

———. "A Letter of Fr. A. de Andrade, S.J.,. Tibet, August 29th, 1627." *Journal of the Asiatic Society of Bengal* (n.s.) 21 (1925): 75–91.

———. "The Jesuits at Agra in 1635–1637." *Journal of the Asiatic Society of Bengal*, 1938, pp. 479–501.

———. "Letters and Papers of Fr. Ippolito Desideri, S.J., a Missionary in Tibet (1716–1721)." *Journal of the Asiatic Society of Bengal*, 1938, pp. 567–767.

Hostetler, Laura. *Qing Colonial Enterprise: Ethnography and Cartography in Early Modern China.* Chicago: University of Chicago Press, 2001.

———. "A Mirror for the Monarch: A Literary Portrait of China in Eighteenth-Century France." *Asia Major* 19 (2006): 349–76.

Hsia, R. Po-Chia. *The World of Catholic Renewal, 1540–1770.* Cambridge: Cambridge University Press, 1998.

Iparraguirre, Ignacio, S.J. *Historia de la práctica de los Ejercicios Espirituales de San Ignacio de Loyola.* 3 vols. Rome: IHSI, 1946–73.

———. *Comentarios de los Ejercicios Ignacianos (siglos XVI–XVIII) Repertorio crítico.* Rome: IHSI, 1967.

Ishihama, Yumiko. "A Study of the Seals and Titles Conferred by the Dalai Lamas." *Tibetan Studies: Proceedings of the 5th Seminar of the International Association for Tibetan Studies, Narita 1989,* ed. Ihara Shōren and Yamaguchi Zuihō, 2:501–14. Tokyo: Naritasan Shinshoji, 1992).

———. "On the Dissemination of the Belief in the Dalai Lama as a Manifestation of the Bodhisattva Avalokiteshvara." *Acta Asiatica* 64 (1993): 38–58.

Johns, Christopher M. S. *Papal Art and Cultural Politics: Rome in the Age of Clement XI.* Cambridge: Cambridge University Press, 1993.

Kaschewsky, Rudolph. "Das Tibetbild im Westen vor dem 20. Jahrhundert." In *Mythos Tibet*, ed. Thierry Dodin, pp. 16–30. Köln: Dumont, 1997.

Kapstein, Matthew. *The Tibetan Assimilation of Buddhism.* Oxford: Oxford University Press, 2000.

———. *The Tibetans.* Oxford: Blackwell, 2006.

Karmay, Samten. *The Great Perfection.* London: E. J. Brill, 1988.

———. *Secret Visions of the Fifth Dalai Lama: The Gold Manuscript in the Fournier Collection.* London: Serindia Publications, 1988.

Klafkowski, Piotr. *The Secret Deliverance of the Sixth Dala Lama.* Vienna: Arbeitskreis für Tibetische und Buddhistische Studien, 1979.

Kreiser, Robert. *Miracles, Convulsions, and Ecclesial Politics in Early-Eighteenth Century Paris.* Princeton, NJ: Princeton University Press, 1978.

Lach, Donald F. *Asia in the Making of Europe.* 3 vols. in 9. Chicago: University of Chicago Press, 1965–.

Lamalle, Edmond. "La documentation d'histoire missionaire dans le 'Fondo Gesuitico' aux Archives Romaines de la Compagnie de Jesus." *Euntes docete* 21 (1968): 131–76.

———. "L' Archivio Generale di un grande ordine religioso: quello della Compagnia di Gesù." *Archiva ecclesiae* 24–25 (1981–82): 89–120.

Landon, Perceval. *Lhasa, an Account of the Country and People of Central Tibet and of the Progress of the Mission sent there by the English Government in the Year 1903–1904.* 2 vols. London: Hurst and Blackett, 1905.

Larner, John. *Marco Polo and the Discovery of the World.* New Haven, CT: Yale University Press, 2001.

Levy, Evonne. *Propaganda and the Jesuit Baroque.* Berkeley: University of California Press, 2004.

Lopez, Donald S., Jr. "Foreigner at the Lama's Feet." In *Curators of the Buddha: The Study of Buddhism Under Colonialism,* ed. Donald S. Lopez Jr., pp. 251–95. Chicago: University of Chicago Press, 1995.

———. *Prisoners of Shangri-la: Tibetan Buddhism and the West.* Chicago: University of Chicago Press, 1998.

Lundbaek, Knud. *Joseph de Prémare (1666–1736), S.J.—Chinese Philology and Figurism.* Aarhus: Aarhus University Press, 1991.

Macdonald, David. *The Land of the Lama.* London: Seeley Service, 1929.

MacCormack, Sabine. *Religion in the Andes: Vision and Imagination in Early Colonial Peru.* Princeton, NJ: Princeton University Press, 1991.

Maggs, Barbara Widenor. "Science, Mathematics, and Reason: The Missionary Methods of the Jesuit Alexandre de Rhodes in Seventeenth-Century Vietnam." *Catholic Historical Review* 86 (2000): 439–58.

Magnaghi, Alberto. "La Relazione inedita di un viaggio nel Tibet del Padre Cassiano Beligatti da Macerata." *Rivista Geografica Italiana* 11, fasc. III (1904): 96–108.

Markham, Clements Markham. "Discovery of Father Desideri's Journal in Tibet." *Geographical Magazine* 3 (1876): 21.

Martin, Dan. "Bonpo Canons and Jesuit Cannons." *Tibet Journal* 15 (1990): 3–28.

Minimaki, George. *The Chinese Rites Controversy from Its Beginnings to Modern Times.* Chicago: Loyola University Press, 1985.

Mungello, David E. "The Reconciliation of Neo-Confucianism with Christianity in the Writings of Joseph de Prémare, S.J." *Philosophy East and West* 26 (1976): 389–410.

———. "Malebranche and Chinese Philosophy." *Journal of the History of Ideas* 41 (1980): 551–78.

———. *Curious Land: Jesuit Accommodation and the Origins of Sinology.* Honolulu: University of Hawai'i Press, 1989.

———. *The Chinese Rites Controversy: Its History and Meaning.* Nettetal: Steyler Verlag, 1994.

Niell, Stephen. *A History of Christianity in India: The Beginnings to AD 1707.* Cambridge: Cambridge University Press, 1984.

Norwick, Braham. "The First Tsha-Tsha Published in Europe." In *Soundings in Tibetan Civilization: Proceedings of the 1982 Seminar of the International Association for*

Tibetan Studies Held at Columbia University, ed. Barbara Aziz and Matthew Kapstein, pp. 73–85. New Delhi: Manohar, 1985.

———. "Locating Tibet: The Maps." In *Studia Tibetica: Quellen und Studien zur tibetischen Lexikographie*, ed. Herbert Franke, 2:301–20. Munich: Kommission für zentralasiatische Studien bayerische Akademie der Wissenschaften, 1988.

Olin, John C. "The Idea of Pilgrimage in the Experience of Ignatius Loyola." *Church History* 48 (1979): 387–97.

———. *Catholic Reform: From Cardinal Ximenes to the Council of Trent, 1495–1563*. New York: Fordham University Press, 1990.

———. *The Autobiography of St. Ignatius Loyola with Related Documents*. New York: Fordham University Press, 1992.

O'Malley, John W., S.J. *The First Jesuits*. Cambridge, MA: Harvard University Press, 1993.

———. "Mission and the Early Jesuits." *The Way* 79 (supp.) (1994): 3–10.

———. *Trent and All That: Renaming Catholicism in the Early Modern Era*. Cambridge, MA: Harvard University Press, 2000.

O'Malley, John W., S.J., and Gauvin Alexander Bailey, eds. *The Jesuits and the Arts, 1540–1773*. Philadelphia: St. Joseph's University Press, 2005.

O'Malley, John W., S.J., Gauvin Alexander Bailey, Steven J. Harris, and T. Frank Kennedy, S.J., eds. *The Jesuits: Cultures, Sciences, and the Arts, 1540–1773*. 2 vols. Toronto: University of Toronto Press, 1999–2004.

Pagden, Anthony. *European Encounters with the New World from Renaissance to Romanticism*. New Haven, CT: Yale University Press, 1993.

Panti, S. Castello. "Nuovi documenti su Ippolito Desideri." In *Miscellanea di storia delle esplorazioni*, ed. Francesco Surdich, pp. 153–78. Genoa: Fratelli Bozzi, 1975.

Perdue, Peter C. *China Marches West: The Qing Conquest of Central Eurasia*. Cambridge, MA: Belknap Press, 2005.

Petech, Luciano. "Il Tibet nella Geografia Musulmana." *Academia Nazionale dei Lincei, Rendiconti, Classe de Scienze Morali*, ser. VIII, vol. 2 (1947): 55–70.

———. "The Missions of Bogle and Turner according to the Tibetan Texts." *T'oung Pao* 39 (1950): 330–46.

———. *I missionari italiani nel Tibet e nel Nepal*. 7 vols. Rome: Libreria dello Stato, 1954–56.

———. "Notes on Tibetan History of the 18th Century." *T'oung Pao* 52 (1965–66): 261–92.

———. *China and Tibet in the Eighteenth Century*. 2nd rev. ed. Leiden: E. J. Brill, 1972.

———. *Aristocracy and Government in Tibet, 1728–1959*. Rome: IsMEO, 1973.

———. "Ippolito Desideri, S.J., 1684–1733." *Indica* 23 (1986): 101–12.

Pinsker, A., S.J. "Mitteilungen des Jesuiten Johann Grueber über Tibet." In *Contributions on Tibetan Language, History, and Culture: Proceedings of the Csomo de Kőrös Symposium Held at Velm-Vienna, Austria, 13–19 September 1981*, ed. Ernst Steinkellner and Helmut Tauscher, pp. 289–302. Vienna: Arbietskreis für tibetische und buddhistische Studien Universität Wien, 1983.

Pommaret, Françoise, ed. *Lhasa in the Seventeenth Century: The Capital of the Dalai Lamas*. Trans Howard Solverson. Leiden: E. J. Brill, 2003.

Puini, Carlo. "Di alcune lettere inedite o ignorate del P. Ippolito Desideri d.C.d.G., missionario nel Tibet." *Al Professore Giovanni Marinelli nel 25° anniversario delle sue nozze*, pp. 5–8. Florence: M. Ricci, 1895.

———. "Lhasa secondo la descrizione che ne fa Ippolito Desideri nella Relazione inedita del suo viaggio nel Tibet." *La Cultura geografica* 6–7 (1899): 71–74.

———. "Il P. Ippolito Desideri e i suoi viaggi nell'India e nel e nel Tibet (1712–1727)." *Studi Italiani di Filologia Indo-Iranica* 3 (1899): i–xxxii.

———. "Il Buddhismo nel Tibet secondo la Relazione inedita del P. Ippolito Desideri." *Studi Italiani di Filologia Indo-Iranica* 3 (1899): 1–61.

———. "Il matrimonio nel Tibet." *Rivista Italiana di Sociologia* 4, fasc. II (1900): 149–68.

———. "Viaggio nel Tibet del P. Ippolito Desideri." *Rivista Geografica Italiana* 7, fasc. X (1900): 565–82.

———. *Il Tibet (Geografica, Storia, Religione, Costumi); secondo la Relazione del Viaggio di Ippolito Desideri 1715–1721*. Rome: Società Geografica Italiana, 1904.

Rahner, Hugo. *Ignatius the Theologian*. Trans. Michael Barry. New York: Herder and Herder, 1968.

Rauty, N. "Notizie inedite su Ippolito Desideri e sulla sua famiglia tratte dagli archivi pistoiesi." *Bullettino Storico Pistoiese* 86 (1984): 3–31.

Rawling, C. G. *The Great Plateau*. London: E. Arnold, 1905.

Rawski, Evelyn S. *The Last Emperors: A Social History of Qing Imperial Insitutions*. Berkeley: University of California Press, 1998.

Richardson, Hugh. "The Fifth Dalai Lama's Decree Appointing Sangs-Rgyas Rgya-Mtsho as Regent." *Bulletin of the School of Oriental and African Studies* 43 (1980): 329–44.

Rockhill, W. W. *The Land of the Lamas: Notes from a Journey through China, Mongolia, and Tibet*. London: Longmans Green, 1891.

———. *Diary of a Journal through Mongolia and Tibet in 1891 and 1892*. Washington, DC: Smithsonian Institution, 1894.

Roscioni, G. C. *Il desiderio delle Indie. Storia, sogni e fughe di giovani gesuiti italianai*. Turin: G. Einaudi, 2001.

Rossi, Paolo. *The Dark Abyss of Time: The History of the Earth and the History of the Nations from Hooke to Vico*. Trans. Lydia C. Cochrane. Chicago: University of Chicago Press, 1984.

Sandberg, Graham. *The Exploration of Tibet: Its History and Particulars from 1623 to 1904*. Calcutta: Thacker and Spink, 1904.

Schlagintweit, Hermann von. *Reisen in Indiën und Hochasiën*. 4 vols. Jena: H. Costenoble, 1869–80.

Schütte, Josef Franz. *Valignano's Mission Principles for Japan*. Trans. John J. Coyne. 2 vols. St. Louis: IJS, 1980.

Sebes, Joseph, S.J. *The Jesuits and the Sino-Russian Treaty of Nerchinsk*. Rome: IHSI, 1961.

———. "A Comparative Study of Religious Missions in Three Civilizations: India, China, and Japan." In *Colloque internationale de sinologie, III: Appréciation par l'Europe de la tradition à partir du XVIIe siècle*, pp. 271–90. Paris: Belles Lettres, 1983.

Selwyn, Jennifer D. *A Paradise Inhabited by Devils: The Jesuits' Civilizing Mission in Early Modern Naples*. Rome: IHSI, 2004.

Shakabpa, Tsepon. *A Political History of Tibet*. New Haven, CT: Yale University Press, 1967.

Sherburne, Richard, S.J. "A Buddhist-Christian Dialog? Some Notes on Desideri's Tibetan Manuscripts." In *Reflections on Tibetan Culture: Essays in Memory of Turrell V. Wylie*, eds. Lawrence Epstein and Richard F. Sherburne, pp. 295–305. Lewiston, NY: Edwin Mellen Press, 1990.

Smith, Jeffrey Chipps. *Sensuous Worship: Jesuits and the Art of the Early Catholic Reformation in Germany*. Princeton, NJ: Princeton University Press, 2002.

Sørensen, Per K. *Divinely Secularized: An Inquiry into the Nature and Forms of the Songs Ascribed to the Sixth Dalai Lama*. Vienna: Arbeitskreis für Tibetische und Buddhistische Studien, 1990.

Spence, Jonathan. *The Memory Palace of Matteo Ricci*. New York: Viking Penguin, 1984.

Sperling, Eliot. "Notes on References to 'Bri-Gung-pa—Mongol Contact in the Late Sixteenth and Early Seventeenth Centuries." *Tibetan Studies: Proceedings of the 6th Seminar of the International Association for Tibetan Studies, Narita, 1989*, ed. Ihara Shōren and Yamaguchi Zuihō, 2:741–50. Tokyo: Naritasan Shinshoji, 1992.

Standaert, Nicholas, S.J., ed. *Handbook of Christianity in China,*. Leiden: E. J. Brill, 2001.

———. *An Illustrated Life of Christ Presented to the Chinese Emperor. The History of the Jincheng shuxiang (1640)*. Nettetal: Steyler Verlag, 2007.

Strasser, Gerhard. "Tibet im 17. Jahrhundert: Johannes Grueber, S.J., seine Reisebeschreibungen und die Frage inrer Veröffenlichung." *Daphnis: Zeitschrift für Mittlere Deutsche Literatur* 24 (1995): 375–400.

Stein, Rolf. *Tibetan Civilization*. Trans. J. E. Stapleton Driver. Stanford, CA: Stanford University Press, 1972.

Sweet, Michael. "Desperately Seeking Capuchins: Manoel Freyre's '*Report on the Tibets and Their Routes (Tibetorum ac Eorum Relatio Viarum)*' and the Desideri Mission to Tibet." *Journal of the International Association of Tibetan Studies* 2 (2005): 1–33.

———. "Jesus as World-Protector: Eighteenth-Century Gelukpa Historians View Christianity." *Buddhist-Christian Studies* 26 (2006): 173–78.

———. "Human Fraud or the Devil's Work? Ippolito Desideri on the Reincarnate Succession of the Dalai Lama." Paper presented at the XV Congress of the International Association of Buddhist Studies, Atlanta, June 23–28, 2008.

———. "An Unpublished Letter in Portuguese by Fr. Ippolito Desideri." AHSI, forthcoming.

Toscano, Giuseppe, S.X. *La prima missione cattolica nel Tibet*. Parma: Istituto missioni estere, 1951.

———. "Pensiero buddhista e pensiero cristiano." *Fede e Civiltà* 60 (1962): 641–741.

———. *Alla scoperta del Tibet. Relazioni dei missionari del sec. XVII*. Bologna: E.M.I., 1977.

———. *Opere Tibetane di Ippolito Desideri*. 4 vols. Rome: IsMEO, 1981–89.

———. "The Death of Lha-bzang Khan According to the Writings of Fr. Desideri, S.J." *Tibet Journal* 7 (1982): 87–92.

———. "The King Lha-bzang Khan and the Jesuit priest Father Desideri." *Tibet Journal* 7 (1982): 58–62.

————. "Contributo del Desideri alla conoscenza dell'Asia nel sec. XVIII." *La conoscenza dell'Asia e dell'africa in Italia nei sec. XVIII e XIX*, pp. 293–302. Naples: Istituto Universitario Orientale, 1984.

————. "Il concetto di śūnyatā nel Desideri." *Orientale Iosephi Tucci Memoriae Dicata*, eds. G. Gnoli and L. Lanciotti, pp. 1465–92. Rome: IsMEO, 1988.

Tucci, Giuseppe. "The Travels of Ippolito Desideri." *Journal of the Royal Asiatic Society*, 1933, pp. 353–58.

————. "L'Italia e l'esplorazione del Tibet." *Asiatica* 6 (1938): pp. 435–46.

————. "L'Italia e gli studi tibetani." *Civiltà*, 1940, pp. 75–84.

————. *Indo-Tibetica*. 7 vols. Rome: IsMEO, 1941.

————. "Le Missione Cattoliche e il Tibet." *Le Missioni Cattoliche e la cultura dell'Oriente*, pp. 224–27. Rome: IsMEO, 1943.

————. "Recensione allo studio del Fazy (vedi R. Fazy)." *Artibus Asiae* 10 (1947): 248–49.

————. *Italia e Oriente*. Milan: Garzanti, 1949.

————. *Tibetan Painted Scrolls*. 2 vols. Rome: La Libreria Dello Stato, 1949.

————. *To Lhasa and Beyond: Diary of the Expedition to Tibet in the Year MCMXLVIII*. Rome: Istituto Poligrafico dello Stato, 1956.

————. *The Religions of Tibet*. Trans. Geoffrey Samuel. Berkeley: University of California Press, 1988.

Vacca, G. "Sui manoscritti dell'opera sul Tibet del Padre Ippolito Desideri." *Bollettino della R. Società Geografica Italiana*, ser. VI, vol. 9 (1932): 525–32.

Van Kley, Edwin J. "News from China: Seventeenth Century Notices of the Manchu Conquest." *Journal of Modern History* 45 (1973): 563–68.

————. "An Alternative Muse: the Manchu Conquest in European Literature." *European Studies Review* 6 (1976): 21–24.

Waddell, L. Austine. *The Buddhism of Tibet, or Lamaism, with Its Mystic Cults, Symbolism, and Mythology, and Its Relation to Indian Buddhism*. London: W. H. Allen, 1895.

————. *Lhasa and Its Mysteries, with a Record of the Expedition of 1903–1904*. London: J. Murray, 1905.

Walker, Daniel P. *The Ancient Theology: Studies in Christian Platonism from the Fifteenth to the Eighteenth Centuries*. Ithaca, NY: Cornell University Press, 1972.

Wegener, Georg. *Tibet und die Englische Expedition*. Halle: Gebauer-Schwetschke druckerei und Verlag, 1904.

Wessels, Cornelius, S.J. "Lettura inedita del P. Ippolito Desideri S.I. scritta da Agra il 21 agosto 1714 al P. Francesco Piccolomini." *Atti e memorie del Convegno de geografi-orientalisti tenuto in Macerata il 25, 26, 27 settembre 1910*, pp. 30–39. Macerata: Giorgetti, 1911.

————. *Early Jesuit Travellers in Central Asia, 1603–1721*. The Hague: Martinus Nijhoff, 1924.

Wind, Edgar. *Pagan Mysteries in the Renaissance*. Rev. ed. New York: W. W. Norton, 1968.

Witek, John W., S.J. *Controversial Ideas in China and In Europe: A Biography of Jean-François Foucquet, S.J. (1665–1741)*. Rome: IHSI, 1982.

Wittkower, Rudolf. *Architectural Principles in the Age of Humanism*. London: Warburg Institute, 1949.

Wittkower, Rudolf. *Selected Lectures of Rudolf Wittkower: The Impact of Non-European Civilizations on the West.* Ed. Donald Martin Reynolds. Cambridge: Cambridge University Press, 1989.

Wylie, Turrell. "Reincarnation: A Political Innovation in Tibetan Buddhism." In *Proceedings of the Csoma de Kőrös Memorial Symposium Held at Mátrafüred, Hungary 24–30 September 1976,* ed. Louis Ligeti, pp. 579–86. Budapest: Akadémiai Kiadó, 1978.

Yates, Frances. *Giordano Bruno and the Hermetic Tradition.* Chicago: University of Chicago Press, 1964.

———. *Art of Memory.* Chicago: University of Chicago Press, 1966.

Zahiruddin, Ahmad. *Sino-Tibetan Relations in the Seventeenth-Century.* Rome: IsMEO, 1970.

Županov, Ines G. *Disputed Mission: Jesuit Experiments and Brahmanical Knowledge in Seventeenth-century India.* Oxford: Oxford University Press, 1999.

———. "Lust, Marriage, and Free Will: Jesuit Critique of Paganism in South India." *Studies in History* 16 (2000): 199–220.

———. *Missionary Tropics: The Catholic Frontier in India (16th–17th Centuries).* Ann Arbor: University of Michigan Press, 2005.

Index

Abraham, 23, 45, 185
accommodation, 12–13, 135–40,
    152–59, 171, 189, 197
Acosta, José de, 80, 89, 277n96
Acquaviva, Claudio, 221n41, 222n49,
    272n54, 277n96
Acquaviva, Rodolfo, 47, 57, 272n54
Adam and Eve, 25, 76, 79, 89, 100,
    232n17, 234n29, 263n92. See also
    primitive revelation
adaptation. See accommodation
Agostino a S. Paschali, 133, 255n7
Agra, 48–49, 53–54, 58–60, 132, 133,
    144, 149, 169, 170, 194, 219n27,
    221n39, 223n56, 258–59n45, 276n94
Ahmadabad, 58
Akbar, 173
Alegambe, Philippe, 22
Alexander the Great, 45, 175–76
Alfaro, Pedro de, 255n5
Almeida, Dom Lopo de, 169
Altan Khan, 105, 111
Amaral, Miguel de, 54, 58, 138,
    223n59, 259n51
Ambrose of Milan, Saint, 118
Amdo, 107–11, 125, 129, 197, 253n87
Amida Buddha, 84, 86, 235n39
Anchieta, José de, 171
Andrade, António de, 47–49, 81, 141,
    146, 147, 161, 187, 204n11, 219n22,
    227n92
Anjos, Alano dos, 48, 49, 219n27
Antoninus of Florence, 83, 233n26
Applicatio sensuum, 26–27, 30, 36, 62.
    See also *Spiritual Exercises*
Aquinas. See Thomas Aquinas
Aris, Michael, 126
Aristotle, 79, 164, 176, 182
Armenians, 54, 146, 158, 189

Arnauld, Antoine, 100
Arrupe, Pedro, 5
Āryadeva, 92, 237n48
Asaṅga, 92
Ascoli, Giuseppe da, 154, 188, 255n8
Aśvaghoṣa, 92
atheism, 90–96, 235n36
Atiśa, 92, 237n48, 249n53
Augustine, Saint, 94, 100–101, 118–19, 157, 177,
    231n12, 233n26, 240n65, 264n99, 274n83
Augustinians, 139, 154, 173
Avalokiteśvara, 75, 89–90, 105–6, 120, 156, 169,
    196. See also Dalai Lama(s)
Avril, Philippe, 221n43
Azevedo, Francisco de, 48, 50, 57, 219n27

Bahadur Shah, 59, 269n31
Bailey, Gauvin, 9
Baius, Michel, 100
Baldinucci, Antonio, 36
Bargiacchi, Enzo Gualtiero, 201n1, 202n2,
    205n22, 260n59
Barros, António de, 138
Barzaeus, Gaspar, 166, 222n49, 234n31
Battelli, Giovanni Cristoforo, 269n35
Batu, 173
Baudino, Giuseppe, 229n110
Baudrand, Michel-Antoine, 266n3
Baudrè, Vautrain, 259n51
Bayle, Pierre, 266n3
Beauvollier, Antoine de, 138
Beijing, 50, 80, 110–11, 129, 142, 147, 150, 153
Bell, Sir Charles, 4
Bellarmine, Saint Robert, 96–99, 150, 154, 156,
    183, 263n92
Benavente, Alvaro de, 139
Bengal, 49, 146, 150, 173, 227n92
Benjamin of Tudela, 46
Bernini, Gianlorenzo, 41–42